PITTSBURGH
LEGENDS AND VISIONS

An Illustrated History

by Eliza Smith Brown

Published by
Heritage Media Corp.
Heritage Building
1954 Kellogg Avenue, Carlsbad, California 92008
www.heritagemedia.com
ISBN: 1-886483-66-3
Library of Congress Control Number: 2002105219

Eliza Smith Brown *Author*
Pittsburgh History & Landmarks Foundation *Photo Editing*
Charles E. Parks *CEO/Publisher*
Lori M. Parks *Editorial Director*
Stephen Hung *Executive Vice President*
Randall Peterson *CFO*

Production
Deborah Sherwood *IT/Production Manager*
Dave Hermstad
Arturo Ramirez

Design
Gina Mancini *Art Director*
Robert Galmarini
Chris Hamilton
Marianne Mackey
Charlie Silvia

Client Services
Aina Grant

Editorial
Betsy Baxter Blondin *Editor-in-Chief*
Betsy Lelja *Softcover Managing Editor*
Mary Campbell
John Woodward

Administration
Kelly Corcoran *Human Resources Manager*
Lisa Barone
Vicki Butler-Hagen
Juan Diaz
Cyndie Miller
Stephanie Stogiera
Vicki Verne

Profile Writers
Karen Ferrick-Roman
Fruma Klass
Amanda Lynch
Art Marino
Jim McCaffrey
Jennifer Miller
John Poniske
Linda J. Poniske
Connie Sievers
Paula Smith
Timothy Trainer
Lauren Trocano

Published in Cooperation with the ***Pittsburgh History & Landmarks Foundation***
www.phlf.org
Printed by Heritage Media Corp. in the United States of America

First Edition

(Endsheet) Maxo Vanka mural
Photo by Clyde Hare

Dedication

For William Welsh Brown Jr., Brendan Fergus Brown and Regina Devlin Kennedy Brown, who share the legacy of seven generations of western Pennsylvania forebears

Table of Contents

Thomas Ondrey Collection

Foreword

The most difficult eras to write about are those closest to and those most remote from our own. The former challenge us to interpret them without the benefit of historical perspective. The latter challenge us to relate to a distant time when even our great grandparents were not yet alive and to recount the stories of that time in an accessible and compelling way.

Pittsburgh Legends and Visions offers an overview of Pittsburgh's history from its founding in the mid-18th century as a military outpost and "Gateway to the West," through its transformation into "The Forge of the Universe" and to its maturity as an industrial and postindustrial metropolis at the Forks of the Ohio.

The usefulness of this book is enhanced by the addition of profiles of businesses and institutions making their mark in Pittsburgh history today. These profiles promise to serve as valuable historical reference materials for future history makers and students of Pittsburgh history.

An admittedly cursory glance at Pittsburgh's development, this volume is offered with full recognition of and homage to (and no small reliance upon) the in-depth scholarship of past writers on the subject, from Neville Craig to James Van Trump and Stefan Lorant, as well as contemporary historians of the city such as Robert Alberts, John Bauman, Frank Bolden, Ronald Carlisle, Carmen DiCiccio, Lu Donnelly, Laurence Glasco, John Hoerr, Walter Kidney, DeCourcy McIntosh, Hax McCullough, Edward Muller, Rob Ruck, Templeton Smith, Franklin Toker, Harley Trice and Joseph Trotter. It is hoped, however, that *Pittsburgh Legends and Visions* will tell the story of Pittsburgh in such a way as to promote interest among a general audience and expand readership in the full range of literature on the subject.

Eliza Smith Brown

(Middle right)
The fountain marks the confluence of the rivers in this silhouette of Pittsburgh at the end of the 20th century. River craft, in one form or another, have been part of the scene for more than 200 years.
Photo by Clyde Hare

(Middle left)
The Monongahela River Valley is viewed from the South Side Slopes, with St. Josaphat's Church in the foreground. The Golden Triangle dominates the skyline. The farthest bridge, the West End Bridge crossing the Ohio River, is a symbolic "Gateway to the West."
Photo by Jim Judkis

Introduction

The great cities of America are legendary. Each carries with it a compendium of stories: tales of exploration; a fight for control of the land; the shift from an agrarian to an industrial economy; struggles for political and economic power; the rise of high culture in the wilderness; the blending of diverse ethnic roots into a rich cultural stew; and the development of a new social order among those who came here to escape the old social order. What elevates those stories to legendary proportions is the magnitude and vitality of effort and achievement embodied in them, coupled with the accumulated memory of a long-continuing drama where every citizen has a role. Throughout each epoch of the city's development, Pittsburgh has attracted many of the nation's best, brightest and most ambitious individuals — visionaries who saw, and seized, opportunity at the Point.

In the case of Pittsburgh, these legends have largely to do with industry and all that comes with it, from the blighted landscape to the patronage of social and cultural amenities. They speak of first conquering, and only much later celebrating, the rivers. Even as the rule of steel as king has waned, the legends yet speak of building a city on the wealth and promise of an industry whose effects have left a permanent mark on the city's social, physical and cultural complexion.

Many of Pittsburgh's historic legends have been cast in a negative light. Regrettably, those are the legends that die hard. Pittsburgh spent the first 100 years establishing itself as an industrial leader, the next 100 building and celebrating a legend and the last 50 trying to live the legend down. Beginning as soon as the early 19th century, visitors and natives alike have seemed to delight in denigrating Pittsburgh for some of the very qualities that fueled and reflected its rise to greatness. The reaction of a traveler in 1834-35 typifies these unfavorable impressions:

> Pittsburg has nothing in its exterior to recommend it. It is a dirty, black place, crooked, confined, and built with regard entirely to convenience for business and economy of room. (Mrs. Ellen H. Blythe, in a letter to her brother, John C. Green, July 22, 1834)

James Parton, an English-born biographer and journalist writing for the *Atlantic Monthly* in January 1868, is said to have referred to Pittsburgh by night as "Hell with the lid taken off." And architect Frank Lloyd Wright, when asked for his advice in revitalizing the city after World War II, offered just two words: "Abandon it!" This, for better or worse, is some of the stuff of which Pittsburgh's legends are made.

Nonetheless, many of the city's legends speak to human ingenuity and tenacity, to the great things that happen when a particular mix of people find themselves together in a particular place and time with specific challenges to meet. These are the legends of building and rebuilding — and rebuilding again — a magnificent downtown. They recount heroic roles played by Pittsburghers in a long series of military and other struggles: the Revolutionary War, the Civil War, the Underground Railroad, the labor movement and more. They tell of inventing world-changing innovations like the air brake, smelted aluminum and human organ transplants. These legends celebrate the ethnic richness that survives in strong neighborhood identities and cultural institutions. They boast of a renowned complex of museums and a world-class symphony orchestra. They point proudly to a series of 20th-century renaissances and a pioneering historic preservation success story that holds *people* in as high regard as the places they inhabit. This is the legacy that will live on, long after the industrial reputation has faded into distant memory.

Throughout this story of Pittsburgh, several major themes lend some continuity to the chronology of important events, trends and visionaries. Like complex literary or theatrical characters that only gradually reveal themselves as a plot unfolds, these themes arise again and again as the story progresses.

Taming and Claiming the Land

In the beginning there was the land and the rivers. Carved out by glacial activity during the Ice Ages more than 12,000 years ago, the terrain was a complex maze of hills and valleys, plateaus and ravines, with elevations ranging from 700 to 1,400 feet above sea level. Its focal point was, and still is, the confluence of the Allegheny and Monongahela rivers to form the Ohio, which ultimately flows into the Mississippi and covers half the 1,852-mile distance to New Orleans. This landscape yields magnificent beauty — marked by drama and an exceptional greenness — that is unmatched in any other American city.

The land offered up a wealth of resources — iron and coal in the hills and valleys and sand in the rivers. The rivers flowed with opportunity, manifested in strategic location for military conflict, steam power for industry and readily accessible transportation routes to unexplored lands farther west.

The theme of taming and exploiting the land was evident from the earliest recognition of the Forks of the Ohio as a prime site for a fort, so prime as to warrant a succession of struggles among the English, the French and the Native Americans for control. It came to the fore as the first coal was mined from Coal Hill (now Mt. Washington) to fuel and supply the foundries and glassworks that began to spring up along the rivers as early as the 1790s. Claiming the land was the dominant theme as Pittsburgh transformed itself into the "Forge of the Universe," boasting more than 500 production centers by the 1870s and cultivating an environment where smoky skies and polluted waters signaled prosperity. With the prosperity came the need to tame the land for habitation and commercial development. Civil engineers mastered the city's precipitous terrain with 17 inclines, including the world's first passenger incline, with hundreds of bridges, countless tunnels and massive earthmoving projects to flatten hills, fill in valleys and raise the riverbanks.

Civic Improvements and Beautification

Yet in the midst of the exploitation was a clear voice crying out for civic improvement and beautification of the urban landscape. Much of this conscience was the echoed voice of national movements that championed public parks, City Beautiful planning, the rise of a "modern" American architecture, urban renewal and historic preservation. Much of it, however, grew out of the vision of local leaders. The voice found its expression in the region's first "rural cemetery" at Allegheny Cemetery, one of the first public parks west of the Allegheny Mountains in Allegheny Commons; the development of four major parks in Schenley, Highland,

A machinist inspects a part of a large construction vehicle at the Anderson Equipment Company in Bridgeville.
Photo by Clyde Hare

Frick and Riverview; the development of the Oakland Civic Center, a never-ending series of building booms; and even in the early migration to the suburbs. It continues to echo in the wake of three renaissances and in the turn-of-the-millenium flurry of public building initiatives, including two stadiums and a convention center.

Patrons and Patronage

In terms of the built environment, a few individuals were responsible for many of the major elements of the cityscape. The Kings of Industry — Andrew Carnegie, Henry Clay Frick, the Mellons, the Heinzes and Henry Phipps — and the King of Commerce, Edgar J. Kaufmann, commissioned the Imperial Age of Architecture that left an enduring mark on Pittsburgh's skyline and streetscapes. Their patronage, and that of many others, extended beyond the built environment to the performing and fine arts, as well as to social and cultural institutions that sought to enhance the quality of life for all who called Pittsburgh home.

Ethnic and Cultural Diversity

"Melting pot" is too bland a phrase to describe the vibrant cultural stew that is Pittsburgh. Beginning in the mid-19th century, a wealth of human capital poured into the city to provide the muscle to run the mills. People came from all over, the Irish and Scots-Irish, Polish, Germans, African-Americans, Italians, and Southern and Eastern Europeans, to name a few. They stayed to weave their respective ethnic heritages into a fabric of unparalleled diversity and beauty. This infusion, coupled with the city's sometimes-isolating topography, manifested itself in a series of distinct ethnic enclaves that survive to this day. As recently as 60 years ago, Pittsburgh had newspapers in 33 different languages. And the diversity is cherished still in architectural icons, social organizations, cultural events and the 40 Nationality Rooms at the University of Pittsburgh.

Rise and Fall of an Industrial Economy

Fueling it all, of course, has been Pittsburgh's economy, its legendary industrial economy that started on a small scale but seemed for a time to be unstoppable in its capacity for growth, its technological innovation, and the breadth of philanthropy it spawned. This legendary economy was sufficiently vigorous to sustain two viable, fully developed rival cities, side by side — Pittsburgh and Allegheny City — which struggled for dominance over one another until Allegheny was finally annexed to Pittsburgh in 1907. Even into the third quarter of the 20th century this legendary economy was reflected in the development of Pittsburgh as a Fortune 500 hub with as many as 50 major corporations headquartered there. Since that time, Pittsburgh has shifted from a reliance on manufacturing to an economic strategy that embraces technology and information as the currency of the future.

As Pittsburgh continues to reinvent itself, the same qualities of tenacity, pride and innovation promise to continue giving form and substance to the legend, regardless of the challenges posed.

The Allegheny River Valley from the North Side, with the Heinz plant to the right of center and Polish Hill across the river, to the left
Photo by Jim Judkis

The Monongahela River Valley is viewed from the South Side Slopes, with St. Josaphat's Church in the foreground. The Golden Triangle dominates the skyline. The farthest bridge, the West End Bridge crossing the Ohio River, is a symbolic "Gateway to the West."
Photo By Jim Judkis

CHAPTER 1

Military/Frontier Outpost

THE DRAW OF THE RIVERS

First impressions are oftentimes prophetic. Perhaps the earliest written impression of Pittsburgh was that of George Washington, who first visited the Point in November 1753. Washington, an ambitious 21-year-old ambassador for British Gov. Robert Dinwiddie of Virginia, was sent with his guide, Christopher Gist, to deliver a warning to French forces in the Ohio River Valley and to recommend a site where the British might build a fort.

English artist George Beck painted Pittsburgh in 1804 during his tour of the western country.
Private Collection

An artist's conception of George Washington's arrival at McKees Rocks; oil on canvas
Pittsburgh History & Landmarks Foundation

While he had been directed to what is now McKees Rocks, Washington advised that the fort be built instead at the confluence of the three rivers at the present-day site of Pittsburgh. His remarks at the time are now legendary: "As I got down before the canoe, I spent some time in viewing the rivers, and the land in the fork, which I think extremely well situated for a Fort, as it has the absolute command of both rivers."

Indeed, by the mid-18th century, the Ohio River and its fork with the Allegheny and the Monongahela were recognized as the key strategic location for controlling the interior of the continent. From this point, the rivers could be navigated northward almost to Lake Erie and southward to New Orleans and the Gulf of Mexico.

Equally insightful were the observations of one 18th-century French visitor, Claude Lezay-Marnezia, who came to the Ohio Valley looking for a promised land where the disenfranchised from revolutionary France could live in harmony with nature. In his *Lettres Ecrites Des Rives de l'Ohio*, Lezay-Marnezia commented on the "superb rivers," "rich prairies," "lavish fertility" and "charming valleys" of the region. He expanded to observe that the quality of the land here "fortifies its inhabitants" for a rigorous, isolated life.

This is the story of those fortified inhabitants and their descendants, whose independent, pioneering spirit sustained them through the initial settlement process and fueled them through two succeeding centuries of growth and achievement.

The rivers are central to the story, although appreciation for them was slow to develop in the 18th century. The Allegheny, extending 325 miles from Pennsylvania into New York and back into Pennsylvania, was used by the French to escape from Fort Duquesne. The Monongahela, 129 miles long, begins in Fairmont, West Virginia, and runs north to Pittsburgh. The Ohio River, 987 miles long and fed by a basin of 203,900 square miles, was known by the French as early as the 17th century. They instead used the Wabash to travel from the Mississippi River to the Great Lakes and Montreal, and to access flour and meat from Illinois, "the bread basket of New France." Nor were the British interested in the three rivers until their mid-century conflicts with the French over the territory.

The Western River system
Pittsburgh History & Landmarks Foundation

Native Americans – Earliest Settlers

It was the Native Americans who first seized upon the site at the forks of the Ohio. By the 1740s, they had established a number of permanent settlements in western Pennsylvania, some dating back as far as 5,000 years. The Seneca, Delaware, Shawnee and Wyandot tribes came in search of resources and opportunity and left behind a legacy of legends and place-names. The Seneca came to escape disease and crop failure. The Delaware and Shawnee came in search of new hunting lands and to flee European settlers on the East Coast. The Wyandot sought allies in their conflicts with the French.

A Native American presence in the region had been established as early as 3000 B.C. at McKees Rocks, where visitors to the area in 1753 described an Indian mound and stockaded village dating to about 1500. Another significant Native American settlement was 18 miles below the forks of the Ohio at Logstown; it thrived between 1747 and 1753 as a village of 40 log cabins where a number of important treaties were negotiated.

Downtown, Trinity Church burying ground on Sixth Avenue was created on the site of an ancient Native American burying mound. As it developed to contain the graves of Pittsburgh's earliest French and English settlers, some Native American interments survived as well. Among them was Red Pole, at one time the Principal Chief of the Shawnee Indian nation.

Trade with the Native Americans was the major attraction that brought the first white settlers to the region. By the mid-18th century, traders from eastern Pennsylvania and Virginia were establishing posts, and companies of land speculators sought to open the Ohio Valley to British settlers. While the number of Native American warriors in the area was probably less than 800, both the French and the British eagerly sought them as allies.

Military Stronghold

The earliest history of the Pittsburgh region is characterized by tension, some of it escalating to actual military conflict, over the land that would someday become the core of Pittsburgh and the opportunity that settlers hoped to find there. The settlement at the Point was truly a garrison town, with five successive forts: Fort Prince George, Fort Duquesne, Mercer's Fort and Fort Pitt, all at the Point, and Fort Fayette on Ninth Street.

The importance of Pittsburgh's days as a military stronghold was amplified by the visionaries who came to fulfill military commitments and went on to play notable roles in civilian life. Ebenezer Denny, Isaac Craig and Henry Bouquet, for example, all came as officers in the military but stayed on to lend their energy and ambition to the growth of the fledgling town.

Access to the new stronghold was by a road first blazed as a trail for the Ohio Company about 1750 by Nemacolin, a Delaware Indian. George Washington and Edward Braddock later improved the road. Extending from Cumberland, Maryland, to the Monongahela River near Pittsburgh, the road became a key route for westward expansion until 1818 when the National Road was completed to Wheeling.

The founding in 1748 of the Ohio Company of Virginia, with its territorial claim of 200,000 acres in the Ohio Valley and its determination to settle the territory, marked a renewal of colonial rivalry between Virginia and New France. Seeking to gain control of the interior by subduing the Native Americans and driving the French from America, Washington's initial trip in the winter of 1753-54 was an eventful, if not successful, one. Over 11 weeks and nearly 1,000 miles, he surveyed the area, developed alliances with the Delaware Indians and made two unsuccessful attempts to talk the French out of their stronghold in the region.

It was on his return from this trip in late December that he and Gist made their perilous and legendary crossing of the icy Allegheny. They started out by raft and fell into the freezing waters before pausing overnight on an island and finally walking across the ice the next morning.

George Washington and Christopher Gist crossing the Allegheny River in December 1753
Carnegie Library of Pittsburgh, Pittsburgh Photographic Library

Following Washington's advice as to the advantages of the Point, the British began to build Fort Prince George there in 1754. The fort, of course, represented a major threat to France's domination of the central portion of the continent. Even before it was complete, a French force with Native American support intervened and replaced Fort Prince George with Fort Duquesne, named for the Marquis du Quesne de Menneville, the governor of New France (Canada). A brilliant military strategist, the Marquis envisioned an all-water route guarded by French forts between New France and Louisiana that would confine the British to the eastern seaboard. The French fort had a six-pointed star of earthworks that surrounded the fort proper, a square with four bastions.

A poster by Andrew Wyeth commemorating Fort Prince George
Pittsburgh History & Landmarks Foundation

War broke out the following year. This territorial dispute in the wilderness beyond the mountains would soon escalate into what might be called the first full-scale global war. The French and Indian War, also known as the War for Empire, marked the decline of the French Empire and creation of the short-lived British Empire on this continent, and set the collision course that would culminate at Lexington and Concord 22 years later. The conflict here drew in France and England and escalated into the Seven Years War (1756-1763) in Europe and Asia, costing nearly one million lives.

Locally, the conflict made for legendary stories. Representing the first major British military presence in this country, Maj. Gen. Edward Braddock and his detachment of 1,459 men came up from Virginia in 1755, with Washington now serving as a noncommissioned aide. About 600 French and Indians ambushed them, however, at Turtle Creek, 12 miles east of Pittsburgh, before they even reached the Point. The battle cost the lives of Braddock, most of his officers, and two-thirds of the British troops. Braddock's defeat left the French once again in control of the Ohio Valley.

Undaunted, the British returned in 1758 under the command of Brig. Gen. John Forbes. Forbes assembled an army of 6,000 men at Raystown, near Fort Bedford, with Swiss-born Col. Henry Bouquet as his second in command. The largest army yet seen in the American colonies, Forbes' forces included Highlanders, Royal Americans and militia regiments from Pennsylvania, Virginia, Maryland, North Carolina and beyond.

Rather than reuse the old Washington-Braddock route, Forbes cut a new east-west route straight across the Pennsylvania Mountains. He fortified his road with forts about 40 miles apart and smaller stockades between them. One of these forts, Fort Ligonier, would serve as

(Far right) General John Forbes, captor of Fort Duquesne, named the little unincorporated settlement Pittsburgh.
Carnegie Library of Pittsburgh, Pittsburgh Photographic Library

The Marquis du Quesne
Carnegie Library of Pittsburgh, Pittsburgh Photographic Library

Forbes' advance base, from which he would launch his final, successful march on Fort Duquesne.

Before Forbes could stage his final takeover of Fort Duquesne, Col. Bouquet reluctantly authorized Maj. James Grant to take an army of over 800 men to reconnoiter. Grant led the expedition to "Grant's Hill" overlooking the fort and could not resist the temptation to try and attack. Instead, some 800 French and Indians rushed from the fort and surrounded Grant's forces. The debacle cost Grant 22 officers and 278 men, and he himself was taken prisoner.

William Pitt the Elder, Earl of Chatham and British Prime Minister: Pittsburgh was named in his honor by General John Forbes.
Pittsburgh History & Landmarks Foundation

The French, in turn, attacked Fort Ligonier. Finally, on November 27, 1758, the British moved in on Fort Duquesne, which they found abandoned and burned by the French.

Within three days Forbes proposed calling the site and the town that would grow there "Pittsbourgh" in honor of William Pitt, Earl of Chatham and British Prime Minister, who authorized construction of a new garrison. On the ruins of Fort Duquesne, the British built the largest and strongest fort in America — Fort Pitt.

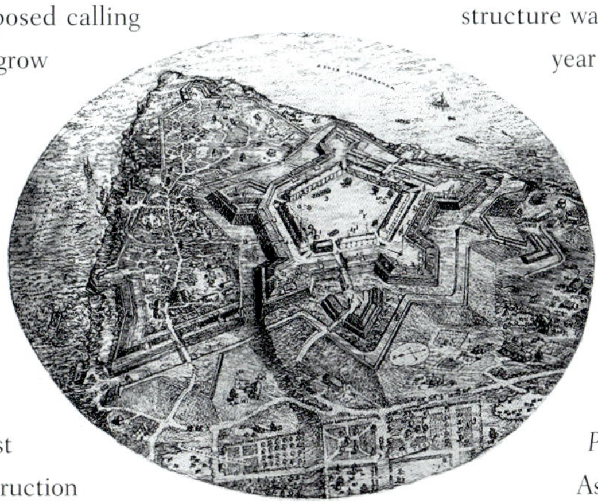

Charles Morse Stotz, architect and student of military history, calls Fort Pitt "the most elaborate and costly fortification erected by the British on their frontier in North America." At the bottom of this 1761 bird's-eye view looking west is the King's Garden, laid out formally but used to raise vegetables for the garrison. The fort withstood an Indian siege in 1763.
Charles Morse Stotz, "Outposts of the War for Empire," Historical Society of Western Pennsylvania, 1985, p. 126; reprinted with the permission of the Library and Archives Division, Historical Society of Western Pennsylvania.

This project, essentially the first relatively permanent building construction at the Point, was under way by early September 1759 and completed in 1761, using local raw materials of timber, coal, clay and limestone. Building the 22-acre fort required the coordinated efforts of hundreds of laborers to cut trees, saw lumber, mine coal, quarry limestone, erect brick yards and kilns, and move massive quantities of earth. This effort also required the ability to execute construction according to the exacting laws and geometrical precision demanded by military engineering. Parts of the fort were reconstructed as part of the Point State Park development in the 1950s.

Ironically, this elaborate stronghold would come to suffer only 10 weeks of attack. In 1763 the new military post with its 630 occupants was besieged by Native Americans under the command of Pontiac, a great Ottawa war chief and ally of the French who united various tribes in his rebellion against British rule. Eight out of 14 frontier forts fell during the summer-long uprising, and some 100 traders and at least 2,000 settlers were killed or taken.

In Pittsburgh all homes and settlements outside the fort were destroyed, leaving 1,000 families homeless. Following Pontiac's defeat in the Battle of Bushy Run in August 1763, the British issued the Proclamation Act, which attempted to keep people out of the western territory and avoid further conflict. Native American threats would continue to curtail development until the 1790s.

Ultimately, floods destroyed much of Fort Pitt. After three of the downstream ramparts were washed away in 1762-1763, the British constructed the Fort Pitt Blockhouse to protect the damaged ramparts. Dating to 1764, the blockhouse is believed to be the oldest building of authenticated date west of the Alleghenies. The five-sided structure was built by Col. Henry Bouquet just one year before his death and survived 130 years of varied occupancy, mutilation and neglect before its salvation by the Daughters of the American Revolution in 1894. Notably, the blockhouse was also the birthplace of Neville Craig, Pittsburgh's first historian and author of *The Planting of Civilization in Western Pennsylvania.*

As local conflicts escalated into national ones, Pittsburgh continued to play a notable role. In

The five-sided Blockhouse, also known as Bouquet's Redoubt, was built in 1764 outside the northwest bastion of Fort Pitt. It still stands on its original site in what is now Point State Park.
Photo by Jim Judkis

response to the struggle at Lexington and Concord that marked the beginning of the Revolutionary War, a public meeting held in a tavern near Fort Pitt on May 16, 1775, elected a committee to represent the county and build a military force. The founding families of Pittsburgh unanimously supported the Revolutionary War. The 8th Regiment of the Pennsylvania line marched east in 1776 to reinforce Washington's floundering Continental Army. One of the most far-reaching impacts of the war on the local scene was the practice of giving land grants to veterans of the conflict.

In the midst of the Revolution, Pennsylvania and Virginia were engaged in a dispute over which colony owned the land that is now southwestern Pennsylvania. Despite that both colonies supported their fellow Americans in Massachusetts, the conflict somewhat hampered the frontier defense effort. Ultimately, the Continental Congress overturned Virginia's claim in 1779. This cleared the path for establishment of a precise Pennsylvania-West Virginia border — engineered by Benjamin Franklin — that expanded the Mason-Dixon line to the west.

While they backed the Revolutionary War effort, Pittsburghers were largely anti-Federalist in their views and were not as eager to embrace the proposed new Constitution that followed the Revolution in 1787. Hugh Henry Brackenridge, who would prove to play a pivotal role in several visionary schemes, was strong in his support and fought tirelessly to secure ratification by Pennsylvania. Finally, with the addition of the Bill of Rights, Pennsylvania became the second state to ratify. That political role won Pennsylvania the epithet of "Keystone State." New Hampshire's ratification as the deciding vote in 1788 prompted great celebration in Pittsburgh over the new law of the land.

In the 1790s the new U.S. government faced great pressures from the frontier to exercise its new power and protect frontier citizens from continued Native American aggression. The federal government built Pittsburgh's fifth and final fort, Fort Fayette, on Ninth Street; and President Washington chose "Mad Anthony" Wayne, a Revolutionary War hero, to lead the decisive expedition against the Native Americans.

After a brief stop in Pittsburgh, Wayne moved his forces 22 miles down the Ohio River to Legionville, where he could prepare them without the distractions of urban life. Rigidly trained and highly disciplined, Wayne's 3,000 men had no trouble prevailing over the Native American forces in the Battle of Fallen Timbers, near Toledo, Ohio.

With this victory, the "Indian menace" was finally put to rest. By confirming the dominance of the English over the Native American population, Anthony Wayne's victory ensured the growth of Pittsburgh and the lands to the west. Ultimately, the Native Americans moved farther west to maintain their independence. They left in the region, however, a legacy of place-names: Monongahela, Allegheny, Ohio, Youghiogheny, Aliquippa, Kittanning, Kiskiminetas and many more.

The government would later sell Fort Fayette and use the proceeds to construct the Allegheny Arsenal in Lawrenceville, which manufactured armaments for the Mexican, Civil and Spanish American wars, as well as World War I.

A Town Takes Form – Early Plans and Incorporation

As the Native American, French and English vied for position, a town took form around the frontier outpost. Pittsburgh's physical transformation from a military post to a city occurred according to two basic plans within the confines of the Allegheny and Monongahela rivers. During the late 18th century both military and civilian leaders laid out the city and began in earnest to enhance it with a built environment, civic amenities and a tentative cultural life.

The first plan, dating to about 1765, was in fact known as the "Military Plan." Laid out by Col. John Campbell, it consisted of four small squares along the Monongahela River bounded by Ferry (now Stanwix Street), Second (now Boulevard of the Allies), Market and Water (now Fort Pitt Boulevard) streets. While limited in scope, just enough to accommodate the small population of traders and workmen, the 1764 plan nonetheless set the orientation of the town's future layout.

Before the plan was further developed, the land around Pittsburgh went through a transition of ownership. It passed to the Penn family as proprietors in 1768. A warrant was subsequently

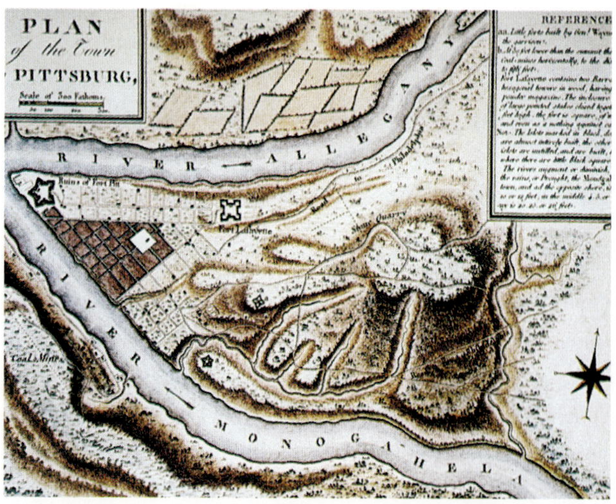

According to a plan published in 1869, this is Pittsburgh in 1795. In the Fort Pitt area, historical liberties have been taken to show the demolished Fort Duquesne, the temporary winter fort, and the final Fort Pitt, all extant and entire together. By 1795 Fort Pitt was largely robbed for its materials. *Pittsburgh History & Landmarks Foundation*

Pittsburgh in 1790, in a 19th-century engraving by J. C. McRae: a view across the Monongahela River with the Point to the left and the prominences now known as the Hill and the Bluff to the right. Fort Pitt has disappeared, the first courthouse has not come to be, and the settlement is not yet a borough. The streets, as yet, exist solely on paper to judge from this rendering of the situation. *Pittsburgh History & Landmarks Foundation*

issued on January 5, 1769, for a survey of the "Manor of Pittsburgh." This survey, completed in May of the same year, consisted of 5,766 acres, some of them within the Triangle.

By an Act of Assembly of November 27, 1779, ownership was transferred to the Commonwealth of Pennsylvania, for which the Penns were given 130,000 sterling pounds and several tracts, or manors, in various areas of the state, totaling 421,015 acres. The manor that included Pittsburgh was again surveyed in the fall of 1783 and the first sale made the following January 22 to Isaac Craig and Samuel Bayard, who purchased 3 acres between the fort and the Allegheny River.

Soon thereafter, in May and June of 1784, the bulk of the town was laid out at the request of the Penns, by George Woods of nearby Bedford, Pennsylvania, and his assistant, Thomas Vickroy. Vickroy's challenge was to reconcile the desire for a logical grid plan with the triangular space allotted. The compromises inherent in that challenge survive in a legacy of triangular lots and acutely angled intersections along Liberty Avenue. Apparently, residents at the time had some input into the layout, according to Vickroy, who added that, "... there was a good deal of conversation, and the ground was viewed by Mr. Woods and the persons who lived at the place to fix on the best plan to lay out the town with the greatest convenience."

Original copies of the 1784 map have not been located, but it was later copied and described. The triangular plan, oriented primarily toward the Monongahela River, consisted of square and rectangular blocks, the streets and alleys being of slightly varying widths. The original lots were apparently 60 feet wide and 240 feet deep, allowing space for a garden and a stable at the rear of each lot.

According to a writer in the *Pittsburgh Gazette* in 1786, five lots within the plan were assigned for churches and burying grounds. Little provision was made, however, for public open spaces, except where necessary for economic purposes. The plan contained a Diamond in the center, crossed by Market Street and Diamond Alley, which was the only major square in the plan and was intended for use as a market, although several public markets were apparently built at different times and in different locations. The 490 lots of this plan constituted Pittsburgh proper until a series of annexations that would begin in 1837.

As the town grew, visitors continued to form favorable first impressions of its natural amenities and its potential for development. Perhaps Louis Brantz, a Philadelphia merchant, drew the earliest sketch of Pittsburgh in 1790. Writing about the Point, he observed that "the view from the spot is in truth the most beautiful I have ever held."

Not long after, in 1796, the French Minister to the United States appointed Gen. Victor Collot to compile "a minute detail of the political, commercial and military state of the western part," including the Ohio and Mississippi valleys. When he visited Fort Fayette, Collot predicted that, "This town, when the Indian Frontier is thrown back, and the roads are rendered practical, will certainly become one of the first inland cities in the United States." With its elevation to Borough status on April 22, 1794, Pittsburgh was on its way toward that destiny.

A painting commemorates the first Allegheny County Courthouse, built in 1794 and demolished in 1852. The public area is the Diamond, now Market Square. This shows the courthouse in its last days, surrounded by market stalls. *Pittsburgh History & Landmarks Foundation*

A log cabin on the south shore of the Monongahela River opposite Pittsburgh. In this painting of 1832 by Russell Smith, a modern phenomenon, a steam packet, is traveling upstream. *Carnegie Library of Pittsburgh, Pittsburgh Photographic Library*

Life and Trade in the Frontier Outpost

Fort Duquesne and Fort Pitt as early trading posts began to set the stage for the larger-scale commerce to come in the 19th century, and the frontier town quickly grew beyond the fort's boundaries. Outside the fort, the 18th-century settlement of Pittsburgh included Native American villages, corn and wheat fields, brick and limekilns, stables and a smithy, saw pits, a cattle pen, a burying place and vegetable gardens.

Beyond the limits of the town, settlers lived on self-sufficient farms. Rather than import goods over the Alleghenies, agents on behalf of the forts traded with local farmers and millers to provide beef, pork and flour. Goods could be transported from Pittsburgh south on the Ohio, setting the stage for growth of boat builders, blacksmiths and gunsmiths to build and repair the necessary equipment.

In response, the town grew. The first census was taken in 1760, counting 149 people, exclusive of soldiers. "Downtown" was the area around the fort; the high ground around Market Square was considered "uptown." By 1783 a German doctor visiting Pittsburgh noted that the town included "perhaps 60 wooden houses and cabins, in which live something more than 100 families."

For these early frontier settlers, life was rugged. The town was dominated by simple log houses, typically less than 20-by-30 feet in size and containing a single room and a loft above, with a large chimney serving two fireplaces. Greased paper covered the windows, some of which also had shutters. The floor was simply beaten down earth. The streets were unpaved, muddy in wet weather and dusty in dry. Trained doctors were rare on the frontier, with only two in Pittsburgh in 1790. The only resorts for illness for most settlers were home remedies or the patent-medicine panaceas sold by itinerant peddlers. Doctors were not highly trained and often relied on a variety of skills for their livelihood. They often worked as preachers, and many sold patent medicines to supplement their income. Undaunted by hardship, however, the population reached more than 1,500 by century's end.

The majority of the region's inhabitants were subsistence farmers, and only a strong belief in a better future could make bearable the creation of a family farm on the Western frontier. The establishment of a farm was backbreaking and often dangerous work.

A farmer would clear a parcel of land for a home and for cultivation of crops using primitive hand tools. The home might initially consist of just a lean-to or shed, which would serve until after the first crop, when a more permanent dwelling was possible. One man could build the log cabin with a heavy axe and a hunting knife. Farming focused on wheat, the region's most widely grown cash crop, but also included corn, barley, rye, hemp, flax, cattle, sheep, hogs, lumber, liquor and tobacco. The yeoman farmer tilled his field by walking behind a wooden plow pulled by an ox or horse, sowed his seeds by hand and harvested his crops with a hand-held sickle or scythe. He supplemented the farming efforts with hunting and trapping of wild turkey, grouse, quail, deer, elk and squirrels.

Pioneers worked from dawn to dusk and had to contend with extreme temperatures, wolves, poisonous snakes and the ever-present threat of Indian attacks. One Frenchman, J. Hector St. John Crevecoeur, who lived as an "American farmer" observed in his *Letters from an American Frontier,* "We never go to the fields but we are seized with the involuntary fear which weakens our labor — we never sit down either to dinner or supper but the least noise immediately spreads a general alarm and prevents us from enjoying our meal."

During this era Pittsburgh first earned its title of "Gateway to the West," with thousands of immigrants passing through each year in search of freedom from the expense and conservatism of life in the seaboard cities, a freedom that they hoped to find in the vast lands to the West. The Ohio River carried some 18,000 pioneers in 1788 alone, and by 1830 fully a third of the American population, or 3.5 million people, lived west of the mountains.

Pausing in Pittsburgh, where land and river traffic met, westward pioneers purchased supplies and bought or built boats.

Commerce thrived. *Niles Weekly Register* in 1786 counted only 38 houses and five stores, but by 1792, according to the American Museum, the town had one clockmaker, two coopers, one skindresser and breechmaker, two tanners and curriers, four cabinetmakers, two hatters, two weavers, five blacksmiths, five shoemakers, three saddlers, one brewery, two tinners, three wheelwrights, one stocking-weaver, one ropemaker and two whitesmiths. By 1794, it was described as a "thriving town" of about 200 houses.

Earliest Industry

The early builders of Pittsburgh exploited its position and resources for transportation and manufacturing and developed a port with an industrial base of coal mining, iron production, glass making and boat building. The enterprising men who built Pittsburgh's early industrial base had migrated largely from England, France, Northern Ireland and eastern Pennsylvania, some in a military capacity, and represented Pittsburgh's first generation of entrepreneurs. Some came with wealth. Others did not. Many entered into businesses that were new to them, but which they recognized held promise for financial success. These early Pittsburghers lived long and worked hard.

A silk waistcoat, c. 1790, worn by George Morgan, a trader, agent for Indian affairs at Fort Pitt, and farmer. *Library and Archives Division, Historical Society of Western Pennsylvania, Pittsburgh, Pa.*

The British were already mining coal for domestic fuel as early as the mid-to-late 1700s from an 8-foot seam in Coal Hill, known today as Mount Washington. Available throughout Allegheny County and the region beyond, coal was quickly seized upon as an efficient and convenient heat source for the early iron and glass industries. And as the technology of industry advanced to steam power and beyond, and railroad service began in the 19th century, coal continued as the primary fuel.

The iron industry had its earliest beginnings toward the end of the 18th century with the opening of the first furnace in Shadyside in 1793, but it was not established as a viable industry until the early 19th century. Likewise, the raw materials for glass — sand, lumber, lead and clay — were abundant in the region, but glass-making would not become a major industry until the next century.

Education and Intellectual Culture

As if to create a veneer of civilization over the rough-hewn quality of frontier and early industrial life, Pittsburgh began to develop some semblance of intellectual culture. Among the amenities of the burgeoning town was the first newspaper west of the Alleghenies, the *Pittsburgh Gazette*.

Hugh Henry Brackenridge, a Philadelphia lawyer who saw the potential of the small settlement, lured two young printers from Philadelphia, Joseph Hall and John Scull, to transport their equipment and their expertise across the Allegheny Mountains in 1786 and begin publication of the partisan paper. Their printing shop was in Scull's home at the corner of Water Street and Chancery Lane; it also served as the town's first post office, with Scull as postmaster.

In an early edition of the *Pittsburgh Gazette*, Brackenridge praised the advantages of the village and predicted that "This town in future time will be the place of great manufactory. Indeed the greatest on the continent. Or perhaps in the world." Some hundred years later, Brackenridge's prediction was not far from the truth.

Other local publications also signaled the development of a civilized community. Scull, in partnership with Hall and later John Boyd, published a series of books and pamphlets, including the *Pittsburg Almanac*, or *Western Ephemeris, For the Year of our Lord, 1788*, the earliest known Pittsburgh imprint extant today. The first novel printed in Pittsburgh — *Modern Chivalry Vol. III of 1793* — was also the work of Brackenridge and was followed by Vol. IV in 1797.

The earliest known school in Pittsburgh was established on Grant's Hill in 1761. Mrs. Pride's day and boarding school for young ladies advertised in November 1786 that students would be taught English, reading and knitting.

Shortly thereafter, Hugh Henry Brackenridge, once again implementing his vision, took the lead in creating Pittsburgh's first true academy. Using metaphors that the locals could embrace, he argued that "academies are the furnaces which melt the natural ore to real metal; the shops where the thunderbolts of the orator are forged."

In 1787 the Pennsylvania legislature granted a charter for the Pittsburgh Academy, incorporated by Brackenridge, along with six Presbyterian ministers, four Revolutionary Army officers,

(Above and right) The McClarren-McCully Schoolhouse at the Depreciation Lands Museum is a replica of a mid-19th-century schoolhouse. *Photos by William Rydberg, Photon*

five lawyers and two physicians, including such first family members as Dr. Felix Brunot, Col. Pressley Neville, Col. William Butler and Nathaniel Bedford, Allegheny County's first physician.

This institution would become the Western University of Pennsylvania in 1819 and the University of Pittsburgh in 1908. Established at a time when the eastern Ivy League schools dominated higher education in this country, the academy represented a significant commitment in the frontier community.

The Penn family granted four lots, bounded by Smithfield, Cherry, Second and Third streets, for the new institution. The first building was a log house, which was augmented by a two-story brick building in 1789. The curriculum was a broad one, including not only the "three R's," but also history, philosophy, Latin, Greek, French and even dancing.

A Rival Emerges – The Town of Allegheny

In an effort to repay its obligations toward the Revolutionary War veterans, Pennsylvania chose to make land grants and designated 3,000 acres north of the Allegheny River as a Reserve Tract for that purpose. A 1783 act of the General Assembly of Pennsylvania established the Depreciation Tract. Veterans could purchase land within the tract using certificates issued to them as partial payment for their military service. These depreciation lands spurred development and brought people who might not otherwise have come.

By 1788 growth in the region had prompted a movement to carve a new county out of Westmoreland. The new county of Allegheny was originally intended to have as its seat a new town by the same name, across the Allegheny River to the north. With that intention, David Redick laid out the new town of Allegheny on the Reserve Tract in 1788. He questioned Pennsylvania executive council president Benjamin Franklin's orders to produce the plan, suggesting that the tract's crater-filled surface would only appeal to inhabitants of the moon! His plan laid out an area a third of a mile square, consisting of 36 smaller squares of four 60-by-40-foot lots each. The four central squares were left open and would ultimately be developed with public buildings. Surrounding the central squares was a grazing commons that would eventually contain a penitentiary, a theological seminary, and a Town Commons and Burying Ground, as well as one of the first public parks west of the Alleghenies. Outside the new town's core was an outlying area of 276 "out-lots" of 8 to 10 acres each, slated for farming.

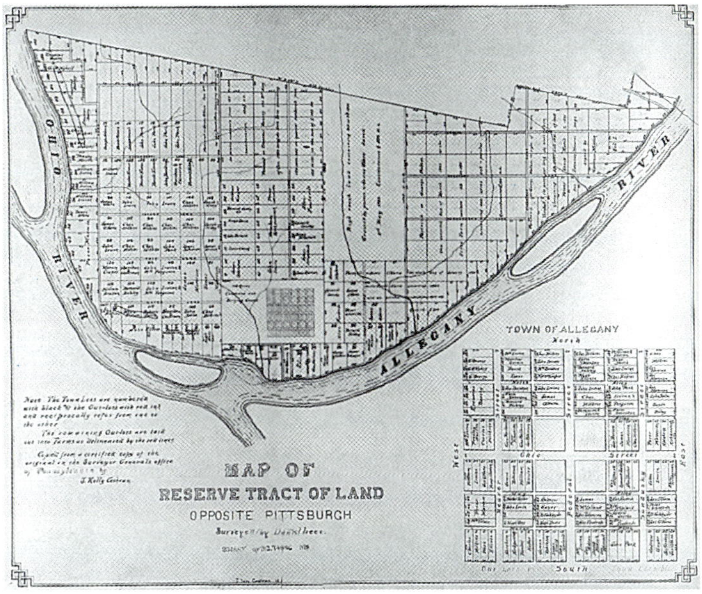

David Redick's survey of "Allegany" Town, its surrounding commons, and the out-lots beyond. The present-day North Side is a little larger. *Carnegie Library of Pittsburgh, Pittsburgh Photographic Library*

In 1791, however, the people of Pittsburgh successfully petitioned to have the county seat established not in the town of Allegheny but rather in Pittsburgh. Thus began a rivalry that was to endure for more than 100 years until Allegheny was finally annexed to Pittsburgh in 1907.

The Whiskey Rebellion

As the 18th century drew to a close, nowhere was the independent spirit of the frontier settlement more fiercely expressed than during the Whiskey Rebellion of 1791-1794. Providing the fledgling federal government in Philadelphia with a valuable lesson in constitutional government, western Pennsylvanians reacted violently in 1791 when a tax was imposed on the chief export of the region. Farmers distilled grain into whiskey and used the profits to buy salt, iron and gunpowder. It was a significant component of their currency, largely playing the role of cash, which was scarce.

Apparently unmindful of the conditions on the frontier, Congress had sought to raise money for its new national Capitol on the Potomac River by imposing an excise tax on whiskey. The tax would be easy to calculate and was a luxury tax designed to discourage the careless use of scarce grain.

Few western Pennsylvanians, including the designated collectors, took the new tax seriously. Congress subsequently amended the law in 1792 and again in 1794 to reduce its burden upon the frontiersmen, and enforcement measures were taken. John Neville, a popular and prominent Pittsburgher, was made chief collector and approached his new assignment with characteristic fervor, serving many writs upon distillers.

Radicals reacted with equal, often violent, fervor. Public response coalesced by July 1794 into a protest group that stormed south (through what is now Mt. Lebanon) to Col. Neville's mansion, Bower Hill, 5 miles south of Pittsburgh, and burned it to the ground. Neville was reportedly among the lucky ones. Another federal excise officer was tarred and feathered. Only then did 13,000 federal militiamen come into the area to squelch the insurrection. With that, the new federal government established its strength and authority.

The End of an Era

The year 1794 marked a turning point for western Pennsylvania in general and Pittsburgh in particular. The Whiskey Rebellion had clarified the relationship between the frontier and the new federal government. With the defeat of Pontiac's Conspiracy and Mad Anthony Wayne's victory at Fallen Timbers, the western lands were made considerably safer for exploration and settlement. And with the designation of Pittsburgh as a borough, its role as the gateway to those lands was well established.

Farmers rally during the Whiskey Rebellion before burning Bower Hill, General John Neville's mansion. This undated linocut on paper is by J. Howard Iams. *Westmoreland Museum of American Art*

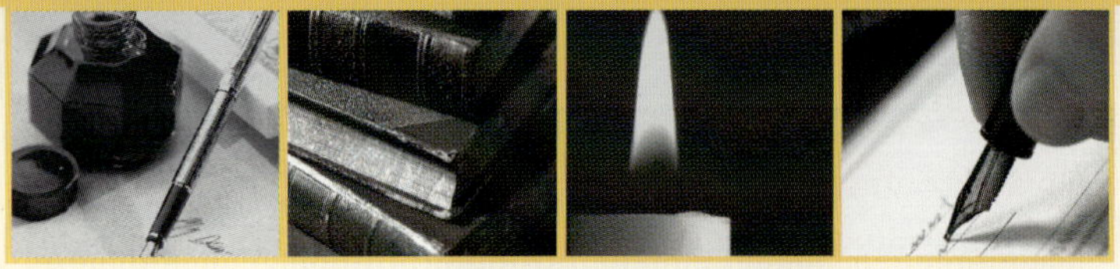

Biographies

Col. Henry Bouquet
Carnegie Library of Pittsburgh, Pittsburgh Photographic Library

Col. Henry Bouquet (1719-1765)

A Swiss-born veteran mercenary soldier, Henry Bouquet came to this county in 1756 as a soldier of King George II and served under Brig.-Gen. John Forbes in his expedition against Fort Duquesne. A student of warfare, he was responsible for the erection of new forts as inspector general of forts from 1756 to 1765 and helped Gen. John Forbes capture Fort Duquesne in 1758. He also assisted in the completion of the Forbes Road, the first direct route across the Alleghenies. Among the building projects to Bouquet's credit was the Fort Pitt Blockhouse. His military expertise also played a role in defeating Pontiac's Conspiracy in 1763 and in freeing 300 white, Indian-held hostages, for which he received public recognition from the king, promotion to brigadier general, and command of the southern district.

John Ormsby (1720-1808?)

Like many of Pittsburgh's founders, John Ormsby came in a military capacity. The college-educated son of a wealthy Scots-Irish family in Ulster, Ormsby served as a colonel in the British army during the French and Indian War, charged with supervising the affairs of the "Six Nations and other northern Indians." As a reward for miltary service, in 1763 Ormsby was given 2,400 acres south of the Monongahela River and therefore became known as the "Father of the South Side." He operated the first ferry across the Monongahela River, beginning around 1775, as well as a tavern and inn frequented by prominent citizens. In 1811 his son-in-law, Nathaniel Bedford, laid out the town of Birmingham. Six streets on the South Side are named for Ormsby family members — Jane, Sidney, Josephine, Sarah, Mary, and Wharton — and Ormsby Avenue is on Mt. Oliver, named for Ormsby's son.

John Ormsby is buried in Trinity Episcopal Cathedral graveyard in Downtown Pittsburgh.
Pittsburgh History & Landmarks Foundation

Gen. John Neville
Pittsburgh History & Landmarks Foundation

Gen. John Neville (1731-1803)

John Neville, of English descent, was a Virginian and a friend of George Washington. Neville came to Pittsburgh in 1775 as part of the militia from Virginia. The Ohio River Island that bears his name was given to him for his services in the Revolutionary War. By 1790 Neville had aquired additional holdings and was a wealthy farmer and slaveholder. As a tax collector during the Whiskey Rebellion, Neville sparked the ire of neighboring anti-federalist farmers, who burned his home, Bower Hill, to the ground in July 1794.

Isaac Craig (1742-1826)

Isaac Craig immigrated to Pennsylvania from Ireland in 1766 and served in the Revolutionary War, participating in Washington's historic crossing of the Delaware River and the infamous winter at Valley Forge in 1777-1778. He first came to Pittsburgh to bring artillery and supplies to Fort Pitt and went on to have a distinguished career as a pioneer industrialist.

Craig and his commanding officer, James O'Hara, went into the glass business, opening the first glassworks west of the Alleghenies in about 1795 and specializing in window and bottle glass. He was later involved in shipbuilding and owned a distillery and a sawmill on the Allegheny River. He served in the elected position of chief burgess. For a time, Craig was the owner and resident of the blockhouse, where his son and Pittsburgh's first historian, Neville B. Craig (1787-1863), was born. Craig ultimately retreated to his 1,000-acre farm on Neville Island, where he lived out his days.

Hugh Henry Brackenridge (1745-1816)

Hugh Henry Brackenridge was Pittsburgh's first big civic booster, one of the earliest visionaries to see Pittsburgh as someplace special. Arriving from Philadelphia in the 1780s, Brackenridge stayed only until 1799. During his short tenure, however, Brackenridge orchestrated the creation of four key elements in establishing Pittsburgh as a civilized town. He established the first newspaper and was instrumental in gaining Pittsburgh its status as the county seat, establishing the First Presbyterian Church and incorporating Pittsburgh's first Academy in 1787.

Hugh Henry Brackenridge, portrayed here by Gilbert Stuart *Carnegie Library of Pittsburgh, Pittsburgh Photographic Library*

James O'Hara (1754-1819)

James O'Hara *Carnegie Library of Pittsburgh, Pittsburgh Photographic Library*

James O'Hara was one of the first and most successful early entrepreneurs of Pittsburgh. He immigrated to Philadelphia in 1772, came to Pittsburgh to serve under Gen. Braddock and ultimately served eight years as an officer and army contractor during the Revolutionary War. He also participated in the Indian wars of the 1790s.

O'Hara became involved in Indian trade but expanded his business interests to include Pittsburgh's first glass factory, two tanneries, a sawmill, the Hermitage Furnace in Westmoreland County, at least one shipbuilding concern and Pittsburgh's first brewery. His Point Brewery near the blockhouse utilized bottles from O'Hara's own glass factory.

Ebenezer Denny (1761-1822)

Born to humble circumstances in Carlisle, Pennsylvania, Ebenezer Denny came to Pittsburgh in 1774 as a dispatch boy for the commandant of Fort Pitt and served in the Revolutionary War under "Mad" Anthony Wayne, rising to the rank of major and participating in the decisive Battle of Yorktown in 1781. He later served during the Indian wars of the 1790s. Establishing himself with his veteran's land grant, Denny went on to acquire additional land and involved himself in business with ownership of the Denny, Beelen & Foster General Merchandise Company, as well as a glasshouse in Manchester. Ultimately he entered politics, becoming treasurer of Allegheny County and the first mayor of Pittsburgh in 1816.

Ebenezer Denny *Carnegie Library of Pittsburgh, Pittsburgh Photographic Library*

CHAPTER 2

Gateway to the West
1800-1845

THE 19TH CENTURY OPENED WITH THE PROMISE OF unlimited growth on the western frontier. By 1800, Pittsburgh had its first iron foundry, glass house and bank. Commercial life for the borough centered on its 63 business establishments, 23 of them general stores. Its population exceeded 1,500. The next 45 years saw tremendous growth in Pittsburgh's economy, built environment and cultural life. Transportation innovations brought the steamboat, the turnpike and the canal to the city. With them, commerce and industry took

This lithograph, titled "View of the City of Pittsburgh in 1817," was made from a sketch by a Philadelphian, Mrs. Gibson, while on her wedding tour of the West. To the right, industrial smoke foretells the future of what seems still to be a village. The first courthouse in Market Square is the most prominent building. *Pittsburgh History & Landmarks Foundation*

off. The city was a bustling place with all the challenges that accompany urban life and the earliest amenities designed to respond to those challenges.

As settlement on the frontier boomed, Pittsburgh's advantages came to the fore. Population in the West grew from an estimated 385,000 in 1800 to 5.7 million in 1840, and most of those pioneers funneled through Pittsburgh. The surrounding terrain made this a logical stopping-off place after the long, arduous trip over the mountains. The rivers offered an easier passage on the next leg of the trip along the inland water system north to the Great Lakes and south through West Virginia, but more importantly west on the Ohio to the Mississippi and points south and west.

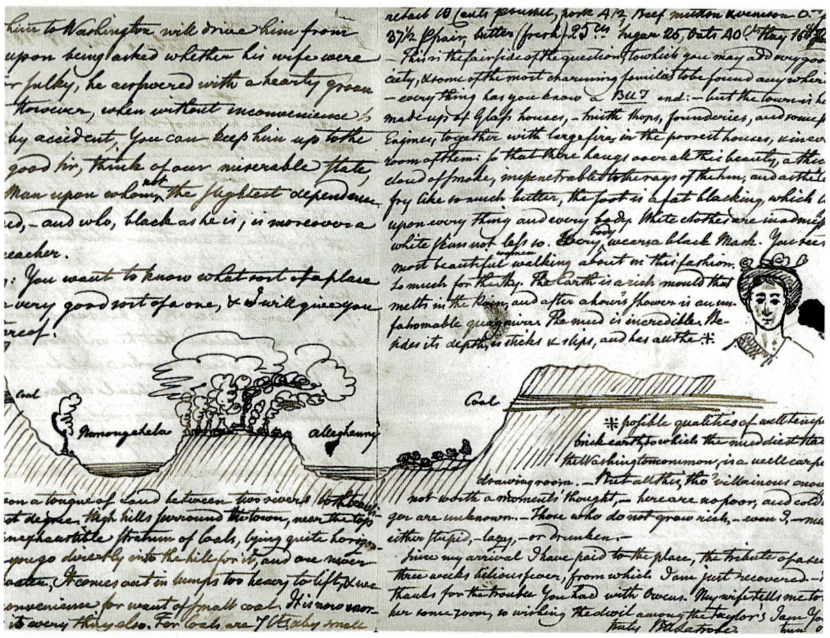

Architect and engineer Benjamin Latrobe, in Pittsburgh in 1813 to set up a shipyard for Robert Fulton, praises the borough to a friend and draws a section of the place. *Pittsburgh History & Landmarks Foundation*

The pioneers passing through Pittsburgh, while in transit and after they had settled in the western territories, created an ever-increasing market for Pittsburgh commerce, as French traveler Michael Chevalier reported in 1839:

> ... the population... creates an indefinite demand for the engines and machines, hollow ware, nails, horseshoes, glass, tools and implements, pottery and stuffs of Pittsburgh. It needs axes to fell the primitive forests, saws to convert the trees into boards, plowshares and spades to turn up the soil once cleared. It requires steam engines for the fleet of steamers which throng the western waters. It must have nails, hinges, latches and other kinds of hardware for houses; it must have white paint to lead them, glass to light them; and all these new households must have furniture and bed linen, for here everyone makes himself comfortable.

With all of this growth, of course, came the need for the settlement to organize. At the request of its citizens, Pittsburgh was incorporated as a city on March 18, 1816, with a mayor, a select and a common council, a recorder and 12 aldermen. With a population of 10,000, including the adjoining communities of Birmingham, Allegheny, Bayardstown and Lawrenceville, the city was poised for continued growth and prosperity. Across the river, the town of Allegheny was subsequently incorporated as a borough on April 14, 1828, but would not achieve city status until April 13, 1840.

The Built Environment

By the time of the incorporation, the number of houses in Pittsburgh had risen from the 200 recorded in 1794 to a total of 960. Industry included four glass houses, two cotton factories, one woolen factory, one paper mill, two sawmills and one flourmill. Smoke and soot already pervaded the atmosphere. With its rapid growth and burgeoning industry, the city failed to impress visitors:

> It is not a wellbuilt city. The south-west part is the most compact, but many years must elapse before it will resemble Philadelphia. Wooden buildings, interspersed with those of brick, mar the beauty of its best streets... Dark dense smoke... rendered it [Pittsburgh] particularly gloomy. *(David Thomas)*

Smoke overhangs this town and descends in the form of fine dust, which blackens every object. *(Zadock Cramer)*

The houses are without any kind of regularity; on one square may be seen a handsome block of brick buildings, occupied by merchants and private families, while, on the next, is a row of one and two story frames, some with their sides, and others with their gable ends on the street, exhibiting a motley assemblage of cordwainers, small dealers, and no small number of those interesting places of refreshment, termed grocery and liquor stores. Nearly the whole town is built in this way. *(Samuel Jones)*

Locally available building materials and tradesmen supported the rapid development of the built environment. The first buildings of Pittsburgh were of logs, some of which were unhewn. Then came rude stone structures made from material quarried nearby, and these in turn were followed by brick buildings, supplied by several local brickyards that produced 4.5 million bricks annually and employed 100 persons. Numerous sawmills and lumber merchants, 23 of them in 1837, supplied lumber, and nails were manufactured locally as well.

Emerging in the midst of a hodge-podge of unimpressive building stock, several significant structures dominated the city. In 1815 the buildings of a public character were all of brick and included five churches and an Academy, as well as the courthouse and market house in the Diamond.

And the building continued apace. By 1826 the borough of Pittsburgh boasted 1,873 buildings: 512 of brick, 913 of frame, 438 "shops, factories, mills, etc." of unspecified materials, and only ten of stone. Among the stone buildings was John Henry Hopkins' Trinity Episcopal Church built about 1824 on Sixth Avenue. In 1826, based on the plans of an architect named Evans, Hannen and Fairman built the Western Penitentiary of Pennsylvania. This massive structure of hewn stone consisted of an octagon covering 2.75 acres across the Allegheny River on the West Commons of the borough of Allegheny.

During the 1830s another small building boom occurred in Pittsburgh and Allegheny. During the year 1837 alone, construction was under way or completed for approximately 33 brick dwellings and stores and 28 brick warehouses, most of which were three or four stories in height. Among the notable additions to the downtown streetscape was the Burke Building of 1836, the city's first true office building and a finely crafted stone Greek Revival commercial front by Pittsburgh's first major architect, John Chislett. The Burke Building was clearly viewed as a significant addition, as it was given a large entry in the Harris 1837 *Directory*, equating its importance with major buildings, industries, institutions and public agencies. Its occupants were eight attorneys who represented a good proportion of the legal community in Pittsburgh at the time, which totaled approximately 50 men.

The Burke Building of 1836 is still downtown on Fourth Avenue. The handsome Greek Revival building by English architect John Chislett was supposedly the first office building in Pittsburgh.
Pittsburgh History & Landmarks Foundation

The Smithfield Street Bridge of 1818, by master carpenter Lewis Wernwag, was the first bridge across the Monongahela River at Pittsburgh. Russell Smith painted this view after a washout by a "freshet" in 1832.
Pittsburgh History & Landmarks Foundation

Nearby the Burke Building stood another significant stone building, the Western University on Third Avenue near Smithfield Street. Other notable additions of the time included the Second Associate Reformed Church at Fourth Street and

Cherry Alley, The Exchange Banking House at Fifth and Wood, a new stone courthouse on Grant's Hill and the Orphan Asylum near the penitentiary in Allegheny. The latter two were designed by John Chislett.

Infrastructure improvements added to the amenities of the urban environment. The borough paved streets and sidewalks, constructed waterworks (1828 and 1844) and introduced streetlights (1816 and 1830). Additional convenience was achieved by Acts of the Assembly of the Commonwealth that took private alleys and lanes for public access, as well as the first attempt in 1836 to reduce the grade of "the Hump," or Grant's Hill, at the eastern edge of downtown.

Pittsburgh as an Inland Port

Pittsburgh's potential could not have been realized had it not been for advancements in transportation, on both land and water. The earliest developments were in the realm of boatbuilding, which had been a thriving industry since the city's earliest days. A Philadelphia publication, *Father Abraham's Almanac*, had predicted as early as 1761, in fact, that Fort Pitt would become a leader in western shipbuilding. And Benjamin Franklin advised in 1770 that sloops and schooners for trade in the West Indies be built on the Ohio River.

Resources for shipbuilding were abundant in the Pittsburgh area: black walnut for frames, white pine and hemlock for masts, rope walks for rigging, iron for fittings and flax for linen sailcloth. Under the capable hands of experienced shipbuilders who settled here from New England, Philadelphia and the Chesapeake Bay, the resources were fashioned into a variety of craft for transporting people, livestock and goods into the western territories.

Somewhat slow to start, production accelerated in the 1790s and reached an estimated $12,000 by the turn of the century. Shipbuilding in Pittsburgh reached a peak between 1803 and 1810. It then ranked third among Pittsburgh's diverse industries with annual production exceeding $40,000 and an estimated eight shipbuilders in operation by 1808. And while during the 1840s, shipbuilding accounted for only about $950,000 of the local manufacturing total of $167 million, it nonetheless played an intriguing role in the city's early history.

The majority of the boats built in Pittsburgh were flatboats, keelboats and barges. Flatboats, measuring between 20 and 100 feet in length and costing roughly a dollar per foot, were the most common and least expensive for downstream travel, popular with both traders and migrating families. Oars for both steering and rowing propelled the flatboats. Used to travel downstream to southern cities, they were often disassembled and sold when they reached their destinations.

Keelboats, designed for upstream travel, were long and narrow with shallow draft and averaged 40 to 80 feet in length. The boatmen walked from bow to stern pushing long poles along the bottom. While the 1,950-mile trip to New Orleans could be made in four to six weeks by flatboat, the reverse trip by keelboat took four months.

Barges were similar in design to keelboats but considerably longer, ranging from 75 to 100 feet with a deeper draft and fitted out with cabins, masts and sails, in addition to their rudders, oars and poles.

Soon, however, under the leadership of a handful of visionaries, boat-building in Pittsburgh adopted a more substantial and far-reaching scale. As the 18th century drew to a close, the industry expanded to include larger, more substantial vessels suitable for trans-Atlantic crossings, beginning with the sloop *Western Experiment* in 1792 and including the two-masted, 50-foot *President Adams* and the 56-foot *Senator Ross*, both of

The second Allegheny County Courthouse, by John Chislett, was completed in 1841. It overlooked Grant Street from the "Hump," an annoying rise in street level that was reduced bit by bit until a final drastic reduction in 1913. Chislett's courthouse burned in 1882. *Pittsburgh History & Landmarks Foundation*

(Far right) A flatboat, steered and propelled by sweeps *Pittsburgh History & Landmarks Foundation*

Two keelboats and a flatboat
Pittsburgh History & Landmarks Foundation

which were war galleys commissioned by Congress in 1798 in preparation for possible war with Spain.

Among the stars of the industry was the firm of Tarascon Brothers, James Berthoud and Company, which launched a series of at least 10 100- to 400-ton vessels between 1802 and about 1806. While most builders fitted their vessels with masts and spars, it is believed that long oars propelled the boats down the Mississippi and the sails were only used in open waters. This boom was short-lived for a variety of reasons: trade restrictions imposed by the Jefferson administration's Embargo Act in 1807; the difficulty of navigating the unimproved upper Ohio; and the lack of adequate banking facilities to invest in the enterprises.

The *New Orleans* as depicted on an early plate (artist unknown)
Library and Archives Division, Historical Society of Western Pennsylvania, Pittsburgh, Pa.

In 1811 the shipbuilding industry took a dramatic turn with the launching at Pittsburgh of the *New Orleans*, a major $40,000 investment and the first steamboat in the West. It followed just two years after the first steam gristmill west of the mountains. Prior to the steamship, it was easier and less expensive to travel from New Orleans to Pittsburgh via the ocean and Philadelphia over the mountains than to travel upstream. Increased river traffic supported the production of 48 steamships between 1812 and 1826 and 48 more between 1826 and 1830.

A second boom in 1840 revived shipbuilding for a period of about 17 years. Established as a leader in the iron industry and equipped with a population of skilled steam engine mechanics, Pittsburgh shared in a national phenomenon of commercial growth and maritime expansion. The first iron-hulled steamboat, the *Valley Forge*, was built at Pittsburgh at that time. The boom was really fueled, however, by federal warship commissions. The *U.S.S. Michigan*, built on the Allegheny and assembled and launched on Lake Erie in 1843, was the first iron warship in the U.S. Navy. The three-masted ship measured 177 feet in length and was kept in service for more than 80 years. Other warship commissions followed.

Building Connections

Pittsburgh's prosperity at this time faced a short-lived threat with the construction of the National Road, the country's first federally funded highway and the first component in the development of a national network of roads. Discussed at the federal level as early as 1797, the National Road actually began in 1811 according to a congressional plan championed by Albert Gallatin, Secretary of the Treasury under presidents Thomas Jefferson and James Madison. It was to have run all the way from Baltimore to St. Louis. As built, the road ran from Cumberland, Maryland, to Vandalia, Illinois, with a significant stretch passing through southwestern Pennsylvania. The National Road followed an earlier path from Wills Creek to the Youghiogheny first forged in 1751 by Christopher Gist for the Ohio Company, in cooperation with a Delaware chief named Nemacolin. Col. James Byrd extended that path in 1759 from Gist's plantation to the Monongahela River at Brownsville.

The *U.S.S. Michigan*, an iron-hulled steamer, was fabricated at Pittsburgh in 1843 for service on the Great Lakes. In its latter day, it was known as the *Wolverine*. It lasted into the 1950s.
Erie County Historical Society & Museums, Erie, Pa.

A late 19th-century reconstruction of a Conestoga wagon and its team: these wagons offered service from Philadelphia to Pittsburgh in 20 days. *Carnegie Library of Pittsburgh, Pittsburgh Photographic Library*

Canal boats *Carnegie Library of Pittsburgh, Pittsburgh Photographic Library*

A Conestoga wagon of 1834 at the Depreciation Lands Museum, Hampton Township *Photo by William Rydberg, Photon*

As the primary road linking the East Coast and the western frontier until the 1850s, the National Road temporarily boosted the stock of rival towns Wheeling and Brownsville. With the arrival of canals and railroads, however, the National Road project was scrapped, ultimately closing its tollhouses in 1905. With that, commercial activity and prosperity were again focused in Pittsburgh.

In the meantime, the completion of the privately financed Pennsylvania Turnpike in 1820 helped to sustain the local economy by reducing the travel time from Philadelphia to less than two weeks. The turnpike was begun in 1795 with the Philadelphia-Lancaster link and eventually cut through the wilderness to connect Harrisburg, Shippensburg, Bedford, Ligonier and Greensburg before reaching Pittsburgh. Paved with stone, it introduced an era of good road building in America.

A more ambitious project, the Pennsylvania Public Works, a canal and rail system begun in 1826 and completed in 1834, shortened the trip from Pittsburgh to the Susquehanna River at Philadelphia to three and a half days. A remarkable feat of engineering, the 395-mile canal system relied upon a series of inclined planes and portage railroads to carry the canal boats across the mountains. As it entered Pittsburgh, the canal passed along the inland side of the Triangle via an 810-foot stone tunnel through Grant's Hill and across a 1,100-foot aqueduct to Allegheny, providing fuller exposure of both cities to outside commerce. Charles Dickens recalled the dreamlike experience of floating along the canal 1842:

> After going through another dreamy place — a long aqueduct across the Allegheny River... we emerged upon that ugly confusion on the backs of buildings and crazy galleries and stairs, which always abuts on water, whether it be river, sea, canal or ditch, and were in Pittsburg [sic].

The canal did not, however, assure Pittsburgh's commercial success, since other competing canal routes were constructed from New York and Baltimore into the western territories. At its peak in 1839, it would carry 1,400 canal boats with 25,000 tons of freight through Pittsburgh. Ultimately, however, the

$25 million project was not a commercial success, and the Pennsylvania Railroad would purchase its right of way when the canal was less than 20 years old.

Industry Booms

By the 1830s, Pittsburgh's economy was no longer dependent upon commerce, but rather upon the region's burgeoning industrial base. The most long-lasting developments of this era were in the realm of industry, particularly in the manufacture of glass and iron. These early industrial entrepreneurs introduced the concept of vertical business integration, took risks and embraced innovation by developing a long list of patents, publications and business entities. Many of their names remain familiar today: Bakewell, Brunot, Dilworth, Gilfillan, Herron, Negley, Neville and Wrenshall, to name a few. Total production for the city grew by 30 percent during the first decade of the 19th century alone, with iron production doubling and glass manufacturing increasing fivefold.

In the manufacture of glass, of course, Pittsburgh and its environs enjoyed an international reputation. Gen. James O'Hara and Maj. Isaac Craig established the city's first glass factory in 1795 on the south side of the Monongahela, just opposite the Point. O'Hara and Craig were not glassmakers by training, but rather visionary businessmen who first had come to Pittsburgh with the military and who saw the potential for a new industry. Pittsburgh quickly became a national glassmaking center. Using raw materials of silica from the sand and potash from the burning of trees and vegetation, the plant was fueled by coal from Mount Washington, then known as Coal Hill. This plant, and the others that followed, produced utilitarian goods for settlers and westward-moving pioneers, such as bottles and window glass. Given their initial investment in the plant, O'Hara and Craig liked to say that the first bottle they produced cost them $30,000. In time they broadened production to include "glassware of all kinds and qualities, with a vigorous export trade." O'Hara and Craig's Pittsburgh Glassworks was the second west of the Alleghenies, preceded only by Albert Gallatin's New Geneva Glassworks in Fayette County.

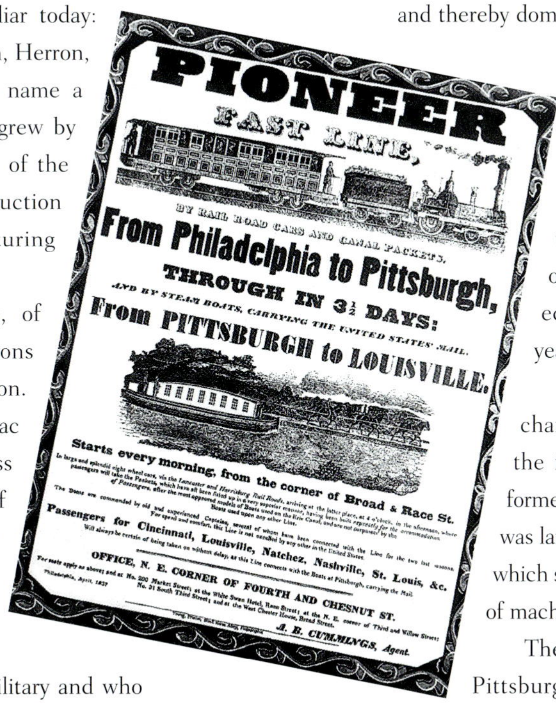

Communications east and west of Pittsburgh in 1837, by rail and canal
Carnegie Library of Pittsburgh, Pittsburgh Photographic Library

By 1815 Pittsburgh was home to at least five glassworks producing $235,000 in glass products. Jones' 1826 *Directory* identifies nine factories producing window glass in the area. Of the four major factories in town, the two major producers of window glass were Pittsburgh Glass Works in Birmingham (7,500 boxes) and Birmingham Glass Works (4,000 boxes). Five additional factories producing window glass were located up the Monongahela and Youghiogheny rivers. By 1837 Pittsburgh had 15 factories, and there were 13 more in nearby Washington and Fayette counties. By the 1880s the number had risen to 51 factories in Allegheny County alone, and western Pennsylvania produced more than a quarter of America's glass.

Pittsburgh's glass producers fought to maintain excellence and thereby domination of the industry. Skilled glassmakers were actively recruited from the East Coast, Germany, France, the British Isles and Belgium. Local Pittsburgh boys as young as 14 provided the unskilled labor, and by the 1810s an apprentice system offered room and board, clothing and education in exchange for several years' work.

This era saw sweeping technological change in the glass industry through the introduction of machine-pressed and formed glass products. This standardization was largely a by-product of the iron industry, which supplied the town with a good number of machinists.

The most famous glass factory in Pittsburgh was Bakewell's Glass House, established in 1808 by Benjamin Bakewell, a transplanted Englishman who came to Pittsburgh to capitalize on the promising new industry. A facile entrepreneur, Bakewell had already made forays into brewing and importing. The glass factory quickly dominated its industry. Bakewell's distinction was that it expanded the industry beyond utilitarian glass and introduced finer products, including leaded crystal, and supplied tableware to three U.S. presidents — Monroe, Jackson and Pierce — for use in the White House. It also exported products to wealthy customers the world over. The business lasted until 1882.

The iron industry got off to a less auspicious start, attributable in part to the difficulty of transporting iron ore over the mountains to Pittsburgh. And it is significant to note that, while Pittsburgh has proudly carried the moniker of "Iron City," iron ore was not indigenous to the immediate area, nor was iron actually manufactured here. The iron industry in Pittsburgh was in fact one of processing, of rolling and forging.

The earliest Pittsburghers and westbound pioneers bought their iron products — tools, cooking utensils and farming implements — from small foundries in outlying Fayette and Westmoreland counties. Yet iron industries had already begun to appear in Pittsburgh at the end of the 18th century, capitalizing on a wealth of nearby resources: natural iron ore deposits in the outlying region, limestone for flux, water power to operate the blast, roads and navigable water to get goods to market and timber to burn for charcoal, which consumed an acre of trees for each day's operation. The first iron operation in Pittsburgh was, in fact, a smelting furnace, opened in 1793 in Shadyside by an Alsatian immigrant named George Ludwig Anshutz in partnership with William Amberson and Francis Beelen, former minister to the United States from the Austrian Netherlands (now Belgium). It closed within two years.

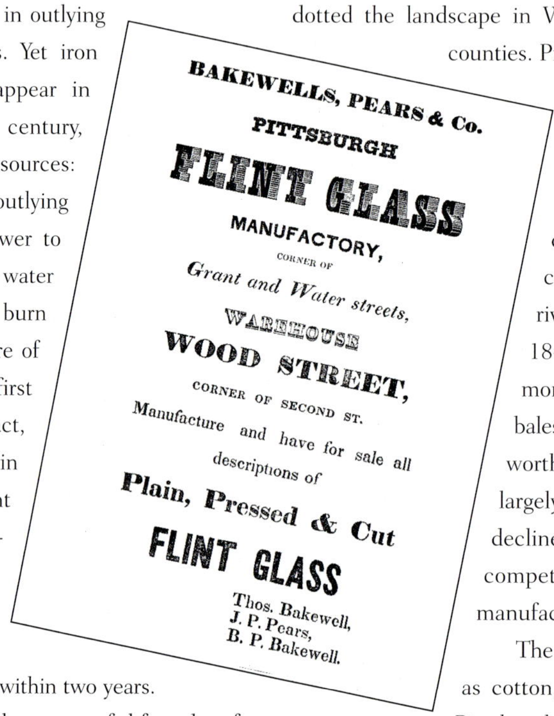

Bakewell advertisement
Carnegie Library of Pittsburgh, Pittsburgh Photographic Library

It was another 10 years before the successful foundry of John McClurg, Joseph Smith and John Gormley was established, which later supplied ammunition for the War of 1812. Initially the industry produced primarily household consumer goods, such as iron kettles; stove pots; and bulk or pig iron for blacksmithing into nails, tools and other implements. It also, however, capitalized on a significant market for cannonballs and other military materials.

But with the first steam-powered rolling mill, built by Christopher Cowan in 1812, and the late introduction of techniques using coke rather than charcoal, Pittsburgh's ferrous-metal leadership was guaranteed. By 1840 iron was the city's largest industry, with annual production of $5 million. It was still only a processing industry, however, securing the iron from rural stone blast furnaces that dotted the landscape in Westmoreland, Fayette and Greene counties. Pittsburgh would not resume smelting iron until 1859.

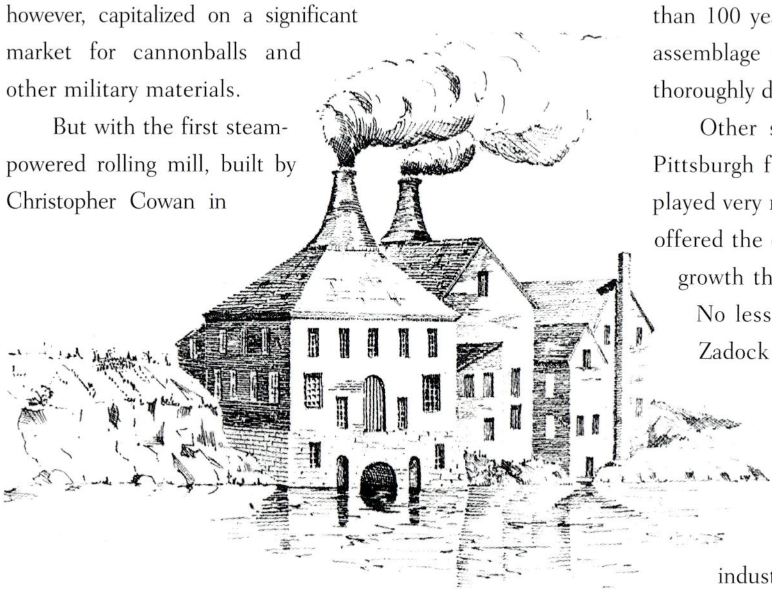

Bakewell's Glass House, 1837
Library and Archives Division, Historical Society of Western Pennsylvania, Pittsburgh, Pa.

Textiles amounted to only a tenth of the size of the iron industry. Cotton manufacturing flourished during the early part of the 19th century, largely supported by the river trade and the War of 1812. By 1847 the city's six factories employed more than 1,400 people, used 12,900 bales of cotton and produced $4.7 million worth of goods. The industry declined largely due to the imposition of tariffs, the decline of river transportation, and intense competition from New England textile manufacturers.

The wool industry, though not as thriving as cotton, nonetheless had a place in early Pittsburgh. The related tannery business, along with the production of leather goods, for which Pittsburgh was recognized as a national leader, also enjoyed a brief heyday in the 19th century. Stockyards and slaughterhouses, leather processors, wool pulleries and soap manufacturers dominated Herr's Island and a stretch of the North Side shoreline for more than 100 years. The last survivor of this integrated industrial assemblage was the Pittsburgh Wool Company, which was thoroughly documented prior to its demolition in 2000.

Other smaller-scale industry boomed as well, making Pittsburgh fairly self-sufficient. Ropemaking and salt plants played very minor roles on the local scene. Neither, however, offered the opportunities for either innovation or large-scale growth that were enjoyed by the city's leading industries. No less than 400 commercial concerns were listed in Zadock Cramer's *Navigator* of 1808. The list included, among other things, makers of tools, building materials, clothing and household goods, as well as building tradesmen, professionals and 33 tavern keepers!

And, of course, banking emerged as yet another industry to serve the growing economy. The Branch Bank of the U.S., organized in 1802, was the first bank west of the Alleghenies. It later merged in 1817 with the Bank of the U.S. to become "The Office of Discounts & Deposits of the U.S." The city's second bank and the first organized with local capital, the Bank of Pittsburgh, was established in 1810.

To Pittsburgh the War of 1812 was more of an economic phenomenon than anything else, originating as a restraint on trade and developing into a naval conflict that brought the issue of American independence again to the fore. As were most of the military conflicts that have drawn upon Pittsburgh industries, this war was good business. A wealth of munitions contracts fed a period of prosperity for the local industries. This short-lived prosperity ended with a depression in 1819. This era also saw the construction of the Allegheny Arsenal in Lawrenceville, a federal project designed by renowned architect Benjamin Latrobe.

Mineral water bottle made in Pittsburgh in mid-19th century
Library and Archives Division, Historical Society of Western Pennsylvania, Pittsburgh, Pa.

Escaping and Expanding the City

As early as 1815, newspapers editorialized on the need for a smoke abatement plan. But for early 19th-century Pittsburghers, the only solution was to leave the center of the industrialized town. Grant's Hill for a time provided refuge from the busy downtown streets. The mixture of residential, commercial and industrial concerns began to break down as Pittsburgh became one of the first American cities to ring itself with suburbs. The importance of residence increased as the city's population and geographical area increased. The fashionable residential area shifted from Water Street in the heart of downtown in 1795 to Penn Street in the second quarter of the 19th century, and ultimately to Allegheny and the East End.

At the same time a series of municipalities sprang up in the surrounding areas, separated from Pittsburgh by the hills and rivers. Some of these were industrialized centers in their own right. In addition to Allegheny, this era saw the development of Birmingham (1811), Sidneyville and the Northern Liberties (1816), Manchester (1832) and East Liberty. The Northern Liberties, including Bayardstown (now the Strip), was annexed to Pittsburgh in 1837, and the others would follow suit in 1867 and 1868.

Ethnicity and Religion in Early Pittsburgh

The earliest European settlers to the region were of English, Irish, Scottish, Scots-Irish and German origins. Until the Native American conflicts were resolved at the end of the 18th century, they did not come so much as settlers from their homelands, but rather in military or trading capacities from Maryland, Virginia and eastern Pennsylvania. These early settlers brought with them their religious traditions and cultural heritage. Of the first families of Pittsburgh, nearly half were of Scots-Irish and New England descent, and they infused their commercial activities with a strong and serious work ethic that characterizes the city to this day. The English tended to bring the most wealth, while the Scots-Irish tended to

(Far left)
The Branch Bank of the United States, from an 1832 painting by Russell Smith
Carnegie Library of Pittsburgh, Pittsburgh Photographic Library

Pittsburgh was a county seat and a market town, as well as a manufacturing town and transportation center. The stone Oliver Miller house, painted by J. Howard Iams, was built south of the city in 1808.
Westmoreland Museum of American Art

The James Armstrong log house of 1803, with an addition of 1839, was built to the north of Pittsburgh. The log house was relocated to the Depreciation Lands Museum in Hampton Township. *Westmoreland Museum of American Art*

One of the wealthiest men in Pittsburgh, George Croghan, built a country villa in what is now Stanton Heights. He eventually added this ballroom of 1835 to Picnic House, decorated by Mordecai van Horne of Philadelphia. The ballroom and its vestibule are now preserved with some alterations in the Cathedral of Learning at the University of Pittsburgh. *Pittsburgh History & Landmarks Foundation*

come from humbler beginnings. What they had in common were careers marked by industry and vision.

The earliest African Americans in this region had come as soldiers fighting on behalf of the French and British armies for control of the land at the Forks of the Ohio. They participated in the construction of Fort Pitt and in provisioning the British military. Soon African-American pioneers followed, both free and slave, who settled along the river ways in some of the county's oldest towns. Most free African Americans held low-wage, low-skill jobs. With the introduction of Pennsylvania's Gradual Emancipation Act in 1780, slaveholding was curtailed even further. That year the Pittsburgh District (including Westmoreland County) registered 691 slaves; by 1790 the newly created county of Allegheny recorded only 159. Nonetheless, with the passage of the first federal Fugitive Slave Law in 1793, some 35 free African-American families organized the local Underground Railroad, with way stations in what are now the lower Hill District, Oakland, Squirrel Hill, Mt. Washington and the North Side. By 1800, Allegheny County counted only 79 slaves, a substantial move toward the elimination of slaveholding in the county by 1840.

Adapting their native traditions to the rugged western Pennsylvania frontier, the immigrants crafted a rich mosaic of local cultures. Religion was no small part of those cultures. For those who had come to enjoy religious freedom, the 1784 plan of Pittsburgh included five lots reserved for churches. By 1815 the city had eight churches representing a full range of Protestant denominations; the *Pittsburgh Directory* of 1842 listed 55.

Reflecting the early dominance of Scots-Irish settlers and tradition, the Presbyterian Church was undisputedly the prominent religious strain in early Pittsburgh, erecting a building as early as about 1786. The First Presbyterian Church was the oldest in Pittsburgh and enjoyed the largest membership. It was led for nearly 49 years by a founder of Pittsburgh, Rev. Francis Herron, who also helped establish Western Theological Seminary in 1825 and was elected to state office.

The Episcopal Church was the second most prominent among the founding families and was centered in Trinity Church downtown. Trinity had begun functioning as a congregation about 1790 and built its first building in 1805 on the triangular plot bound by Sixth Avenue, Wood Street, and Liberty Avenue (now the site of the Wood Street transit station). The congregation grew quickly and constructed a new building in 1825 on the site of the current church, which was erected in 1872.

Other denominations prospered as well. The German Reformed Church was built in 1790 on the corner of Sixth

The First Presbyterian Church was built in 1802 and fronted on Wood Street. In 1814, during his short-lived stay in Pittsburgh, the brilliant architect Benjamin Latrobe added the porches and the transepts on either side.
Carnegie Library of Pittsburgh, Pittsburgh Photographic Library

Avenue and Smithfield Street. Methodism, led by John Wrenshall, followed in 1796.

Pittsburgh's African-American population began to establish itself in earnest during the first half of the 19th century, with the church as the focus of the community. The first black church in Pittsburgh, Bethel African Methodist Episcopal, was founded downtown in 1818 when the African-American population numbered only 185. This church would later be destroyed in the Great Fire of 1845 when the congregation moved to the Hill District. From that foundation the community grew in strength and numbers, creating institutions to promote their closely held values of education, gentility and high culture.

A second AME church was organized in 1837-1838 in Allegheny City. When Pittsburgh's new public school system excluded blacks in 1834, they created a school of their own, prompting the city to open the all-black Miller Street School in the Hill District three years later. Also in 1834, in response to a Commonwealth law that disenfranchised black residents, Pittsburgh blacks joined their brethren statewide in protest. The community celebrated cultural attainments, and produced such internationally renowned stars as Henry O. Tanner, an award-winning painter, and Hallie Q. Brown, an elocutionist. Yet black Pittsburghers in the early 19th century faced segregation in theaters, restaurants and hotels, and were occasionally attacked by white mobs.

Following the French evacuation of Fort Duquesne in 1758, Catholicism would not even begin to take hold for half a century. It was not until 1843 that Pittsburgh Catholics secured their own bishop, and the first Jewish congregation would not appear until 1853.

Cultural and Intellectual Life

It was during this early period that Pittsburgh began to develop a legitimate cultural and intellectual life, with notable initiatives in art, music, literature, drama and science. According to the *Pittsburgh Mercury* in 1813, these activities had to be aggressively pursued, lest frontier life "retard the progress of the human mind, and the liberal culture of science and literature."

Local artists like Russell Smith, David Blythe and the members of the Wall family not only enriched the quality of life in the burgeoning city, but also provided much of the visual documentation of the period. Some believe that Pittsburgh had an art museum and gallery as early as 1828. Perhaps the earliest, and certainly the longest lived, commercial art concern was the J.J. Gillespie Gallery, opened in 1832. Gillespie's was frequented by David G. Blythe (1815-1865), destined to become one of Pittsburgh's great talents. Blythe came to Pittsburgh in 1831 as an apprentice to another artist, Joseph Woodwell, in his woodcarving and furniture business. Later, in 1841, William Coventry Wall opened a shop for "Plain and Fancy Portrait and Picture Frames." Wall, along with his brother Alfred S. Wall and his nephew A. Bryan Wall, formed a family dynasty of painters who were among the first in Pittsburgh to pursue art as a livelihood. Other art initiatives of the early 19th century included the Pittsburgh Art Association (1859) and the Pittsburgh Academy for Instruction in Drawing and Painting (1855).

Music, too, captured the imagination of early Pittsburghers who founded the Pittsburgh Philharmonic Society in 1812, the Pittsburgh Musical Society in 1818 and the Mozart Society in 1838.

Built in 1790, this was the first of five churches on the corner of Sixth Avenue and Smithfield Street for the German Evangelical congregation.
Pittsburgh History & Landmarks Foundation

Despite the opposition of the town's Presbyterian leaders, Pittsburgh became possibly the best theater town in the Ohio Valley. As Henry M. Brackenridge noted in his *Recollections,* "the better class of society in the early time occasionally endeavored to amuse themselves with amateur theatricals." As early as the 1790s, according to the *Pittsburgh Gazette*, the officers in the garrison amused themselves by staging farces and other productions. Drama during this era found its first home on the top floor of the courthouse in 1803, where physicians, lawyers and mechanics performed Shakespeare, comic operas and the popular farces of that era. Three dramatic societies were active by 1812. Taverns also served as venues.

The city's first theater building opened nine years later at Third Avenue near Smithfield Street, a rather modest frame structure that held 400 persons, but was rarely used after 1826. Then, in 1833, Pittsburgh entrepreneurs spearheaded construction of the Pittsburgh Theatre, a fine, substantial establishment on Fifth Avenue between Smithfield and Wood streets. Most probably designed by prominent Philadelphia architect John Haviland, the 1,200-seat theater was considered an elegant establishment, with tiers of rose-colored boxes and crimson upholstery with brass nails. The theater opened with productions of *Busy Body* and *Of Age Tomorrow.* It was later known as the Old Drury. Other venues included the New National, the Apollo and the Pittsburgh Grand Opera House.

Literary and other interests found their voice in the Quintilian Society, the Franklin Society, a Historical Society (1834), an Institute of Arts and Sciences (1838) and the Pittsburgh Permanent Library Association (1816) of 500 volumes. The Permanent Library, a private membership organization, was nonetheless housed in the public setting of the courthouse on Market Square, with an initiation fee of $10 and annual dues of $5, but open only on Saturday evenings. Also housed in the courthouse was the Pittsburgh Chemical and Physiological Society (1813).

Formal primary and secondary education was not yet a thriving concern during this period. It was not until 1834 that Pittsburgh established a public school system, with two common schools opening the following year. In fact, when the city was incorporated in 1816, less than a quarter of school-age children actually attended school. At the same time, a number of private institutions were established, including Duff's Mercantile College (1840), a Catholic school (1844) and a handful of girls' boarding schools in the 1820s and 1830s. Although the Adelphia Free School (1816) and Union Society (1818) attempted to extend educational opportunities to poor children, neither was a success.

Nor did higher education blossom during the early 19th century. The Pittsburgh Academy was rechartered in 1819 as the Western University of Pennsylvania (which would become the University of Pittsburgh in 1908). It suffered a number of fires and by mid-century was still only graduating a few students. A number of women's colleges also appeared during this period. The Presbyterian Church established Pittsburgh Female College and the Episcopalians countered with the Bishop Bowman Institute. The Presbyterian Church also founded the Western Theological Seminary in Allegheny in 1825. Yet the presence of these institutions, however few and small they may have been, was important to a regional society that tended to keep its children local.

Pittsburgh also continued to develop during this period as a printing center, supplying a variety of books and other printed material to the westward-moving pioneers, who bought almanacs and books on religion, government and music, as well as textbooks, presumably for homeschooling of children in isolated pioneer settings. Zadock Cramer, one of the leaders in the printing business, opened a bookstore, which was believed to be Pittsburgh's second and known as "Sign of the Franklin Head"

The second building from the right is the Pittsburgh Theatre ("Old Drury"), built in 1833 and said to have been by the prominent Philadelphia architect John Haviland. *Carnegie Library of Pittsburgh, Pittsburgh Photographic Library*

in 1800 on Market Street between First and Second streets. Cramer quickly expanded into bookbinding and publishing and ultimately established a circulating library. By 1815 he had published 70 books and pamphlets, including the *Pittsburgh Almanack*.

Perhaps the most important book produced locally was *The Navigator*, a river guide authored by Cramer (and printed by John Scull) that detailed the Ohio Valley to the Mississippi River through woodcut maps and descriptive text that were updated almost every year beginning in 1801. By 1856 the city was home to some 35 printing firms. After mid-century, however, the rise of printing centers in the Eastern seaboard cities of Boston, New York and Philadelphia eclipsed Pittsburgh and the industry declined here.

The city's growth also supported the publication of additional newspapers to augment the *Pittsburgh Gazette*, the first newspaper west of the Alleghenies, which Hugh Henry Brackenridge had begun publishing in 1786. Under the leadership of John Scull, Joseph Hall, and Neville Craig, the *Gazette* represented the voices that fought to expand the nation and abolish slavery. The *Pittsburgh Gazette* became a daily in 1833 and would ultimately grow to become the *Pittsburgh Post-Gazette*.

As Scull became more conservative and Brackenridge became more liberal, Brackenridge in 1800 launched an anti-Federalist paper, *Tree of Liberty*, which only survived for a few years. The *Commonwealth* operated from 1805 until 1818 and was subsequently renamed the *Statesman*. More newspapers followed in rapid succession: the *Mercury* (1811), the *Pioneer* (1812), the *Western Gleaner* (1813), the *Record* (1814), the *Statesman* (1820), the *Allegheny Democrat* (1824), the *Western Journal* (1826), the *American Manufacturer* (1830), the *Pittsburgh Times* (1831), the *Daily Bulletin* (1837), the *Daily American* (1840), the *Pittsburgh Chronicle* (1841) and the *Daily Morning Post* (1842). By 1842, reflecting the city's prosperity, Pittsburgh boasted six dailies and 12 weeklies, three of them published in German.

Caring for our Own

In the spirit of Jacksonian democracy, the early 19th century saw a surge of social conscience that manifested itself in a variety of agencies to help the poor, the orphaned and the otherwise disadvantaged. Like most cities that were beginning to experience the ill effects of industrial and urban development, Pittsburgh created a benevolent culture that operated both through the churches and independently.

Pittsburgh's first poorhouse was established in 1818, an Asylum for Orphans in 1832 and the Pittsburgh Provident Society and Pittsburgh and Allegheny Relief Society in 1839. A Humane Society was organized in 1813 to "alleviate the distress of the poor — to supply the wants of the hungry, the naked and the aged — to administer comfort to the widow, the orphan and the sick," all on annual dues of $2. The Erin Benevolent Society, an Irish relief agency, operated from at least 1819 to 1826. Other organizations devoted themselves to reforms such as temperance or abolition.

Fire Levels the City

Illustrated in 1840 by an engraving published in Edinburgh, Scotland, Pittsburgh was a bustling city recovering from the panic of 1837 and the subsequent depression. Iron was the core of the economic structure, representing nearly $5 million in annual production. With a population of 21,115, the city had 50 churches and a five-year-old public school system, as well as gas lighting, a water system fed by reservoir on Grant's Hill and a volunteer fire department.

Pittsburgh in 1840 from Grant's Hill. The Hill, as it is now called, was largely unpopulated and served as a recreation and military exercise ground. *Pittsburgh History & Landmarks Foundation*

(Far right)
The Great Fire,
April 10, 1845
Photo by William Rydberg, Photon

(Right)
The Smoky City in 1843 — this is a view toward the Pittsburgh that Charles Dickens visited in 1842, looking up the Ohio from Saw Mill Run. Three years after Dickens' visit, much of the city was effaced by fire. The smoky structure in the foreground is a saltworks.
Painting by Russell Smith, Carnegie Library of Pittsburgh, Pittsburgh Photographic Library

Pittsburgh from two miles down the Ohio River just before the Great Fire
Carnegie Library of Pittsburgh, Pittsburgh Photographic Library

Charles Dickens, during his visit to Pittsburgh in 1842, characterized the city at that time:

> It certainly has a great quantity of smoke hanging about it, and is famous for its ironworks... It is very beautifully situated on the Alleghany [sic] River, over which there are two bridges; and the villas of the wealthier citizens, sprinkled about the high grounds in the neighborhood, are pretty enough.

This era of growth and prosperity came to an abrupt halt with the devastating fire of April 10, 1845. Believed to have started as a woodshed laundry fire at the corner of Ferry and Second Avenue, the conflagration quickly spread along the Monongahela side of the city and consumed 56 acres, or 24 blocks, of Pittsburgh's core, destroying nearly 1,000 buildings, with losses estimated in the millions. Almost 12,000, or more than a third, of the city's population were left homeless, although the fire claimed only two lives. The magnitude of the disaster was exacerbated by a very dry spring, windy conditions that day, the poor quality of the municipal water service and the city's reliance on a volunteer fire department.

The fire consumed the Monongahela House and five other hotels, Western Pennsylvania University, the Custom House, the *Daily Chronicle* office, the mayor's offices, and the engine house of the Vigilant Fire Company. It also destroyed three churches, two bookstores, Globe Cotton Textile Mill, two glass houses (including the Benjamin Bakewell Factory) and several iron works. "Iron and glass were melted as thoroughly as when passed through furnaces," reported William Johnston. The Monongahela Bridge was all in flames within seven minutes of being ignited. The *Pittsburgh Gazette* survived sufficiently to report on the calamity: "Nothing was spared — very little saved. The progress of the fire as it lanced and leaped with its forked tongue from house to house, from block to block and from square to square was awfully magnificent."

"View of the Ruins of the City of Pittsburgh from Boyd's Hill," a lithograph after a painting by William C. Wall
Pittsburgh History & Landmarks Foundation

The only pre-fire building surviving to this day is the Burke Building, which stands juxtaposed to an icon of 20th-century Pittsburgh, Philip Johnson's PPG Place complex.

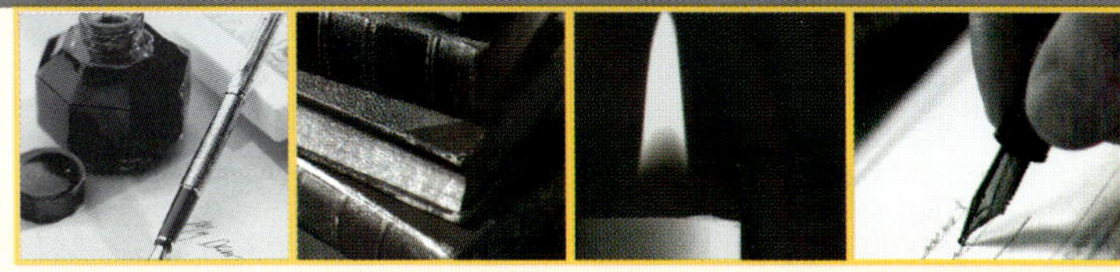

Biographies

MIKE FINK (1770-1823)

Pittsburgh's extensive river traffic made for a life rich in folklore. Earning the status of folklore legend, Mike Fink was a real-life boatman who typified the boisterous, muscular, crude personalities (about 3,000 of them after the War of 1812) who made their life on the rivers. Like his compatriots, Fink was a character brimming with confidence and contention:

> "I'm a Salt River roarer!... I love the women an' I'm chockful o' fight! I'm half wild horse and half cock-eyed alligator and the rest o' me is crooked snags an' red-hot snapin' turkle... I can out-run, out-jump, out-shoot, out-brag, out-drink, an' out-fight, rough-an'-tumble, no holts barred, ary man on both sides the river form Pittsburgh to New Orleans an' back ag'in to St Louiee."

Other stories of the river appear notably tame by comparison.

The legendary Mike Fink, as portrayed by William Gropper
Carnegie Library of Pittsburgh, Pittsburgh Photographic Library

Neville B. Craig
Carnegie Library of Pittsburgh, Pittsburgh Photographic Library

NEVILLE B. CRAIG (1787-1863)

Born in the historic Fort Pitt Blockhouse, which his father Isaac Craig had converted to a dwelling, Neville Craig fittingly went on to become Pittsburgh's first historian. A Princeton graduate, he distinguished himself as a scholar, writer and lawyer, and as the "fearless, crusty, keen" editor of the *Pittsburgh Gazette* from 1829 to 1841. Neville Craig's first and last names survive as street names in the Oakland section of Pittsburgh, which began to develop during the last decade of the 19th century on the Craig farm, "Bellefield."

John Chislett
Photo by Clyde Hare

JOHN CHISLETT, ARCHITECT (1800-1869)

The first Pittsburgh architect whose work is relatively well known is Englishman John Chislett. He studied in Bath, England, before coming to America. He was practicing architecture in Pittsburgh by 1833 and maintained an office as "architect and fancy painter" on Federal Street in Allegheny in 1837.

CHAPTER 3

Iron City

1845-1875

ACCORDING TO YOUNG THOMAS MELLON, THE 1845 fire cleared Pittsburgh's core and set the stage for a new era of development. "Instead of depression, it gave an impetus to every kind of business." With relief money coming in from as far away as London, Pittsburgh rebuilt itself and by 1850 was again a dense, busy urban center. Within four years of the great fire, the city appeared in a colored lithograph as a bustling place, the riverfront lined with boats and small-scale industry. Its population exceeded 45,000, and

Pittsburgh is shown in a lithograph of 1859 by William Schuchman, with the second Courthouse and the towers of St. Paul's Cathedral dominating the skyline. To the left is Allegheny. Vignettes show the nearby communities of Manchester (bottom left) and Birmingham (bottom right). *Pittsburgh History & Landmarks Foundation*

annual production from manufacturing was estimated at $50 million. Over the ensuing decades, the city increased in population, in territory and in amenities. This was the beginning of an epoch of expansion that would last for nearly 100 years.

The first through train from Philadelphia at East Liberty near Pittsburgh, December 10, 1852 *Carnegie Library of Pittsburgh, Pittsburgh Photographic Library*

Enter the Rails – a City Transformed

As Pittsburgh emerged from the ashes, it was transformed by the introduction of the Pennsylvania Railroad. With the arrival of the first train in 1851, the region began the shift from a consumer-based economy to one built on large-scale production of iron and, ultimately, steel.

Improvements in roads, the introduction of steamboats and the construction of canals had initially provided cheaper and faster means of transportation, but they had all posed limitations. Roads were slow and expensive; steamboats were useful only on navigable rivers; and canals not only posed geographic limitations, but often froze in the winter. The beginning of the Age of Steam, which had come to America in the late 1820s, took another quarter century to reach Pittsburgh. Yet when it did, the steam railroad etched an indelible mark on the face of business and the built environment.

The Baltimore and Ohio Railroad had been chartered in 1827, just two years after the completion of the Erie Canal, in an effort to restore Baltimore's position as the dominant eastern city in the western trade arena. It began construction on the first commercial railroad in the United States on July 4, 1828, but would not reach its western terminus at Wheeling on the Ohio River until well after 1850, and only reached Pittsburgh considerably later.

After 1850, railroads boomed, especially in northern states. The federal government actively encouraged railroad construction by providing generous land grants to railroad companies. Following on the heels of Millard Fillmore's first railroad land-grant act in 1850, by 1857, 45 railroads received about 18 million acres of land from the government and by 1860 over 30,000 miles of track interlaced the Northeast and the Midwest.

Pittsburgh's first railroad was the Ohio & Pennsylvania Railroad (later the Pennsylvania), which connected New Brighton in the Beaver Valley to the west with Allegheny City on October 6, 1851. But it was the Pennsylvania Railroad (PRR), chartered by the General Assembly of Pennsylvania in 1846, that first succeeded in 1852 in providing the link from the east to Pittsburgh, cutting three days off the time required to travel on the Pennsylvania Mainline Canal. The 249-mile stretch from Harrisburg was an engineering triumph, crossing the

Allegheny Mountains via the famous Horseshoe Curve in Blair County and the 3,612-foot Summit Tunnel under the Gallitzin Mountains, eliminating the last 150 vertical feet of the Horseshoe Curve. The project was overseen by engineer John Edgar Thomson (1808-1874), who was elected president of the railroad that year and for whom Andrew Carnegie would name his first successful Bessemer steel works in North Braddock in 1873.

Initially the Pennsylvania Railroad extended only to Turtle Creek, about 12 miles east of Pittsburgh, where a 28-mile gap was traversed by stagecoach before the tracks resumed their eastward connection. Then, on December 10, 1852, the first truly cross-state Pennsylvania Railroad train trip crossed the mountains from Philadelphia and arrived at East Liberty. A large crowd of politicians, industrialists, civic leaders and common folk gathered in the village to celebrate the opening of the new line. It had taken six days to travel from Philadelphia to Pittsburgh by stagecoach in 1812 and about 16 days for freight on the Conestoga wagon to complete the nearly 300-mile trip. By contrast, a one-way trip on the PRR from Philadelphia to Pittsburgh took 15 hours in 1856. An editorial in the *Pittsburgh Gazette* proclaimed, "fifteen hours from Pittsburgh to Philadelphia ought to satisfy the fastest of this fast generation." Railroad service from Pittsburgh west to Chicago opened in 1856.

With its east-west route complete, the PRR purchased the Mainline Canal, including the Allegheny Portage Railroad, in 1857 for $7.5 million. The railroad did not cause the decline of steamboat freight travel on western waters, however, until after the Civil War. The disruption of river travel during the war, together with greater railroad construction during and after the war, put an end to the brief but glorious era of the antebellum steamboat world so celebrated by Mark Twain and others.

Over the next 30 years, the PRR expanded dramatically, acquiring so many short lines that by 1860 it already had a near monopoly of all rail traffic through Pennsylvania from Chicago. This transportation revolution fueled urban growth in the west such that cities like Cincinnati, St. Louis and Chicago had populations exceeding 100,000 each, and Pittsburgh had 50,000.

The railroad's impact was not only in its links to eastern and western markets, but also in its seemingly endless demand for tracks and fuel, which provided an enormous boost to the iron and coal industries after the 1840s. By 1880, Pittsburgh would be served by more than 14 separate lines.

Telecommunications Hint at Globalization

On the eve of the Civil War, trains and steamboats carried passengers and freight, as well as letters, newspapers and other sources of information. With the invention of the telegraph by Samuel Finley Breese Morse (1791-1872), the stage was set for a revolution in long-distance communication in the nation and, indeed, the world. In 1847, just three years after Morse's first telegraph transmission on a federally sponsored line from Washington, D.C. to Baltimore, the *Pittsburgh Post* was the first city newspaper to use the new communication technology for news coverage. On July 9, 1850, the recently elected president Zachary Taylor suddenly died and was succeeded by Millard Fillmore, his vice president. The news of his death was carried over the country in rapid time, due to the new "magnetic telegraph." By the eve of the Civil War, all newspapers in Pittsburgh were using the telegraph in their news-gathering activities.

It would be another quarter century before the telephone would be introduced in Pittsburgh. The "speaking telephone" was demonstrated at the Monongahela House in 1877 to Thomas R.A. David, head of the Central District and Printing Telegraph Company, who was suitably impressed. First used in business that year, it did not reach the residential consumer until some years later.

A mid-Victorian dry-goods store at 1805 Carson Street on the South Side, an area that until 1872 had been the borough of East Birmingham. *Pittsburgh History & Landmarks Foundation*

The Urban Environment in the Iron City

Prosperity and vision soon manifested themselves in Pittsburgh's built environment as the city reinvented itself after the 1845 fire. Within 15 years, the city was ranked 16th in the nation, and Pittsburgh and Allegheny City had a collective population of nearly 125,000 people, with about 10,000 houses and 100 different industries.

Documented for curious readers nationwide on the pages of *Harper's Weekly*, *Ballou's Pictorial* and *Gleason's Pictorial Drawing Room Companion*, Pittsburgh and Allegheny during the 1850s boasted a collection of relatively substantial new buildings. Among them were a domed courthouse on Grant's

(Above)
The Monongahela House as it was around 1900
Library and Archives Division, Historical Society of Western Pennsylvania, Pittsburgh, Pa.

The Duquesne Depot as it was during the Centennial Celebration of 1858
Carnegie Library of Pittsburgh, Pittsburgh Photographic Library

Hill, a customhouse and a newly rebuilt Monongahela House hotel, as well as 17 other hotels. Several monumental churches also made their marks on the urban skyline: St. Mary's German Catholic Church in Allegheny City (still standing); the First Presbyterian Church on Sixth Avenue in Pittsburgh, which would be replaced shortly after the turn of the 20th century; Trinity Episcopal Cathedral next door; and St. Paul's Cathedral at Fifth Avenue and Grant Street, second only in size to New York's St. Patrick's. Also notable was the Duquesne Depot of the Pennsylvania Railroad at the Point, where Pittsburghers celebrated their centennial in 1858.

By the 1870s, Pittsburgh and Allegheny City would boast no less than 87 banks, including 27 national banks. They enhanced the built environment with monumental designs that bespoke security for the millions they safeguarded and represented the major architectural idioms of the age, most predominantly Italianate, Second Empire and Classical. Dollar Bank on Fourth Avenue is the only survivor of this large collection of banks.

Population growth soon taxed the physical limitations of the central city, hemmed in as it was by the three rivers and the slopes of Grant's Hill. Development pressures intensified as industrialization brought changes to the quality of life that were not all positive. Those who could began to flee to outlying areas to escape the smoke and congestion. During the latter half of the 19th century, the outlying areas grew in earnest. In time, the city would grow by annexation of those suburbs, adding another 100,000 to the population.

Already, a number of small towns had cropped up along the riverfronts close to the Point. These towns typically supported a variety of industrial concerns and developed in somewhat irregular grid patterns. Birmingham, on the south side of the Monongahela River, had been laid out in 1811 by John Ormsby's son-in-law, Nathaniel Bedford, and Isaac Craig, the glassmaker, and had been named after Craig's hometown in England. It was incorporated as a borough in 1826. An adjacent town of Sidneyville was laid out at the same time. Shortly after Birmingham and Sidneyville were laid out, in 1816 George A. Bayard and James Adams laid out the Northern Liberties borough, which originally consisted

A lithograph from c. 1870 of Birmingham (in the foreground) with the cities of Pittsburgh and Allegheny beyond
Pittsburgh History & Landmarks Foundation

Birmingham and East Birmingham in 1872, the time of their annexation by Pittsburgh
Pittsburgh History & Landmarks Foundation

of two towns: Bayardstown, extending from 11th through 26th streets, and Lawrenceville. The Northern Liberties was incorporated in 1829, Lawrenceville was incorporated as a separate borough in 1834, and the Northern Liberties was annexed to the city of Pittsburgh in 1837, the only borough to be annexed before 1867.

By 1857 nine municipalities existed in the area around the Triangle: the city of Pittsburgh, Allegheny City, and the boroughs of Manchester, Duquesne, Lawrenceville, East Birmingham, Birmingham, South Pittsburgh and West Pittsburgh. Several more had been established by the time Pittsburgh underwent a sudden expansion in the five years between 1867 and 1872. The annexation occurred first within the confines of the Allegheny and Monongahela rivers, as the city limits were expanded in 1867 to include Lawrenceville borough and the townships of Pitt, Oakland, Peebles, Liberty and Collins. In the same year and the one following it, Allegheny City annexed Manchester Borough, Reserve Township, Duquesne Borough (along the Allegheny River), and two parcels of unnamed land. The second wave of annexation came in 1872, as 27 square miles south of the Monongahela river were added to the city of Pittsburgh, and the city of Allegheny doubled its size.

Other annexations would follow during the last decade of the 19th century and the first seven years of the 20th. This sustained growth spurt would eventually culminate in the annexation of the city of Allegheny and its population of 129,000 to the city of Pittsburgh in 1907.

Accompanying this growth spurt, the city's infrastructure began to reflect its growing prosperity and prominence. The consolidation of areas separated by rivers and hills required the consideration of increased communication among them. Until 1818 the only access across the rivers was by ferry. The first two bridges across the Monongahela and the Allegheny Rivers were simple wooden structures on masonry caissons. Three decades later, in 1846, John Roebling introduced the concept of wire cable suspension

"On the Monongahela," oil on canvas, 1860, by William Coventry Wall
Westmoreland Museum of American Art

in bridge design. The Sixth Street bridge, his second in the city, showcased the new technology and was acknowledged as the finest in the world. Roebling would later go on to build the Brooklyn Bridge. Despite the new technology, the city continued to have wooden covered bridges as late as 1874.

Allegheny Cemetery, incorporated in 1844, was planned by John Chislett as a Romantic landscape. *Photo by Clyde Hare*

(Opposite page, top right) A mid-19th century rolling mill. Workers are rolling a small channel iron in this labor-intensive operation. *Carnegie Library of Pittsburgh, Pittsburgh Photographic Library*

(Opposite page, top left) The glassworks of Atterbury & Company in the late 19th century *Library and Archives Division, Historical Society of Western Pennsylvania, Pittsburgh, Pa.*

Further outward, a new set of communities was developing. Communities like Sewickley, Edgewood, Evergreen Hamlet, East Liberty, Hazelwood and Swissvale offered idyllic village or "suburban" living that proved to be a welcome relief from the dense, dirty quality of urban life. Inadequate transportation initially remained an obstacle to the outward movement. Until the Pennsylvania Railroad reached East Liberty and Shadyside in the 1850s, horse-drawn streetcars took two hours to make the run from East Liberty to downtown. Even as late as 1860, Pittsburgh did not have a single upper-class neighborhood. Families tended to scatter over a wide region. Only later did wealthier families begin to congregate in Allegheny City.

For those who did not have the luxury of moving out, temporary relief from urban conditions was available at nearby Grant's Hill, which functioned as a sort of park. A bit farther out in Lawrenceville was Allegheny Cemetery, established in 1844 as the nation's sixth major rural "park" cemetery. Used as Pittsburgh's primary burial ground, Allegheny Cemetery came to provide a verdant escape from the smoke, noise and congestion that came hand in hand with industrialization.

The Forty-third Street Bridge across the Allegheny River was built in 1870. Some river bridges were wooden covered at this time, and all were private and charged tolls. *Carnegie Library of Pittsburgh, Pittsburgh Photographic Library*

Early Visionaries of the Industrial Era

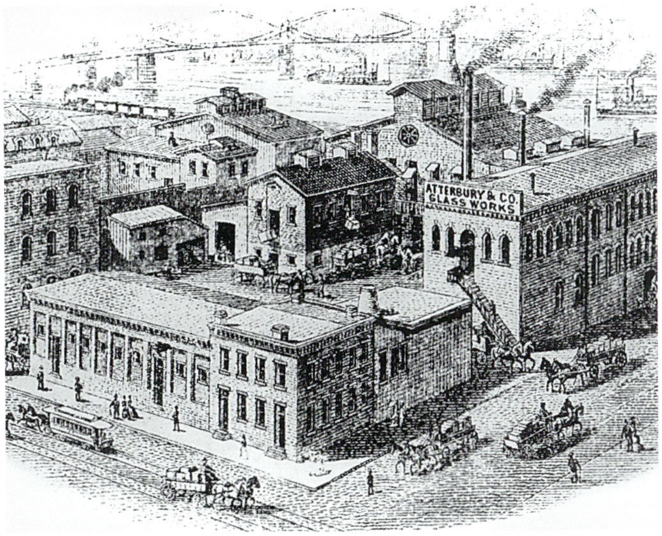

As in each era of Pittsburgh's legendary story, the iron age spawned its share of visionaries who saw potential in the city and its resources, seized opportunity and created new industries to operate as cogs in the city's mighty manufacturing machine. These individuals, in concert with the financial and human capital that fueled their businesses, led the Pittsburgh region from an economy and a lifestyle that was based in agriculture and small-scale commerce to one that lived and breathed industry.

As Pittsburgh boomed into the "Forge of the Universe," it became an internationally renowned center for transportation, production and innovation, with 500 manufacturing concerns fueling the economy and the beginnings of great fortunes. Fahnestock's *Pittsburgh Directory*, published in 1850 at the beginning of this era of expansion, already cited some staggering statistics:

- 13 rolling mills employing 2,500
- 30 foundries employing 2,500
- At least 25 glass factories employing over 1,000
- Five large cotton factories and many smaller ones employing 1,500

These major operations were joined by other establishments involved in such industries as iron casting, soda ash manufacturing, copper rolling, white lead production and more. Total annual product in Pittsburgh and the vicinity exceeded

(Bottom left)
In this *Harper's Weekly* wood engraving of 1873, workers are tapping the "iron notch" of a blast furnace.
Pittsburgh History & Landmarks Foundation

(Below)
Making cylinder glass for window panes, in the 1870s
Pittsburgh History & Landmarks Foundation

Across the Monongahela, in this view of c. 1900, is the Clinton Furnace of Graff, Bennett & Company (left of center). *Archives Service Center, University of Pittsburgh*

(Right)
A blast furnace in 1871, with the lid raised so a "top filler" could dump a barrow load of charge — iron ore, coke, and limestone (which, when melted, absorbed some of the impurities and became slag). *Carnegie Library of Pittsburgh, Pittsburgh Photographic Library*

(Far right)
The bottom of a blast furnace. It appears that the "iron notch" has just been tapped, and the furnace crew is guiding the hot metal into the molds that will form it into pigs, small ingots for melting in foundry furnaces. *Carnegie Library of Pittsburgh, Pittsburgh Photographic Library*

A postcard of the Eberhardt & Ober Brewery, late 19th century
Pittsburgh History & Landmarks Foundation

$30 million, coal consumption was estimated at 12 million bushels, and imports by river and canal that year were more than 500,000 tons.

Using iron from rural blast furnaces in Westmoreland, Fayette and Greene counties, Pittsburgh's iron foundries and rolling mills were already booming when the Clinton Furnace was constructed on the South Side in 1859 by Graff, Bennett & Company. It was only the city's second furnace and the first coke-burning blast furnace in the immediate area. By 1874, 11 blast furnaces produced 144,000 tons of metal. By the end of the 1870s, 15 blast furnaces turned out 300,000 tons of metal. In the meantime, iron would be surpassed by steel.

One of the earliest of the visionary industrialists, Samuel M. Kier, chose not to follow his father in the salt-producing business, but rather to try his luck as a merchant in Pittsburgh. After a rocky start and the disappointments of the 1837 depression, Kier moved into a series of successful ventures, including a company that operated boats on the Pennsylvania Canal. The turning point in his career came with the discovery of oil as a troublesome by-product in his father's salt wells. Seizing the opportunity, Kier first marketed the oil as a medicinal cure-all, and only later realized its potential for lighting lamps. Importing the oil in barrels down the Allegheny River, Kier became the world's first oil refiner, eclipsing his other accomplishments in the manufacture of firebrick, operation of a pottery, coal mining and steel production. He ultimately became an early partner in what would become Jones and Laughlin Steel Corporation.

Brewing had appeared on the local manufacturing scene as early as 1803 with James O'Hara's Point Brewery, built near the Fort Pitt Blockhouse. O'Hara's Brewery utilized glass bottles from his South Side glass factory and operated until fire destroyed it in 1813. Zadock Cramer's 1804 edition of the *Almanac* lists the production of beer and porter in Pittsburgh at 900 barrels annually. From two breweries in 1807 to five in

1837, employing 60 workers, the brewing industry established a foothold that would only continue to grow. The industry expanded greatly after the 1840s with the influx of a large immigrant German population to the city. Men like Straub, Vilsak, Ober and Eberhardt opened many of the new and successful breweries that would come to dominate the industry in the second half of the 19th century. By 1870 Pittsburgh's 52 breweries would post sales of $4.8 million, lagging only slightly behind the year's $5.4 million in steel production!

Operating on a smaller scale were the visionaries who represented the upper middle class. These merchants, bankers and brokers, doctors and lawyers, and other professionals, many of whom left secure businesses in eastern cities like Baltimore and Philadelphia, risked their careers and oftentimes their own capital to establish speculative ventures and follow the lure of economic prosperity that Pittsburgh offered. The commercial infrastructure they built supported the city's renowned industrial empire.

Visionaries Turn to Activism

During the mid-19th century, Pittsburgh also grew in stature as a focus of trendsetting thought and activism. The same risk-oriented individuals who brought their vision to the business arena applied it to influence politics and affect social change. The city became a stronghold for abolitionism and early labor organization and saw the founding of the Republican Party here in 1856.

The Rev. Charles Avery
Carnegie Library of Pittsburgh, Pittsburgh Photographic Library

The antebellum period was a crucial time for the region's African-American population, not only to build a community in Pittsburgh, but also to respond to the national crisis that centered on the slavery issue. The local black community prior to the Civil War resembled that in most northern cities, with Pittsburgh's African-American population hovering around 2,000 people (less than 5 percent of the city's total) who were impoverished and subject to racial discrimination. Nonetheless, the community had established the first black church in the Pittsburgh area as early as 1818 and over the years supported a growing number of institutions, including several benevolent societies, Lincoln Cemetery, a militia company and a temperance society.

The Great Compromise of 1850, enacted by the U.S. Congress, consisted of several parts, including the Fugitive Slave Law, negotiated by Henry Clay. The Fugitive Slave Law amended and strengthened the previous law of 1793 permitting slave owners to pursue and capture runaway slaves. The effect of this legislation in Pittsburgh, as through much of the North, was to galvanize a defiant opposition to slavery among abolitionists, religious leaders and intellectuals. On September 30, 1850, the *Pittsburgh Daily Gazette* reported that "a meeting of the citizens of Allegheny County opposed to the fugitive slave law, without distinction of party, was called in the Diamond," drawing "a tremendous concourse of persons." Rev. Charles Avery and others issued a public cry for open resistance to the law, saying, "every man who accepts a commission under it should be branded with the mark of infamy." The following day, politicians led a meeting at the Allegheny Market House (which stood on the current site of Allegheny Center) and drew up a resolution calling for a congressional repeal of the law, which they called "an outrage on constitutional liberty not to be tolerated."

Despite this opposition, the immediate effect of the Fugitive Slave Law was a massive flight to Canada. One anti-slavery newspaper, *The Liberator*, reported that just days before the September 30 meeting in Pittsburgh, some 100 fugitives had already left Pittsburgh, including all of the black waiters from a single hotel, with an additional 200 leaving over the next month.

Those who remained, however, joined with the city's established anti-slavery community, led by both white and black abolitionists, and played a vital role in helping others either to remain or to flee safely. In some cases, they raised the money to buy the runaways from the slave hunters. Anti-slavery papers like the *Pittsburgh Daily Gazette* printed compelling personal stories of local and national fugitive cases, with citizens frequently banding together in aggressive, vigilant pursuit of the slave hunters.

The movement generated a great deal of inter-racial cooperation as blacks and whites banded against a common enemy. Among the leaders of this effort were John B. Vashon, Martin R. Delany, Rev. Charles Avery and Jane Gray Swisshelm. Delany, an African American, published the abolitionist newspaper *The Mystery* and promoted Black Nationalism. Avery (1784-1858) not only dared to acknowledge the social and biological equality of blacks and to fight slavery, but in 1849 he founded the Avery Church and Avery Institute (later Avery College), a school for blacks in Allegheny City. Swisshelm, an advocate of both abolition and women's rights, made her impact as a journalist, newspaper editor and national lecturer.

The natural consequence of this strong anti-slavery sentiment was active participation in the Underground Railroad, a story that remains shrouded in mystery, given its defiance of national law, the lack of written records and the consequent reliance on oral tradition to pass it along. This dramatic story, as described by historian Irene Williams, had to many "the excitement of piracy, the secrecy of burglary, the daring of insurrection." Yet others would characterize it as a quiet, discreet effort that took advantage not only of the local political and social climate, but also of ready river transportation and the region's terrain with its wooded hills, deep ravines and deep underbrush.

Several sites in Pittsburgh and the surrounding area are commonly regarded as having served as stations on the Underground Railroad. Among them are the Bigham House, now a part of Chatham Village on Mount Washington, and a Shadyside house at 4841 Ellsworth Avenue.

Civil rights activism continued after the Civil War, with the passage in 1869 of the 15th Amendment to the Constitution, guaranteeing the right of blacks to vote in Pennsylvania. And by 1875, protests by black Pittsburghers finally succeeded in making Pittsburgh one of the nation's earliest cities with a desegregated school system.

Still other activists turned their attention to the issues that faced the variety of skilled and unskilled artisans and laborers that made up the working class: carpenters, blacksmiths, mill hands, mechanics, tailors, boot makers and others. Early initiatives had represented broad spectrums of workers, including the Pittsburgh Manufacturing Company (1819), a cooperative warehousing and marketing entity; the Pittsburgh Central Labor Union (1836), a consortium of 14 craft organizations; and

In 1963, the Rev. Elijah Pettus shows the entrance to a stop on the Underground Railroad in the North Side's Avery Memorial Church. *Carnegie Library of Pittsburgh, Pittsburgh Photographic Library*

the Iron City Industrial Congress (1849), which represented some 23 organizations. As time went on, the unions represented more specialized constituencies, such as the Sons of Vulcan (1858), that comprised iron puddlers and other laborers.

The laboring class also championed issues of more general interest. The Workingman's Party of the 1830s, for example, fought for the protective tariffs that they viewed as critical to the survival of the laboring class, but also worked for free public education and the elimination of debtors' prisons. The unions would not become strong forces, however, until the next phase of industrial development.

It was not until Pittsburgh-based activism manifested itself in the founding of the Republican Party in 1856 that the laboring class found a widely audible voice. The party that would launch Abraham Lincoln into the presidency had its roots in a meeting on Washington's birthday at Lafayette Hall on Wood Street in Pittsburgh. Lincoln would, in fact, win the largest majority in Allegheny County of any county in the United States. A crowd of 500 delegates representing 24 states and two territories assembled as a national organization to arrange a convention at Philadelphia and to select their candidates for the upcoming election. Their platform: free labor, free soil, and free men. Obviously pivotal in the national political context, the new party

The Columbiad cannon, product of the Fort Pitt Foundry
Carnegie Library of Pittsburgh, Pittsburgh Photographic Library

held particular significance in Pittsburgh, which was effectively reduced to a one-party town for the next 75 years or so.

The Civil War – A City Invested

Given the anti-slavery sentiment that dominated the regional mindset, and the fact that its economy was based on the very industries that war demanded, Pittsburgh not surprisingly threw itself into the war effort, both in the trenches and on the production lines. Pittsburgh's commitment to the Civil War was reflected not only in the 24,000 Allegheny County men sent to fight with the Union forces, but also in the measurable boost it gave to the local economy. Already established in armament production during the Mexican War, Pittsburgh sealed its position as the nation's military supplier during the Civil War. It was arguably the Civil War demands for weapons, locomotives and ironclad boats, in fact, that first launched Pittsburgh into industrial giant status.

The Fort Pitt Foundry, located at 28th Street in Allegheny, furnished the Union army with 10 million pounds of shot and shell and almost 3,000 cannon. Its 15-inch Columbiad, the biggest gun in the world, was 190 inches long; loaded with 35 pounds of large grained powder, it could shoot shells of more than 300 pounds to a distance of 4 miles. Guns manufactured at Pittsburgh armed the *Monitor*, the Union's first ironclad vessel.

Social Fabric and Quality of Life in the Iron City

By the beginning of the Civil War, a third of the population was European-born, with Irish and Germans as the largest groups, followed by the English, Scots and French. In 1850, 10,000 Irish immigrants, fleeing the potato famine in their homeland, comprised more than 21 percent of the city's population. They worked in factories and as domestics. Germans, largely concentrated in Allegheny City and lending it the nickname of "Deutschtown," were heavily engaged in the brewing and canning industries.

Pittsburgh began to develop those aspects of social, educational and cultural life that elevate a city to legendary status and create an enduring heritage. The institutions that arose represented both high and low culture.

The first public high school, Central High School, opened in 1855 opposite the customhouse. By 1870 the city boasted 16,000 high school graduates and more than 9,000 college graduates. Pittsburgh became a pioneer among large cities in 1875 when it desegregated its schools.

Augmenting the academic opportunities introduced by the Pittsburgh Academy in 1787, Pennsylvania College for Women was incorporated in 1869 and opened in the fall of 1870 under the auspices of the Presbyterian Church. It joined the ranks of prestigious women's colleges such as Mount Holyoke (1837) and Vassar (1861), but actually predated Wellesley (1870), Smith (1875) and Bryn Mawr. This forward-thinking institution would later come to be known as Pennsylvania College for Women (1890) and later still as Chatham College (1955). Slightly later, in October 1878, The Pittsburgh Catholic College of the Holy Ghost opened its doors with an enrollment of 40 students and a faculty of seven.

Pittsburghers moved in the years before the Civil War to establish institutions for emergency and other medical care. Perhaps it was a wake-up call from the disastrous fire of 1845, which exposed the inadequacies of the city's emergency services. Or perhaps it was a reaction to the conditions of urban life. *The Pittsburgh Post*, for instance, reported a total of 400 deaths in two weeks during the city's worst cholera epidemic in 1854. During the years that followed, the Sisters of Mercy opened their first hospital in Pittsburgh in 1847, the Pittsburgh Infirmary (later Passavant Hospital) was established in 1849 as the oldest Protestant hospital in the city, Western Pennsylvania (West Penn) opened in 1853, and the Allegheny Medical Society was organized as a branch of the State Medical Society. St. Francis Hospital was founded in 1865 to cater to a largely German Catholic clientele.

From Iron City to Steel City

For a time, Pittsburgh's dominance as the Iron City was challenged. Bethlehem Iron Company had a major operation in the eastern end of the state and a concentration of furnaces in the counties to the east of Pittsburgh — Armstrong, Venango, Clarion, Fayette, Westmoreland, Indiana and Cambria — represented 75 percent of all western Pennsylvania iron production. The major western Pennsylvania competitors were the Cambria Iron Works at Johnstown and the Brady's Bend Iron Works in Armstrong County, built originally as the Great Western Iron Works. Brady's Bend figured nationally for setting industry standards, pioneering the use of coke instead of charcoal, increasing furnace size, rolling the first T-rails west of the Alleghenies in 1846, and introducing the notion of integrated production, with a rolling mill right at the site of the iron furnace. With a capital investment of more than $1 million, four operating furnaces by 1872 and a work force of 1,500 men at its peak, the Brady's Bend Iron Works was a viable contender. The company closed shortly after the Panic of 1873, however, just about the time that Carnegie was introducing Bessemer steel production outside of Pittsburgh.

The challenge quickly fell away as Pittsburgh underwent yet another transformation from Iron City to Steel City. As technology and transportation changed, the age of iron became the age of steel, and industrial activity shifted in the 1840s from rural areas producing agricultural tools, grates, stoves and wagon wheels, to the county's urban centers producing rail to meet the enormous demands of the burgeoning railroad industry.

The battle of the *Monitor* (right) and the *Virginia*, or *Merrimack*
Pittsburgh History & Landmarks Foundation

Biographies

John A. Roebling
Carnegie Library of Pittsburgh, Pittsburgh Photographic Library

JOHN A. ROEBLING (1806-1869)

A German-born renaissance man whose interests spanned architecture, engineering, philosophy and music, John Roebling was a visionary who came to western Pennsylvania in 1831 with his brother, Karl, to establish a German farming community in a setting where independent thought and free enterprise were encouraged. More importantly, Roebling was an entrepreneur who founded the nearby town of Saxonburg in 1841 and built there the world's first factory for making wire rope and cables. One of the first applications of this new technology was to pull railroad cars across the Allegheny Mountains on the portage railroad of the Pennsylvania Canal. Roebling then turned to developing innovative wire cable suspension bridges. In 1844-45, he built his first, an aqueduct across the Allegheny River as part of the Pennsylvania Canal. After the 1845 fire, he designed another suspension bridge across the Monongahela River at Smithfield Street, which took seven months to build and stood for 40 years. The innovative design utilized cast-iron towers with cables suspended from pendulums. Roebling later took this Pittsburgh-born technology to New York and is best known today as the designer of the Brooklyn Bridge, which he did not live to see completed.

Martin Robinson Delany
Carnegie Library of Pittsburgh, Pittsburgh Photographic Library

MARTIN ROBINSON DELANY (1812-1885)

Martin Delany was one of the earliest and most prominent leaders of Pittsburgh's black community. As one of the nation's most outspoken abolitionists, he established *The Mystery,* an anti-slavery newspaper, in the 1840s and worked with Frederick Douglass to publish *The North Star*, another popular paper, in 1847. Many historians recognize Delany as "The Father of Black Nationalism" for promoting pride among blacks in their African roots. He would ultimately go on to Harvard Medical School and be commissioned a major of the 104th U.S. Colored Troops, one of the highest military appointments of a black man at the time, by President Lincoln. It was not until closer to the Civil War, however, that Pittsburgh's African-American population would find strong support in the city's strong white abolitionist community.

Thomas Mellon
Carnegie Library of Pittsburgh, Pittsburgh Photographic Library

THOMAS MELLON (1813-1908)

Judge Thomas Mellon was the first of his legendary family to achieve prominence in Pittsburgh. Arriving in Pittsburgh as a boy in 1823, he grew to leave a permanent mark on the business life of the city. He studied at Western University, practiced law and built the basis of a family fortune in real estate and business. An attorney and a judge, Mellon founded the bank in 1870 that bears his name. His human legacy was the success of his four sons and three grandsons: Thomas Alexander (1844-1899); James R. (1846-1934); Andrew W. (1855-1937); Richard B. (1858-1933); Richard K. (1899-1970); and Paul (1907-). Representing the American Dream at its fullest expression, Mellon maintained that "any man who cannot get rich in Pittsburgh within ten years is a fool." Mellon family philanthropy continues to benefit civic, social, educational and religious organizations and initiatives.

Jane Gray Swisshelm (1815-1884)

Jane Gray Swisshelm, best known as an ardent abolitionist, distinguished herself first as a journalist and an advocate of women's rights. Born in 1815 in a log cabin on the site of the former Gimbels Building across from Trinity Cathedral downtown, Jane Grey Cannon adopted her family's strict Calvinist beliefs, as well as a great penchant for learning and for art. Her short-lived marriage to James Swisshelm in 1836 took her to live in Louisville for a brief period, where she witnessed firsthand the inequities of slavery. Returning to Pittsburgh, she campaigned tirelessly on behalf of both women and blacks in the *Spirit of Liberty*, a Pittsburgh abolitionist newspaper, and later on the pages of her own anti-slavery paper, *The Pittsburgh Saturday Visiter*, which she founded in 1848. Moving to Minnesota in 1857 and again editing a newspaper, she became a national figure, lecturing extensively and returning to Pittsburgh about 1865.

Jane Gray Swisshelm
Carnegie Library of Pittsburgh, Pittsburgh Photographic Library

David Gimore Blythe (1815-1865)

David Blythe was born in East Liverpool, Ohio, to Scottish parents and came to Pittsburgh at the age of 16 as an apprentice to woodcarver and cabinetmaker Joseph Woodwell. After completing his apprenticeship in 1834, he traveled and spent three years in the Navy before embarking on a career as an artist. Before finally settling again in Pittsburgh in 1856, Blythe completed a larger-than-life statue of Lafayette for the dome of the Fayette County Courthouse, as well as a "mile-long" panorama of the Allegheny Mountains. During his most productive years in Pittsburgh, the last nine years of his life, he painted the satirical genre scenes for which he is best known.

David Gilmore Blythe portrays himself (left) with a sculptor in front of J. J. Gillespie's Wood Street gallery.
Carnegie Library of Pittsburgh, Pittsburgh Photographic Library

(Bottom left)
"Oh! Susanna"
Library and Archives Division, Historical Society of Western Pennsylvania, Pittsburgh, Pa.

Stephen Collins Foster (1826-1864)

Stephen Foster ranks as both an American legend and as a pioneer in the music business. Born to a wealthy Pittsburgh family in Lawrenceville, Foster was well educated and became a professional songwriter who celebrated the various ethnic traditions of the country's immigrant population. He wove them into a rich legacy of over 200 songs that captured the essence of simple life in a relatively new and open society. Sympathetic to the abolitionist cause, Foster sought to humanize the characters in his songs and to reform black-face minstrelsy, a powerful force in popular culture at the time. He also pioneered the notion of songwriting as a business with artistic property issues, crafting hand-written contracts with his publishers and struggling to secure copyrights and royalties for future earnings on his work. Nonetheless, Foster died penniless, but left behind enduring contributions to our cultural heritage, among them "Oh! Susannah," his first big hit, along with "My Old Kentucky Home," "Old Black Joe" and "Jeanie with the Light Brown Hair."

Stephen Collins Foster, pictured in an ambrotype of around 1850.
Carnegie Library of Pittsburgh, Pittsburgh Photographic Library

CHAPTER 4

Smoky City — City Beautiful

1875-1920

THE NEXT 45 YEARS SAW AN UNRIVALED FERVOR of growth and activity. This was the great epoch of expansion. Industry boomed, particularly in the service of a nation at war, giving rise to steel towns up and down the rivers and establishing Pittsburgh as a financial center with dozens of what would come to be known as Fortune 500 headquarters. Immigration and annexation swelled the population of the city from 86,000 to nearly 600,000 and the metropolitan area to more than 1.3 million, continuing to add to its ethnic and cultural mix.

(Far right) The Harvard-Yale-Princeton Club interior *Pittsburgh History & Landmarks Foundation*

Two of the Isabella Furnaces, on the Allegheny River at Etna, were built in 1872, and a third was added before 1900. All had been rebuilt by the 1900s when this picture was taken, and have skip bridges ascending to the tops to charge them mechanically. This was a furnace company, a producer of iron only, and its annual product was 441,000 tons of iron of various chemical compositions. *Carnegie Library of Pittsburgh, Pittsburgh Photographic Library*

With the growth, much of it unbridled, came attempts to enhance the built environment, launch a cultural movement commensurate with the city's economic stature and improve the social order. Civic improvements and cosmetic urbanism during this period yielded much of the infrastructure and monuments that are treasured as part of the urban fabric. The city embarked on a building boom that gave birth to its physical character and many of its historic icons. Under the watchful eyes of a handful of patrons, both commercial and cultural development flourished, as did a wealth of private clubs catering to every taste and demographic. At the same time, in response to the darker aspects of industrialization, Pittsburghers developed a strong social conscience and sought to improve their quality of life.

The Harvard-Yale-Princeton Club building in the heart of the business district began as workers' housing in the 1890s. In the background is the German Evangelical (now Smithfield United) Church of 1925. *Pittsburgh History & Landmarks Foundation*

It was during this time that the city's name underwent a change in spelling. Under orders from the U.S. Board of Geographic Names, the "h" was dropped in 1891. As a result of continuing citizen protest, however, the "h" was restored in 1911.

An Industrial Economy with Steel as King

The story of steel in Pittsburgh assumes an almost melodramatic tone with Andrew Carnegie and Henry Clay Frick as central characters. The bitter rivalry that developed between these two industrial giants dominated the industry from 1900 to 1919. But beyond the steel industry, beyond all industry, Carnegie, Frick and other titans of business left indelible marks on the city through their visionary real estate schemes and their philanthropy.

Pittsburgh factories had been manufacturing crucible steel in very small amounts prior to 1875 for specialty uses such as springs and cutlery. The true transformation of Pittsburgh from the iron city to the steel city, however, occurred rather precipitously with the introduction of the Bessemer process from England and the construction of Carnegie's Edgar Thomson Works in 1875 at North Braddock, 11 miles down the Monongahela River from the Point.

While visiting Sheffield, England, Carnegie toured Henry Bessemer's new factory and recognized the growing importance of iron and steel. Upon his return, Carnegie resigned from the Pennsylvania Railroad in 1865 to form the Keystone Bridge Company, build a steel-rail mill and buy out the Homestead Steel Works. By 1888 he controlled several steel plants at Homestead, Duquesne and Braddock.

The Bessemer process, already patented in England in 1855, made steel making cheaper and more efficient by removing impurities from newly smelted iron, or "hot metal," in its molten state. This made the difference between producing hundreds of pounds at a time and tons at a time. With the blister steel or crucible processes, small lots of iron had to be exposed to carbonization by charcoal for a day or so. With Bessemer steel, the heat of the hot metal burned off the impurities when ordinary air was blown through a batch for about 20 minutes. Named for the president of the Pennsylvania Railroad, its major client, the Edgar Thomson Works was the earliest high-volume steel plant in the area, producing steel by the open-hearth method. In 1875 the works rolled the first 60-foot steel rails in the United States and boasted a daily capacity of 375 long tons. It remains one of the few U.S. plants still operating today.

The *New York Herald* in 1893 summarized the production of steel as follows:

> The eighth wonder of the world is this;
>
> Two pounds of iron-stone purchased on the shores of Lake Superior and transported to Pittsburgh; Two pounds of coal mined in Connellsville, manufactured into coke and transported to Pittsburgh; One pound of limestone mined east of the Alleghenies and brought to Pittsburgh; A little manganese ore; — mined in Virginia and shipped to Pittsburgh; and these 4.5 pounds of material manufactured into 1 pound of solid steel and sold for 1 cent. That's all that need be said about the steel business.

Eleven miles up the Monongahela River stood the Edgar Thomson Works at North Braddock, 1876. *Pittsburgh History & Landmarks Foundation*

A Bessemer plant in the 1880s — in the foreground a works locomotive moves two white-hot billets. *Pittsburgh History & Landmarks Foundation*

From 1870 to 1900, steel production in the Pittsburgh region increased sevenfold, from 3.2 million tons to 29.5 million tons. During the second half of the 19th century, the number of iron and steel mills in Pittsburgh rose from 25 to 94 and the employment in them from 5,500 to more than 45,000. At the same time, the overall population grew from 49,000 to 534,000.

In the 1890s competition among the large steel makers became increasingly intense, characterized by integration of mining, production and transportation, and by consolidation. In 1899 Carnegie consolidated his various holdings into the Carnegie Steel Company. He sold his company in 1901 for approximately $480 million to one of his chief competitors, J.P. Morgan, who combined it with his own Federal Steel and 10 other companies and formed the first billion-dollar corporation: United States Steel Company. At the time, the $1.4 billion value of the new company was said to be double the cost of running the federal government for a single year. The U.S. Steel powerhouse garnered an instant monopoly with control of nearly two-thirds of the nation's steel market and substantial ownership of assets ranging from iron ore to railroads to ships.

In this *Harper's Weekly* wood engraving of 1888, workers are removing coke from beehive ovens. Above, a mule draws a larry car with a new charge of coal. *Pittsburgh History & Landmarks Foundation*

Meanwhile, Carnegie rival Jones & Laughlin Limited was developing as an independent operation. Having been founded in 1853 as American Iron Works by John and Bernard Lauth in the East Birmingham neighborhood on the south side of the Monongahela, the business was soon joined by Samuel Kier (who had earlier distinguished himself in the oil business) and Benjamin Franklin Jones. Kier and Jones had already partnered in the iron industry with an iron furnace and forge in the Allegheny Mountains. By 1861 B.F. Jones and James Laughlin took ownership of American Iron Works and renamed it American Iron Works — Jones & Laughlin's.

J&L adapted to the rapid changes in the industry, progressing from its early production of wrought iron, rails and spikes to Bessemer steel production in 1886. By 1894 it was out of the wrought iron business and producing only steel. The comapany's Eliza Furnace of 1858 across the Monongahela from American Iron Works was one of the first blast furnaces built in Pittsburgh and the first of six by that name.

Steel production at J&L increased dramatically during this period, from seven tons per day in 1853 to 5,000 tons per day by 1907, when the company built a new plant 26 miles down the

Ohio River at Woodlawn (later renamed Aliquippa) and created a new 415-acre community to support it. One of the region's early company towns, it developed into an independent borough in 1909. The new plant permitted a diversification of products beyond structural steel and sheet metal to include steel wire products, tin plates, seamless tubing, steel barrels and welded pipe.

J&L's stronghold would continue to grow over the next 30 years, and it became by World War II the fourth-largest steel producer in the world with an annual capacity of more than 4.8 million tons and employment of over 45,000 workers. It would remain family controlled into the 1930s and independent until its merger with LTV in 1974, beginning a 20-year decline that characterized the entire industry locally.

And the steel industry would reach far beyond this region through its products and its innovators. Structural steel made at Ambridge would find its way into the Empire State Building, the Chrysler Building, and the Verazano and Golden Gate bridges. Pittsburgh was home to the world-renowned steel mill designer and engineer, Julian Kennedy, between 1879 and 1920. At the age of 27, after realizing that smelting iron was a chemical and not a physical procedure, he doubled the capacity of Andrew Carnegie's blast furnaces. He went on to patent dozens of other techniques that resulted in major reductions in the cost of steel and consequently in the cost of living. He also built mills and railroads all over the world and helped to engineer the locks on the Panama Canal.

Coal beds near Pittsburgh provided the world's finest bituminous coal for producing the coke that fueled the iron and steel industries. It was also the primary fuel for home heat at a time when most other major cities were using wood. Even without the region's industrial plants, the domestic use of coal would have been enough to earn Pittsburgh the title of smoky city.

The birth of the aluminum industry in Pittsburgh marked yet another breakthrough in industrial innovation. The most plentiful metallic element in the earth's crust, aluminum was so difficult to extract that its value exceeded that of gold or silver. The 6-pound aluminum cap placed on the Washington Monument in 1884 was the largest piece of aluminum in the world at that time. Two years later, 22-year-old Charles Martin Hall, working in a woodshed laboratory with makeshift equipment, discovered the electrolytic process that would make large-scale aluminum production possible and economical.

After a two-year search for financial backers, Hall found Capt. Alfred E. Hunt, who had founded the Pittsburgh Testing Laboratory in 1883, and assembled a group of seven initial investors. With the breakthrough technology and $20,000 in venture capital, they formed the Pittsburgh Reduction Company, later renamed the Aluminum Company of America. Its first employee was Arthur Vining Davis, later known as "Mr. Aluminum," who ultimately served as both president and chairman of the company.

The new company's first plant was in a two-room corrugated tin building on Smallman Street, where the first commercial batch of aluminum made by Hall's process was poured into a small sand mold on Thanksgiving night of 1888. Before long, the plant was producing 50 pounds of metal per day. Aluminum was no longer a precious metal, as the little plant was selling it in 1,000-pound lots for only $2 per pound.

The next challenge facing the fledgling aluminum industry was product development and marketing. It became apparent that aluminum was a good material for cooking utensils because it was lightweight, bright, a good heat conductor and easy to clean. As the company outgrew its original plant, it opened a new plant in New Kensington in 1891. One of Pittsburgh's earliest "advanced materials," aluminum would find applications in aviation, architecture, furniture, automotive design and numerous other areas.

The founding of H. J. Heinz Company represented the vision of yet another Pittsburgh entrepreneur. From an early age, Henry John Heinz peddled vegetables from his parents Sharpsburg vegetable garden, and ultimately developed an entirely new industry in food processing. His first innovation was to pack horseradish in clear glass bottles to showcase the product's purity. In 1869, at the age of 25, he partnered with two brothers to form Heinz & Noble Company. Despite bankruptcy after just five years in business, Heinz persevered and began again, initiating construction in 1888 of the factory complex on the north shore of the Allegheny River.

The company was renowned for its enlightened approach to employee management, and was awarded a gold medal at the 1899 Paris Exposition for its high-quality factory conditions and generous employee benefits. Women, in particular, were given free medical and dental care, weekly manicures if they handled food, library privileges, free concerts, lectures and classes, quarterly dances and use of a swimming pool and gym on the premises. Proud of his accomplishments and eager to use his superior workplace as a marketing tool, Heinz was the first American industrialist to open his plant operations to public scrutiny through guided tours.

By the time Heinz incorporated his company in 1905, it was the country's largest producer of pickles, vinegar and

A family coal mine was illustrated in a wood engraving: *Every Saturday*, March 11, 1871. *Pittsburgh History & Landmarks Foundation*

ketchup, as well as the largest grower and manufacturer of sauerkraut, pickling onions and horseradish, the second largest mustard producer and the fourth largest olive packer. It employed 2,800 people worldwide.

Heinz was also notable for taking the initiative to promote government regulation of his industry in order to gain the industry increased respectability. His work culminated in the passage of the Pure Food Law in 1906 and the birth of the modern food processing industry.

Drawn to Pittsburgh in 1867 by its entrepreneurial atmosphere, George Westinghouse likewise introduced new technology and industries to the region. Westinghouse had already invented the air brake and other railroad devices and found in Pittsburgh both the manufacturing capability and the markets for his products. In 1869 he organized the Westinghouse Air Brake Company, followed by Union Switch & Signal Company in 1882. Also in the early 1880s, he entered the gas business. Westinghouse's purchase in 1885 of basic alternating current patents laid the foundation for organization of the Westinghouse Electric and Manufacturing Company, which fostered widespread use of electricity for both commercial and residential applications.

A lesser-known industrial innovation in Pittsburgh was its role in supplying the world's radium, half of it, in fact, between 1913 and 1922. The Standard Chemical Company of Pittsburgh, organized by Joseph Flannery and the first to commercially produce radium in America, mined radium-bearing ores in Colorado, extracted them in a Canonsburg plant, and refined them at the Radium Research Laboratory in Oakland. It took 500 tons of carnotite ore and six months of work to produce one gram, which was worth about $120,000. Its applications were wide: cancer treatment, luminous dials, fish bait and fertilizer.

Labor Flexes Its Muscle

As industrialization bifurcated society and created stresses between the "haves" and the "have nots," Pittsburgh proved fertile ground for the development of the labor movement. Pioneering organizational efforts and violent clashes tell a story of a determined working class that fought hard to bring about change.

The Great Railroad Strike of 1877 was the first national strike in the United States. The strike was rooted in a depression that had begun in 1873 and would see 4 million unemployed laborers over the ensuing seven years. Those who did work saw their income decline by 50 percent. A revolt of the community against the Pennsylvania Railroad, the strike began in Martinsburg, West Virginia, in July 1877 and spread to Pittsburgh on July 19.

Rioting went on for two days and created a national sensation. *Harper's Weekly* reported on the rioting "by a howling mob whose deeds of violence were written in fire and blood." Thomas Scott, president of the Pennsylvania Railroad at the time, described it with horror: "Such a scene of riot, arson and bloodshed as can never be erased from the memory of its people." The strike was over by August 1, 1877, but the rioting had already caused damage in excess of $5 million and destroyed 1,383 freight cars, 104 locomotives and 66 passenger trains, as well as the Union Depot and Hotel and about 168 private properties. Philadelphia militia came into Pittsburgh to squelch the uprising. All told, this first national strike left 100 dead, 20 of them in Pittsburgh, including three children.

Pittsburgh continued as a center for labor activities. Under the leadership of Samuel Gompers and Thomas Armstrong, the American Federation of Labor (AFL) was founded at a convention in November 1881 in downtown Pittsburgh. Armstrong also founded the Pittsburgh-based *National Labor Tribune* and ran unsuccessfully for governor in 1882. A statue of him in North Side's West Park is a tribute from the workers who underwrote it. The "United Labor Day" parade on September 3, 1887, drew approximately 12,000 union marchers, according to the *Labor Tribune*:

> As the long column wound its sinuous course across the Smithfield Street Bridge, out Carson and Sarah Streets, far away into the south side, and returning by the Tenth Street Bridge, the head of the column reached Fifth Avenue and the rear was still crossing the Smithfield Bridge from the point of rendezvous.

The banners carried that day represented issues that still speak for labor leaders: "Educate, Agitate and Organize" and "Equality Before the Law/Our Rights to Organize."

The turning point in the struggles between labor and management was the 1892 Lockout and Strike at the Homestead Works just south of Pittsburgh along the Monongahela River. Pittsburgh Bessemer Steel Company had built the massive facility that manufactured steel boiler plates, structural steel and beams; and Andrew Carnegie later bought it. In the time leading up to the strike, ironically, Carnegie had conceded that "The right of the workingmen to combine and to form trade unions is no less sacred than the right of the manufacturers to enter into association and conference with his fellows..." The crisis that followed belied his words.

The bloody and violent labor dispute known as the 1892 Homestead Strike began as a conscious attempt by company management to destroy the Amalgamated Association of Iron and Steelworkers, which had been formed in 1876. This union represented nearly 10 percent of the American Federation of Labor (AFL) membership in 1892, although only 800 of the 3,800 workers at the massive Homestead plant were members. On June 30, 1892, the date that the union's three-year contract with the Carnegie Steel Company was scheduled to expire, plant manager Henry Clay Frick discharged all of the steel workers and hired 300 Pinkerton guards to protect the facility and the replacement workers, or "scabs." What followed on July 6 was a momentous battle between labor and management waged on the shores of the Monongahela River. Pinkerton guards on two barges fell under attack. The standoff was finally broken when the governor called in National Guard troops and Gen. Snowden led 8,000 troops from Philadelphia on July 13, 1892, but not before at least seven workers and three Pinkertons had been killed.

The state militia protected the mill and the scab workers until November, when the Amalgamated Association called off the strike. Mill workers returned to work at lower wages and union members were blacklisted. Defeated, the union remained broken for 40 years until the New Deal would introduce laws to ensure labor-management bargaining. In the wake of the so-called Battle of Homestead, Frick declared, "Our victory is complete and most gratifying. I do not think we will ever have serious labor troubles," while Carnegie, who had been out of the country during the July confrontation, simply declared, "Life is worth living again."

News of the Homestead Strike of July 6,1892, was publicized nationwide. *Carnegie Library of Pittsburgh, Pittsburgh Photographic Library*

A similar dispute had occurred the year before in Morewood, Westmoreland County, when Pinkertons hired by the Henry Clay Frick mines killed 17 striking coke oven workers. Reportedly, 17,000 men and women attended a mass funeral for the victims.

Several pioneer unions were founded in Pittsburgh subsequent to the Homestead Strike. Among them were the Ironworkers (1896), Boilermakers and Sheet Metal Workers; the Bakery, Confectionery and Tobacco Workers (1895); and the Carpenters, Painters, Bricklayers, Plasterers, Plumbers and Electrical Workers. Yet in the aftermath of the Homestead Strike, Carnegie's plants operated non-union for the next four decades, as did most major steel mills in the country. When the movement revived, it tended to favor "company unions" rather than the outside organizers represented by the Amalgamated Association, American Federation of Labor and, later, the Congress of Industrial Organizations (CIO). Even nationally, union membership was apparently a low percentage of the overall labor force, with less than 3 percent enrolled in 1900, reaching less than 16 percent by 1940. Nonetheless, national averages for weekly working hours dropped from 72 in 1870 to 40 in 1920.

In the years that followed, several additional labor-driven events figured prominently. A two-month strike in 1909 at the Pressed Steel Car Company in McKees Rocks involved more than 4,700 workers and ended in a confrontation with police in which 12 workers were killed. While not successful, the struggle did demonstrate that diverse ethnic groups could find unity in the labor forum. The Westinghouse Strike of 1914 involved 11,000 workers in a battle for a countywide industrial union. Electrical workers descended on the Edgar Thomson Works in Braddock, precipitating a bloody struggle that ended in two workers' deaths. The 1919 Steel Strike, also a failure, involved 365,000 workers under the direction of William Z. Foster and National Committee leaders.

Brewing a Cultural Stew

Behind the industrial growth and the labor unrest was a growing immigrant work force, introducing a rich ethnic diversity that the region still enjoys. As the phenomenon of the steel town evolved, it brought with it a whole new wave of immigration and social change. The new high-volume steel-making demanded large numbers of unskilled laborers. Initially, Carnegie raided the Cambria Iron Works at Johnstown for good men. The high demand soon exceeded local supply, however, and prompted immigration from eastern and southern Europe.

The interior of St. Nicholas Russian Orthodox Church, McKees Rocks
Pittsburgh History & Landmarks Foundation

To the older, established workers, who had strong unions by this time and enjoyed good wages, the unskilled immigrants were cheap competition.

Between 1880 and 1900 Pittsburgh's foreign-born population doubled. This new wave of immigrants came not from England, Ireland, Scandinavia and Germany as in the past, but rather from the eastern and southern European countries of Poland, Hungary, Slovakia, Italy and others. By 1900 the local population included more than 114,000 from Poland and Austria-Hungary, nearly 100,000 from Russia and the Baltic States, and more than 100,000 from Italy. The immigrants tended to settle in ethnic enclaves, many of which remain strongly ethnic to this day. The Poles created a close-knit community in Polish Hill. Germans dominated Troy Hill. Bloomfield became an Italian enclave. Eastern Europeans settled in McKees Rocks, the Russians in Squirrel Hill.

With the population swelling faster than municipal services could accommodate, many immigrants faced a bleak existence, living in crowded tenements with inadequate sanitation and limited amenities. Yet they created in their new communities a cultural richness that celebrated the traditions of their homelands. By the end of this period, Pittsburgh had newspapers in 33 languages. The newspapers are gone, but other remnants still thrive. Onion-domed church towers rise above the working-class housing of riverfront mill towns. Ethnic festivals showcase food, music, dance and crafts that have been kept alive here for more than 100 years.

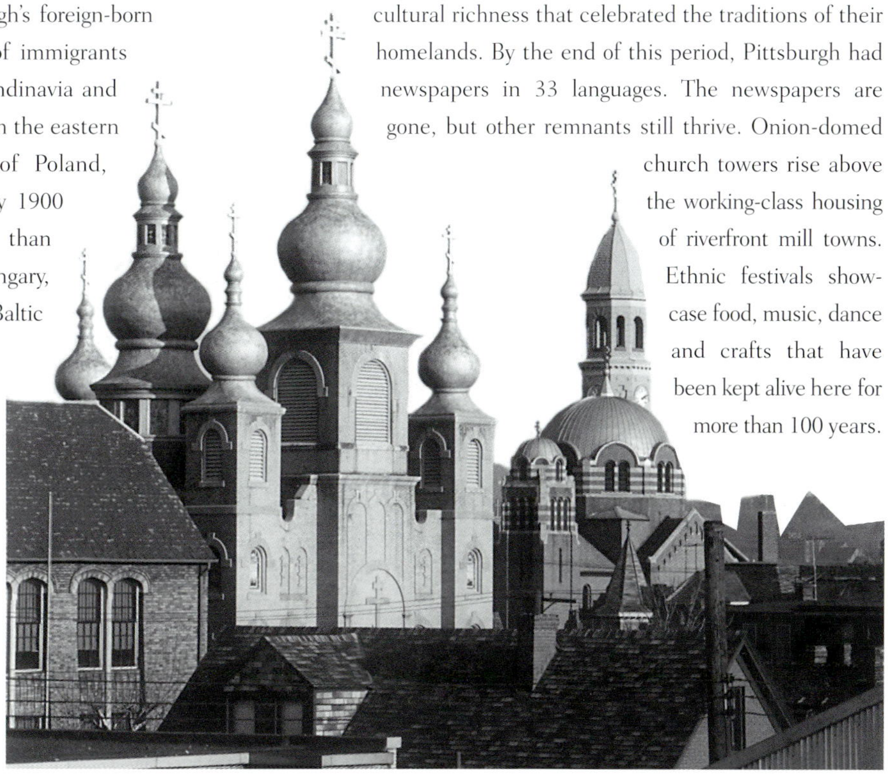

Cultural diversity, exemplified by religious buildings in the "Industrial Bottoms" of McKees Rocks, on the Ohio River. From left to right, the school of St. Mark's Roman Catholic Church, for a Slovak congregation; St. Nicholas Russian Orthodox Church; St. Mary's Ukrainian Orthodox Church; and the tower of Holy Ghost Byzantine Catholic Church.
Pittsburgh History & Landmarks Foundation

The spire of St. Matthew Roman Catholic Church and the domes of St. Casimir's (now closed) on the South Side
Photo by Jim Judkis

Unfortunately, diversity was not always embraced with enthusiasm. Some contemporaneous writers described the immigrant population in the most derogatory of terms: "brute-like people," "illiterate, docile, lacking in self-reliance and initiative," "beaten men from beaten races, representing the worst failures in the struggle for existence." Even Woodrow Wilson stooped to denigrating the nation's newest population in 1902: "Men of the lowest class... out of the ranks where there was neither skill nor energy, nor any initiative or quick intelligence."

Indeed, this rich cultural stew would need decades to simmer before it was widely palatable. As Israel Zangwill predicted in his 1908 Broadway play, *The Melting Pot*, "The real American has not yet arrived. He is only in the Crucible, I tell you — he will be the fusion of all races, the coming superman."

Company Towns

Industrialization on this enormous scale spawned a whole series of riverfront industrial towns, the most prominent being steel towns: Homestead, McKeesport, Duquesne, Clairton, Aliquippa, Ambridge and more. These towns, many developed according to the classic company town model, dominated the valleys around Pittsburgh and took on identities all their own.

In the steel towns, the companies often gave buildings and services that promoted social stability and encouraged the populations to depend on the company. Braddock was the site of the world's first Carnegie Library, dedicated in 1889, which initially included books and a collection of historical artifacts, but which in 1893 added an auditorium, gymnasium and social hall, and public baths. In Homestead, Carnegie donated a library, club and concert hall in one building, Henry Clay Frick gave a park, and Charles Schwab gave a vocational school — all after the violent labor struggle of 1892. In Duquesne the steel plant supplied free electricity to the churches.

In some company towns, management developed the entire built environment as well as the support services. Towns such as Presston, created by the Pressed-Steel Car Company, a portion of Natrona developed by Penn Salt Manufacturing Company, and Pittsburgh Plate Glass Company's Ford City contained enclaves of uniform housing and commercial development that served as ever-present reminders of the companies' power.

The Dark Side of Industrialization

Both literally and figuratively, industrialization had its dark side. Smoke, soot and overcrowding were taking their toll as the overwhelming impact of "progress" proved to be a drop in the quality of life for the common man. "A month in Pittsburgh would justify anyone in committing suicide," said Herbert Spencer in the 1870s. Indeed the city was the blackest, dirtiest city in the United States. Writing in 1883, Willard Glazier got a bit more specific: "the smoke sinks, and mingling with the moisture in the air, becomes... a consistency which may almost be felt as well as seen... In truth, Pittsburg is a smoky, dismal city, at her best."

While most agreed that these conditions were a drawback to life in the city, a few enterprising individuals had the audacity to

The domes of St. John the Baptist Ukrainian Catholic Church on the South Side
Photo by Jim Judkis

Union Station, when it was new in 1905: a grand architectural gesture of the Pennsylvania Railroad surrounded by the chaos of the Golden Triangle. Beyond the station is a trainshed where steam locomotives idle. The view beyond is greatly obscured by smoke, although one can see the Penn Incline. On the hill, right of center, is the old Central High School of 1874.
Pittsburgh History & Landmarks Foundation

suggest that the smoke held benefits as treatment for "lung and cutaneous [skin] diseases." At the very least, the smoky conditions were the tangible evidence of prosperity. The city's earliest promotional campaign, launched in 1901 by iron magnate William L. Scaife, touted Pittsburgh's natural resources and hardworking entrepreneurs as the sources of the city's economic growth and industrial prowess. Claiming the title "Workshop of the World," Pittsburgh professed a larger mission of promoting worldwide progress.

Reflecting the trend among progressive reformers nationwide to improve the quality of life for average people and building upon the fledgling social reform efforts of the 19th century, Pittsburgh developed a social conscience of its own during the early years of the 20th century. Great attention was given to the impact of industrialization on the quality of life in and around the city. Perhaps the most representative occurrence of this phenomenon was the initiation and development of the *Pittsburgh Survey*, a critical investigation of the city conducted between 1907 and 1914. Funded by the Russell Sage Foundation, it was the first attempt in the United States to study life and labor of ordinary people in one industrial city in a comprehensive and systematic manner. Statisticians, social workers, engineers, lawyers, physicians, economists, labor investigators and city planners examined the Pittsburgh community's quality of life. They looked at such issues as housing, food, sanitation, play space and health care.

The survey, which arguably helped to fuel Pittsburgh's negative image between the two world wars, also became a model for other cities through its four books, two collections of articles and a traveling exhibition aimed to promote liberal social reform. It concluded that "Pittsburgh forgot that beside every furnace and every engine stood a man and that man was hers... She has not yet learned how to work without wastefulness and destruction."

The city's newfound social conscience also manifested itself on a smaller scale, with the creation of settlement houses and service agencies that sought to assimilate European immigrants and black migrants into their new environment and help to alleviate some of the hardships associated with poverty and urban living. Among the more prominent of these efforts were Kingsley House, likened to Jane Addams' work at Hull House in Chicago; Sarah Heinz House; Irene Kaufmann House; and the Urban League.

The Urban League sought to address these issues for the black community. Associated Charities had already been established in 1908 to coordinate social welfare activities of various organizations. With the Great Migration well under way, black workers, some with families, were arriving daily in boxcars at Union Station; more than 25,000 arrived between 1900 and 1917, the bulk of them during the last two years.

The Monongahela Incline up Mount Washington was the first passenger incline in the Pittsburgh area, though coal-carrying inclines had preceded it. Founded in 1870, it was augmented in 1883 by a vehicular incline, seen here to the left. The latter track was demolished in 1935, at which time steam power was replaced by electricity. *Carnegie Library of Pittsburgh, Pittsburgh Photographic Library*

Contrary to the promise of good wages and a better life, they found inadequate housing, unsanitary conditions, crime, rampant alcoholism and racial tension. In response, three men joined forces in 1914 to address problems of "health and sanitation, temperance, vice suppression, civic action, education and race relations." They organized "The Association for the Improvement of Social Conditions in the Hill District of Pittsburgh." Then, in 1915, a group of white and black citizens formed the Pittsburgh Council for Social Service Among Negroes. Hearing of a national interracial organization, the National League on Urban Conditions Among Negroes, which was at work in 18 northern cities, the council decided to establish an affiliate in Pittsburgh and became the Urban League of Pittsburgh in 1918. The Urban League has continued to combine a basic commitment to social welfare with an equal commitment to social change.

Civic Improvements and High Culture in the Gilded Age

Chaotic growth and squalid conditions accompanied industrialization. Yet the prosperity it brought yielded both the pride and the money necessary to realize major civic improvements and support high culture in what would come to be known as the Gilded Age. This brief period of unbridled wealth would end in 1913 with the income tax imposed by the 16th Amendment to the Constitution.

Pittsburgh responded to the park and City Beautiful movements that were sweeping the East in the practical manner that characterizes most of its development. Beginning with provisions for parks and other major urban amenities in the 1870s, this response broadened in time. Admittedly, much of the early civic consciousness was in the form of ordinances, which may or may not have been enforced, and new bureaus for their administration. Regulations of the 1880s and 1890s were concerned with such problems as building materials and sidewalk widths. The Department of Public Works, established in 1895, acquired a long list of subsidiary bureaus over the subsequent decade: parks, city property, assessment of water rents, light, filtration, construction, highways, sewers and surveys. The actual effectiveness of these bureaus would be difficult to assess.

Among the more unique additions to the late 19th-century cityscape were Pittsburgh's inclined planes, or inclines, which numbered at least 17, more than any city in the world. Built to conquer Pittsburgh's precipitous terrain, these inclines were built on a scale commensurate with that of the city's booming industry and ranked as engineering feats in their size and design. Each carried a distinction of some sort. Although the earliest incline was mentioned in the *Pittsburgh Gazette* in 1854, they did not become common until the 1870s. Privately built and operated, they served a variety of purposes, transporting passengers, freight and vehicles to support industry, commerce and real estate development. Of course, only two of Pittsburgh's inclines survive, serving both daily commuters and as novelty amusements. They provide a glimpse, however, into an innovative technology that once served as daily transportation.

The leading designer of Pittsburgh's inclines, Samuel Diescher, was born in Budapest in 1839 and moved to Ohio in his late 20s. He emerged as an industry leader, designing most of the heavy inclined planes in the United States. After building one in Cincinnati, he moved to Pittsburgh in the early 1870s and went on to design 10 of Pittsburgh's inclines. It was a family business, including his father-in-law, John Endres; his wife, Caroline Endres Diescher; and their three sons, all trained as engineers. The author's great-great-grandfather, John M. McRoberts, designed two of the city's inclines.

The first of Diescher's inclines, the Monongahela, opened in 1870 and by the 1890s was carrying close to a million passengers per year. It still survives and, at 35-percent grade, is one of the steepest inclined planes in the world. The largest ever built was the Penn Avenue, or 17th Street Incline, which connected the Strip and the lower Hill District beginning in 1883. The 840-foot incline was designed to carry 20 tons of coal down from the Minersville area of the Hill and could accommodate up to 100 passengers, in addition to wagons, horses and other cargo. The Penn Incline Resort, an entertainment complex, opened at the top in 1889 and operated for over 60 years. Built in 1882 and surviving only until about 1900, the Fort Pitt Incline connected Second Avenue and the Bluff and consisted of iron cars measuring 16 feet by 38 feet to carry teams of horses.

Among the later passenger inclines were the Nunnery Hill, built in 1887 around a 70-degree curve from Allegheny City's Federal Street Railroad Station to the neighborhood of Fineview. The Troy Hill, connecting the neighborhood's German residents with their jobs at the H.J. Heinz plant, also hauled freight and wagons but lasted only from 1887 to 1898. The Mt. Oliver of 1871 was both popular and long-lived, carrying passengers up Mount Washington from the south side for 80 years. The Knoxville followed in 1890. With its 2,644-foot length around an 18-degree curve, it was the longest ever built in Pittsburgh. Castle Shannon No. 1, operating on Mount Washington from 1890 to 1964, was the last to carry vehicles as well as passengers.

Two inclines in Allegheny City, the Ridgewood and Clifton, were built to provide access to new housing developments in the 1890s, but both were short lived. The Norwood (Penny) Incline at McKees Rocks carried passengers to Norwood Hall, an entertainment complex, for a fare of 1 cent.

Around the turn of the 20th century, private civic groups delivered a great deal of rhetoric expressing their concern for "the beautification of the city." According to the Pittsburgh Art Society, interested in "the artistic and the material progress of the city...," this concern was "a wholesome sign of the times." Similarly, the Civic Club professed an interest in urban amenities and boasted of its influence in obtaining legislation between 1895 and 1906 regarding pure water, garbage, playgrounds and expectoration in public spaces, as well as in the development of model tenements. More important with respect to the general physical configuration of the city and its possible improvement, the Civic Club in May 1906 joined the Pittsburgh chapter of the American League of Architects in sponsoring a lecture by Mr. Albert Kelsey of Philadelphia on:

> "A Pittsburgh Possible," showing what a magnificent city might be built here, instead of the haphazard conglomeration which now appears within the embrace of our three rivers.

Yet beyond these rather vague expressions of noblesse oblige, the late 19th and early 20th centuries saw considerable changes in the urban infrastructure, as well as unrealized plans. Between 1890 and 1895 alone, the Department of Public Works added 11 bridges. As early as 1906, Pittsburgh began to examine the possibility of a subway system when the Pittsburg Subway Company applied to city council for municipal consent. It would be about another 80 years before the city would have such a system.

In planning for its urban infrastructure, the powers in Pittsburgh characteristically thought on a large scale. Though far less grand in conception than the sort of plans being done by Daniel H. Burnham at the same time in other major cities, a

(Bottom left)
The Pittsburgh, later the Knoxville, Incline descended to the 1100 block of Bradish Street on the South Side. It ran between 1890 and 1961, and was one of two local inclines to have a curve. This photograph is from between 1915 and 1930. *Carnegie Library of Pittsburgh, Pittsburgh Photographic Library*

(Below)
The "Hump," a rise that had long caused trouble was lowered in 1912 or 1913. This is Diamond Street (now Forbes Avenue). The Courthouse is to the left, and to the right is the present location of the City-County Building. *Carnegie Library of Pittsburgh, Pittsburgh Photographic Library*

The grand stair of the courthouse as it was when completed in 1888 *Pittsburgh History & Landmarks Foundation*

series of plans attempted to bring order and amenities to the city's core. A 1904 plan prepared by the Pittsburgh chapter of the American Institute of Architects called for the removal of the Hump (finally completed in 1913) and the opening up of the streets at the base of Grant's Hill. In addition to an open public square for monuments, the plan proposed a symmetrical grouping of public buildings. Neither this proposal nor one for effective slum treatment was realized.

Six years later, the Civic Improvement Commission sponsored a study of the city's problems by a team led by Frederick Law Olmsted Jr. titled "Pittsburgh Main Thoroughfares and the Down Town District" of 1910. The study offered practical recommendations, yet forwarded a more far-reaching vision for capitalizing on the city's assets. It addressed the regional steam railroad system, flood control, parks and playgrounds, the water and sewer system, a building code and — an idea whose time had not yet come — the organization of a smoke abatement control that would counsel and cooperate with factories to improve "the Pittsburgh atmosphere without hampering its industrial success."

The plan imposed no new axial streets or grand avenues on the existing plan but proposed only to widen the main thoroughfares. Public buildings were to be grouped in a landscaped area next to the existing courthouse and jail. The adjacent Hump was to be leveled. Linking these buildings and the entire civic industrial area was to be a system of trees and pathways along the waterfront of both rivers. The waterfront, in turn, was to be exploited for commerce, green space and recreation. Looking beyond the downtown area, the plan proposed community parks and isolated rural parks, as well as tunnel access to the suburban South Hills with the Liberty Tubes, completed in 1922 and opened in 1924, and the Liberty Bridge in 1928. Aside from these concessions, however, the plan did not take the regional approach that was becoming common by this time, particularly in Burnham's work.

Subsequent to Olmsted's report, the city established its first planning department. Also in 1911 the city organized an art commission to provide design reviews for new buildings, bridges and other structures.

Into this context of civic planning entered a downtown commercial building boom that remains unmatched, even in Pittsburgh's much-touted mid- to late-20th-century renaissances. Downtown was abuzz with construction, as the fruits of industrialization began to manifest themselves in so-called "cathedrals of commerce" bankrolled by the patrons of the day: Carnegie, Frick, Mellon, Phipps and others. From 1893 to 1906, 350 new buildings were constructed in downtown, and the residential commercial mix in the triangle became purely commercial. It was during this period, in 1914, that the central business district earned the title of "The Golden Triangle" from the *Saturday Evening Post*.

The first major addition to the city's skyline has also remained its most significant: the Allegheny County Courthouse and Jail by Henry Hobson Richardson. This, the third courthouse to be built in Pittsburgh, was the culmination of a design competition among four leading architects of the day. Richardson was a popular choice. In an 1885 poll of 75 architects, five of the Top 10 buildings named

Allegheny County Courthouse and Jail, c. 1900 *Carnegie Library of Pittsburgh, Pittsburgh Photographic Library*

(Far left)
The courthouse tower stands tall and visually strong, impressive even among the taller business buildings.
Photo by Jim Judkis

(Left)
The lions on the courthouse front sit high above the street today. Before the Grant's Hill Hump was lowered, the lions were close to the street.
Photo by Jim Judkis

The grand stair of the courthouse
Photo by Jim Judkis

as significant were designed by Richardson. And although he did not live to see the project completed in 1888, Richardson himself considered it to be the crowning achievement of his career, saying "If they honor me for the pigmy things I have already done, what will they say when they see Pittsburgh finished?" Richardson's design represented such a departure from the standard revival styles of the time to have earned the title of a style all its own: Richardsonian Romanesque. Its rock-faced stone idiom, with minimal ornament and massive rounded arches, was not only refreshing in its simplicity, but also unashamedly expressive of its structural elements and efficient in its ventilation systems. Just 11 years after its completion, the jail was deemed too small, and local architect Frederick J. Osterling was commissioned to double its size.

The courthouse is important not only in its hint at a modern architectural idiom, but also for the design talent that it attracted to the Pittsburgh area. Among those who came as part of Richardson's team and stayed to build prominent practices of their own were Shepley Rutan & Coolidge and Alden & Harlow, very popular among prominent Pittsburghers as architects for their personal homes.

With the stage set by the monumental new Allegheny County Courthouse, Andrew Carnegie launched a commercial

Murals in the courthouse entrance hall, painted in the 1930s by Vincent Nesbert
Photo by Jim Judkis

The upper part of the Park Building, as it was before a cheap remodeling in the 1960s
Pittsburgh History & Landmarks Foundation

Progress on the Union Arcade, a real-estate speculation by Henry Clay Frick, as of July 20, 1916.
Pittsburgh History & Landmarks Foundation

boom with his construction of the Carnegie Building in 1895, a 13-story office building that who were the first steel skeleton-framed structure in Pittsburgh. It was designed by Longfellow, Alden & Harlow, who were designing the new Carnegie Institute in Oakland at the same time. Following close on its heels was the Park Building of 1896, designed by New York architect George Browne Post, which now survives as the city's oldest standing skyscraper. Over the next two decades alone, industrialists, banks and speculators transformed the skyline with more than 25 buildings of 12 stories or more. In the process, they helped to forward the development of a modern architecture that would incorporate new building technology and a design aesthetic that rejected the historical revival styles of the 19th century.

Fourth Avenue developed as Pittsburgh's answer to Wall Street, with money from the region's industrial success pouring into the various financial institutions that lined the street. By 1908 the Pittsburgh Stock Exchange and 20 banks were located in and around Fourth Avenue, and the amount of capital held in Pittsburgh's banks was second only to that in New York. Among them were Pittsburgh National Bank (originally the Peoples Savings Bank), Colonial Trust Company, Industrial Bank, Union Trust, Fidelity Trust, Pittsburgh Bank for Savings, Dollar Savings Bank, Commonwealth Trust and Union National Bank.

Other major buildings that came with this boom included the Oliver Building, the Frick Building, the Benedum-Trees Building and the Keenan Building. More than a dozen of these were by D.H. Burnham, the Chicago architect credited with developing the new high-rise genre.

Although the city had basically stabilized its boundaries by 1908, minor annexations continued through the early 20th century. These areas, located to the north of the newly annexed north side and to the south of the Monongahela River, were mostly residential communities.

As the downtown building boom gathered momentum, what some would call the second founding of Pittsburgh was occurring in Oakland. Oakland had begun as a suburb in the 1840s and was annexed to the city in 1867. Much of it, however, remained as farmland until the 1890s. The transformation of Oakland was masterminded by Andrew Carnegie as philanthropist and Frank F. Nicola as speculator.

Carnegie, grateful for the library made available to him as a youth by Col. James Anderson, sought to make books and culture available to the public through a single institution — Pittsburgh's "palace of culture" — incorporating a library, a music hall, a natural history museum and an art gallery. First offered to the city in 1881, the idea was not accepted until 1890, when a board of prominent Pittsburghers assembled; authorization by the city to build in Oakland came the following year. As with many monumental building projects of the late 19th century, the founders chose to conduct an architectural competition, which attracted 97 American architects. The successful firm was Longfellow, Alden & Harlow, a prominent practice with offices in Boston and Pittsburgh.

Carnegie Mellon University's Hamerschlag Hall (formerly Machinery Hall) of 1913, with the University of Pittsburgh's Cathedral of Learning in the background
Photo by William Rydberg, Photon

Citing the need for such an institution in an 1890 letter to English Prime Minister William Gladstone, Carnegie said that Pittsburgh "has never been anything but a center of materialism; it has never had a fine hall for music, nor a museum, nor an art gallery, nor a public library." While certainly small initiatives in these arenas have appeared since the city's earliest days, Carnegie's new complex was unprecedented in its scale and grandeur. Just as conceived, Carnegie's new institute served as the central cultural hub for many years. From 1896 to 1910, the music hall was the home of the first Pittsburgh Symphony.

By 1899, just four years after the building was dedicated, it proved too small, and Carnegie offered funds for a significant expansion and renovation. Alden & Harlow, now in practice without Longfellow, designed the expansion in 1904-1907, a grand design in the style made popular by the Ecole des Beaux-Arts in Paris. The largest building in Alden and Harlow's portfolio, the institute covered nearly 5 acres of ground, with almost 20 acres of floor space, 165,000 square feet of cut stone on the exterior and 6,000 tons of marble on the interior. The success of the project was reflected in its inclusion in the 11th edition of the *Encyclopaedia Britannica* (1910-1911) as representative of the large-scale, modern American museum. The vision would come to be expanded even further in the late 20th century with the construction of the Sarah Scaife Gallery in 1974, and most recently the addition of the Carnegie Science Center in 1991 and the Andy Warhol Museum in 1995, both on the North Side.

The art gallery had as its central vision the collection of contemporary works from around the world. To that end, Carnegie conceived the first International in 1896, an annual juried exhibition of paintings by the great painters of the time, with the expectation that the museum would purchase the prize-winning canvases. The exhibition attracted the masters of the day — Matisse, Monet, Picasso and Rouault — and began to build the permanent collection of the Museum of Art. Today, the International is held every few years and continues to serve as a benchmark event in the exhibition and collection of contemporary art.

At the first meeting of the Associated Artists of Pittsburgh in 1910, the Carnegie Institute is in the background.
Carnegie Library of Pittsburgh, Pittsburgh Photographic Library

Carnegie collected on the same large scale that characterized his industrial pursuits. The Hall of Architecture is the sole survivor among some 20 that once existed in capital cities around the world. Following an accepted practice at the turn of the century, the institute purchased life-size plaster reproductions of the great architectural and sculptural treasures of the past, 144 in all. Likewise, the Museum of Natural History sought to collect the finest dinosaur fossils by purchase or expedition and began amassing a collection that would grow to 700,000 pounds of fossils between 1909 and 1922.

As his "palace of culture" was taking form, Carnegie began work on a "learning factory" next door. He established the Carnegie Technical School with a $1 million endowment to the city in 1900. Henry Hornbostel (1867-1961), a partner in the New York practice of Palmer and Hornbostel, won the competition to master plan the new school in 1904. Construction of the original campus took 19 years, from 1904 to 1923, and the school was renamed Carnegie Institute of Technology in 1912. Much later, in 1967, it would become Carnegie Mellon University.

Building upon the foundation established by Carnegie's new institute and fledgling university, Frank F. Nicola laid out his Schenley Farms development beginning in 1905. Nicola envisioned a "model city" on a sylvan tract of farmland that he had purchased from Mary Schenley's estate for $2.5 million. The expansive Schenley Farms development, adjoining Schenley Park, would provide a fine residential enclave adjoining a monumental civic complex and combine the concepts of model suburb and City Beautiful.

An established developer, Nicola had been responsible for building the Schenley Hotel in 1898 (now the student union of the University of Pittsburgh) which was Pittsburgh's first large, steel-framed "skyscraper hotel." "Perched on the edge of a cornfield," the Schenley Hotel gave instant legitimacy to the new civic center and hosted many notable guests including Eleanor Duse and professional baseball players.

Building on that success, Nicola's new Schenley Farms project took off quickly, and half of the original lots were sold by 1909. Eight major buildings were erected between 1910 and 1916, as well as Forbes Field in 1909. Residential construction began in 1906, and by the 1930s the residential area was essentially filled. Nicola ruled the development with an iron hand. He actively recruited clubs such as the Concordia Club and the Oakland Turnverein and imposed strict building codes and policies for landscape treatments.

This development presented a major opportunity to a handful of architects who were favored by the patrons of the day. Major institutional buildings developed during this civic and cultural boom included the Masonic Temple (1914), the Young Men and Women's Hebrew Association (1924), the Mellon Institute (1937), the Twentieth Century Club (1930) and the Pittsburgh Athletic Association (1911), displaying the versatility of architect Benno Janssen; and the Schenley Apartments (1922), Webster Hall Hotel (1924) and Soldiers and Sailors Memorial (1911), all by Henry Hornbostel. Also included was the Syria Mosque (1916) by Huehl, Schmid and Holmes.

The Twentieth Century Club after remodeling in 1930 by the society architects Janssen & Cocken
Pittsburgh History & Landmarks Foundation

Frank Nicola was not alone in his vision to create a discrete and ideal family community at the turn of the century. Out in the Chartiers Valley, four miles southwest of Pittsburgh, Frank Thornburg conceived and developed a residential enclave that would become the borough of Thornburg. Arriving in Pittsburgh from Iowa in 1899, Thornburg teamed up with his cousin David to create the Thornburg Land Company and acquired 250 acres of the family farm. Another cousin, Samuel Thornburg McClaren, served as the principal architect for the Land Company, which constructed 70 houses by 1917. Inspired by the arts and crafts movement through frequent visits to California, the Thornburgs and McClarren created an exceptional collection of Queen Anne, Shingle Style, Tudor, English Cottage, Colonial Revival, Craftsman Bungalow and California Mission idioms, executed with an abundance of boulders, cobblestone and rubblestone. Like its urban counterpart, Schenley Farms, this pioneering suburban development has remained largely intact to this day. The community also enjoyed its own golf links, tennis courts and spring-fed water system.

After the initial establishment of the new cultural district in Oakland, the building focus resumed downtown where a number of obstacles presented themselves. Not the least of these was the terrain. Between 1911 and 1913, the final campaign was waged to lower Grant's Hill, affectionately known as the Hump. Begun in the 1830s and continued in a succession of projects, the 70-year effort ultimately lowered the hill at the eastern end of downtown 60 feet to its current level. This massive earthmoving triumph opened up additional land for development and forced the redesign of at least two landmark buildings in downtown. Both Richardson's Courthouse and the Frick Building found themselves with exposed basements that had to be transformed into new first floor entrances. The lowering of the Hump also prompted construction of several other significant downtown landmarks. Among them were the William Penn Hotel, the Union Arcade, and the City-County Building.

Urban Oases – A Park System and Other Amusements

Pittsburgh jumped on the bandwagon early with the nationwide movement to provide professionally designed public parks in major cities. Beginning with Olmsted and Vaux's 1858 design for New York's Central Park, major American cities began to build large urban parks in a pastoral style. This style was inspired by growing democratic ideals and social concerns, coupled with a sense of responsible land stewardship. The designers of these parks combined agricultural methods, civil engineering techniques and artistic principles to shape the land.

The tenets of the parks movement were first embraced locally by forward-thinking officials in Allegheny City as a solution to the problem of dealing with 84 acres of underutilized open space in the midst of a squalid urban environment. The city fathers sought to provide what they called "breathing places" for the citizens. Named for its previous use as a public grazing land, the "Allegheny Commons" represented an intensive eight-year effort, from 1869 to 1876, to develop an oasis of green in keeping with the best examples of its day. The city established a park commission that studied comparable initiatives in the major east coast cities, hired the New York landscape firm of Mitchell and Grant, and went about implementing a plan that incorporated grand avenues, public gardens and fountains, a rustic, rock-lined lake for boating and swimming, a bandstand and extensive plant materials that included at least 820 trees, thousands of shrubs and tens of thousands of bulbs and annuals. It also included construction of the first Phipps Conservatory in 1887. The conservatory was a scaled-down precursor to the one that Phipps would build in Schenley Park in 1893.

It was approximately 15 to 20 years after the creation of the Allegheny Commons that the story of Pittsburgh's four great parks; Schenley, Highland, Riverview and Frick began. As these parks developed, they combined the principles of the parks movement with the new City Beautiful aesthetic gaining momentum at about the same time. City Beautiful principles were promoted by the 1893 World's Colombian Exposition and the redesign of Washington, D.C. by the McMillan Commission with Frederick Law Olmsted Jr. in 1901.

The movement really took off locally with the appointment in 1880 of Edward Manning Bigelow as the city's engineer and ultimately as its first director of public works. Known as "The Father of Pittsburgh's Parks," Bigelow described himself as "a visionary dreamer who tried to put his dreams into action." And indeed he did.

Schenley Park was launched with Bigelow's appeal to Mary Schenley in 1889 to donate 300 acres of farmland to the city. The Schenleys, living in England, had actually offered to sell the land to the city as early as 1869, but the effort was defeated in referendum. It was followed by other false starts. Finally, in 1889, upon learning of Mary Schenley's intention to sell "the Mount Airy tract" to developers, Edward Carnahan on behalf of Bigelow literally raced to London, beating the real estate agent by two days, and returned with her commitment to donate the land. That initial 300 acres was augmented by purchases of an additional 136 acres, 121 of them from Mary Schenley, as much a businesswoman as a philanthropist.

Bigelow hired William Falconer as the superintendent of Schenley Park in 1896, and Falconer introduced to Pittsburgh the most advanced standards of botany, horticulture and landscape architecture. Little of the park is truly natural; the contours of the land and the plant materials reflect a very conscious

Frick Park as it was in the 1930s
Pittsburgh History & Landmarks Foundation

process of design. In 1896 Falconer's nursery, which would supply the city parks, contained more than 73,000 trees and shrubs and over 34,000 hardy perennials. He planted with full and rather prophetic confidence: "Besides, our city won't be smoky all the time." The park was continually enhanced with amenities and became a hub of activity. Among the additions over the years were a massive electric fountain, a zoo, a band shell, a casino for ice skating, theater, opera and bowling, a horse racing track and a merry-go-round.

The jewel of Schenley Park, Phipps Conservatory, was a gift to the city from industrialist and philanthropist Henry Phipps. Having made his fortune in steel as a partner of Andrew Carnegie and in real estate, Phipps wanted to "erect something that will prove a source of instruction as well as pleasure to the people." Under the direction of the prestigious New York firm of Lord and Burnham, the new $110,000 conservatory took shape within one year, with its nine display houses featuring "silvered" domes, glass vaults and a Richardsonian Romanesque stone entrance. When it opened on December 7, 1893, it was the largest conservatory in the United States and boasted the finest collection of tropical plants, secured from the World's Columbian Exposition in Chicago that same year. Over the next seven years, Phipps and the city would add three more display houses and nine growing houses. The conservatory was operated by the city of Pittsburgh for 100 years until a 1993 agreement privatized the management and expanded its mission to include not only display, but education as well.

Highland Park, though completed after Schenley, was actually initiated before. Bigelow, trained as a civil engineer, also had an entrepreneurial real estate bent. His scheme for a parks system for Pittsburgh had begun as somewhat of a clandestine effort to acquire land around the city's new reservoir about 1870. When 360-acre Highland Park opened in 1893, its feature attractions were two large reservoirs and a zoo. Christopher Magee and associates at the Fort Pitt Traction Company expanded the zoo in 1898 in an effort to capitalize on trolley lines from the city.

Not wanting to be outdone by the city of Pittsburgh, the rival city of Allegheny quickly set about developing a park of its own. Shortly after Schenley Park was officially dedicated in 1889, Allegheny's Mayor William Kennedy organized a citizens' committee, which in five years collected $110,000 from about 400 contributors. They acquired 275 acres that were carefully planned to give the appearance of virgin woodlands.

Riverview Park was built around the Allegheny Observatory, first established in 1860 through the generosity of William Thaw and first directed by Samuel Pierpont Langley (1834-1906). Its chief early utility was in astronomically establishing the correct time, information that proved marketable to other cities and to the Pennsylvania Railroad, which in fact supported the observatory for many years. But by 1894 the observatory had become useless and was rebuilt between 1900 and 1912 with monies raised by astronomer John Brashear (1840-1920) and donated by Henry Clay Frick.

The father of Pittsburgh's parks did not live to see the birth of the city's largest urban oasis, Frick Park, which was designed by nationally known New England architect Guy Lowell. Bigelow died in 1916, one year before Henry Clay Frick executed a will that provided for the park. When he died in 1919, Frick

The Casino Restaurant of 1899 in Kennywood was originally an open-air pavilion. Glass windows were added in the 1940s and festive canopies now cover the terrace.
Photo by Jim Judkis

The giant carousel built by William Dentzel and Company was brought to Kennywood in 1927. Restored in 1976, it is one of the last merry-go-rounds built with such elaborate hand-carved animals and ornamentation.
Photo by Jim Judkis

left 151 acres to the city, estimated at the time to be worth about $1 million, along with a $2 million trust fund to cover maintenance and improvements. By 1942 the trust had obtained an additional 306 acres.

Schenley and Highland parks were actually designed to be linked to each other and downtown as part of a larger network of green space linked by two scenic roadways. This "Emerald Necklace" was conceived to imitate the ones developed by Frederick Law Olmsted in Boston, Buffalo and Louisville. Bigelow Boulevard (formerly Grant Boulevard until Bigelow's death in 1916) was designed as an extension of Grant Street to connect downtown with Schenley Park. Beechwood Boulevard was to connect Schenley and Highland parks via what is now Washington Boulevard.

Meanwhile, on a bluff above the Monongahela River 12 miles south of Pittsburgh, between the mill towns of Homestead and Duquesne, and directly across from Carnegie's Edgar Thomson Works, development began on Kennywood Park. Kennywood was a project of the Monongahela Street Railway Company, which connected Pittsburgh with the mill towns of the Monongahela River Valley via Oakland and Squirrel Hill.

In 1898 the company leased a 141-acre wooded farm, known as Kenny's Grove, which had been a popular picnic spot since the time of the Civil War. They immediately set about building a dance pavilion, casino (restaurant), a merry-go-round and a small artificial lake, all meticulously landscaped and magnificently lit with thousands of incandescent bulbs at a time when electricity was still a novelty to the average Pittsburgher. Before long, these attractions were joined by many others, including the first roller coaster in 1902, a three-way, figure-eight toboggan, 85 feet wide and 225 feet long, with a 70-foot-long incline. By 1905 Kennywood advertised more than 100 attractions. It has been a family-run business for most of its history.

The Monongahela Street Railway Company sought to boost evening and weekend ridership, and in the process created a sylvan setting for mill town residents, who could ride there for a fare of just 5 cents. With supplemental service and special excursion rates on the Pennsylvania Railroad, Kennywood attracted people from as far away as New Castle, Erie, Washington

(Pennsylvania), Youngstown, Cleveland, Canton, Columbus and Wheeling. Widely advertised for company and organizational picnics, the park marketed itself as the poor man's country club:

> Golf is all right and you probably enjoy your Country Club privileges, but how about the fellows in the mill or factory who have neither the opportunity nor price of golf? An outing, with an opportunity for a bit of recreation, would bring more of a thrill to him and his family than your game of golf brings to you. It is not too late to book a picnic date for your employees at Kennywood Park.

And, in fact, the annual Kennywood picnic became a Pittsburgh institution. The first large nationality picnic there was the gathering of the Scottish clans in 1899, followed by the Serbians, Russians, Slovaks, Carpathians, Irish, Hungarians, Polish, Croatians and Italians, each bringing native music, foods, dances and languages.

When the park opened on May 30, 1899, the *Pittsburgh Index* prophetically reported that "Kennywood is bound to become famous from the very start." Indeed, Kennywood today is recognized as both a National Historic Landmark and as the "Roller Coaster Capital of the World." Once one of over a dozen area trolley parks and amusement resorts, Kennywood is one of only two that survive, the other being Idlewild Park in Latrobe, about 30 miles east of the city.

Suburban Growth

The latter part of the 19th century saw the growth of additional suburbs to accommodate Pittsburgh's growing population and provide a retreat from the industrial atmosphere of the downtown. These suburbs developed most heavily to the east of downtown, between the rivers.

At least one of the outlying suburban areas, which were eventually annexed to the city, traces its beginning to the 18th century. The Turner family first settled Squirrel Hill in 1764, at the time when the first streets were being laid out around Fort Pitt and the population of Pittsburgh was only about 140. The path from the Point eastward was along Forbes Trail (now Avenue) and on to Squirrel Hill, a hunter's paradise. Gen. John Forbes had used Forbes Trail when he dislodged the French from Fort Duquesne in 1758, and it remained the primary eastward route from Pittsburgh until 1800.

After its annexation in 1868 as a suburban metropolitan community, it continued to grow slowly until improved transportation in the 1890s prompted sudden increased migration. In 1893 the streetcar line to Squirrel Hill began operations, traveling through Schenley Park, up the ravine on the south side of Forbes and up to Murray Avenue, which was not paved. The car tracks were laid on ties from Forbes Street to Browns Bridge, where they crossed the river to Homestead. This development plus the construction of the bridge over the Panther Hollow ravine on Forbes Street led to a land boom that inflated prices from $500 per acre to $5,000 per acre.

The East Liberty Valley, too, developed early. The Greensburg Pike, running through the valley, succeeded the Forbes Trail as the main road to the east about 1800. Penn Avenue was part of that original pike. About 1800, Jacob Negley purchased the property from what is now Highland Park to Penn Avenue. He cleared the white oak and hickory from the area now bounded by Penn Avenue, Highland Avenue, Stanton Avenue and North Negley Avenue, and the current North Negley neighborhood early became a popular residential district around East Liberty. Major transportation routes continued to run to and through the area, including both street railways and the Pennsylvania Railroad, creating a hub at the heart of the neighborhood. Between 1860 and 1900, East Liberty became the second-largest business district and the most fashionable residential area in the Pittsburgh region.

Point Breeze, to the south of East Liberty, was laid out by 1895 and developed in the early 20th century as a residential suburb for wealthy industrialists and businessmen. Penn Avenue, Fifth Avenue and the train, cable and trolley systems afforded easy access to downtown. Designed as the quintessential fashionable suburb, Point Breeze reflected the influence of the parks movement in its plan of grassy circles and wide esplanades.

East Liberty in the late 19th century
Carnegie Library of Pittsburgh, Pittsburgh Photographic Library

As the fashionable area of the city moved out to this end of town, the urban amenities that normally accompany such development followed. Of course the city already had its great park cemetery, Allegheny. With the development of the East End, however, three more beautiful cemeteries were laid out in a short time: Homewood (1878), Calvary (1886) and Smithfield (1887). Eventually Homewood would surpass Allegheny as the place for prominent people to be buried.

The city also continued to grow through annexation, as it had in the mid-19th century. The city limits had been expanded in 1868 to include Lawrenceville borough and the townships of Pitt, Oakland, Peebles, Liberty and Collins. In the same year and the one following it, the city of Allegheny annexed Manchester borough, Reserve Township, Duquesne borough and two parcels of unnamed land. The second wave of annexation had come in 1872, as 27 square miles south of the Monongahela River were added to the city of Pittsburgh, and the city of Allegheny doubled its size.

In 1906 came the passage of "An Act to enable cities that are now, or may hereafter be, contiguous or in close proximity, to be united, with any intervening land other than boroughs, in one municipality." Allegheny City, with a population of over 129,000, was annexed to the city of Pittsburgh the following year and became known thereafter as the North Side. Several other boroughs, mostly on the South Side, were annexed during the 1890-1907 era. Appreciable increases in the population of Pittsburgh of course accompanied this vast physical growth.

This gasoline station of c. 1915 made exuberant use of terra cotta, a fashionable building material of the time. *Carnegie Library of Pittsburgh, Pittsburgh Photographic Library*

CLUB LIFE

Club life served as a focal point for life across all social and economic sectors, bringing together people with common interests and backgrounds. In keeping with a nationwide club boom that endured from the 1860s through World War I, Pittsburgh developed its share of business and social clubs, many of which survive to this day. Here members could meet with like-minded people, perhaps conduct business, discuss the problems inherent in rapid industrialization and urban growth, begin to forge solutions and find welcome respite from the rigors of the outside world.

Just as Pittsburgh was embarking on its leap from Iron City to manufacturing metropolis, business leaders founded the Duquesne Club in June 1873. Certainly not Pittsburgh's first club, the Duquesne Club has nonetheless remained the city's premier business club for more than 125 years. The founding members represented a who's who of newly wealthy, self-made entrepreneurs, the majority of them in their 20s and 30s. This group represented the new elite in Pittsburgh, as the economic power shifted from merchant families to industrialists. More than a third of the earliest members derived their livelihood from iron and steel. By the time of the momentous 1901 celebration to mark the creation of United States Steel Corporation in the club's main dining room, 28 of the 41 "Carnegie Millionaires" were members of the Duquesne Club.

Originally housed at 259 Penn Avenue, the Duquesne Club moved in 1879 to leased quarters at 19 Sixth Avenue. At the time of the move, a number of younger members decided to stay behind and establish a new club, the Pittsburgh Club, "conceived in discontent and born in rebellion." It would go on to have a quieter history.

After less than 10 years in the new location, the Duquesne Club engaged the renowned Boston architectural firm of Longfellow, Alden & Harlow to design a stately new brownstone clubhouse at 325 Sixth Avenue which opened in 1890. The new building utilized the new steel frame technology that would soon transform the city's skyline. Subsequent additions in 1904 and 1929 would accommodate expanded facilities and a larger membership. This "Eveless Eden," as the *Pittsburgh Dispatch* called it in 1889, catered to its elite membership with the finest food and service, offering a menu with a staggering breadth of choice and several dining rooms. The club also began early on to amass a significant art collection, a tradition that continues to this day, featuring significant works by artists such as Frederick Remington, Charles Russell and George Hetzel. Long a bastion of conservative, white, Anglo-Saxon males, the Duquesne Club would ultimately pioneer the notion of social inclusion in clubs by opening its membership to Jewish members in the mid-1960s, to women in 1980 and to African Americans in 1981.

Private clubs were not all focused on social and business concerns. In 1882 a small group of managerial and professional Pittsburgh men formed a study group for their own enrichment and edification, which they called the Junta, in memory of Benjamin Franklin's Junto, which he formed for craftsmen in London and later in Philadelphia. For more than 100 years, 10 meetings have been held each year at which scholarly papers are presented on an assigned subject and all present are invited to comment on the subject.

As Oakland developed into the city's civic center, it attracted its own share of clubs, many of which Frank Nicola actively recruited. Among those that found their homes there between 1900 and 1920 were the Concordia Club (1874), the Twentieth Century Club (c. 1890s) and the Pittsburgh Athletic Association (1908).

The Twentieth Century Club could be seen as the response of Pittsburgh's female elite to the Duquesne Club or groups like the Junta. How progressive the name must have sounded to the Pittsburgh community in 1894! It carried the promise of new ideas and forward-thinking to launch the city's leading women into the coming age, prepared for the anticipated myriad of changes that the new century would most certainly bring — changes in social and political thought, in national economic policies, in international relations, in science and technology, in the built environment and much more. Clearly, the founders perceived themselves as sitting poised on the cutting edge of modern life. They drew their intellectual inspiration from the New Century Club in Philadelphia, an organization whose members gave lectures instead of using outside speakers.

The Twentieth Century Club members' hunger for new ideas spawned a lecture series that has presented more than 2,000 programs during the past 100 years. The lecturers — ambassadors, foreign correspondents, artists, poets, activists, business people, historians, politicians, royalty, refugees, musicians, philosophers, architects, actors and actresses, Pulitzer Prize-winning authors and others — collectively have offered a well-rounded education to rival most liberal arts programs in the country. Before the proliferation of modern mass media, members relied heavily on these outside lectures to

The Duquesne Club in downtown Pittsburgh was built in 1887 to the designs of Longfellow, Alden & Harlow. *Pittsburgh History & Landmarks Foundation*

bring them in-depth analysis of world affairs, with distinguished speakers such as Jacob A. Riis of New York, Miss Jane Addams of Hull House in Chicago, Dr. Woodrow Wilson, then of Princeton University, Julia Ward Howe, John Quincy Adams, Booker T. Washington, W.E.B. Dubois, Mrs. Theodore Roosevelt, Jr. and Dr. Margaret Mead. As time went on, the focus broadened to include a wider range of subjects.

Like their purely social counterparts, political clubs provided camaraderie to their members. Both founded in 1884 and both boasting more than 700 members, the Americus Republican Club and the Randall Club for Democrats catered to the social and political leanings of their respective memberships in the private settings of their clubhouses. Both also reached outward, however, to create larger spheres of influence. The Americus Club's activities and campaign leadership came to be nationally known. Likewise, the Young Men's Republican Tariff Club also enjoyed a large membership and a private clubhouse.

The desire to mingle with like-minded folk also spawned a number of exclusive clubs in the outlying residential areas that attracted the wealthy from Pittsburgh and Allegheny even before the age of automobiles would give rise to a host of country clubs after 1920. Elite enclaves like the Pittsburgh Golf Club and Allegheny Country Club provided sylvan venues for such gentrified sports as golf, tennis, and swimming, as well as purely social gatherings for city's power class. Later, the Mellons established the exclusive Rolling Rock Club at Ligonier, thereby opening the rolling farm country of Westmoreland County to development with lavish estates and rustic farms.

The wealthier residents of Pittsburgh and Allegheny City also fashioned even more remote escapes for themselves, primarily in the Allegheny Mountains to the east of the city. One of the earliest, the South Fork Fishing and Hunting Club, enjoyed a brief and ill-fated history on a hill above Johnstown. Chartered in 1879, the club was conceived as a rustic resort for a select group of Pittsburgh businessmen, many of them young, who would ultimately control much of the city's commercial infrastructure. Of the 61 members in 1889, 38 were officers, partners or owners of business firms ranging from real estate to steel, seven were attorneys and four were bankers. Many were direct business associates. They built a hotel and 14 cottages on a property of 600 acres that included Lake Conemaugh and the earthen dam that contained it. What gained the South Fork Club its notoriety, however, was not the secluded enclave of prominent Pittsburghers, but rather the disastrous collapse of the dam and consequent draining of Lake Conemaugh on May 31, 1889, down the valley and into the city of Johnstown. The Johnstown Flood, the greatest national tragedy of the post-Civil War era, left more than 2,200 people dead and caused substantial property damage.

Many ethnic and working class social clubs also flourished at this time. The 1875 City Directory lists over 200 lodges and other clubs. By 1920, the number had more than doubled to meet the recreational, benevolent, temperance, civic, commercial, political, educational. musical and social interests of Pittsburgh's growing population.

By 1900 the African-American community had an active club life, centered primarily in the Hill district. Among the most prestigious were the Loendi Club, Aurora Reading Club, Goldenrod Social Club and White Rose Club, which emphasized social and cultural activities. A number of clubs promoted the cultural life of the community through literary reading and discussions: the Aurora Reading Club, the Frances Harper League, the Wylie Avenue Literary Society, the Homewood Social and Literary Club, the Emma J. Moore Literary and Art Circle, and the Booker T. Washington Literary Society.

White fraternal lodges excluded African-American members, who established all-black chapters of their own, many of which — such as the Elks, Masons, Odd Fellow, Knights of Pythias and True Reformers — emphasized community improvement. Community leaders also helped raise funds for a Home for Aged and Infirm Colored Women," an institution that survives today as the Lemington Center, as well as a Working Girls' Home and a Colored Orphans' Home, among others. Churches were also active in community affairs, while more than 25 women's clubs devoted themselves to charity and social interaction.

The End of an Era

By the end of this era, the face of industrial Pittsburgh was cast. The bulk of its labor pool had arrived. The major industries were established. The four top industrial players — Carnegie, Frick, Heinz and Westinghouse — had all died, three of them in the same year of 1919, leaving powerful industrial empires. Pittsburgh was established as a bourgeois town. Labor had been squelched and would remain so until the 1930s. The Gilded Age had arguably drawn to a close with the introduction of the income tax. The city had prospered under the industrial demands of World War I. The nation had emerged victorious. It was now time for the mature city to examine the foundations of its stature and find balance between the demands of heavy industry and the needs of its people.

Biographies

Andrew Carnegie
Carnegie Library of Pittsburgh, Pittsburgh Photographic Library

Andrew Carnegie (1835-1919)

Andrew Carnegie, who would become the dominant figure in the post-Civil War American steel industry, was born in Dunfermline, a village near the eastern coast of Scotland. Poor and with little formal education, he came to the United States at the age of 13 and settled in Allegheny City. His first job was as a bobbin boy in the Blackstock Cotton Mill for $1.20 per week, then in a telegraph office, and subsequently for the Pennsylvania Railroad. A natural entrepreneur, Carnegie introduced the first Pullman sleeping cars and became head of the western division of the Railroad in 1859.

On a visit to Sheffield, England, Carnegie toured Henry Bessemer's new factory and recognized the growing importance of iron and steel. He resigned from the Pennsylvania Railroad to form the Keystone Bridge Company in 1863 and the Pittsburgh Locomotive Works and the Union Iron Mills in 1866, beginning what would become a legendary empire. Carnegie built a steel-rail mill, bought out the Homestead Steel Works and by 1888 controlled several steel plants at Homestead, Duquesne and Braddock.

In 1899 Carnegie consolidated his various holdings into the Carnegie Steel Company, which he sold to J.P. Morgan in 1901 to create the United States Steel Company, the nation's first billion-dollar business. Retiring at age 65 with a guaranteed income of $1 million a month, Carnegie devoted the rest of his life to philanthropy, donating more than $350 million to various causes. Carnegie's charitable influence extends well beyond the Pittsburgh region. He established more than 2,500 libraries and founded the Carnegie Institute of Pittsburgh, the Carnegie Institution at Washington, the Carnegie Foundation for the Advancement of Teaching, the Carnegie Endowment for International Peace and the Carnegie Corporation of New York.

Henry Phipps
Carnegie Library of Pittsburgh, Pittsburgh Photographic Library

Henry Phipps (1839-1930)

Henry Phipps was born in Philadelphia to English parents and moved as a child to Allegheny City, where he lived next door to Mrs. Margaret Carnegie and her two sons, Andrew and Thomas. Joining forces with Andrew and Thomas Carnegie, Phipps orchestrated what has been called the first important steel merger in history, culminating in the Edgar Thompson Works, the first plant west of the Alleghenies to manufacture steel rails. As second in command and financial steward of the Carnegie Steel Company, he built a personal fortune of $100 million. Like his fellow Carnegie partners, Henry Clay Frick and Henry Oliver, Phipps invested millions in local real estate and made his mark on the downtown skyline, although only one of his buildings survives today: the Fulton Building, now the Renaissance Pittsburgh Hotel.

Phipps gave generously to charity and public welfare, with an emphasis on medical concerns, including the war on tuberculosis, a psychiatric clinic at Johns Hopkins University and his Henry Phipps Institute in Philadelphia, the first organization ever formed to fight a single disease in hopes of eliminating it. Phipps also sought to make a difference by bankrolling sanitary public housing facilities. By far his most enduring contribution to the quality of life in Pittsburgh, however, was his gift in 1893, of Phipps Conservatory in Schenley Park, which eclipsed and outlived an earlier conservatory he had erected in Allegheny City's West Park during the 1880s.

Henry W. Oliver (1840-1904)

Henry W. Oliver
Carnegie Library of Pittsburgh, Pittsburgh Photographic Library

Henry Oliver, of Scot-Irish descent, emigrated with his family as a child in 1842. An optimistic innovator, Oliver began as a messenger boy but ultimately made his career and his fortune in steel, railroads and mining. As a young man in 1863, he started a small nut and bolt manufacturing business that was the precursor to the Oliver Iron and Steel Company. A founder of the Pittsburgh and Lake Erie Railroad, he introduced a number of improvements, including the steel railroad car. Through his Oliver Mining Company, he pioneered development of the Mesabi ore district in Minnesota. Like many of his peers, Oliver also made a mark in commercial real estate, leaving the Oliver Building (1908-10) as one of his most lasting legacies.

H.J. Heinz (1844-1919)

H. J. Heinz
Carnegie Library of Pittsburgh, Pittsburgh Photographic Library

Henry John Heinz was born to German parents on the South Side. Educated at Lutheran Church schools and Duff's Business College, he took over his father's brickyard at the age of 21. As early as age 10, Heinz had begun to sell the surplus from his parents' garden. By 1869 he had formed the H.J. Heinz Company and had 6,000 acres of fruits and vegetables. By 1900 the company had 1,000 to 2,000 workers, depending upon the season. When Heinz died in 1919, the business employed 6,523 people and processed crops from 100,000 acres.

In addition to his influence as a trend-setting and enlightened industrialist, Heinz left behind an enduring legacy of philanthropy as well. His Point Breeze mansion offered a public conservatory and museum, he built a settlement house near his Allegheny City plant in memory of his wife Sarah, and of course generations of descendants have continued to apply the Heinz fortune to philanthropy in a wide range of causes.

George Westinghouse (1846-1914)

Still another visionary of the age was George Westinghouse, born in Central Bridge, New York, the son of an inventor of agricultural machinery. He went on to become an inventor in his own right, as well as an industrialist, and during his lifetime obtained about 400 patents, including his railroad air brake. In 1865 he patented a device for replacing derailed freight cars on tracks. After coming to Pittsburgh, he founded the Westinghouse Air Brake Company in 1869. By the early 1880s the company had developed interlocking switches and a complete railroad signal system; this technology was capitalized into the Union Switch and Signal Company in 1882. Westinghouse also made forays into the energy business. After discovering oil on his East End estate, Homewood, he established gas companies and developed technologies to make natural gas available for both commercial and residential use. Subsequently attracted to electricity, Westinghouse pioneered the use of electric lighting in his own residence. With the founding of the Westinghouse Electric Company in 1886, he effectively brought about the use of alternating current in the United States, applying it to generating and transmitting apparatuses as well as appliances.

George Westinghouse
Pittsburgh History & Landmarks Foundation

Christopher Lyman Magee
Carnegie Library of Pittsburgh, Pittsburgh Photographic Library

Christopher Lyman Magee (1848-1901)

Christopher L. Magee was born and educated in Pittsburgh and grew to develop, in collaboration with William Flinn, the city's first political machine. Elected to the post of city treasurer by the age of 23, he also served as a fire commissioner, secretary of the State Republican Committee and a delegate in a number of Republican National Conventions. On the private side, Magee made profitable investments in the early development of natural gas and in real estate. In 1884 he bought the *Times* newspaper and built its circulation from 1,500 to 60,000. He was also organizer and president of the Duquesne Traction Company, controlling 32 miles of street railway, and director of four other railway companies, two banks and the Allegheny Electric Light Company. At his death, the bulk of his estate went to establish Magee Women's Hospital in memory of his mother.

Henry Clay Frick (1849-1919)

Like Carnegie, Henry Clay Frick was born in humble circumstances but grew to become a leading industrialist and philanthropist. Frick's birthplace was the agrarian village of West Overton, southeast of Pittsburgh, where his family was involved in agriculture and the distillery business.

Henry Clay Frick
Carnegie Library of Pittsburgh, Pittsburgh Photographic Library

While working as a distillery bookkeeper, Frick developed an interest in the business of making coke from coal and entered that business in 1871 with the organization of Frick, Overholt & Co. He eventually began building ovens to supply coke to the Pittsburgh market. As head of the H.C. Frick Coal and Coke Company with Andrew and Thomas Carnegie and Henry Phipps, he owned 3,000 acres and 1,022 coke ovens centered in Westmoreland and Fayette counties. Eventually the business grew to 40,000 acres of coal with 11,000 beehive ovens and an annual capacity of 7 million tons of coal. Frick became known as the "Coke King" and achieved millionaire status at the age of 30.

As chairman of Carnegie Steel Company, Frick figured prominently in one of labor's most memorable struggles. While attempting to break the landmark 1892 Strike at Carnegie's Homestead mill, he was shot and stabbed by Alexander Berkman, a Russian-born anarchist. Frick survived the attack, and Berkman was imprisoned for 13 years at Western Penitentiary and subsequently deported. Frick participated in the formation of J.P. Morgan's United States Steel Corporation in 1901 and became one of its first directors.

An avid collector of "pictures," Frick amassed a valuable art collection, most of which he moved to New York City to create the Frick Collection. Some of the collection remains at Clayton, his home in Point Breeze, which is operated as a museum of the Frick family and the Gilded Age. Frick also gave considerable sums to hospitals, educational institutions and the city of Pittsburgh, including the 151 acres that constituted the core of Frick Park.

William Flinn (1851-1924)

William Flinn
Carnegie Library of Pittsburgh, Pittsburgh Photographic Library

William Flinn was born in England to Irish parents, but was in fact a lifelong Pittsburgher. Like his fellow political boss, Christopher Magee, Flinn went to work early and positioned himself for power at a young age. He was elected a fire commissioner in 1877 and went on to serve both in the state house of representatives and as a state senator, as well as chairman of the Republican City Executive Committee of Pittsburgh for 20 years and as a delegate to several Republican National Conventions. Founding the contracting firm of Booth and Flinn in 1877, Flinn proved successful in business as well. His other business interests included the Duquesne Lumber Company, Pittsburgh Lumber Company, Sharon Water Works Company and directorships of several oil, natural gas and coal companies.

Andrew Mellon
Carnegie Library of Pittsburgh, Pittsburgh Photographic Library

Andrew Mellon (1855-1937)

Andrew W. Mellon held many prominent positions during his lifetime, including: secretary of the treasury under presidents Harding, Coolidge and Hoover; ambassador to Great Britain; banker; art collector; and founder of the National Gallery of Art.

Mary Roberts Rinehart (1876-1958)

Mary Roberts Rinehart
Carnegie Library of Pittsburgh, Pittsburgh Photographic Library

Mary Roberts Rinehart was born in Allegheny City. She grew to distinguish herself as an author and a journalist. The *Saturday Evening Post* regularly published her work, and in 1915 sent her abroad as a foreign correspondent, a role she also performed for the War Department in World War I. She became best known, however, for her more than 50 books, eight plays and hundreds of short stories, poems, travelogues and special articles, which sold over 10 million copies by the time of her death. Three of her plays ran concurrently on Broadway. By far her most popular works were her mystery stories, introducing a new genre crafted with a unique combination of mystery, crime, love and humor. It was in one of her critically acclaimed mystery books that Rinehart coined the phrase, "The butler did it."

The legendary Joe Magarac
Pittsburgh History & Landmarks Foundation

Joe Magarac

A mythical but highly symbolic figure, Joe Magarac was a hero to the thousands of ethnic immigrants who came to Pittsburgh during the late 19th century. He symbolized their pride in the hard work and long hours that fueled the "Workshop of the World." Magarac (Slovak for "jackass"), it was said, was the strongest steelworker in Pittsburgh. Local lore said that he could measure the consistency of a ladle of molten steel by tasting it and that he ended his life by jumping into a blast furnace, thereby improving the quality of the metal. A statue of Magarac was suggested in lieu of the fountain when Point State Park was developed, and his image survives in the monumental bronze reliefs that were salvaged from the demolished Manchester Bridge of 1915 and are now on display next to the Pittsburgh Children's Museum.

■ PITTSBURGH LIVABILITY

■ POPULAR RECREATION

■ AT WORK

■ PITTSBURGH IN POSTCARDS

As the 19th century approached its end, Pittsburgh was still a raw place, reckless of its environment. A few people realized that something must be done, and officials, employers, architects and planners worked to accomplish something better.

The fabulously rich industrial city was just beginning to learn how to spend money on itself, to create places like the Carnegie Institute, Schenley Park or Kennywood where people could take a break from work and enjoy the arts and recreation.

A natural gas flare occurs near Pittsburgh: *Harper's Weekly*, November 7, 1885. Natural gas offered promise to mitigate the prevailing smoke pollution, although the coal-burning excursion boat *Geneva*, and its like, would always number among the exceptions.
Pittsburgh History & Landmarks Foundation

A rough commute during the Flood of 1907
Pittsburgh History & Landmarks Foundation

Festivities on the Monongahela River during the Pittsburgh Sesquicentennial of 1908 — to the right is the old Point Bridge, removed in 1927. The wooden coal barges in the foreground are tied up at the Monongahela Wharf, and across the river is the Clinton Furnace.
Pittsburgh History & Landmarks Foundation

Water filtration was one of Edward Manning Bigelow's contributions to Pittsburgh. The Mission Pumping Station on the South Side Slopes was built in 1912.
Archives Service Center, University of Pittsburgh

The irony of naming this hillside street in Hazelwood "Sylvan Avenue" is apparent. By 1907, when this picture was taken, Jones & Laughlin's coke-oven fumes had killed all vegetation.
Carnegie Library of Pittsburgh, Pittsburgh Photographic Library

Popular Recreation

The Schenley Park band shell, c. 1900
Carnegie Library of Pittsburgh, Pittsburgh Photographic Library

Little Hip Park, c. 1910, on the Allegheny River; Union Station, at one corner of the Triangle, is on the skyline at the center.
Pittsburgh History & Landmarks Foundation

The Homestead Grays, championship baseball team, 1913
Carnegie Library of Pittsburgh, Pittsburgh Photographic Library

A sculling race on the Monongahela River
Pittsburgh History & Landmarks Foundation

At Work

Bottling in the early 1890s
Carnegie Library of Pittsburgh, Pittsburgh Photographic Library.

The Glass Manufacturing Company in Tarentum: casting and rolling sheets of plate glass
Carnegie Library of Pittsburgh, Pittsburgh Photographic Library

Switch engine, c. 1880
Carnegie Library of Pittsburgh, Pittsburgh Photographic Library

Pittsburgh Plate Glass workers, 1887
Carnegie Library of Pittsburgh, Pittsburgh Photographic Library

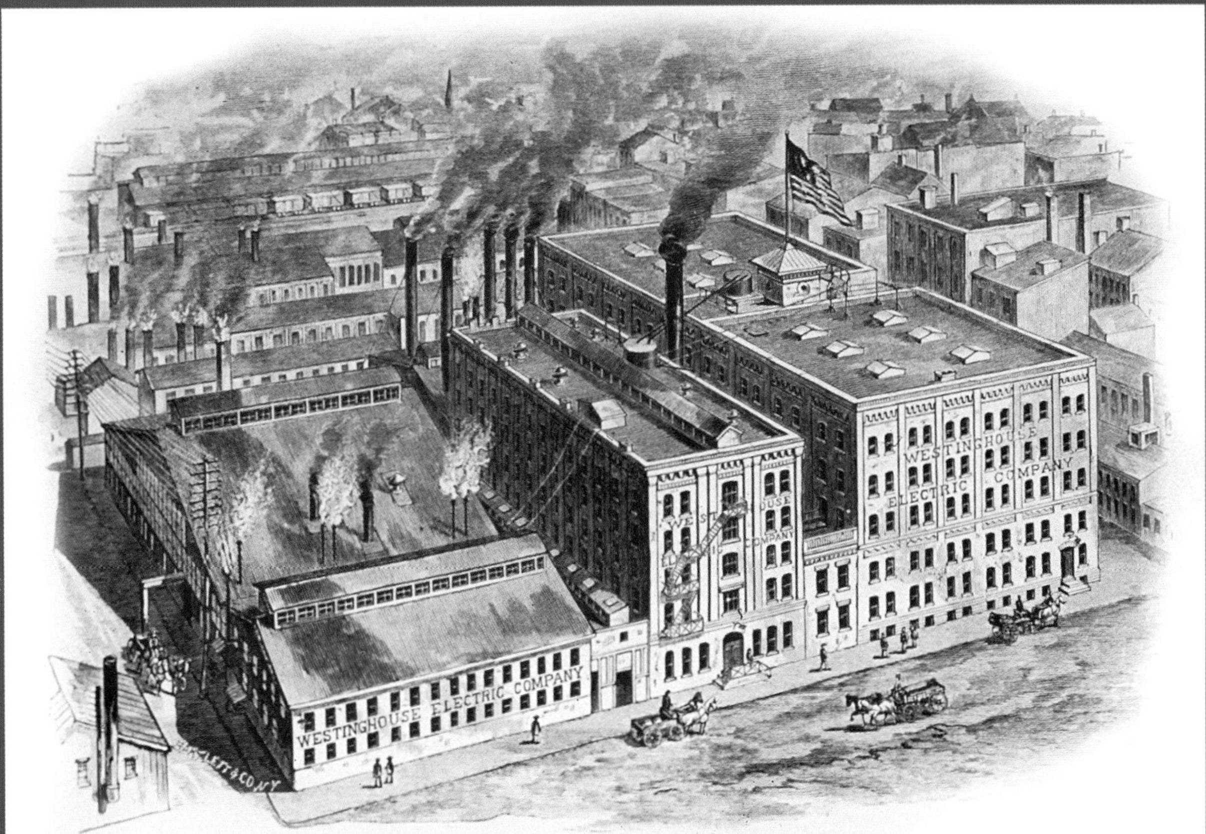

At the Heinz plant, 1903: a meeting of sales managers at the Men's Roof Garden
Pittsburgh History & Landmarks Foundation

An 1888 view of the Westinghouse Electric Company when it was still in the Strip District
Pittsburgh History & Landmarks Foundation

At the Heinz plant, c. 1905: hand-wrapping cans of baked beans
Pittsburgh History & Landmarks Foundation

An outing of employees from the Heinz plant in Allegheny: to the rear is the plant's gatehouse.
Pittsburgh History & Landmarks Foundation

(Above)
Boy glass workers from a postcard marked 1907
Pittsburgh History & Landmarks Foundation

(Top right)
Coal miners from a postcard marked 1905
Pittsburgh History & Landmarks Foundation

(Middle right)
A view of the Homestead Works in Munhall, postmarked 1909
Pittsburgh History & Landmarks Foundation

(Bottom right)
The Triangle from the North Side, c. 1910: the Sixth Street Bridge of 1892 is to the right. Flanking its entrance are two real-estate ventures of Henry Phipps: the Fulton Building to the left (now the Renaissance Pittsburgh Hotel) and the Bessemer Building (now gone) to the right.
Pittsburgh History & Landmarks Foundation

The short-lived Luna Park in Oakland, c. 1905
Pittsburgh History & Landmarks Foundation

Westinghouse white-collar workers homeward bound: at the East Pittsburgh Station, c. 1910
Pittsburgh History & Landmarks Foundation

Iron workers, 1900s
Pittsburgh History & Landmarks Foundation

The Irene Kaufmann Settlement from a postcard marked 1914
Pittsburgh History & Landmarks Foundation

The home of an ironmaster, the Singer House built in Wilkinsburg in 1865, in a postcard marked 1911
Pittsburgh History & Landmarks Foundation

West View Park, on the North Side: the lake and "Dip the Dip" from a postcard stamped 1914
Pittsburgh History & Landmarks Foundation

CHAPTER 5

Progress in the Face of Hard Times

1920-1945

WITH ITS INDUSTRIES WELL ESTABLISHED AND subsequently tested during World War I, Pittsburgh faced a new age presenting a new set of challenges. Despite the victories of the preceding half century — military, industrial, philanthropic, cultural, civic improvement — the city and its people would now enter a brief period that seemed largely overshadowed by hard times and sacrifice. Yet in its characteristic resourcefulness, the city also achieved advances that showcased the genius of a new generation of visionaries.

Pittsburgh c. 1940: this may have been an unusually clear day. At the Point there is a tiny park at the junction of the two bridges. *Pittsburgh History & Landmarks Foundation*

This photograph by the locally renowned Luke Swank shows the North Side in the 1930s with the Gulf (left) and Koppers buildings prominent on the downtown skyline. *Carnegie Library of Pittsburgh, Pittsburgh Photographic Library*

Not only had World War I taken its toll, with 1,500 Allegheny County men killed in action, but the city was still reeling from an influenza epidemic in 1918 that had taken another 2,052 lives. Peacetime brought production cutbacks and declining wages. At the same time, the coal industry was in the doldrums due to overproduction. Tensions mounted between labor, with its democratic ideals, and management, with its confident attitude that it knew best. Immigration was cut through three successive laws in 1921, 1924 and 1929, fragmenting families who had left loved ones behind in their homelands. Prohibition forced leisure activity into hiding. Depression hit. The city was devastated by flood. The nation dove headlong into another global conflict. And the physical city deteriorated into a dirty, shameful embarrassment. Ultimately, this decline would galvanize city leaders into action.

A Facelift for the Aging City

In an effort to respond aggressively to the *Pittsburgh Survey* of 1907 to 1914 and Olmsted's plan of 1911, the business elite formed a citizens' committee bent on improving the city's infrastructure: its streets, waterways, railroads, parks and playgrounds. For 20 years, from 1921 to 1941, the committee issued a publication called *Progress*, which served as the official voice for the revitalization agenda. Similarly, the Chamber of Commerce launched the short-lived but intense Pittsburgh Forward promotional program in January 1926, which was designed to "sell Pittsburgh to Pittsburghers." The full scope of the reforms these initiatives sought would not be realized until the creation in 1943 of the Allegheny Conference on Community Development, a public-private partnership established to drive the successive Renaissances of the second half of the 20th century. Yet progress was made between the wars.

A view of the Jones & Laughlin Pittsburgh Works around 1931: in the foreground are the Eliza blast furnaces within the Pittsburgh Works of J&L, whose South Side plant is visible across the Monongahela. *Carnegie Library of Pittsburgh, Pittsburgh Photographic Library*

With the "Hump" fully removed along Grant Street and the Pennsylvania Railroad yards removed from the northern end in 1929, the way was paved for several more major buildings. While the earlier buildings were attributable to individuals like Carnegie, Frick and Oliver, this next wave was partially the result of corporate and public patronage. At the northern end, the Koppers Building was completed on the eve of the Depression, in 1927-29, and the Gulf Building, Federal Reserve Bank and the U.S. Post Office followed in 1930-32. The City-County building and the Grant Building anchored the southern end of Grant Street. Pittsburgh patrons, then and now, typically sought their design talent from outside the city.

Yet exceptions occurred as well; notable among designs by local architects during this era were the Union Trust Building by Frederick J. Osterling, the William Penn Hotel by Janssen & Abbott, expanded by Janssen & Cocken, the City-County Building by Edward B. Lee with Palmer, Hornbostel & Jones, and the Grant Building by Henry Hornbostel and Eric Fisher Wood.

The University Takes Off and Soars

With the Oakland Civic Center already established under the direction of Andrew Carnegie as philanthropist and Frank Nicola as developer, there entered a third figure whose vision would not only change the physical face of Oakland, but also change the face of philanthropy. John Gabbert Bowman, a former college president and director of the American College of Surgeons, was recruited in 1921 by the trustees of the University of Pittsburgh as its chancellor and charged with creating a modern university. At the time, the center of Oakland, part of the Frick estate, was open land occupied by a few Victorian houses. The university was more than $1 million in debt and sorely needed teaching space, faculty and an endowment. Over the next 24 years, Bowman would go about building all three and, under his leadership, enrollment would grow from about 2,300 to some 23,000 students.

(Above)
A tour bus pauses in Schenley Plaza before an East End trip in 1922. In the background is the Carnegie Library.
Pittsburgh History & Landmarks Foundation

(Top far left)
The 535-foot-high Cathedral of Learning and Heinz Chapel dominate this scene of the Civic Center from around 1950.
Pittsburgh History & Landmarks Foundation

(Above center)
In 1927 the John Eichleay Jr. Company successfully moved this mid-Victorian residence to a new location, thus clearing the site for the University of Pittsburgh. In the background the Cathedral of Learning rises.
Eichleay Holdings Inc., Pittsburgh, Pa.

(Left)
The Pittsburgh Civic Center in Oakland, c. 1932
Carnegie Library of Pittsburgh, Pittsburgh Photographic Library

(All three photos) The Greek, Irish, and Armenian Nationality Rooms in the University of Pittsburgh's Cathedral of Learning
Photos by H.K. Barnett

On the advice of R.B. Mellon, the new chancellor developed a plan for a fresh start at the university in the form of a major new building. Bowman conceived of a new academic skyscraper that would serve as an expression of courage, "an inspiration, a witness to the spirit of hope and achievement of Pittsburgh, both to itself and to the world." The new building would be 52 stories high, 27 stories higher than the Oliver Building, Pittsburgh's highest building at the time. Moreover, he saw it as a regional project and set about raising the necessary $15 million funding with that objective. A somewhat controversial character, Bowman persevered tirelessly against indifference, skepticism and open opposition.

The planning, design and construction of the new building was a long and arduous process. Bowman purchased the Frick land with $1.5 million given by the Mellons. As his architect, he selected Charles Z. Klauder, a recognized leader in Collegiate Gothic design whose portfolio already included buildings at Yale, Princeton, Cornell, Brown and Wellesley. No doubt Bowman thought that, as the nation's 12th-oldest university, the University of Pittsburgh deserved a structure befitting the Ivy League. In 1925 he set about to raise $10 million and collected more in the first five months than had been raised in the previous 138 years of the university's history.

Construction began in September 1926, but the steel skeleton did not start going up until May 1928. The columns were the largest and strongest used in Pittsburgh to that date. In October 1929, just three days before Black Tuesday and the onset of the Great Depression, the structure of Bowman's skyscraper was complete. The project still continued to progress. To keep it moving along and provide some relief to unemployed workers, the Civil Works Administration sent a force of more than 1,200 tradesmen to work on the building for four months. Reduced from his original vision of 52 stories, it was nonetheless an impressive 42 stories with a Commons Room that soared 52 feet high and covered one-half acre. The first classes moved into a very unfinished building in 1931, with no elevators, heat or plumbing.

Over the next few years, work would continue intermittently until its ultimate completion in 1937. The Heinz Chapel, Stephen Foster Memorial and the first four of the Nationality Rooms were also added during that period. Perhaps the most collective reflection of Pittsburgh's broad ethnic roots, the Cathedral's Nationality Rooms celebrate the architectural and artistic traditions of 25 different countries in a classroom setting. Of the city's population in the 1920s, a fifth were foreign born and a third were the children of immigrants. Bowman courted this constituency for the Nationality Rooms, acknowledging that the immigrant population brought not only industrial brawn but also a rich cultural heritage.

The cost of the overall project would also change over the years, mounting to an estimated $32 million. Bowman was innovative in his approach to raising the necessary funds for the project. His campaign included all sectors of society, including 97,000 children, who each contributed a dime in exchange for a certificate of participation. At the other end of the spectrum, Bowman introduced the notion of corporate philanthropy, with U.S. Steel's in-kind contribution of 7,142 tons of steel rods, bars, girders and beams valued at $250,000.

But above all, Bowman was a visionary who saw the building as transcending steel, masonry and a monumental budget. He touted the building to University trustees, faculty, leading citizens and the press with great symbolism:

> Pittsburgh is known as a center of wealth and of industry. It is known for the making of steel, glass, aluminum, and machinery. The idea of Pittsburgh's vast tonnage is in the minds of millions of people here and over the country. But tonnage is only one phase of Pittsburgh. There is a way of thinking here, a way of doing, an inward spirit and imagination. Out of things of the spirit, out of imagination, the tonnage has come.
>
> The new building is to express that spirit of achievement with such force and sublimity that the whole world will understand. The building is high. It is not high, though, just for the sake of being high. It is only with height that stones can talk the language of courage and sublimity. Such a building belongs in Pittsburgh.

Dubbed the "Cathedral of Learning" by a Scottish draftsman in Klauder's office, the building was also referred to by Bowman, in a jovial moment, as the "Learning Tower of Pisaburgh."

Beyond Bowman's legendary cathedral project, the university made other strides during this difficult period. It opened regional campuses in Johnstown, Erie and Uniontown in the late 1920s. It founded the Falk School as a sort of laboratory project for its education students. It launched the University of Pittsburgh Press in 1936, with the introduction of the *Historical Survey* (a 10-volume work on western Pennsylvania history funded by the university), the Buhl Foundation and the Historical Society of Western Pennsylvania. It constructed its first stadium, which held 67,000 seats and was twice the size of Forbes Field and the largest in the country at the time.

Given recent history, perhaps the most visionary move by the university during the 1920s was the new medical center conceived to "save" Pitt Medical School and launch it into its next phase of growth. The medical center was a relatively new concept in the field of medicine, with only about eight in existence nationwide, beginning with Johns Hopkins in 1899. Bowman, of course, with his medical background, embraced the idea. The then dean of the medical school, Dr. Raleigh Russell Huggins, called for a group of teaching hospitals with more than 1,000 beds, lab and lecture rooms for 400 students, an outpatient department, clinical and diagnostic labs for advanced study and research, a nursing school and home, and dormitories.

The new University of Pittsburgh Medical Center became the nucleus for an assemblage of several other established hospitals: Children's (chartered in 1887), Presbyterian (chartered in 1893), Eye and Ear (1895), Magee-Women's (1911) and the Falk Clinic (1928). By 1930, though not complete, the Medical Center was well on its way. It was there, in 1932, that Vitamin C was synthesized for the first time. Countless innovations would follow.

African Americans Season the Cultural Stew

Pittsburgh's black community grew during a phenomenon known as the Great Migration. By 1900 the city's black population had reached 20,350, making Pittsburgh the sixth-largest black community in the country. Until World War I this growing community was relegated to the menial service jobs that white workers did not want. The region's mills, mines and factories employed them only as temporary strikebreakers. Wartime production demands, coupled with ethnic hostilities and the consequent cutoff of European immigration, however, opened the manufacturing job market to black workers. They came to western Pennsylvania from the deep south, especially Georgia and Alabama, in a wave, swelling the local black community between the two World Wars from 25,000 to 50,000 in Pittsburgh and from 5,000 to 23,000 in the neighboring mill towns of Aliquippa, Homestead, Rankin, Braddock, Duquesne, McKeesport and Clairton.

In response, the local black community found itself divided between the established, light-skinned, educated "Old Pittsburghers," with their institutions of high culture, and the dark-skinned, working-class migrants with their more popular tastes. The result was a rich cultural mix that embraced and nurtured a full range of cultural and recreational activities, from opera to jazz, from literature to sand lot baseball. This rich diversity would later earn the intersection of Wylie and Fullerton avenues in the Hill District the title of "Crossroads of the World," a term coined by Claude McKay, the leading poet of the Harlem Renaissance.

The black community shared an interest in high culture and created

Frank Lloyd Wright described the Cathedral of Learning as the biggest keep-off-the-grass sign in the world. *Photo by William Rydberg, Photon*

Mary Cardwell Dawson, founder of the National Negro Opera Company *Carnegie Library of Pittsburgh, Pittsburgh Photographic Library*

The 50th anniversary of the light bulb was celebrated in 1929. *Carnegie Library of Pittsburgh, Pittsburgh Photographic Library*

The complete canalization of the Ohio River was celebrated on the Monongahela Wharf in 1929. In the middle ground, the Wabash-Pittsburg Terminal Railway bridge disappears into the haze. *Pittsburgh History & Landmarks Foundation*

three concert and symphony orchestras. One was led by William A. Kelly, a coal miner and graduate of Oberlin College, one by Dr. A.R. Taylor, who had played in the Toronto Civic Orchestra, and a third by local contractor David Peeler. Pittsburgh would later become home to the National Negro Opera Company, founded by Mary Cardwell Dawson in 1941, which performed over the next two decades not only for local audiences, but also in Washington, D.C., Chicago and New York.

The Great Depression and the WPA

For some, the bleak conditions of the urban environment were merely an inconvenience for an otherwise bourgeois lifestyle rich with amenities. For many others, however, they were part and parcel of a larger picture that included physical decay and social disorder. As long as smoke signified prosperity, it could be rationalized to at least a certain extent. With the coming of the Great Depression, however, smoke signified little more than dirt, and Pittsburgh's thriving industries suffered the same financial blows and losses of confidence that plagued businesses nationwide.

The Great Depression hit Pittsburgh particularly hard. With the 1929 crash and the economic decline of 1930, nationwide productivity and prices in every industry dropped precipitously. None declined as much as iron and steel, however, which suffered an 83 percent drop in productivity and a 20 percent drop in price. Mill workers lost their jobs and depended upon breadlines and the relief strategies of the New Deal. In 1934 one-third of Pittsburgh's employable population was without work. This left 176,156 people looking for jobs.

The upper middle class suffered somewhat less. Those who had saved found their buying power increased by lower prices. But all were affected by the general decline in business and in morale.

The federally funded Works Progress Administration (WPA) program of the 1930s put people to work and funded many projects that improved the quality of life and many built environment enhancements that survive today. WPA projects exhibited an astonishing diversity. They included mapmaking, research and survey projects, mural painting, literacy projects, sewing projects and even a WPA Symphony. The most enduring were the public infrastructure projects. For example, the WPA funded all the stone bridges and walls in Schenley Park, Riverview's Valley Refuge Picnic Shelter and the prominent stone entrances to Frick Park.

Labor's Voice Is Finally Heard

In issues related to labor struggles, management's long-standing attitude was best expressed by Calvin Coolidge who professed that "What's good for business is good for America."

Maxo Vanka painted these murals in 1939 and 1941 in St. Nicholas Church in Millvale. (Below) Detail shows Parishioners dedicating their church.
Photos by Clyde Hare

The Steel Strike of 1919, also known as the Red Scare, was crushed by accusing the strikers of being communists. Events in Germany, Russia and Hungary at the time only served to feed the scare.

(Above and right) The murals show a startling contrast between the reality of life in the new world and the memory of traditions in the homeland. *Photos by Clyde Hare*

Nonetheless, it was during this period that the labor movement finally gathered sufficient momentum to present a formidable force. In 1931 a group of 60,000 unemployed workers, known as "the Reverend James Cox's unemployed army," rallied at Pitt Stadium in Oakland; 12,000 of them took the cause onward in a march to Washington. On June 17, 1936, Philip Murray, John L. Lewis and nine other organizers founded the Steel Workers Organizing Committee (SWOC) in the Grant Building. The following year, the Congress of Industrial Organizations (CIO) held its founding convention at the Islam Grotto at the corner of Allegheny and Ridge avenues on the North Side. During the summer of 1936, the first open-air Steel Rally was held in McKeesport's Cycler Park, and the first SWOC meeting was held in West Field, Homestead.

It was also during this period, in 1934, that Roosevelt signed the Fair Labor Standards Act, addressing child labor and establishing the 40-hour workweek. The history of labor and the struggles associated with it in the mills around Pittsburgh inspired a number of artistic creations. Prominent examples include Maxo Vanka's frescos at St. Nicholas Croatian Church in Millvale, as well as a glass insert at 300 Sixth Avenue depicting an iron puddler and the John White Alexander murals of 1907 at the Carnegie Museum of Art, which depict the Saga of Steel, with one panel devoted to the Crowning of Labor.

Pittsburgh Under Water

Long plagued by flooding, Pittsburgh had found itself under water on a number of occasions. The record-breaking flood of

1907, when the water crested at 38.7 feet, had made abundantly clear the power of the three rivers to stop the city in its tracks.

The most devastating flood, however, was the Saint Patrick's Day Flood of 1936, which inundated 36 acres of the triangle for a full week, killing at least 70 people, injuring 3,500 and leaving more than 110,000 homeless. Swelled by heavy rains and melting snow, the rivers crested at more than 46 feet, the highest in Pittsburgh's history, with water at 20 feet in some downtown streets. With not only water damage, but also fires and the flood of debris, including barges, cars, docks and boats, property loss was estimated near $200 million. The city was without running water, electricity, telephone lines and gas service for several days. Industry was stilled, transportation systems ground to a halt, and schools closed.

Pittsburgh was paralyzed, and the National Guard and Red Cross were brought in to maintain order and help the refugees. Drinking water was hauled in from as far away as Philadelphia. Nonetheless, *The Pittsburgh Press* continued to publish with the help of presses in nearby towns. Among the news stories published was an announcement of President Roosevelt's appropriation of $25 million in Works Progress Administration funds to help with the cleanup and a city council appropriation of $1 million for flood relief.

Ultimately, the flood precipitated a decline in property values of $10 million. However, it did leave a positive legacy; by summer, Congress had passed a flood-control act, establishing support for flood-control improvements in the district. Those improvements would include upstream dams along the Allegheny and the Monongahela.

Pittsburgh over water

Under pressure from political and civic groups, Allegheny County embarked in 1924 on a massive road and bridge improvement program, known as the "Ultimate Highway System." The plan called for radial connections to the suburbs, new boulevards along the rivers, and bridges across both the rivers and the deep ravines. Building on Olmsted's 1910 vision for Pittsburgh and the 1918 Citizens Committee on City Plan of Pittsburgh, the plan was spurred on by several factors. The U.S. War Department issued an assessment that six Allegheny River bridges were obstacles to navigation. Booming industrialization of the river valleys and a tenfold jump in car registrations between 1910 and 1921 ultimately taxed the existing highway system beyond its limits.

While the Ultimate Highway System was never fully realized, its most dramatic legacy was the bridges. Between 1924 and 1932, the county invested an estimated $47 million in 99 new bridges. The plan was championed by Joseph G. Armstrong, a former mayor and director of Pittsburgh's Department of Public Works, who was elected chairman of the Allegheny County Commissioners in 1923. Armstrong pushed through a $29 million bond issue, created the Department of Public Works and set to work on monumental projects such as the Washington Crossing Bridge, the 1,598-foot-long Westinghouse Memorial Bridge, the West End Bridge and the "Three Sisters" at Sixth, Seventh and Ninth streets. The 460-foot main span of the Westinghouse Bridge carrying the Lincoln Highway 200 feet above the valley floor was the longest reinforced concrete bridge

The St. Patrick's Day Flood, 1936
Pittsburgh History & Landmarks Foundation

This 1932 view shows the way to the South Hills suburbs. The south end of the Liberty Tubes penetrated Mount Washington south of the Monongahela River. *Archives Service Center, University of Pittsburgh*

Election day, November 1923: a polling place at the Irene Kaufmann Settlement *Carnegie Library of Pittsburgh, Pittsburgh Photographic Library*

in the western hemisphere. It was considered comparable in magnitude to other engineering feats of its time, such as the Hoover Dam, the George Washington Bridge and the Holland Tunnel.

Ultimately, Armstrong's administration fell under attack by political rival Charles G. McGovern. As county controller, McGovern issued a report in 1926 lambasting Armstrong's Department of Public Works as a "den of patronage," a "huge parasite living off the public treasury" and perpetuating "monumental waste." Within five years, McGovern was elected commission chairman and went about reducing the size of county government by approximately 4,800 jobs. He fired the entire Department of Public Works and replaced only 10 percent of the workers. A new Allegheny County Authority was conceived to capitalize on New Deal opportunities but never achieved what the Department of Public Works had. Among the monumental legacies of this era, however, was the Homestead High Level Bridge of 1937.

Political Turnabout

The 1920s and 1930s saw a new interest in the exercise of political power, fueled largely by the participation of a new class of voter: women. As in the rest of the country, Pittsburgh women had lobbied long and hard to win the right to vote. Led by tenacious innovators like Jeannie Bradley Roessing, Mrs. Julian Kennedy, Mary Bakewell and Daisy Lampkin, they advocated education and participation. Once they had laid the groundwork, the suffragettes took to the streets on May 2, 1914 in a parade that brought widespread attention to the controversial issue. Finally, a half century after the 15th Amendment to the Constitution had enfranchised the nation's black men, the 19th Amendment granted suffrage to women in 1920 and spawned a powerful new political action group. The Allegheny County League of Women Voters, the League of Women Voters of Greater Pittsburgh and the Lucy Stone Suffrage League for African American Women were all formed to promote political responsibility and activism.

The restructuring of the Department of Public Works was symptomatic of a larger move toward reform in the city's political structure, largely championed by the newly enfranchised. In 1934 the city that had been a stronghold of Republicanism found that the GOP was not responding to its needs and, consequently, turned its back on Lincoln's party. Mirroring national trends, Democrats assumed control of city government, which they would hold to the present day.

Better Housing

Housing quality became a major issue during this period. A dramatic split had long been evident between the homes of the wealthy and those of the masses. The grandest homes in Pittsburgh, clustered on the North Side's Ridge Avenue in the

East End and further out in Sewickley, were massive mansions, with dozens of opulently decorated rooms, that reflected the prosperity of the industrialists and rivaled the palaces of their peers on the East Coast. The vast majority of those homes have long since been demolished as "white elephants."

Listening to station KDKA on an Aeriola, Jr., built by Westinghouse in 1921
Carnegie Library of Pittsburgh, Pittsburgh Photographic Library

The other end of the spectrum was characterized by overcrowding and unsanitary conditions. In 1934, for example, three out of four houses on the lower North Side had no hot water and no bathrooms. Nine out of 10 had no furnace.

These conditions prompted two very different approaches to improving the quality of housing. The greatest success during this era was the planned community of Chatham Village on Mt. Washington. In 1929 the Buhl Foundation initiated an experimental for-profit, large-scale housing project for limited-income families. The foundation assembled a design team that included Clarence S. Stein and Henry Wright of New York, whose innovative plans for Radburn, New Jersey, and Sunnyside Gardens, Long Island, had already won national acclaim, as well as the Pittsburgh firms of Ingham and Boyd, architects, and Griswold & Kohankie, landscape architects. With its 197 units on 46 acres, Chatham Village introduced to Pittsburgh the notion of separating automobile traffic by relegating it to the perimeter and created an idyllic setting of clustered Georgian buildings surrounded by shared pastoral landscaping.

On a much larger scale, Terrace Village in the Hill District was one of Pittsburgh's first public housing projects and one of the country's largest when Franklin D. Roosevelt dedicated it in 1941. Capable of housing more than 11,000 people, the $15.5-million project covered 15 acres and was considered an exciting innovation. Built at the same time as the smaller, 1,700-person Bedford Dwellings, Terrace Village was conceived as a means of replacing substandard housing in the lower Hill and of accommodating families displaced by the 1941 Homestead mill expansion. Pittsburgh's new public housing was originally intended for a fully integrated population but would eventually shift with the neighborhood demographics to become predominantly occupied by African Americans.

SUBURBS

Suburbanization, a trend in which Pittsburgh had taken the lead since the mid-19th century, found new impetus in the era between the two World Wars. Already well established in Thornburg, the suburban ideal was continually reinterpreted in outlying areas with the advent of the automobile age. By 1929 more than 5 million cars were produced. The Model T cost only $500. This wide availability supplanted the role of the trolley as the primary suburban link, and true suburban development began in earnest with communities such as Mt. Lebanon and Fox Chapel emerging as fashionable new addresses. The South Hills Trolley Tunnel had begun the process as early as 1904, but the Liberty Tunnel in 1924 and Liberty Bridge in 1928 spurred a true suburban boom in the South Hills. Opening day of the bridge saw a mile-long procession of cars. Developers of the new suburbs laid out picturesque plans, establishing patterns of development and scales of architecture that created an open, yet intimate community ambience. With the stage thus set, the postwar American dream would ultimately manifest itself in an explosion of suburban growth.

DIVERSIONS

In the face of hard times, Pittsburghers devised a broad variety of diversions. Much leisure time was devoted to the activities that occupied the rest of America: movies, baseball, clubs, dances, amusement parks and more. Yet even in their pursuit of leisure, Pittsburghers displayed a pioneering spirit and spawned a host of legends, many of which survive today in beloved institutions.

Westinghouse engineer Frank Conrad pioneered radio broadcasting as an entertainment medium with the first musical broadcast in 1919. In November of the following year, the Westinghouse radio station broadcast election results, peppered with musical numbers. Before long, radio became the focus of home entertainment until the postwar development of television.

The Pittsburgh Symphony was revived in 1927 by Edward Specter, who built a world-class orchestra with conductors Otto Klemperer, Victor De Sabata, Fritz Reiner and William Steinberg.

Nightspots in the Hill District attracted whites and blacks alike who came to hear some of the nation's finest jazz musicians, many of whom found their start in Pittsburgh. Among them were Lena Horne, Billy Strayhorn, Kenny Clarke, Art Blakey, Earl "Fatha" Hines, Roy Eldridge, Leroy Brown, Mary Lou Williams, Louise Mann and Maxine Sullivan. The nightspots they frequented — places like the Crawford Grill, the Fullerton Inn, the Humming Bird, Derby Dad's, Harlem Bar, Musician's Club, Sawdust Trail, Ritz and the Bailey Hotel — lent vibrancy to the neighborhood.

One of the most divisive issues of the 1920s was Prohibition, as legislated by the 18th Amendment to the Constitution. Attempts to legislate morality did not quench the thirst of the working class, particularly as they suffered exploitation at the hands of the upper classes. Nor did Pittsburgh's elite adhere to the rules imposed to make the city "drier than the Sahara." In fact, with its abundant speak-easies and private clubs, Pittsburgh offered a variety of drinking venues for all sectors of society, over 500 by some accounts. These were fueled by some 10,000 stills in Allegheny County alone and thrived until the repeal of Prohibition in 1934. In the year of 1928 alone, well over 37,000 people were arrested for drunkenness, earning Pittsburgh a national reputation as a wet town.

The established sport of baseball found new energy in the emergence of the Negro National Leagues and its legendary local teams, and Pittsburgh became a national center of black

(Right and opposite page) A streetcar suburb from the 1900s, Mt. Lebanon became an automobile suburb in the 1920s. Here are views from Mayfair Drive and Mission Hills. *Pittsburgh History & Landmarks Foundation*

baseball. The Pittsburgh Crawfords grew out of a collection of neighborhood clubs in the Hill and boasted five Hall of Famers in 1936: Satchel Paige, Josh Gibson, "Cool Papa" Bell, Oscar Charleston and Judy Johnson. The Homestead Grays, a team formed as early as 1913 and comprised of steelworkers, won eight out of nine Negro National League titles. This era also saw Arthur Rooney's Pirates (later the Steelers) play their first football game.

World War II Fuels the Industrial Economy and Taxes Resolve

Like the rest of the country, Pittsburgh was heavily invested in World War II. Its economy boomed, many of its men were drafted or enlisted and those left behind worked hard and abided by the rules of rationing.

By World War II Pittsburgh was undeniably the nation's primary supplier of machine tools, iron, steel, aluminum, foundry products, electrical machinery, coal, glass, railroad cars and switches, safety signals, air brakes and more. Pittsburgh had already established itself as the "Arsenal of the Nation" as early as the Civil War, a role that continued through World War I. After the attack on Pearl Harbor, orders began to flood in from the Allies in 1939. The local economy geared up to meet the demand. Factories producing armor plates, engines, anti-aircraft guns, shells and ships rose to capacity production, and workers in key industries were protected from the draft. Major companies launched expansion programs. Iron and steel production alone increased 202 percent between December 1941 and January 1943. Moreover, an estimated 40 percent of the landing craft used in World War II was manufactured in and around Pittsburgh, with a heavy concentration at the Dravo shipyard on Neville Island.

To meet the increased demand and to compensate for the portion of the workforce that had gone to war, the work week was lengthened and tens of thousands of women were recruited as production workers.

Shortages and rationing affected a broad range of products: wheat flour, gasoline, rubber, liquor, cigarettes and silk stockings, to name a few. Rationing coupons were issued to control consumption. People rode bicycles or used public transportation instead of driving. A single pair of silk stockings might be expected to last for a year or more.

Biographies

(Above)
Barney Dreyfuss
Carnegie Library of Pittsburgh, Pittsburgh Photographic Library

BARNEY DREYFUSS (1848-1932)

Barney Dreyfuss, born in Germany, came to Pittsburgh at the age of 17 and became a legendary figure in the world of sports. He bought the Pittsburgh Pirates in 1899 and led the team on a climb to greatness over his 32-year ownership. Under Dreyfuss, the Pirates would win six National League pennants between 1901 and 1927, as well as two World Series championships in 1909 and 1925, the team's last successful World Series campaign until 1960.

JOHN KANE (1860-1934)

John Kane epitomized the notion of enduring hard times. Born in Scotland, he had minimal education and worked in a coal mine through his childhood before coming to the United States in 1879. Kane worked variously as a steelworker, gandy dancer (railroad man who stamps gravel between the ties), street paver, house painter, carpenter and amateur boxer; and his life was tainted with tragedy. As a painter, however, he developed a lively, detailed, primitive style for capturing Pennsylvania landscapes and Pittsburgh cityscapes on beaver board. Of his Pittsburgh work, Kane said, "I paved its streets, made its steel, and painted its houses. It is my city; why shouldn't I paint it?" His works were discovered in 1927 when one of his pictures was accepted for the Carnegie International, and he won a prize two years later. Museums began to seek out his work, but he died in relative obscurity.

(Right)
John Kane and his painting the "Frankstown Avenue Bridge"
Carnegie Library of Pittsburgh, Pittsburgh Photographic Library

John Gabbert Bowman
Carnegie Library of Pittsburgh, Pittsburgh Photographic Library

JOHN GABBERT BOWMAN (1877-1962)

John Bowman was recruited to the city in 1921 by the board of trustees at the University of Pittsburgh to develop a modern university. He had already distinguished himself as the youngest college president in the country, taking charge of Iowa State at the age of 34, and as the first director of the American College of Surgeons. Seeing the opportunity to create a great institution, Bowman accepted the trustees' offer and moved to Pittsburgh. When he arrived, the university was more than $1 million in debt and sorely needed teaching space, faculty and an endowment. As chancellor of the university from 1921 to 1945, Bowman was the mastermind behind the development of the Oakland campus. A somewhat controversial character, Bowman worked tirelessly to convince the city's business and civic leaders to embrace — and fund — his grand scheme for the university. Bowman's vision included an educational skyscraper and a great medical center. His most prominent legacy is the campus centerpiece, the $32 million Cathedral of Learning, completed between 1927 and 1938. Also under his leadership, university enrollment rose from about 2,300 to approximately 23,000 students.

Edgar Kaufmann (1885-1955)

Born in Pittsburgh, Edgar Kaufmann greatly expanded the department store business that had been founded by his ancestors in 1870. As owner of Kaufmann Department Store, he was Pittsburgh's "King of Commerce" and peer to the city's "Kings of Industry." Committed to making Pittsburgh a thriving cultural center, Kaufmann would prove to be a key figure in the city's renaissance. In addition to commissioning Frank Lloyd Wright's legendary "Fallingwater" home at Bear Run, Kaufmann was an avid patron of the arts, financed the Light Opera Company and donated over a million dollars toward construction of the $22 million Civic Arena.

(Above)
Edgar Kaufmann
Carnegie Library of Pittsburgh, Pittsburgh Photographic Library

(Far left)
Robert L. Vann
Carnegie Library of Pittsburgh, Pittsburgh Photographic Library

Robert L. Vann (1887-1940)

Robert Vann was one of the first black graduates of the University of Pittsburgh School of Law and became one of Pittsburgh's most influential African-American leaders during the 1920s through the 1950s. He is best known as the publisher and editor of the *Pittsburgh Courier*, Pittsburgh's African-American newspaper, which enjoyed an international reputation and distribution. With 14 editions and a weekly circulation of 400,000, the paper reached all 48 states in addition to Europe, Canada, the Philippines and the West Indies. Vann is also remembered for his role in quietly promoting a neighborhood desegregation agenda. After moving to Monticello Street in Homewood in 1911, he later bought additional houses in the neighborhood for family and friends. White protest to this trend resulted in "the battle of Monticello Street," a nonviolent residency conflict, and many whites moved out to Wilkinsburg.

Daisy Lampkin (1888-1965)

Daisy Elizabeth Lampkin, political activist and pioneer civil rights reformer, adopted Pittsburgh as a young adult. Born in Washington, D.C., and raised in Reading, Pennsylvania, she moved to Pittsburgh in 1909 at the age of 21 to marry William Lampkin, a clerk for Pittsburgh Gage and Supply Company. Once there, she quickly made her mark in a variety of causes from women's suffrage and social service to civil rights. In 1915 she became the third president of the Negro Women's Equal Franchise Federation, later the Lucy Stone Suffrage League. During the great migration from the south, which brought nearly 50,000 blacks to Pittsburgh between 1910 and 1930, Daisy Lampkin was instrumental in establishing free clinics. She also led the African-American community far beyond its quota in Liberty Bond drives during World War I and organized the first American Red Cross Chapter among African-American women. As soon as women gained the right to vote, Lampkin entered the political arena and was chosen as an alternate delegate to the National Republican Convention twice during the 1920s.

Mrs. R. Templeton Smith
Carnegie Library of Pittsburgh, Pittsburgh Photographic Library

Mrs. R. Templeton Smith (1889-1964)

Eliza Jane Kennedy, daughter of steel mill engineer Julian Kennedy, symbolized the spirit of reform that characterized Pittsburgh politics after 1920. Born in Pittsburgh, she completed her education at Vassar College in 1912 before marrying fellow Pittsburgher R. Templeton Smith. After vigorous campaigning for women's suffrage, she dedicated her life to educating women to use their newly won right effectively. Working at the local level, Mrs. Smith organized the Allegheny County League of Women Voters and gathered a following by providing lectures on government and programs to root out corruption. She and her troops succeeded in getting thousands of phantom voters off the registration rolls, closely monitored the activities of City Council and raised money to hire a private accounting firm to audit the city books, resulting in a jail sentence for the mayor. When a conservative Democrat unexpectedly became mayor in the Roosevelt landslide of 1932, he appointed Mrs. Smith as budget advisor. She and the public auditor prepared a budget eliminating payroll padding and illegal expenditures of all kinds. Upon her death, Congressman Robert Fulton eulogized Mrs. Smith as the "conscience of Pittsburgh."

CHAPTER 6

Renaissance City

1946-2000

PITTSBURGH EMERGED FROM THE INTENSE, SINGLE-minded focus of the war years intent on recasting its image. Through aggressive public-private partnerships, business and political leaders sought to diversify the economy, enhance the built environment and earn the Steel City a new title: Renaissance City. This renaissance first manifested itself in the built environment and more recently has found its expression in the rise of a new economy that is hoped to eventually fill the enormous void left by the demise of the steel industry.

Pittsburgh in the mid-1950s, with the Point and Manchester bridges in the foreground: the land has been cleared at the Point for Renaissance I, and the skyscrapers of Gateway Center have just been completed.
Pittsburgh History & Landmarks Foundation

The beginning of a new attitude toward the city was already evident in a $38 million plan that the Pittsburgh Regional Planning Association had commissioned from renowned urban planner Robert Moses in 1939. Moses' plan dealt mostly with traffic problems, allocating traffic to the riverfront areas, but it also marked a new comprehensive concern for amenity in the city and introduced a bold plan for Point State Park. Moses concluded his report by saying:

> It [Pittsburgh] has been so engrossed in business that it has only recently got around to a consideration of the incidental problems which business creates — problems of comfort, convenience and beauty.

While Moses' contention ignores the series of civic-improvement efforts that preceded his plan, it is certainly true that the next wave of redevelopment initiatives, beginning post-World War II, would prove to have a much larger impact on the city.

By the end of World War II, Pittsburgh was in a sorry state. *Time* magazine's 1949 commentary on Pittsburgh described:

> ...a noisy, grimy giant sprawled across a coal seam, gobbling up ore from Mesabi and spewing out molten steel. It squatted, black and ugly, on the hills between the Allegheny and the Monongahela, training mill towns up and down its river valleys... Smoke from its stacks and its chimney pots, as from its blast furnaces hung over its head in a never-dissipated cloud... It was a city better seen at night. Then it had a mystery, beauty and grandeur — a mammoth black patchwork, spotted with the pink blossoms of the Bessemers, hung with lights stretching out between pale river highways... In the daytime it emerged in all its sprawling ugliness.

Others simply described the city as "an esthetic abortion, a municipal hovel, a mining town on a vast scale."

At the same time, the economic engine that had both fueled the region's prosperity and sullied its environment faced serious threats. Equipment was worn out by the production

(Far left)
The outline of the Civic Arena and the new roads are superimposed on this view of the lower Hill from the mid-1950s.
Pittsburgh History & Landmarks Foundation

The Civic Arena as built, boasting the world's largest retractable roof, October 1960
Pittsburgh History & Landmarks Foundation

demands of war. Increasing competition, domestic and international, challenged Pittsburgh's domination of the steel industry. The city and the region were at a crossroads, and aggressive intervention was required to stay the decline.

The critical turning point in this sequence of events came in 1946 with the passage of the city's smoke abatement ordinance, which had actually been initiated in 1941. The ordinance specified that all smoke-producing fuels be burned in mechanical equipment that controls smoke. The first targets were industry, commercial buildings and railroads, followed by residential furnaces and stoves a year later. Facing widespread challenges, the legislation was subsequently pursued at the state level. As in many arenas, Pittsburgh emerged as a leader with national smoke abatement legislation in 1947.

Richard King Mellon, a Republican, broadened his sphere of influence when he enlisted Mayor David L. Lawrence as a bridge between the Democratic Party and Pittsburgh labor. Seizing the opportunity for a new, clean city, Mellon and Lawrence forged the public/private partnership that would orchestrate Renaissance I. Together, they formed the Allegheny Conference on Community Development and drew in the city's power people. Mellon told his friends: "Don't let business interfere with your civic enterprise."

Mellon envisioned a city cleared of "drab relics of half a century," a city with clean air and water, more efficient transportation routes, better housing and a more robust tax base. Already he had helped to launch a number of catalytic projects countywide: a new airport and new highways and bridges. His Mellon-U.S. Steel Building (now Three Mellon Bank Center) of 1952, Alcoa Building of 1953 and Mellon Square of 1955, covering several city blocks of premium real estate, have been called a $38 million token of faith in Pittsburgh's future. The

The Langenheim house of 1885 on Liverpool Street in Manchester as it was in 1967 when the Pittsburgh History & Landmarks Foundation received it for preservation and eventual restoration
Pittsburgh History & Landmarks Foundation

This photograph of September 14, 1988 shows a partially stripped open-hearth plant at J & L's South Side Works being demolished. *Photo by Thomas Ondrey*

(Opposite Page) Beginning in 1966, the Pittsburgh History & Landmarks Foundation worked with neighborhood residents to create the first historic preservation district in the nation primarily for African Americans; the first federally funded historic district program administered by community residents; the first preservation programs using Title I urban-renewal funds for the restoration of houses for low- to moderate-income residents; and a series of incentive programs designed to combat displacement and encourage longtime residents to stay and become part of the revitalized community. The Manchester Citizens Corporation now continues the neighborhood restoration. *Pittsburgh History & Landmarks Foundation*

Blast-furnace and stove ruins at Duquesne in 1988 — production stopped at the Duquesne Works by May of 1984, and demolition was well under way by November 1988. *Photo by Thomas Ondrey*

Allegheny Conference also spawned the Regional Industrial Development Corporation (RIDC) in 1955 and ACTION-Housing in 1957.

Before it was completed, Renaissance I would see $500 million in new projects. The centerpiece was the transformation of the Point, where 23 acres of warehouses, exposition buildings and other substandard urban fabric were cleared to make way for Point State Park with its Fort Pitt Blockhouse and Museum, as well as the four-tower Gateway Center with its $50 million in new office buildings, co-financed by Equitable Life Assurance Company.

A key component of the Renaissance I campaign was the phenomenon of urban renewal, which advocated the wholesale clearing of entire neighborhoods to make way for new development. Pittsburgh's three largest urban renewal projects during Renaissance I were Allegheny Center, East Liberty and the lower Hill District. For Allegheny Center, a mixed-use center in the heart of the North Side, the core buildings of Allegheny City's historic center were demolished, the streets eliminated and a ring road constructed around the new development. East Liberty saw demolition, construction of a ring road and creation of a pedestrian mall through the neighborhood's commercial center. In the lower Hill, substandard but historic housing was cleared to make way for the new Civic Arena, which was completed in 1960.

It has been argued that the lower Hill project in particular was an effort at social engineering, as it forced the relocation of hundreds of African-American and Jewish families and broke the political alliance that the two groups had forged. Many of the Jewish families moved to Squirrel Hill, while the African Americans settled largely in nearby Homewood, marking a pattern of segregated settlement that persists to this day.

In reaction to the massive clear-and-rebuild strategies embraced in the 1950s and 1960s, Pittsburgh has emerged as a national, and in fact international, leader in engaging historic preservation as a tool for not only enhancing the built environment, but for building economic momentum and improving the quality of life as well. This leadership was initiated by Arthur P. Ziegler, Jr. and James D. Van Trump in 1964 with the founding of the Pittsburgh History & Landmarks Foundation (Landmarks). Beginning with the deteriorated 19th century housing on the North Side, Landmarks championed both neighborhood preservation and large scale commercial renovation and adaptive use, best manifested in their successful transformation of Station Square, beginning in 1976. Public officials and private developers visit Pittsburgh from the world over to learn from these successes.

Foundations of the Cold Rolling Mill at J&L's Pittsburgh Works, December 1986
Photo by Clyde Hare

Five historic Pittsburgh & Lake Erie Railroad buildings, now restored and adapted for new uses, form the nucleus of Station Square, a mixed-use development opposite downtown Pittsburgh.
Photo by Jim Judkis

Steel Dethroned

While the postwar civic improvement strategies were at work, Pittsburgh remained an industrial and corporate center, with 50 Fortune 500 headquarters at its peak. It was not long, however, before the industry that was Pittsburgh's backbone and had made its reputation began to decline. By the early 1980s the steel industry was in serious trouble. Labor historian John Hoerr, writing on the demise of the steel industry, quoted Joseph Odorcich, USW vice president and union reformer: "One of the problems in the mills is no union man would trust any of the companies. To the average union man, they're always crying wolf. And the wolf finally came."

According to Hoerr, the steel industry here lost its competitive edge for a number of reasons. The growth of foreign steel contributed to an excess in steelmaking capacity. Alternative materials, such as plastic, aluminum and ceramics, began to replace steel in a myriad of applications. American "minimills" were able to produce steel with more efficient equipment and lower labor costs. Pittsburgh companies had failed to invest in upgrades. Perhaps the most influential factor was the continuing labor-management conflict that had overshadowed the industry from its outset. After 50 years of organized labor, unions and management were still not effectively working together to improve work processes, introduce innovations, or make mutual wage concessions. The result was deadlock.

Whatever the cause, the undeniable effect was vivid. The industry that had been building to a crescendo for over a century took less than five years to fall. This era arguably rivaled the Great Depression for economic decline and all of the social problems that came with it. Steelworkers had risen to become the highest-paid industrial laborers in the United States. But between 1979 and 1987, the five-county Pittsburgh metropolitan area lost 127,000 manufacturing jobs. Those jobs were replaced by nearly 76,000 service-type jobs, but they could not compare in either skill or pay level. Particularly in the riverfront mill towns, the tax base declined. The population aged. Young people left in search of opportunity elsewhere. As Hoerr described it, "an entire industrial culture was overthrown and trampled into the dirt within a few years."

In the midst of worldwide economic upheaval, the steel industry in general, and U.S. Steel in particular, slipped into the doldrums, culminating in a 184-day shutdown of U.S. Steel plants in a labor dispute. U.S. Steel closed plants in Homestead, Duquesne and McKeesport. Having diversified through the purchase of two large energy companies, U.S. Steel changed its name to USX. Wheeling Pittsburgh closed its Monessen plant in 1986, while J&L's South Side works was torn down. Related industries declined as well, closing dozens of other manufacturing plants.

The towers of Renaissance II (left to right): Fifth Avenue Place; Dominion Tower; and PPG Place *Photo by Clyde Hare*

A large relief of a moving locomotive announces the original purpose of the Pittsburgh & Lake Erie Railroad's headquarters building. *Photo by Jim Judkis*

The Renaissance Continues

Meanwhile, the city embarked on yet another facelift operation, Renaissance II, which was championed by Mayors Richard Caliguiri and Tom Murphy. This rendition saw the arduous construction of the light rail transit and subway system that had replaced Pittsburgh's legendary trolleys and transformed the downtown skyline with construction of seven new office towers: One Mellon Bank Center, One Oxford Center, Fifth Avenue Place, PPG Place, CNG Tower and Liberty Center. This new renaissance also placed a new emphasis on the waterfronts that industry was beginning to vacate.

By 1985 Pittsburgh had sufficiently transformed itself to earn the title of America's Most Livable City from Rand McNally's *Places Rated Almanac*.

(Opposite page)
When opened in 1901, the P&LE passenger room was one of the finest Edwardian interiors in the city, marked by great richness and decorative detail. *Pittsburgh History & Landmarks Foundation*

The 550-seat Grand Concourse Restaurant opened in 1978 in the old passenger waiting rooms. *Pittsburgh History & Landmarks Foundation*

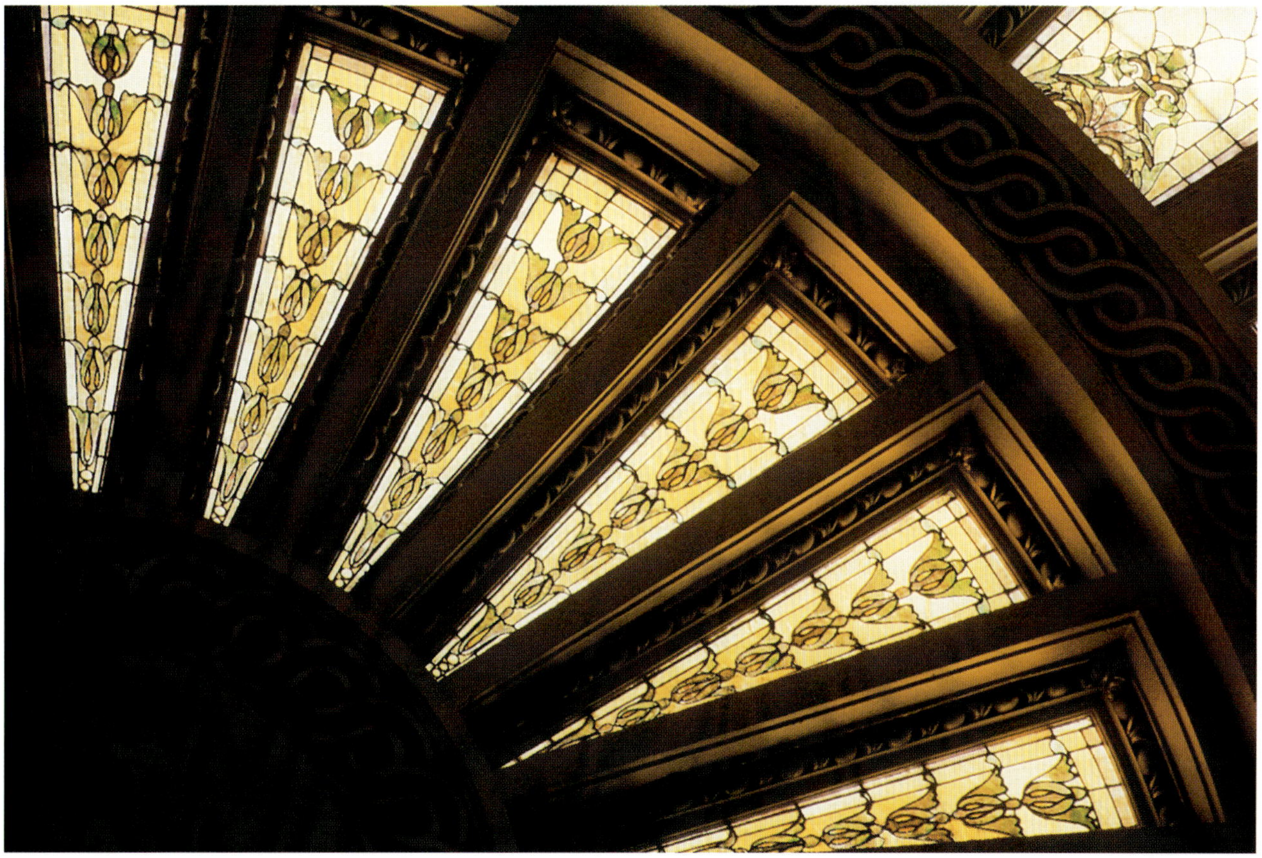

After much cleaning, polishing, gilding and re-touching, the interior gleams like new and the barrel-vaulted stained glass ceiling soars above the restaurant. *Photo by Jim Judkis*

Biographies

David L. Lawrence
Carnegie Library of Pittsburgh, Pittsburgh Photographic Library

David L. Lawrence (1889-1966)

A colorful character and one of the drivers behind Pittsburgh's legendary Renaissance, David Lawrence was a native Pittsburgher who rose to become mayor of Pittsburgh from 1946 to 1958 and governor of the Commonwealth of Pennsylvania from 1959 to 1963. Lawrence believed fervently in cities and in change and was highly adept at working the political system to achieve it. Speaking at an Urban Design conference at Harvard's Graduate School of Design in 1956, Lawrence explained that his grand design had been "the acceptance of a belief that a city is worth saving." Seeking a balance between the practical and the ideal, he added that, "it is very necessary for the practical among us to be constantly challenged by those who want to do it better, to be compelled to make hard compromises instead of easy ones, to stretch and pull at the dollar sign and the land available and the needed uses until that which is done is admittedly the very best that can be done." His public-private partnership methods, of course, have become models for urban improvement.

Richard King Mellon
Carnegie Library of Pittsburgh, Pittsburgh Photographic Library

Richard King Mellon (1899-1970)

Richard King Mellon, born into a dynastic family, was chairman of Mellon Bank, an avid conservationist, and a dominant figure in the financial, industrial, and civic life of Pittsburgh for many years. He took to heart his father's admonition to "live where you work and work where you live." In between service in both World Wars, Mellon took leadership of the family business interests at the age of 35. As governor and president of T. Mellon and Sons, he oversaw a business empire with controlling interests in Gulf Oil, Koppers and Alcoa, as well as strongholds in U.S. Steel, Westinghouse Air Brake, the Pennsylvania Railroad, Pittsburgh Plate Glass and Pittsburgh Consolidation Coal. He created the R. K. Mellon Foundation in 1947.

R. K. Mellon is perhaps best remembered for introducing the notion of public-private partnerships, and using his influence to spearhead a legendary revitalization effort. A staunch Republican, he sought an alliance with Democratic mayor David L. Lawrence following World War II. They shared a vision of a Pittsburgh free of smoke, devastating floods, and blighted areas, and enhanced by efficient transportation, decent housing, and appealing public spaces. Mellon's contributions were recognized by the U.S. Chamber of Commerce when it named him "a great living American."

William Steinberg (1899-1978)

William Steinberg was a legendary character in Pittsburgh's cultural arena. Born in Cologne, Germany, he studied orchestra direction at the Cologne Conservatory and held several posts with prominent institutions, including the Cologne Opera, the Frankfurt Opera and the German Theatre in Prague before Nazi pressures prompted him to leave Germany and establish the Palestine Symphony Orchestra with Bronislav Hubermann in 1936. Arturo Toscanini brought him to New York as deputy conductor of the NBC Orchestra from 1938 to 1941. He then went on to a series of prominent guest and permanent positions with the San Francisco Opera, the Buffalo Philharmonic Orchestra, the London Philharmonic Orchestra, the New York Philharmonic Orchestra and the Boston Symphonic Orchestra. By far his longest-standing contribution was as conductor of the Pittsburgh Symphony Orchestra from 1952 through 1976, during which time he built it into a world-class musical institution.

William Steinberg
Carnegie Library of Pittsburgh, Pittsburgh Photographic Library

Rachel Carson
Carnegie Library of Pittsburgh, Pittsburgh Photographic Library

Rachel Carson (1907-1964)

From her humble beginnings on a small farm in Springdale, Pennsylvania, Rachel Carson grew up to set in motion the modern environmental movement. She attended Pennsylvania College for Women, now Chatham College, and went on to teach and earn a master's in marine zoology from Johns Hopkins University, teach zoology at the University of Maryland, and work at Chincoteague before joining the U.S. Fish and Wildlife Service as its first woman employee. Her early writings — *Under the Sea Wind*, *The Sea Around Us*, and *The Edge of the Sea* — celebrated the wonders of nature. Through her writing and research, Rachel Carson became increasingly aware of the destruction to the natural environment wrought by mankind's indiscriminate use of chemicals. She fought the conventional wisdom that man was destined to control nature and in 1962 published *Silent Spring*, which eloquently articulated the concept of ecology. Thoroughly researched and sensitively written, *Silent Spring*, and Rachel Carson herself, were viciously attacked by chemical companies, doctors, university agriculture schools and others. During this time she stood firm and let the book speak for itself — which it did, by remaining on the bestseller list for almost a year and appearing in numerous translations. Ultimately, Rachel Carson's message began to gain widespread followers and she became an international symbol of the widespread environmental movement. Rachel Carson did not live to see the phenomenal impact of her efforts. She died of cancer in 1964, two years after *Silent Spring* was published.

■ STEEL

As the 1950s opened, it looked as if the Steel City would go on forever.

A giant open-hearth plant was to be built at J & L in the mid-1950s, and the tallest blast furnace in the region would go up in 1961. In the next three decades, U.S. Steel, Alcoa, and PPG would raise proud towers, each showing off its owner's product.

It is business as usual as the Monongahela River flows past the two halves of Jones & Laughlin Steel's Pittsburgh Works. On the right bank, the Eliza blast furnaces are downstream and the Hazelwood Coke Plant is in the foreground. On the left bank, the massive open-hearth steel plant opened in the 1950s.
Pittsburgh History & Landmarks Foundation

The Aliquippa Works of J & L grew to a length of seven miles along the Ohio River.
Pittsburgh History & Landmarks Foundation

Sunset over the Triangle, with the Eliza Furnaces in the foreground: May 1966
Photo by Clyde Hare

The Dorothy Six blast furnace at U. S. Steel's Duquesne Works was 297 feet high: the tallest in the Pittsburgh region.
It was blown in in 1963 and was toppled in 1988, three days after this photograph was taken.
Photo by Thomas Ondrey

The steelworker and his world: standing on a teeming platform, a worker releases the gas from the steel that is being poured into an ingot mold so the pressure does not build up and explode, May 1962.
Photo by Clyde Hare

A worker inspects a bloom about to be rolled into sheet steel, early 1960s.
Photo by Clyde Hare

This scene from a U.S. Steel plant shows gas being removed from a ladle of steel, June 1962.
Photo by Clyde Hare

The main gate of U.S. Steel's Homestead Works was eight miles up the Monongahela River from downtown Pittsburgh. This plant was famous for its structural mill and notorious for the 1892 labor dispute. All this, photographed in 1964 for *National Geographic*, has disappeared.
Photo by Clyde Hare

At U.S. Steel's Edgar Thomson Works in Braddock in 1987,
the faint pink glow indicates that steel is still being made,
although the rate of production has declined.
Photo by Thomas Ondrey

A view of the J & L Hazelwood Coke Plant in 1985 with hillside houses in close proximity
Photo by Thomas Ondrey

Looking east in the morning toward the Carrie Furnaces of U.S. Steel in Rankin — the year is 1988. The church steeple of St. Michael the Archangel Greek Catholic Church is just visible. The hillside homes are in Braddock and North Braddock.
Photo by Thomas Ondrey

POSTSCRIPT

Pittsburgh Beyond 2000

WITH THE DEMISE OF STEEL, NEW ECONOMIC engines have come to dominate the region as the arenas for the next generation of innovators, a generation dealing in currencies of technology and information, of medicine and education. As Pittsburgh has looked for a fresh identity and new strategies to boost a floundering economy and forge a direction for the future, it has once again spawned and attracted a host of trailblazers who promise to keep alive the tradition of legends and visions. In their constant quest to build the New

Economy, this new generation is proving ever mindful that success will depend not only on technological innovation and business acumen, but also on the quality of life available to the city's inhabitants.

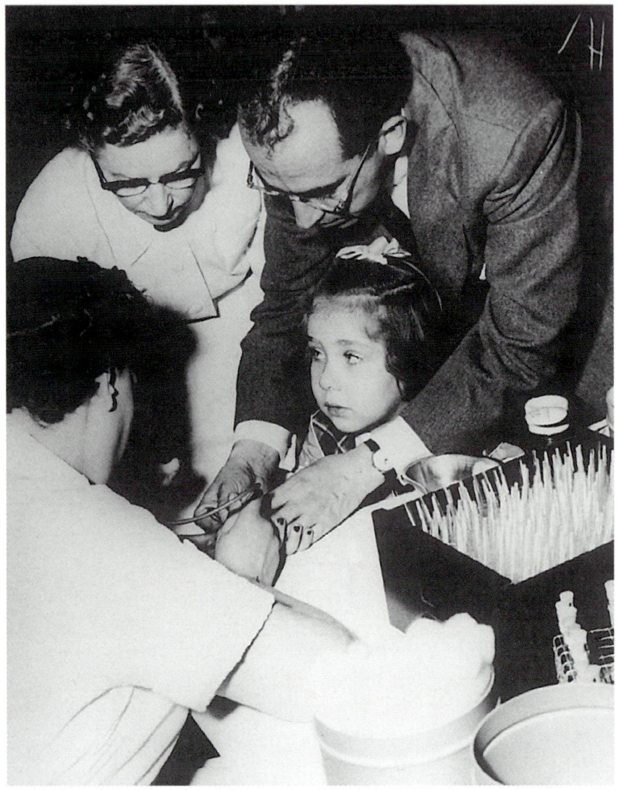

(Above)
Pittsburgh in 2001, from a mile down the Ohio River
Photo by William Rydberg, Photon

(Top far right)
Doctor Jonas E. Salk administering polio inoculations in 1954
Carnegie Library of Pittsburgh, Pittsburgh Photographic Library

Looking toward the North Side with the towers of Allegheny General Hospital rising well above the neighborhood
Photo by William Rydberg, Photon

University of Pittsburgh researcher and physician Bora Baysal in his lab at Western Psychiatric Institute and Clinic, UPMC Health System
Photo by Jim Judkis

Traditionally noted for significant medical developments, Pittsburgh's hospitals and universities have long made international news with innovations such as Dr. Jonas Salk's polio vaccine in the 1950s and Dr. Thomas Starzl's pioneering success with organ transplants in the 1960s. The first intensive care unit, the first bronchoscope and the first electron microscope were all developed here.

During the last quarter of the 20th century, the hospitals and universities not only became the region's largest employers, but also earned status as international leaders in research and technological advances. The first aeromedical transportation system in the northeast, Lifeflight, debuted in Pittsburgh in 1978. The University of Pittsburgh Medical Center (UPMC) was voted one of the top 12 hospitals in the country by *U.S. News* and *World Report* in 1999 and ranks as one of the top 10 institutions in National Institutes of Health (NIH) funding. UPMC now receives $200 million annually with larger increases over the last decade than any other institution in the nation.

Likewise on the business side, Pittsburgh is distinguishing itself as an emerging center for robotics, information technology, biotechnology, advanced materials, advanced manufacturing and envirotech. Pittsburgh ranked 13th in the *Wall Street Journal's* 2000 Hot Spots. The number of new technology firms

A view from the South Side Slopes, looking toward the University of Pittsburgh and its medical complex in Oakland
Photo by Jim Judkis

Heinz Field, home of the Pittsburgh Steelers, under construction in the summer of 2001
Photo by William Rydberg, Photon

PNC Park in its inaugural season
Photo by William Rydberg, Photon

in the region has increased significantly since 1990, encompassing a full range of pursuits in the areas of biotechnology, advanced materials and manufacturing, environmental technology, software engineering and more. Employment for some 250,000 people has been generated by technology companies and technical positions within non-technology companies. Since its founding in 1983, the Pittsburgh Technology Council has grown to rank as the nation's largest regional technology association. With the involvement of major successes like FreeMarkets Online, Fore Systems, Seagate Technologies, Tissue Informatics, Automated Healthcare and Precision Therapeutics, Pittsburgh is becoming a major player.

Recognizing the critical role that innovation will continue to play in the story of the Pittsburgh region, government is also reinventing itself with a more regional focus. Allegheny County Executive Jim Roddey's New Idea Factory, a 200-member committee, has generated over 100 strategies for improving the region's economic climate.

Much of the venture capital to fuel this new economic engine has its roots in the fortunes of Pittsburgh's original entrepreneurs. Joined by transplants who enjoy the synergy of a critical mass of technology innovators, new generations of some of the city's oldest families are turning their attention, talent and investments to developing this so-called "New Economy."

Crossing the Roberto Clemente Bridge, formerly the Sixth Street Bridge, on the way to a Pirates' baseball game at PNC Park
Photo by William Rydberg, Photon

Roberto Clemente in bronze
Photo by William Rydberg, Photon

In addition, a number of ancillary industries have begun to emerge and become inextricably part of Pittsburgh's identity. Among them is the film industry, which first appeared here as early as 1914 with *The Perils of Pauline*, but which produced only seven major movies in Pittsburgh prior to 1970, including the original version of *Angels in the Outfield* (1951) and *Night of the Living Dead* (1968). Beginning in about 1970, however, the city has actively recruited movie makers and secured no less than 110 film projects over the ensuing 30 years, among them box office successes such as *The Deer Hunter* (1978), *Flashdance* (1982), *Silence of the Lambs* (1990) and *Wonder Boys* (1999).

More dominant, however, is the business of sport, which has evolved from a community-based recreational activity to an industry in its own right. With the construction of two major new stadiums in 2001 — the 38,000-seat, $262 million PNC Park for baseball and the 65,000-seat, $281 million Heinz Field for football — and a possible new hockey arena on the way, sports are expected to play a major role in Pittsburgh's economic engine. These "cathedrals of sport," as they have been called by designers at the architectural firm of HOKSport, are becoming the downtown's newest landmarks, dominating prime riverfront sites.

Like the generations before them, Pittsburgh's latest crop of visionaries and innovators is leaving its mark on the rest of the city's built environment as well. While Pittsburgh patrons have traditionally looked outside the city for architects on major

(Above)
The riverfront headquarters of Alcoa, designed by The Design Alliance, opened in 1998.
Photo by William Rydberg, Photon

(Top far right)
The Mellon Client Service Center and Mellon Green, both designed by Burt Hill Kosar Rittelmann Associates, offer a welcome oasis in the heart of downtown.
Photo by David Lamb

(Below)
Benedum Center for the Performing Arts, a grand 1920s movie house.
Photo by William Rydberg, Photon

projects, many have come to recognize the local design talent. Firms like Burt Hill Kosar Rittelmann Associates, L.D. Astorino Associates, Bohlin Cywinski Jackson, The Design Alliance and Urban Design Associates, among others, are not only having dramatic impact on Pittsburgh's cityscape, but are also being called upon for significant, visible projects nationwide.

On a smaller scale, community development groups and the Community Design Center of Pittsburgh are working in tandem to facilitate quality architecture and urban design in the city's neighborhoods and to foster community reinvestment and citizen participation.

Since 1984, the Pittsburgh Cultural Trust has led the charge, revitalizing the 14-block Cultural District of downtown. The process had begun under the leadership of Jack Heinz and his son, Sen. John Heinz, with the catalytic transformation in 1971 of Heinz Hall as a new home for the Pittsburgh Symphony Orchestra. The Trust's first project, the $43 million Benedum Center for the Performing Arts, set the stage for over 14 cultural facilities, public parks and plazas, private developments and other infrastructure enhancements. Most recent additions include the O'Reilly Theater, home of the Pittsburgh Public Theater, and the Renaissance Pittsburgh Hotel in the former Fulton Building.

Others are seeking to capitalize on the region's natural resource assets. Finally realizing the vision first set forth in Olmsted's 1910 report on Pittsburgh, riverfront enhancement has become a top priority. Under the direction of the Riverlife Task Force, the city's latest public-private partnership is crafting and implementing a comprehensive plan to enhance rivefront commercial development, cultural and recreational opportunities and environmental stewardship. At the same time, the Friends of the Riverfront is developing the Three Rivers Heritage Trail, a 37-mile linear park along all the rivers that links Herr's Island on the Allegheny with amusement parks on the Monongahela and will ultimately connect with other trails to provide recreational access between Pittsburgh and Washington, D.C. Augmenting these efforts is a project of the Pittsburgh Cultural Trust, the new Allegheny Riverfront Park, a 35-foot-wide pedestrian oasis that extends for 4,000 feet along the Allegheny River on the edge of downtown, as well as Alcoa's new world headquarters across the river.

Moving inland, the Pittsburgh Parks Conservancy was founded with the goal of preserving Pittsburgh's four great parks — Schenley, Highland, Riverview and Frick — and

enhancing their value as featured amenities in the lifestyle of the city. Through successful fund-raising and highly visible restoration projects, the Conservancy has demonstrated the potential for the effort.

Grasping onto the growing promise of heritage tourism as an industry, the Steel Industry Heritage Corporation (SIHC) is working to preserve, promote and interpret the historic, cultural, natural and recreational resources of steel and related industries in southwestern Pennsylvania and to promote economic development through their creative reuse. The SIHC is active in the development of the seven-county Rivers of Steel National and State Heritage Area and a unique urban national park site at the Homestead Works. It is transforming "brownfield" sites into productive "greenfield" developments, including at least 11 river landings. It is also working to keep alive folklife traditions such as metalworking, needlework, instrumental music, song, dance, crafts and storytelling. Through these efforts, the SIHC is expecting to attract 840,000 annual visitors and generate nearly $60 million per year in revenues as well as 1,100 jobs with a gross annual payroll of $16 million.

The turn of the millennium also saw a number of innovative cultural groups thriving in the region. Adding to the list of long-established arts organizations, groups such as The Mattress Factory, the City Theatre, the Manchester Craftsmen's Guild, Pittsburgh Filmmakers and the Society for Contemporary Craft are pushing artistic agendas that challenge traditional media and presentation.

To ensure that the host of business opportunities and lifestyle amenities do not go unnoticed, a number of groups have arisen to retain young talent and promote the city to outsiders. Pittsburgh Regional Authority (PRA) is southwestern Pennsylvania's leading economic development agency, promoting the 10-county Pittsburgh region to businesses for expansion or relocation. A more grass-roots operation, the Pittsburgh Urban Magnet Project (PUMP) was founded in 1995 to attract and retain young and young-thinking people in the region. As a forum for a variety of issues, PUMP educates and advocates to promote growth of existing and new enterprises and to make Pittsburgh into a more dynamic and engaging place in which to live.

These are the legends of the new Pittsburgh. More of them are yet emerging as the city continues to reinvent itself in response to changing times. Behind these 21st century legends will be a lively and diverse population, fueled by vision and tenacity, who, like two centuries of their forebears, will meet the challenges with energy and innovation, ensuring Pittsburgh a continued presence on the frontier.

(Opposite page, bottom right)
Heinz Hall for the Performing Arts, home of the Pittsburgh Symphony, formerly a 1920s movie palace
Photo by William Rydberg, Photon

(Far left)
The lobby of the Renaissance Pittsburgh Hotel, formerly the Fulton Building
Photo by William Rydberg, Photon

The Carrie Furnaces along the Monongahela are to become the centerpiece of a national park celebrating Pittsburgh's steel heritage.
Pittsburgh History & Landmarks Foundation

The riverfront park along the Allegheny
Photo by William Rydberg, Photon

■ PITTSBURGH TODAY

As a tow with mixed cargo passes the Golden Triangle, business architecture old and new dominates a post-industrial scene. Around the Triangle, houses, trees, and streets of neighborhood shops occupy the hillsides and river plains, as ever, though no longer with smoke and fire as elements of the scene.

A tow of four barges on the Monongahela passes by Fort Pitt Boulevard.
Photo by William Rydberg, Photon

The three- to five-story Victorian buildings along Fort Pitt Boulevard give a human scale to Pittsburgh.
Photo by Jim Judkis (above) and photo by William Rydberg, Photon (right)

MYERS
247
Piccolo
Piccolo

(Top left)
An ornamental detail from a Fort Pitt Boulevard building facade
Photo by Jim Judkis

(Top right)
The Pittsburgh Technology Center stands on the old J & L steel site. The University of Pittsburgh's Center for Biotechnology and Bioengineering, by Bohlin Cywinski Jackson (1992), was built where the strip mill used to be.
Photo by Jim Judkis

A view up the Monongahela shows the Smithfield Street Bridge in the foreground and the PNC Firstside Center just beyond. The banking operations center was designed by the LDA-L.D. Astorino Companies and completed in 2000.
Photo by William Rydberg, Photon

The Tenth Street Bridge is Pittsburgh's only conventional suspension bridge, and the South Side is visible beyond. The hills, valleys and rivers give Pittsburgh its special vividness and drama.
Photo by Jim Judkis

When seen from afar, the hillside houses seem like brushstrokes on an Impressionistic canvas. Two churches served by the Passionist Fathers appear in the scene also. At one time the churches were connected by a hillside garden with Stations of the Cross.
Photo by Jim Judkis

St. Vincent de Paul
Society
Geoffrey Boehm Chocolates
OCTOBER IS
NAT'L PASTA
MONTH

Victorian buildings give character to East Carson Street on the South Side. This is now a City Historic District.
Photo by William Rydberg, Photon

(Top left)
Public steps are common on Pittsburgh's sloping streets.
Photo by Jim Judkis

(Top right)
Eighty-eight distinct neighborhoods comprise the city of Pittsburgh, and many of them retain their strong ethnic character.
Photo by William Rydberg, Photon

A view from Arlington Avenue looking up over the South Side Slopes to Oakland beyond
Photo by Jim Judkis

(Top right)
Liberty Avenue in Bloomfield, one of Pittsburgh's many ethnic neighborhoods
Photo by William Rydberg, Photon

(Left photos)
Pausing for a moment in Oakland, outside the Cathedral of Learning and Phipps Conservatory
Photos by William Rydberg, Photon

(Bottom right)
Pittsburgh's Strip District is a vital marketplace and entertainment district. To the left is St. Stanislaus, the oldest Polish Catholic church in the city.
Photo by William Rydberg, Photon

Acres of glass and an obelisk:
PPG Place, downtown Pittsburgh
Photo by William Rydberg, Photon

Smallman Street in the Strip District: The Senator John Heinz Pittsburgh Regional History Center, at left, is one of several cultural institutions located in the Strip District.
Photo by William Rydberg, Photon

Market Square, downtown Pittsburgh
Photo by William Rydberg, Photon

One of two surviving inclines, the Duquesne Incline takes passengers 400 feet above the river for a view of the Golden Triangle below and the Pittsburgh region beyond.
Photo by William Rydberg, Photon

Partners Table of Contents

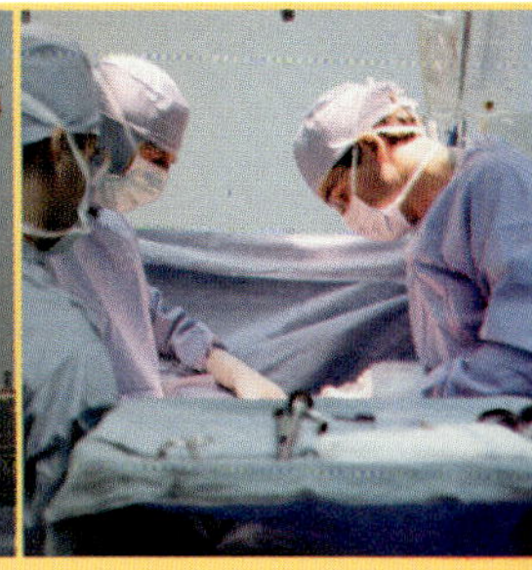

Building a Greater Pittsburgh

Providing and improving working and living space for area residents, Pittsburgh construction, real estate and related industries flourish.

Bricklayers & Allied Craftworkers Union Local 9

FOR MORE THAN A CENTURY, Bricklayers & Allied Craftworkers Union Local 9 has steadily contributed to the growth of Pittsburgh and western Pennsylvania — brick by brick and row by row — providing much more than the mortar filling the gaps in between.

Local 9 participates in Pittsburgh's annual Labor Day Parade.

Since its founding at the close of the Civil War, the Bricklayers & Allied Craftworkers Union has helped to support the lives and families of its membership through better working conditions, higher wages, benevolent health care and retirement programs, apprenticeships and training, and the clout of collective bargaining. In many ways, the union has filled the gaps in the walls of the community that are often the byproducts of urban growth.

Many Become One

With 2,800 members, including both active and retired craftsmen, Bricklayers & Allied Craftworkers Local 9 is an amalgam of the many local bricklayers, stonemasons and tile setters unions that were originally established throughout the western Pennsylvania region. The International Union of Bricklayers & Allied Craftsmen, which is part of the AFL-CIO, was officially chartered on October 17, 1865. The local bricklayers unions throughout western Pennsylvania were initially established during the same time frame as the international union, beginning with the Bricklayers Union of Pittsburgh, Allegheny and vicinity, which met regularly as early as 1864, and followed by Local 10 in Chester City (now Clarion), which was chartered in 1869. From Erie to Washington, Clarion to New Castle, and Warren to Johnstown, Local 9 represents the many craftsmen who work with brick, stone, cement, marble, plaster and tile. The union includes bricklayers, plasterers, cement masons, stone and marble masons, pointer-caulker-cleaners, tile setters, finishers, and the artisans who create mosaic and terrazzo works in tile.

Bricklayers & Allied Craftworkers Local 9 is an important contributor to Pittsburgh's strong sense of community and family as indicated by this photo from the annual picnic of Tile Layers and Helpers from 1915. *University of Pittsburgh Historical Archives*

Made up of many separate, former locals with different names — Local 2, Bricklayers; Local 33, Stone Masons; Local 20, Finishers — today's Bricklayers & Allied Craftworkers Local 9 represents bricklayers and craftsmen throughout the entire western portion of the state. Local unions from Pittsburgh, Greensburg, Erie, Washington, Warren, Johnstown, Clarion, Beaver and New Castle were consolidated into Local 9 in 1995 under the direction of the international union. All of the former locals throughout western Pennsylvania are now served through Local 9, which is headquartered in Monroeville.

The legacy of Local 9 rests in the hard work and struggle of the local unions that preceded it, organizations that were truly building blocks in the foundation of the labor movement that swept the nation during the industrial revolution and helped to establish a more humane treatment of workers that America knows today. Pittsburgh has been a prominent city in the history of labor's organization and enrichment of society, and Bricklayers & Allied Craftworkers Local 9 continues to contribute to the region's growth and sense of community.

A Worthy Trade

Although bricklaying and working with stone, cement, marble, plaster and tile are among the most arduous and physically taxing trades, they are also among the most rewarding. A craftsman can touch and see the fruits of his labor on a daily basis, bring an artistic, creative flair to his work, and continue to enjoy that work for years to come. For many people, bricklaying and related crafts are gratifying vocations, especially under the improved working conditions that Local 9 and the many other locals of the International Union of Bricklayers & Allied Craftworkers have worked to establish over the years.

Because bricklaying and related crafts expose a craftsman to the elements, working through all types of weather conditions, the union's efforts at its inception more than a century ago were directed toward a shortening of the workday. At the time, the workday was as long as the period of daylight (anywhere from 12 to 14 hours depending upon the time of year). Such conditions put considerable wear and tear on the bodies of these craftsmen, and the union successfully achieved an initial

Local 9 members assembled the large granite blocks comprising the old Allegheny County Jail, which was constructed in the late 1800s. *Allegheny County Department of Public Works*

Local 9 members constructed the redbrick façade of the new Allegheny County Jail in 1994. *Allegheny County Department of Public Works*

The observation deck of the old Greater Pittsburgh Airport took shape in 1949 thanks to Local 9 members. *Allegheny County Department of Public Works*

Local 9 members performed block work at the new Pittsburgh International Airport, ranked among the most modern airports in the world. *Allegheny County Department of Public Works*

reduction to 10 hours, then the eight-hour working day that has become the modern standard. The union contributed greatly to the political will that led to the establishment of the U.S. Occupational Safety and Health Administration (OSHA), which has established safety standards for all occupations.

Today, the union focuses on serving both young and old members, providing important apprenticeship and pension/retirement programs. Through its apprenticeship program, the union guarantees that the quality of its craftsmen remains at a consistently high level. The four-year, 6,000-hour program supports the union's commitment to contractors to provide well-trained, highly competent craftsmen to their building projects. Every year, Local 9 conducts required apprenticeship classes such as blueprint reading, stewards training and OSHA 500, as well as many hours of hands-on training. At the completion of the four-year apprenticeship program, a journeyman craftsman joins the ranks of building tradesmen. Local 9 President Bucky Donkin says, "Our greatest challenge in the foreseeable future is to train good apprentices and try to preserve what the past generations have worked so hard to achieve in making this a great union."

And just as the apprenticeship program establishes competency standards for journeymen, the union's pension program rewards retiring craftsmen for their hard work, commitment and dedication to their time-honored trade, enabling them to retire with a sense of pride, dignity and accomplishment.

Helping the Community

Bricklayers & Allied Craftworkers Local 9 has an active community service program through which the union gives back to communities throughout Pittsburgh and western Pennsylvania, many of which its craftsmen helped to build.

Union members volunteer countless hours to community projects such as building baseball dugouts, concession stands and recreational facilities. Working with Habitat for Humanity, Local 9 members help to build homes for low-income families. They also volunteer services in senior citizen centers and retirement communities, and annual contributions to the United Way fund a range of community services.

Bricklayers & Allied Craftworkers Local 9 has been and will continue to be an important resource, the mortar holding many bricks together, in the walls of western Pennsylvanian communities.

Bricklayers & Allied Craftworkers Local 9 represents bricklayers, plasterers, cement masons, stone and marble masons, pointer-caulker-cleaners, finishers, and tile setters. *Allegheny County Department of Public Works*

Continental Real Estate Companies

CONTINENTAL REAL ESTATE Companies transformed one of Pittsburgh's most historic sites — U.S. Steel's abandoned Homestead Works — into The Waterfront, the city's newest family destination and one of the most ambitious commercial redevelopment efforts in the nation.

The former mill's 12 mighty stacks, which once billowed smoke and steam and symbolized Pittsburgh's industrial power, now watch over a $300 million, 260-acre modern mixed-use development that blends the pride of the city's past with its economic future. The Homestead Works was the setting for one of Pittsburgh's most historic events, the infamous Homestead Strike, during which striking workers fought 300 hired Pinkerton guards in a battle that served as one of the defining moments in the American labor movement. It also produced the steel for the battleships and tanks that helped win World War II and for America's most majestic bridges and buildings, including the Empire State Building. At one time, Homestead Works was the largest steel mill in the world. It closed in 1987.

The site, which spans three townships (Homestead, Munhall and West Homestead) and fronts the Monongahela River about five miles southeast of downtown, sat idle for 10 years until Frank Kass, chairman of Continental, a Columbus, Ohio-based developer of shopping centers, office buildings and multifamily developments, created his vision for redevelopment. Kass believed a mixed-use approach — combining upscale and value retailers with entertainment, condominiums, office space and recreational opportunities — would transform the reclaimed site into a bustling economic center.

Bordered on one side by the Sandcastle Water Park and on the other by the Homestead Business District and the KennyWood Amusement Park, The Waterfront site seemed perfectly suited for Continental's mixed-use development. However, there was one hurdle to overcome: addressing the $32 million of public infrastructure required to support the development while working with three different municipalities. Kass championed the project's potential and persuaded all three taxing bodies to fund the infrastructure improvements through the sale of tax-exempt bonds. The Commonwealth of Pennsylvania contributed a $6.3 million grant to fund the on-site road system.

The Waterfront is unique because it combines 700,000 square feet of traditional shopping (The Market), with 500,000 square feet of specialty retail and entertainment space (The Town Center), 217 luxury apartments and a 150-slip marina (The Docks). The Market includes best-of-class large format retailers, including Target, Lowe's Home Improvement and Giant Eagle, the region's leading grocer. The Town Center features a 5,000-seat Loews Cineplex Theatre, Barnes & Noble bookstore, Dave & Buster's (a dynamic entertainment facility), and many other unique restaurants, retailers and entertainment venues. The entire development was designed to support pedestrian and bicycle traffic, giving it a quaint, small-town feel.

Continental made a special effort to capture the historic ambiance of the site. The smokestacks remain, now lit up at night, along with other historic artifacts. The Homestead Hi-Level Bridge runs over the site, providing scale and towering archways. Period-style gaslights, Victorian architecture and river views complement the historic atmosphere.

The Waterfront represents more than the rebirth of a historic area — it also provides new economic life for the surrounding communities.

The 12 preserved original brick smoke stacks commemorate the heritage of The Waterfront site.

Mariani & Richards, Inc.

THE STORY OF THE AMERICAN dream goes something like this: A person has an idea for a business but very little money. Hard work, sweat and perseverance eventually provide all the capital that's needed to get the business up and running, turning the idea into a success story.

The results far exceeded Ed Mariani's own American dream when he started his waterproofing business in 1949. But with help from a little old lady, a catchy advertising slogan and a big rainstorm, it's the path his business would take.

Born in 1915 in the east end of Pittsburgh, Mariani grew up among the old brick buildings of the city. After graduating in the class of 1938 from Duquesne University, Mariani tackled a brief stint investigating company credit histories at Dunn & Bradstreet. World War II soon led Mariani into the Air Force, where he obtained the rank of major. In 1946 Mariani headed back to his hometown to seek work, encountering little in the way of an income that could provide for his growing family.

In the course of working as a life insurance agent, Mariani called on a former fellow military officer, Herb Sullivan. Sullivan was in the home-building business and was looking to expand into remodeling. Though it piqued Mariani's interest, he knew very little about construction. But with a $1,000 investment by Sullivan and mentoring by Sullivan's superintendent, Buddy Richards, the business came to life.

Mariani & Richards opened shop on Saw Mill Run Boulevard and hoped that business would pick up. One day, an older lady stopped by and asked about getting rid of the water in her basement. Mariani looked into the matter, researching proper procedure at the Carnegie Library Technical Department. Armed with an interior drainage plan, Mariani and his crew went to work. And so began the waterproofing business for which Mariani & Richards has become known.

The business slowly expanded, and by 1951 Mariani & Richards was handling about 50 projects a year and had seven employees. The business moved to Squirrel Hill and beefed up its advertising efforts. A job in Stanton Heights yielded surprisingly fateful results: the son of the couple who hired Mariani & Richards for the project worked in the advertising business at Goldman and Shoop. He recommended advertising their waterproofing business on WDTV. A one-minute spot at 11:15 p.m. cost $100 — a big sum of money for a growing business in 1951. The television commercial produced a slogan still famous in Pittsburgh today: "Aw, Dry Up." In fact, the *Pittsburgh Post-Gazette* ran an article in 1994 calling it "the favorite of the unctuous pitchman for waterproofing cellars being heckled by the off-screen voice saying 'Ah Dry up.'"

Three weeks of advertising didn't produce the results Mariani and Richards wanted, but a terrible rainstorm did. The

Sacred Heart Church, Shadyside (before restoration) — a total stone restoration brought this historic landmark to life and added years to protecting and preserving its exterior surface.

(Far right) Sacred Heart Church, Shadyside (after restoration)

television advertising coupled with the bad weather caused leaky basements all over town. The phone at Mariani & Richards rang off the hook, solidifying its presence as a reputable waterproofing business.

The Pittsburgh landscape provided a way to further expand the business. With old brick buildings peppering the city, Mariani literally spotted his next inspiration. The company purchased a hanging scaffold and started soliciting masonry restoration work. Mariani stopped at old buildings and inquired about restoration, knocking on doors to drum up business. Suppliers the company worked with provided more than materials; they also produced some leads. Projects for masonry and concrete restoration work came in and have since become a large part of the business.

For example, Frank Lloyd Wright's Fallingwater, a historic western Pennsylvania landmark, was in need of restorative concrete work when the moisture from the atmosphere and the waterfall built to flow through the lower level contributed to the erosion of the concrete and reinforcements. And the U.S. Department of the Interior contracted Mariani & Richards to restore the masonry on the home of Albert Gallatin, the first U.S. Secretary of the Treasury under Thomas Jefferson, after a fire damaged the historic home.

Other Pittsburgh landmarks have also been touched by the work of Mariani & Richards, including Carnegie-Mellon University Fine Arts building, Carnegie-Mellon University Hunt Library, the Station Square Complex, AT&T Building, Somerset County Courthouse, Sacred Heart Church, buildings within Penn State University — and the list goes on.

Mariani & Richards' restorative services have also taken the company outside of Pennsylvania and into Illinois, West Virginia, Ohio and, notably, South Carolina after Hurricane Hugo ripped through Charleston. Historic homes, apartment buildings and churches were in need of skilled craftspeople to restore the buildings to their former glory. The citizens of Charleston took their town and their town's history and buildings very seriously, and the sight of Mariani & Richards' crew working on their buildings even drew a few spectators. The company, true to its reputation, painstakingly restored many of Charleston's old landmarks down to their original Irish bricks.

With the addition of Ronald Freeborough in 1976, president of the company since 1988, the family-owned Mariani & Richards has progressed from a small start-up doing odds and ends for homeowners to a major force in the masonry restoration and waterproofing services for the area's commercial and institutional industries. Skilled craftspeople who have been with the company for years and a reputation synonymous with quality have propelled the business into a premier position within Pittsburgh.

AT&T Building along Grant Street — the entire exterior was cleaned and all joints were resealed.

Today, Mariani & Richards, Inc. is a $5 million a year business with some 70 employees and upward of 300 jobs a year. Its reputation as a quality restorer has come not just through nearly 50 years of doing work in the Pittsburgh area but also through restoring and preserving buildings of great historical significance.

The history of Mariani & Richards is as precious as the buildings that the company restores. It's an American dream come true — born one brick at a time.

Restoration completed on Mudge House, Carnegie Mellon University

Oxford Development Company

THERE IS A FORCE THAT IS RESHAPING the face of the Pittsburgh region and that force is Oxford Development Company, a full-service commercial real estate firm. The company pioneered the development of regional shopping malls and led Pittsburgh's second renaissance in the 1980s with construction of its landmark headquarters building, One Oxford Centre.

Founded in 1962, the company evolved from a predecessor, Don Mark Realty, which had operated in Pittsburgh's Oakland section. In the early 1960s, company leaders foresaw that consumers would continue to abandon urban retail shops and flock to the shopping malls springing up in the growing suburbs.

Oxford Development's first major success as a shopping-mall developer was South Hills Village, which opened in 1965. The mall enjoyed instant acceptance, and within a few months of leasing, its 1 million square feet of retail space was fully occupied by 120 tenants. Its two levels of outdoor parking — a first for the region — made two levels of retail stores easily accessible to shoppers.

The first jewels of downtown Pittsburgh's Renaissance II are the four octagonal buildings of One Oxford Centre. Completed in 1982, the vari-storied structures, which rise to 45 floors, are home to Oxford Development and other prominent firms.

Strengthening its prominence, the company went on to develop the Monroeville Mall in a rapidly growing region east of Pittsburgh. Containing 1.3 million square feet of space, along with parking and annexes, the shopping facility opened in 1969. With the development of adjoining land stretching into the present, this 260-acre site now includes a hotel, an apartment building, a fitness club, an exposition center, office facilities and additional retail outlets.

In the 1970s Oxford Development expanded its operations southward to develop malls in West Virginia and Florida.

In 1978, under the leadership of Edward J. Lewis, chairman and chief executive officer, the company invested in two acres of county-owned land in the heart of downtown Pittsburgh. Signaling the start of Pittsburgh's famed Renaissance II, ground was broken in 1980 for construction of One Oxford Centre, and the first tenants moved into the building in 1982. Prominent on Pittsburgh's skyline, the vari-leveled complex consisting of four connected octagonal towers — clad in alternating bands of silver-gray aluminum and reflective glass — rises as high as 45 stories. Entered through a dramatic five-story atrium, the structure houses Oxford Development's headquarters and other office facilities, as well as 50,000 square feet of retail space.

Also changing the face of Pittsburgh were other Oxford Development projects, including the renovations of the historic, marble-walled Frick Building and the James H. Reed Building.

Beginning in the late 1980s, Oxford Development expanded its business to include real estate services. Today the firm consists of four operating divisions: real estate development, property management, leasing and brokerage services, and operating services. Through affiliated companies, Central Property Services and Bakewell Corporation, Oxford Development provides commercial cleaning services and parking facility management.

Today's Oxford Development Company ranks as one of Pennsylvania's largest private real estate firms. At its Pittsburgh headquarters and regional offices throughout the state, the company's more than 1,700 employees provide expertise in a wide array of services. Among them are tenant representation, brokerage, leasing, real estate development and consulting, and construction and property management.

Oxford Development has managed, developed, owned or sold more than 40 million square feet of commercial space — enough in size and type of structure to make up a small city.

This space includes office buildings, health and fitness facilities, warehouse and distribution units, retail centers, hotels, high-tech data centers, medical satellite facilities, apartments, exhibition centers and airport retail shops. In 2000 the company added Dominion Tower to its portfolio of Pittsburgh landmarks. This significant architectural statement is a 32-story office structure in the heart of the city's Golden Triangle.

To ensure a successful real estate development project, Oxford Development's team of professionals serves clients with market analysis, site selection and planning, government-approval processing, project financing, design and construction, and project management. Oxford Realty Services acts as the firm's leasing unit.

Playing a major role in the renovation of Pittsburgh's landscape, Oxford Realty Services has leasing responsibility for such notable projects as the Gimbels Landmark Building, Penn Avenue Place, One Oxford Centre and Dominion Tower.

In Thorn Hill Industrial Park, northwest of Pittsburgh, Oxford Realty Services represents Keystone Commerce Center. The 180,000-square-foot industrial building provides 24 feet of space from floor to ceiling and is suitable for warehouse, distribution, research and development, and light manufacturing operations.

Oxford Realty Services has managed transactions that stretch across the nation and the world through its affiliation with Oncor International, an organization of top-ranked commercial real estate firms. The affiliate, Oxford Realty Services/Oncor International, draws on more than 2,900 professionals around the globe to staff projects outside the Pittsburgh area. This organization consists of about 180 full-service offices in more than 30 countries.

Oxford Development has managed, developed, owned or sold more than 40 million square feet of commercial space – enough in size and type of structure to make up a small city.

Through their community service as well as their professional involvement, Oxford Development's executives contribute to the vitality of the Pittsburgh region. Chairman Lewis serves on the board of directors of the United Jewish Federation Investment Committee, Pittsburgh Downtown Partnership, Jewish Healthcare Foundation of Pittsburgh and the University of Pittsburgh Medical Center. Vice Chairman Mark E. Mason sits on the board of trustees of the World Affairs Council of Pittsburgh as well as the boards of several national organizations. David M. Matter, president and chief operating officer, is former board chairman of the Allegheny County Regional Asset District and Pittsburgh Water and Sewer Authority and is chairman of the Greater Pittsburgh Chamber of Commerce. He is a member of the board and executive committee of the Pittsburgh Regional Alliance and serves on the boards or committees of various other civic and community development groups.

In the 21st century, renovating the face of Pittsburgh and western Pennsylvania remains the primary focus of Oxford Development Company. Its real estate professionals are continuing to develop facilities designed to make shopping more convenient, entertainment more exciting and work space more desirable for the people of Pittsburgh.

Added to Oxford Development's properties in 2000 was the monumental Dominion Tower, capped by a distinctive curved crown. The 32-story art deco office building graces Pittsburgh's Golden Triangle.

Pennsylvania Drilling Company and Penndrill Manufacturing

PENNSYLVANIA DRILLING COMPANY has been drilling holes in Pennsylvania for 100 years. In its earliest days, the company located coal and mineral deposits, determining their quality and planning mining excavation. Offices were also opened in remote areas of New Mexico to drill for potash (potassium nitrate, used in explosives), and in Utah for uranium.

THEN:
With a steam core drill, drilling for minerals in the West in the 1920s

Pennsylvania Drilling Company doesn't do much mineral drilling these days, although President Thomas Sturges still keeps a 3-inch cylinder of bright pink potash as a paperweight and a reminder of his company's history.

Today Pennsylvania Drilling Company drills for engineers, construction project managers, geologists and other scientists. No bridge, tunnel, dam or major building project can be planned before the geology of the foundation site is known. And when earth, ground water or riverbeds have to be checked for contaminants, or when precise sampling cores are needed for landfills or waste-lagoon sites, Pennsylvania Drilling Company's advanced technology and experienced staff produce exact, efficient results with minimal site damage. The drills use a diamond-core barrel, producing a single 2- to 7-inch-diameter core, like coring a pineapple. The cores are turned over to the scientists and engineers for analyses, and Pennsylvania Drilling Company moves on to drill somewhere else.

In 1947 the company developed its own manufacturing arm, a small machine shop it named Penndrill, to produce specialized equipment it needed but wasn't available anywhere else. Today Penndrill's state-of-the-art computer-controlled machining equipment supplies the entire industry with a complete offering of drilling tools and equipment.

NOW:
With a CME-85 Auger/Core Drill, drilling sample borings for a power plant in 2000

When special tools and modified equipment are needed for a particularly complicated job — and needed fast — Penndrill's dependability and innovation stand out. Because most of the Penndrill staff members have worked in the field themselves, they have a broad understanding of industry problems — and what lost field time means.

What makes this company different from its competitors is the difficulty of the jobs it takes on. For example, if heavy drill equipment must be brought to the top of a steep hill, one solution would be to bulldoze a road up the hill. But because bulldozing can loosen boulders and cause rock slides, Pennsylvania Drilling Company sometimes opts to bring in the equipment by helicopter — 5,000 to 8,000 pounds at a time.

"We used to drill holes for coal and water," says Sturges. "Now we drill foundation-investigation holes for highways and monitoring wells for hazardous waste monitoring. That's really all we want — to keep right on doing what we're good at, and to keep evolving into a company than can seize opportunities as they arise."

Pennsylvania Drilling Company and its offspring, Penndrill, will do just that. As long as engineers, scientists and government research teams need dependable, accurate data about the earth and its resources, they will continue to rely on the innovative expertise of this industry leader.

Ryan Homes

THE PITTSBURGH RENAISSANCE was the name given to the resurgence of the city's growth in the years following World War II. As Pittsburgh redefined itself as a major city in America, Pittsburgh city leaders considered innovative plans for improvement. A prominent figure in the redevelopment process was Edward Ryan, a local businessman and home builder. Following an increase in the population base coupled with a growing economy, a significant need for affordable family housing became apparent to Ryan. Accordingly, Ryan established a home construction company in 1948 that has remained a stronghold in the building industry for over half a century. His brother, James, accompanied him in helping Americans fulfill their dreams of owning a home.

In the late 1950s the "Smoky City" was changing in design, demographics and development. Ryan was a realist and a visionary whose ideas transformed the home-building industry. While constructing a home for his family, he realized the advantages of a specialized labor force utilizing individual expertise. Ryan's emphasis on insulation reduced heating costs; and his innovative closed-wall system, in which homes are assembled in a lumberyard and then delivered to the property site, also lowered costs. When Ryan observed that the price of purchasing a lot and then building a home was higher than the price of purchasing a house and property together, he became a Pittsburgh leader in designing and building planned residential neighborhoods. These neighborhoods consisted of a variety of home styles located in a "community within a community" with playgrounds, clubhouses, pools and trails.

These early years of refinements in construction built a solid foundation for Ryan Homes that endures into the 21st century. The Ryan Homes tradition of integrity blended with an appreciation of today's lifestyles appeals to prospective homeowners but also has won the company numerous outstanding design awards. Individuality in each Ryan home is expressed by the finest building materials, flexible floor plans and a selection of amenities. An energy-saving package and a nondeductible, 10-year, fully transferable warranty are also available. And to honor personal commitment, a company representative walks through each new home and confirms attention to every detail.

This dedication to the consumer is comprised of many aspects. In 1987 NVHomes Inc. of Virginia acquired Ryan Homes and changed its name to NVR Inc. As a result, the company has been traded on the American Stock Exchange under the symbol NVR. An affiliate mortgage company, NVR Mortgage, offers prospective Ryan homeowners financing through NVR Inc. Another affiliate, NVR Settlement Services Inc., a residential title and settlement agency, provides assistance for closing on a new home.

Grady Gaspar, Ryan Homes division manager for Pittsburgh, believes these high professional standards contribute to ultimate customer satisfaction. Statistics reveal that over 60 percent of Ryan homeowners are previous customers, demonstrating that the company has achieved its objective. Ryan Homes extends throughout most of the southwestern region of Pennsylvania, with offices in nine additional states. One of 10 top builders in the United States, it has provided homes for over 200,000 families. For more than 50 years the American dream remains a reality with Ryan Homes.

Ryan Homes conducts extensive consumer research to reflect what homeowners prefer in designs.

Prospective Ryan homeowners may select from a variety of interior and exterior styles.

Soffer Organization

WHEN ANDREW CARNEGIE FIRST surveyed Pittsburgh's three rivers, he envisioned a future built on steel and trimmed with economic success. Decades later, in 1950, when Joseph Soffer looked toward Pittsburgh's suburbs, he also saw a future called mixed-use land development.

Soffer Realty started in the late 40s as a small real estate business, buying and selling homes and building early shopping centers, like Norwin Towne Square. In the early 60s the company became Soffer Organization and Joseph Soffer's initial vision was realized as Penn Center East, a massive suburban complex of large-scale commercial, retail and residential facilities.

Today Soffer Organization is one of the largest private real estate developers of office buildings in Pittsburgh, according to Joseph's son and current President and CEO R. Damian Soffer. Staying ahead of the curve by following industry trends and encouraging a team effort allows Soffer Organization to remain competitive in a market where suburban land development continues to grow.

Building Six of Soffer Organization's Technology Park at Penn Center West

Employing close to 100 people, Soffer is committed to making technologically advanced, environmentally friendly buildings with plenty of people amenities. "Outdoor space for indoor people" has become its land development philosophy. The company's leasing and management philosophy likewise remains simple: Give tenants the best services and amenities because satisfied tenants are worth the extra cost. Caring about current and future tenants and their needs is what sets Soffer Organization apart. In fact, the National Association for Industrial and Office Parks named R.Damian Soffer the 2000 Developer of the Year.

With elaborate landscaping budgets, Soffer's building complexes abound with waterfalls, hiking trails, lush flower beds and outdoor eating areas. A perfect example of Soffer's development philosophy is Penn Center West, a 90-acre office park equidistant to downtown Pittsburgh and the Greater Pittsburgh International Airport. The complex features office buildings with landscaped atriums and original artwork commissioned by R. Damian Soffer, a comprehensive on-site conference center and a comfortable yet contemporary design.

R. Damian Soffer, a former international art dealer who returned to Pittsburgh to help lead the family business, remains the creative force behind his company's many ambitious projects, including the South Side Works being built on the former LTV Steel site along the Monongahela River. Many years in the making, this joint venture with the city of Pittsburgh will bring a lifestyle punch to the riverfront. South Side Works plans to offer up to 500,000 square feet of high-performance office space, 300,000 square feet of lifestyle retail entertainment, 300 residential units, a Pittsburgh Steelers practice field, nine restaurants, a hotel and marina. Soffer hopes this multipurpose complex will be a riverside jewel that attracts more young people to work and live in Pittsburgh.

Believing in Pittsburgh's great potential drives Soffer Organization to create more pleasurable environments for people to work and live. Says R. Damian Soffer, "The days of corporate headquarters and steel giants are giving way to technology and e-commerce and we're prepared for those times." Joseph Soffer's steel will and R. Damian Soffer's future vision, displayed in the success of the Soffer Organization, are leading Pittsburgh's transformation from a steel giant to a vibrant, youthful city.

As it turns out, Andrew Carnegie's vision wasn't so far off, thanks to the vision of companies like Soffer Organization.

Pittsburgh History & Landmarks Foundation

Business & Finance

Banks, investment and financial services companies, as well as personnel and insurance providers support a host of Pittsburgh organizations.

Dollar Bank

WITH ITS ROOTS DEEPLY TIED TO the people, commerce and values of Pittsburgh since 1855, Dollar Bank has grown to become a large, full-service, regional bank serving individuals and business customers throughout western Pennsylvania and northeastern Ohio.

Over the past century and a half, the bank has invested billions of dollars in millions of lives and thousands of businesses. Today, Dollar Bank operates more than 50 offices and loan centers throughout the Pittsburgh and Cleveland metropolitan areas.

Independence Is the Key

In this age of mega-mergers in the banking industry, Dollar Bank remains fiercely independent and committed to providing the highest quality of banking services to individuals and businesses for many more years to come.

As a mutual institution, it has no stock to sell. As a well-capitalized bank, it has no reason to sell. This means that consumers and businesses alike will continue to find Dollar Bank available as an option to meet their needs.

Relationships Built on Experience

In business, experience matters, and it matters at Dollar Bank too. Business men and women who come to the bank find themselves in the hands of tenured, hard-working banking officers backed by a team of financial experts.

> In this age of mega-mergers in the banking industry, Dollar Bank remains fiercely independent and committed to providing the highest quality of banking services to individuals and businesses for many more years to come.

Many of the Bank's business customers have been working with the same team of banking officers for more than a dozen years. These Dollar Bank teams work virtually without walls to insure that the best interests of the customer remain paramount.

If the business customer needs financial specialization, these officers can connect him or her with colleagues in the commercial real estate, cash management or corporate lending departments. Combining their desire to build relationships with their depth of experience, these officers can help with a wide variety of projects. The local manufacturer needing to respond to increased demand can secure a line of credit to expand his operation. The franchiser can find the funds she needs to open another outlet in a new market area. The team of physicians wanting to buy a building to house their booming practice can get the guidance and financing needed to do it right.

A well-respected commercial real estate lender, Dollar Bank is often asked to take the lead on a number of sophisticated development projects. Working with federal, state and local government officials, the bank recently helped reclaim an abandoned steel mill site by financing the construction of a new headquarters building for a national manufacturing corporation. High-tech companies have turned to Dollar Bank to finance the construction of unique, state-of-the-art office/lab/production facilities. Anxious to help save and retool older buildings in the region, the bank has financed the conversion of several former school buildings into apartment buildings specially designed for senior citizens.

Innovation for Better Service

Driven by the desire to provide the highest level of customer service, Dollar Bank's leaders always have been innovators in the industry. The bank was the first in the region to offer telephone bill paying in the mid-1970s. Its online banking system, called NetBanking, earned Dollar Bank a ranking as one of the top 10 banks in cyberspace. The system was even selected by the prestigious Smithsonian Institution to be part of the permanent Computerworld Smithsonian Innovation Collection.

Business customers can put cyberspace to work for them too with CashAnalyzer. This state-of-the-art, PC-based system allows businesses as well as governmental and nonprofit organizations to monitor their cash flow, make sound cash management decisions and conduct banking transactions online in a secure environment 24 hours a day, 7 days a week.

Some of the bank's innovations are high touch, not high tech, including its approach to Private Banking. Believing that medical and legal professionals, corporate executives and business owners have a unique set of financial needs, Dollar Bank's Private Banking Department provides these high net worth individuals with a single point of contact for all their banking needs. Every Private Banking customer is assigned a seasoned relationship officer who has the experience and the authority to move freely within all the bank's departments to address the customer's needs, whatever they may be.

At the other end of the economic spectrum, Dollar Bank was the first bank in the region to recognize the need for and provide credit counseling to low- and moderate-income borrowers, who had been shut out of the housing market because of poor credit, too much debt or inadequate income.

Beyond Basic Banking

When businesses are faced with funding new equipment purchases, they often want an alternative to borrowing. That is why the Dollar Bank Leasing Corp. was founded. From vehicles to communication systems, from short term to long term, this wholly-owned subsidiary of the bank has the sophistication and skill to handle the leasing needs of many businesses. Whether the lease is for $1,000 or $1 million, businesses can and do get quick answers, often within 24 hours.

When buying property, borrowers and lenders alike need to know the property is free and clear of any liens. Dollar Bank's full service title insurance agency, The Flenniken Corp., can help by examining titles, issuing title commitments and insurance policies and assisting in loan closings. Although Flenniken's customers are usually those of the bank, even non-Dollar Bank customers can use this important service.

One of the biggest frustrations faced by residential mortgage borrowers is having their mortgages sold to a giant, out-of-state mortgage company. That is what led Dollar Bank to establish its own mortgage servicing subsidiary, The Mortgage Service Center.

Dedicated to servicing the mortgages originated by the bank, this subsidiary even helps borrowers who run into economic hard times by providing mortgage foreclosure guidance enabling the borrower stay in their homes, repair their credit and pay off their loans.

COMMITTED TO COMMUNITY

The bank's commitment to community is reflected in the support it has given to some of the annual events that have become part of the fabric of Pittsburgh and its neighborhoods. Each year, the Dollar Bank Jamboree brings local and national country music talent to Point State Park for a free day of family fun and music. Concession and activity proceeds are donated to the Boys and Girls Clubs of Western Pennsylvania.

Every September, the streets of Pittsburgh are filled with runners 12 years old and younger participating in the Dollar Bank Junior Great Race. Sponsored in part by Dollar Bank, this event encourages physical and financial fitness for families and raises money for the Richard S. Caliguiri Amyloidosis Fund.

MANY OF THE BANK'S BUSINESS CUSTOMERS HAVE BEEN WORKING WITH THE SAME TEAM OF BANKING OFFICERS FOR MORE THAN A DOZEN YEARS. THESE DOLLAR BANK TEAMS WORK VIRTUALLY WITHOUT WALLS TO INSURE THAT THE BEST INTERESTS OF THE CUSTOMER REMAIN PARAMOUNT.

Whether with individuals, small businesses, corporations or nonprofit organizations, relationships have always been built on a sound mixture of responsibility and trust. That is what set Dollar Bank apart in the minds of its customers since 1855. That is what has made it the oldest continuously operating bank in Pittsburgh, and that is what will carry Dollar Bank into the future.

Female heads of households have the opportunity to learn how to become homeowners with a Dollar Bank-sponsored, free, half-day seminar designed specifically for them. Called Mortgages for Mothers, participants learn about credit, the mortgage process and most importantly, that they really can become homeowners.

Here for the Future

At its core, banking has always been a business of responsibility and trust. The leaders of Dollar Bank feel an intense responsibility to provide products and services that grow out of an understanding and feel for their communities. The customers trust that Dollar Bank will be there to meet their needs in the future.

Federated Investors, Inc.

JOHN F. "JACK" DONAHUE WANTED to work for himself and sell a product in which he believed — mutual funds — when he founded Federated Investors, Inc. with two Central Catholic High School friends in Pittsburgh in 1955. Donahue, Richard B. Fisher and Thomas J. Donnelly combined youth, determination and courage with an entrepreneurial spirit to grow the firm into a world-class investment management company, which now manages more than $125 billion in assets and is traded on the New York Stock Exchange under the ticker symbol FII.

Federated Investors employees at the New York Stock Exchange — Federated Investors (NYSE: FII) became a publicly traded company in May 1998.

Employing nearly 2,000 people, Federated today manages more than $125 billion in 175 different domestic and international equity, fixed-income and money market investment products.

The trio of high school friends, who had become two mutual fund sales guys and a lawyer, had much at stake when they founded Federated Investors. Each had a young family; by 1958 they were supporting 12 children between them and had more on the way. So they persevered, trudging through the streets of Pittsburgh, knocking on doors to introduce the concept of mutual fund investing. The idea was slow to catch on in those early days, but they could not afford to fail. They maintained faith in their enterprise through the help and support of family and friends. And as the mutual fund industry grew and prospered, so did Federated Investors, ultimately reaching heights the founders had never imagined.

Today Federated ranks within the top 5 percent of all U.S. managers of money market, fixed-income and equity funds based on assets under management. With offices in Pittsburgh, Boston, New York City, Dublin and Frankfurt, the company now has about 1,800 employees, including 1,600 in its Pittsburgh headquarters. Two founders, Donahue and Fisher, continue to be active in the company. John F. Donahue is chairman of the board, and his son, J. Christopher Donahue, is president and chief executive officer.

With more than 175 different domestic and international equity, fixed-income and money market investment products, Federated Investors delivers a diversified product lineup to financial intermediaries and institutions to help them reach a variety of investment goals for their clients. Federated has long supported financial intermediaries and has firmly believed in the importance of professional advice from its inception. Today, with more investment options than ever, professional advice has never been more important. Product performance, breadth and innovation combined with superior customer service and one of the largest wholesaling sales forces in the industry have enabled Federated to achieve substantial asset growth throughout its 45-year history.

Innovator of Industry Firsts

Federated's pioneering, visionary approach to cash management resulted in explosive growth in the 1970s when the company launched the first money market fund (Money Market Management, Inc.) and achieved its first $1 billion in managed assets. Federated spearheaded legislation to make it possible for

mutual funds to enter previously untapped markets, particularly bank trust departments. Federated essentially helped to create the bank mutual fund business. Before bank trust departments began using money funds, the mutual fund industry experienced limited growth. While at one time bank assets in funds did not even exist, today, as a result of Federated's efforts, bank mutual fund assets represent roughly 25 percent of the entire mutual fund industry.

During the 80s and 90s, the company became a major player in the fixed-income market, introducing the Government Income Securities Fund, Inc. (GISI), and expanded its family of funds into international markets with the introduction of the Federated International Equity, Federated International Income and Federated World Utility funds. Federated was instrumental in the creation of the first high-yield fund and today remains a leader in the high-yield market with approximately $5 billion under management.

The expansion of Federated's domestic and international equity assets to 34 different funds defined the significant growth of the 1990s. Today Federated's extensive product line covers a full spectrum of asset classes and market capitalization including growth, growth and income, and value. This broad base of equity products combined with Federated's extensive distribution system has enabled the equity product line to produce more revenue for Federated than any other class of assets under management. While the company was adding to its equity lineup during the 1990s, in May 1998 Federated completed an initial public offering (IPO) and began trading on the New York Stock Exchange under the trading symbol FII. The IPO gave Federated increased visibility as well as the capital to continue to grow through strategic acquisitions.

Global Reach

Although international products had been a part of Federated's fund offering for 16 years, the establishment of Federated Global Investment Management Corp. — a dedicated global/international investment unit headquartered in New York City — in 1995 marked a new era for the company. With key contributions from Federated Global, the firm has grown its international assets more than tenfold since 1991 to approximately $8 billion. Through a family of 13 mutual funds, Federated currently offers a variety of core international investments, along with the regional focused funds and innovative sector offerings.

Recognizing other opportunities related to the developing global economy, Federated has also expanded its reach by teaming up with international partners. Federated has been instrumental in making cash management products available to financial communities outside the United States, which has led to the establishment of Federated International Management Limited (FIML) in Dublin. FIML administers five offshore funds marketed to international investors comprising global banks and multinational corporations.

Federated also has developed a partnership with LVM Insurance Company, one of the largest insurance companies in Germany and Austria. The partnership formed Federated Fonds-Service GmbH, a joint-venture company that markets six retail mutual funds, which are managed by investment teams in New York City and Pittsburgh, to LVM's 3 million insurance customers through a sales force of more than 2,300 agents.

Remaining True to Its Roots

Federated remains committed to growth of assets under management through organic growth as well as through strategic acquisitions. The firm will rely on the same values of hard work, integrity, innovation, and devotion to customer service that defined the firm and its founders when Federated Investors was born 45 years ago. These values have been the foundation from which Federated has grown to become an integral part of the Pittsburgh skyline as well as worldwide financial markets.

Founded in Pittsburgh in 1955, Federated has a rich history of supporting the local community — including the Pittsburgh Pirates and Pittsburgh Steelers in Three Rivers Stadium.

Federated Investors Tower has been home to Federated since 1986. The tower recently became a widely recognized part of the downtown Pittsburgh skyline when the Federated logo was assembled atop the 27-story building.

Fiserv

THE MASSIVE MARBLE-PILLARED edifices dotting Pittsburgh's business district amply demonstrate that the city has built its history as much on banking as on steel and aluminum mills, glass factories and pickle plants. Some of the nation's largest financial institutions have their roots in the city and continue to make it their home.

One part of the city's banking business is changing rapidly with the growing Pittsburgh presence of Fiserv, a high-tech provider of information services. The company's systems have allowed financial institutions to move away from the stodgy image of accountants in green eyeshades grinding out stacks of reports to a new vision of electronic networks that record and track detailed customer information and transactions at incredibly high speeds.

Fiserv Pittsburgh occupies a contemporary facility on the edge of the Allegheny River. *Photo by Jeff Comella*

Milwaukee-based Fiserv, Inc., parent firm of the Pittsburgh operation, reduces paperwork for more than 10,000 banks and thrift institutions worldwide. The company is the nation's largest provider of information technology services for the financial industry and the second largest U.S. manufacturer of credit cards and other plastic cards.

James C. Puzniak, president of Fiserv Bank Servicing Division II

The Pittsburgh unit of Fiserv supplies a comprehensive suite of integrated systems and services for data processing and information management. It provides custom-tailored hardware and software for call centers and back-office operations, as well as systems to run Internet banking and ATMs throughout the country and around the world. The company's services include information technology support for account and transaction processing, lending systems, data warehousing and financial management.

Fiserv also provides electronic commerce products and services as well as revolving credit and electronic funds transfer services. Through its customer relationship management systems and services, the company greatly improves customer convenience, helps call-center contact management agents increase customer satisfaction and makes them more effective salespeople. These systems also help market managers design new products and services to meet evolving customer needs, allow banks to seize market opportunities at low risk, automate back-office operations to boost efficiency and enhance service, and to improve financial management.

A vital member of the city's growing high-technology industry, Fiserv employs a staff of over 700 that includes a high percentage of software developers and engineers, in addition to business analysts and customer service representatives. In view of the company's prominent role, the Pittsburgh Technology Council named Fiserv one of the region's fastest-growing technical companies in both 1999 and 2000.

The roots of the Fiserv Pittsburgh operation date back to 1960, when a major Pittsburgh financial institution set up a data processing outsourcing business. Fiserv, Inc., purchased the profitable business in 1993 and a year later the operation moved into a modern, 10-story

At Fiserv Pittsburgh highly skilled banking analysis, systems engineering and technology experts work together to develop effective information technologies.

building near the Allegheny River in Pittsburgh's Golden Triangle. Later, the business expanded to occupy one story of an adjacent building, and more expansion is on the drawing board.

By taking over many operations for financial institutions, Fiserv allows them to reduce personnel and eliminate the need to purchase their own hardware, operating systems and applications software. More importantly, the company's systems free the banking staff to concentrate on customer sales and service. The Fiserv custom outsourcing function currently processes more than 10 million core accounts for 124 clients nationwide. More than 325 million on-line transactions are processed each month.

One of Fiserv's most successful software solutions is InformEnt, a complete enterprise-wide data warehousing system that collects and transforms data from diverse systems into a single source for comprehensive, timely, accurate and easy-to-use information about customers, products and profitability. Among its many advantages, InformEnt fosters more effective decision making, more personalized service and better customer relationships.

InformEnt also helps financial institutions identify new markets and develop marketing campaigns, launch new banks and develop other ways to expand the business. Further, the system lets an institution know what products are selling well and how the firm is faring compared with its competition.

Another major Fiserv service is the Contact Management Sales and Service product suite, a contact management, campaign management, target marketing and workflow system that supplies a financial institution's service agents with important customer information, critical handling instructions and a detailed record of previous contacts. The product suite is designed for sophisticated call centers, which have evolved from customer service departments into personalized banking relationship managers. Call center agents not only handle client questions and help solve problems but also sell additional products and services. The Contact Management Suite gives the agents online instructions and prompts, aids in problem solving, fulfills literature requests and responds to customers' inquiries from a bank's Web site.

Besides its central role in the banking community, Fiserv also is active in the region's charitable events. The company supports the Make-A-Wish Foundation, American Heart Association, American Cancer Society, Susan B. Koman Breast Cancer Foundation, United Way and the Salvation Army's holiday gift collection, among others. Employees also take part in an annual People Make the Difference Week. Among the week's events, participants toss coins from the upper floor of the headquarters atrium, with proceeds going to charity, and those employees who drop a quarter into a container six floors below qualify for a paid day off.

Looking toward the future, James C. Puzniak, president of Fiserv Bank Servicing Division II, which includes the Pittsburgh operation, plans to enhance the company's lead in electronic services that allow clients to bank where, when and how they wish. The company makes it convenient for customers to conduct their business person-to-person, through an ATM machine, by phone or by Internet, which is the most promising growth area for tomorrow's banking. More and more, Fiserv is transforming the image of banking from a snail-like operation, with customers waiting in long lines for the next available teller, to a high-tech, high-speed electronic business.

As part of the company's commitment to effective partnerships, Fiserv Pittsburgh associates regularly review clients' needs.

Mellon Financial Corporation

MOST PITTSBURGH NATIVES WILL agree that the city of three rivers is known for more than a few things: terrific sports teams, a revitalized downtown, old steel mills and the Mellon name. What many don't realize is that the industrial revolution out of which Pittsburgh's steel mills were born began with an investment from a bank — T. Mellon & Sons' Bank.

The year was 1869, and on Smithfield Street sat a storefront operation furnished with a safe, a desk, an iron stove and some chairs. Retired Judge Thomas Mellon, an Irish immigrant, and his sons, Andrew W. and Richard B., had the opportunity to invest $10,000 in a man whose vision would change the industrial landscape: Henry Clay Frick. Mellon's investment provided both the capital and the fuel needed to drive a revolution. The bank has been funding dreams ever since.

In 1902 T. Mellon & Sons' Bank joined the national banking system as Mellon National Bank. Two years later it expanded the business by forming a foreign bureau that provided banking services for customer activity outside of the United States.

Throughout the 1920s Mellon's regional banking business was thriving. But with the impact of the Great Depression, FDR declared a bank holiday on March 4, 1933, in an effort to stabilize the financial system. Many banks across the nation closed their doors and never opened them again. But foresight and perseverance allowed Mellon to stay open and form Mellbank Corporation, a bank holding company for many western Pennsylvania banks. Both Mellon and the Mellbanks survived the stock market crash and continued providing much needed capital to the region.

After the crash and World War II, Mellon merged with Union Trust Company to become Mellon National Bank and Trust Company. The new company prospered in the post-war era as the banking house with the fifth-largest lending limit in the country. The merged organization was making its presence known and supplied loans to America's largest corporations, such as Ford and Alcoa. By the time the post-war era came to a close, Mellon ranked as one of the nation's largest banks.

Mellon soon capitalized on another vision that catapulted the organization into the future, becoming the first bank to buy a computer. In 1955 the model, an IBM 650, referred to by most as the "electronic brain," offered the same

One Mellon Center, Pittsburgh

power as today's pocket calculators. Its potential was what captured the vision of Mellon leaders. In 1958 Mellon automated its clearinghouse operations. Three years later, it became the first to sell software applications to other banks. By 1974, Mellon became one of the first banks to offer automated teller machines and allow international direct deposit.

In the early 1980s Mellon became more than a corporate banking institution. Retail expansion included mergers and acquisitions. Among them were Philadelphia-based The Girard Company; CCB Bancorp, Inc. of State College; Northwest Pennsylvania Corp. of Oil City; and Commonwealth National Financial Corporation of Harrisburg. By 1990 Mellon had purchased 54 branch offices — and later all — of PSFS, a leading savings institution in the Philadelphia market, from Meritor Savings Bank.

The company had survived a stock market crash, the Great Depression, two World Wars, major technological change and even natural disasters, and it had never lost money.

Meanwhile, the banking industry was changing, and Mellon saw the need to generate revenues beyond loans and fee-based services such as cash management. With the acquisition of The Boston Company in 1993 and a landmark merger with The Dreyfus Corporation six months later, Mellon surged to a position as a leader among bank managers of mutual funds. Mellon's presence as a banking and corporate powerhouse was furthered by its 1998 acquisitions of Denver-based Founders Asset Management, London-based Newton Management Limited, Miami-based United National Bank and Los Angeles-based 1st Business Bank.

Judge Thomas Mellon

In 1999 Mellon produced a new leadership team set to move the bank forward into a new century of global financial services. Led by Chairman and Chief Executive Office Martin G. McGuinn, the strategic focus of Mellon, now called Mellon Financial Corporation, was sharpened to become the best-performing financial services company, with a clear focus on serving customers and emphasizing its fee-based businesses.

Overall, Melon's asset management companies comprise the sixth-largest asset management group in the United States and one of the largest worldwide, with approximately $2.8 trillion in assets under management, administration or custody, including more than $500 billion under management.

The goal remains to give customers greater convenience, service, information and choice with the right balance between high-tech and "high touch." In fact, Mellon was named one of the three top banking-related companies in the United States in the *InformationWeek* 500 annual survey of top information technology innovators. And in a survey conducted by *Financial Times,* Mellon was ranked one of the five most respected global financial services companies.

That kind of innovation and service is keeping the name of Mellon consistent with the benchmark services for which it is known. From the birth of the steel, coke and aluminum industries to the evolution of one of today's largest global financial services companies, Mellon Financial Corporation continues to make its mark on Pittsburgh — and the world.

The PNC Financial Services Group

WITH ROOTS REACHING AS FAR back as the 18th century, including a bank that counted John Quincy Adams, Daniel Webster and Henry Wadsworth Longfellow among its depositors, The PNC Financial Services Group has grown through business development and acquisitions to become one of the largest diversified financial services firms in the United States.

Although many native Pittsburghers associate PNC with just one of its formative organizations — Pittsburgh National Bank — today's PNC comprises a strategic blend of acquisitions and internally developed businesses that are national in scope and span financial services markets outside of traditional banking. Drawing from its success as a major regional bank (the 1983 merger of Pittsburgh National Bank and Provident National Bank presaged the acquisition of numerous successful banks in Pennsylvania and adjoining states), today's PNC employs 26,000 people across the country and operates both traditional banking and asset management and processing businesses.

PNC Park is more than a new baseball park — it's a symbol of PNC's commitment to the economy, culture and people of Pittsburgh.

PNC Bank continues to be a leader in each of its primary regional markets: Delaware, Kentucky, New Jersey, Ohio and Pennsylvania. PNC Bank provides retail, small business and corporate banking services, has the ninth-largest ATM network, is a top 25 small business lender, has the ninth-largest treasury management business and is Pennsylvania's largest private placement agent.

A National Financial Services Company

While PNC Bank continues to expand in regional markets, the rest of PNC has become a growing national force in investment management and financial services. PNC has evolved to become a major national financial concern because of the organization's commitment to build new businesses and provide consistently high levels of innovation, technology and service to customers and shareholders.

Many of PNC's competitively positioned growth businesses — PNC Advisors, PNC Real Estate Finance, PNC Business Credit, PFPC and BlackRock — are national organizations with national marketing outreach. PNC Advisors is a top 10 manager of trust, high-net-worth and wealth management services, working along with its Hilliard Lyons and Hawthorn subsidiaries. PNC Real Estate Finance is one of the nation's leading providers of commercial and real estate finance products and services for investors and developers. PNC Business Credit is the nation's 10th-largest asset-based lender. PFPC, with headquarters in Delaware, is the nation's largest full-service mutual fund transfer agent. BlackRock, based in New York City, is the seventh-largest publicly traded asset manager, providing asset management services for nine out of the 10 largest U.S. companies.

These businesses grew as a result of the corporation's strategy to diversify PNC's mix of businesses. Over the past decade, PNC has evolved through the development and acquisition of nontraditional banking businesses. Important acquisitions include Hilliard Lyons, Midland Loan Services, BlackRock and First Data Corp.'s Investor Services Group (ISG).

Leveraging Technology for Growth

Advanced technology and automation have fueled PNC's growth while adding customer and shareholder value. PNC has leveraged technology not only to increase efficiencies but also to drive revenue growth through the introduction of leading-edge, technology-based products and services.

PNC's innovative approach has resulted in data center and information processing capabilities that have supported the growth of PNC's diversified businesses, establishing a solid technological foundation for the development of best-of-class businesses. The corporation's commitment to technology has also led to numerous online firsts in the financial services industry.

PNC Capital Markets offered the first municipal bond offering over the Internet, and nearly 25 percent of eligible retail customers bank online with PNC — one of the highest penetrations in the country.

Commitment to the Community

Chairman, President and CEO James E. Rohr is a leader involved in many civic, cultural and educational boards and initiatives in southwestern Pennsylvania.
©Mark Bolster

An important PNC corporate value is to invest in the communities where PNC does business. Many of the corporation's community initiatives focus on Pittsburgh, the home of PNC's corporate headquarters. But wherever the location, PNC's commitment of financial and human capital is multifaceted, focusing on the local economy, culture and people.

One example of how PNC's business objectives coincide with community needs is the PNC Firstside Center, a major new downtown building that is creating jobs for the residents of Pittsburgh while supplying PNC with a state-of-the-art, consolidated technology center.

PNC's support of local entertainment and culture is evident throughout Pittsburgh. The Pittsburgh Pirates major league baseball team plays its home games at PNC Park. PNC is the official bank of the Pittsburgh Steelers professional football team. PNC is a corporate partner and contributor to the Pittsburgh Cultural District, supporting Pittsburgh's music, arts and theater scenes.

Through The PNC Foundation and local United Way campaigns, PNC helps to stimulate regional economic development through the support of health and human services, culture and art, and other organizations that enhance living and working environments and improve the quality of life throughout southwestern Pennsylvania. In fact, PNC is one of only 6 percent of banks to earn an outstanding rating for community reinvestment, under the terms of the Community Reinvestment Act (CRA), from The Office of the Comptroller of the Currency. The CRA evaluation rates a bank's ability to provide loans, investments, access to services and outreach efforts in the low- to moderate-income communities it serves.

In addition to corporate efforts, PNC's Promise to Neighborhood Children program encourages PNC employees to volunteer time to programs focused on the well-being of children and youth. Through this initiative, PNC employees are pledging 1 million volunteer hours involving activities for children who need extra adult guidance and caring. From learning how to overcome obstacles and gain self-confidence to exploring reading and literacy activities, Promise to Neighborhood Children helps children become the best they can be.

From the 1800s to the new millennium, PNC has grown from a local bank into a national financial services leader, remembering along the way the people in the communities it serves.

PNC Firstside Center is creating jobs for the residents of Pittsburgh while supplying PNC with a state-of-the-art, consolidated technology center.

Yanni & Company Investment Advisors

Yanni & Company provides meaningful, measurable, and lasting value to clients.

YANNI & COMPANY INVESTMENT Advisors provides comprehensive, customized investment counseling for clients with investment portfolios ranging from $600,000 to $50 million. Motivated and knowledgeable professionals with access to proprietary tools and information, which have been gathered and maintained for over 25 years, as well as state-of-the-art systems and technology, gives Yanni & Company a competitive edge. Drawing information and expertise from its institutional roots, Yanni & Company develops investment plans for clients, allowing them to tap into a firm with the experience and reputation otherwise available only to those with over $50 million in assets.

Yanni & Company Investment Advisors is ready to provide its customized services for individuals and institutions investing $600,000 to $50 million.

Yanni Partners, Inc. and its predecessors have been providing investment consulting services to the institutional market place for over 25 years. With the proliferation of investment options throughout the 1980s, private investors and smaller institutional clients began to seek the wisdom of objective investment professionals to help them navigate the investment waterways. The answer came in 1990 with the creation of Yanni & Company Investment Advisors.

One key reason for Yanni & Company's success in helping clients meet their investment goals, is its commitment to remaining an independent and objective advisor. Yanni & Company does not sell any products nor does it accept any compensation from any source other than its clients. By remaining independent and operating strictly from clients' fees, Yanni & Company sticks with its clear-cut objective of choosing the best investment vehicles for its clients, with no qualms about possible conflicts of interest that could arise if the company were benefiting from selling commissioned products.

While providing services typically not found at this asset level, Yanni & Company dedicates itself to customizing its advice. Clients consistently meet and work with an Investment Strategist, who is one of the firm's principals. That means every time clients speak with their advisor, they are also speaking with an owner. The company advocates face-to-face meetings with clients at least quarterly. Strategists speak even more often with new clients and longtime investors who feel more comfortable discussing their investments more frequently. The company delivers personal attention by assigning no more than 20 clients to each Strategist.

Already Yanni & Company has developed multigenerational relationships with clients, continuing to serve the same families, as parents pass along their assets to children and grandchildren. Clients feel comfortable knowing these dedicated professionals will be active in the field for years to come and will provide the same level of stewardship and commitment to their children and grandchildren.

Yanni & Company will nurture these long-term relations as it steadily grows; continuing to provide needed expertise in this niche market while maintaining the personal touch so necessary for successful investing.

Satisfied clients have become the best advocates for Yanni & Company and have referred approximately 95 percent of the company's existing clients. Clearly, Yanni & Company provides meaningful, measurable, and lasting value to clients.

Yanni Partners, Inc.

EXCELLENCE, INTEGRITY AND respect form the cornerstone of Yanni Partners, Inc. The institutional investment-consulting firm begun in 1976 by James E. Yanni has delivered its promise of providing consulting to institutional portfolios so that the client can provide the resources necessary to fulfill its mission. That means that Yanni Partners' clients — corporations, hospitals, colleges and universities, endowments, foundations, labor unions, municipalities and religious organizations — can expect their assets to be monitored with an eye toward economic efficiency, proper diversification and controlled risk.

Although Yanni Partners serves clients in 25 states, the company that grew from the Fiduciary Consulting Group remains employee owned, firmly planted in Pittsburgh.

The firm made the strategic decision to develop its own in-house analytical capability to evaluate investment management firms for its clients so that it could vouch for the accuracy of the information it collects on behalf of its clients, rather than to rely on outside sources for the same information. This fact alone strengthens Yanni Partners' reliability in the marketplace. The value of their investment analytics is in the interpretation of the information provided by the deep staff of professionals that is in place to service their growing client base. The nearly 40-person firm is unique in that the senior consulting staff is composed of individuals whose educational, training and work experience is exclusively in portfolio analytics, with each senior consultant possessing an advanced degree along with the Chartered Financial Analyst designation. Unique to competitors, Yanni Partners requires the support staff to have this same educational background. The consulting support team is enrolled in the three-year course of study to obtain the Chartered Financial Analyst designation, and that depth of knowledge translates to creative, effective portfolio solutions for the clients. Yanni Partners consultants average 14 years of investment experience in treasury management, portfolio management, asset/liability management as well as plan sponsor experience. The staff's singular location in Pittsburgh provides an atmosphere for collaborative research, allowing the clients to benefit from the "best thinking" of this group of professionals.

Because Yanni Partners is strictly independent and provides no other services beyond institutional consulting, the firm keeps its focus on the client's best interest. The company obtains no benefit from recommending certain investment firms or investment products. Its advice is uncompromised.

Yanni Partners places a premium on interacting with clients to determine their business needs, their financial goals and their risk tolerances so that the portfolio can be positioned to meet the objectives of the clients. The firm provides a yearly symposium, the largest in this region, to discuss market trends, forecasts and investment issues specific to its client base. In this age of the information explosion, Yanni Partners believes that clients need solid explanations to make wise portfolio decisions in a volatile, confusing marketplace.

This client focus has allowed Yanni Partners to retain clients, in some instances, dating to when the company first formed. It has moved smoothly into the next generation of ownership and is forging new client partnerships across the country. A hallmark of Yanni Partners' success is that the majority of clients arrive on the recommendations of satisfied customers.

Yanni Partners continues to deliver on its promise of service. Their excellence in portfolio analytics allows hospitals to have the necessary resources to provide quality care to their communities, labor unions to provide retirement benefits to give dignity to their membership, colleges and universities to provide quality education and training, and nonprofits to continue their beneficial work. Yanni Partners' client commitment allows their clients to deliver on their promises as well.

The financial consultants at Yanni Partners are dedicated to serving their clients with data generated by in-house specialists.

Allegheny Personnel Services

ALLEGHENY PERSONNEL SERVICES has sported quite a few addresses on its letterhead since it opened in 1972. Its first was a one-room shop in the Jenkins Arcade, decorated with homemade drapes and secondhand furniture. Company founder Nancy Thomas typed out invoices on a manual typewriter and wrote paychecks in longhand.

A Monroeville branch opened in 1978 and allowed the growing firm to serve the corporate presence along the Parkway East corridor. Soon after, the firm took out 10 rooms in the Arrot building to expand its downtown presence. In 1988 several large contracts and the firm's complete automation necessitated a move to Two Oliver Plaza. The Moon Township branch opened in 1989 followed by a Wexford office in 1992.

With the firm's purchase by Personnel Group of America (PGA) in 1996, Allegheny Personnel Services (APS) became part of a billion-dollar, publicly held company and an elite network of nationwide temporary staffing companies. The acquisition also took the firm right back where it had started. Its downtown offices are now located in Fifth Avenue Place at the site of the old Jenkins Arcade.

Allegheny Personnel Services, a Personnel Group of America Company, has offices at Fifth Avenue Place as well as five other locations in the Pittsburgh and Harrisburg areas.

Today Allegheny Personnel Services offers temporary, permanent and temporary-to-hire staffing for businesses of all kinds. In addition to traditional temporary and seasonal noncore work force needs for administrative, secretarial, clerical, data entry and mail room employees, APS also trains telemarketing and call center associates as well as light technical and light industrial employees. Its six locations together supply more than 5,000 temporary employees to Pittsburgh businesses each year.

Although this seems a far cry from Thomas' one-room firm of yesteryear, a closer look reveals that what is important to the people of APS remains unchanged. Loyalty, commitment and responsiveness have always been the keys to APS' success, and they remain as such.

Affiliation with Personnel Group of America has given APS an infusion of technological and financial resources, but management and decision making remain local and autonomous. APS account executives take the time to know and understand their clients' businesses so they can do the best job of matching temporary associates to the specialized skill requirements of each client. With its fully automated service delivery system, APS can offer more efficient and timely service as well as customized reporting and invoicing.

APS' most valuable assets, however, are its people. The firm takes great pride in its associates' high level of training and their commitment to quality. Each APS branch is equipped with an automated software training center so associates can hone their skills and increase their marketability to a wide range of clients. Vacation, benefits and financial packages are available to long-term temporary associates who enjoy the flexibility and variety of temporary work. For the career "temp" or for anyone looking for a fresh start in the professional world, APS is the open door to a world of opportunity.

Pittsburgh has successfully negotiated the transition into the new economy. And Allegheny Personnel Services has been there, bringing innovative staffing solutions to old and new client companies alike.

Provident Agency

FIREFIGHTERS ARE OFTEN touted as heroes, saving property and lives. Today numerous emergency personnel are paid to risk life and limb, but in 1903, as today, most of Pennsylvania's firefighters remain volunteers. Third-generation family-owned Provident Agency, begun in 1903 by Willard Hopkins as a general insurance agency, quickly realized these heroes had no financial safety net.

In 1928, Provident began insuring western Pennsylvania volunteer firefighters, who had long been considered uninsurable by other insurance companies. And because more firefighters have died from stress-induced heart attacks than anything else, Provident pioneered heart attack coverage in 1962.

As the second-largest emergency personnel insurer in the United States, Provident is now licensed in 48 states and in the last three years has added satellite offices in Indianapolis, Indiana, Chattanooga, Tennessee, and York, Pennsylvania. Provident's ability to offer first class coverage and service has enabled emergency service organizations to recruit and retain their members, and accordingly, resulting in sustained growth and success for Provident.

According to President Chris Martin, while the volunteer pool shrinks, the retention of volunteers is vital to maintaining the high quality of service residents rely on. Volunteer services save Pennsylvania taxpayers millions each year. By providing benefits to volunteers, like disability coverage, group life and pensions, organizations can reward their volunteers with more than just a word of thanks.

A community-minded company, Provident supports organizations that make a difference, like the Coalition for Christian Outreach, the Highmark Caring Program, Hill District Ministries, Pittsburgh Experiment, and the Pittsburgh Leadership Foundation. Company leaders also have firsthand knowledge of the dangers emergency personnel face. Four Provident employees are members in volunteer fire companies and have served in both line and administrative capacities. Another employee is an RN and former paramedic.

The Provident management team of Barry Balliet, Dave Gibson and Ulrich Mauser, along with the rest of the staff is politically active, taking major roles with the Pennsylvania Fire and Emergency Services Institute and National Volunteer Fire Council, which is an advocacy group to Congress. To remain abreast of current issues and industry concerns, Provident employees connect with the nation's fire service leaders at the Congressional Fire Services Institute in Washington, D.C. The company assists in the education of state and federal legislatures about emergency services and the role they play in society.

Community involvement, commitment to affordable quality insurance and a cutting-edge approach to insurance products and coverage help Provident maintain high client retention in a business where loyalty is rare. In Allegheny County, Provident insures over 90 percent of the county's 215 departments and a number of those have been insured continuously for over half a century.

Provident plans to continue its steady growth, offering full-coverage insurance to firefighters and other emergency personnel, enabling the nation's heroes to continue being heroes.

Education

Pittsburgh educational institutions provide citizens of all ages with learning opportunities in diverse subjects and environments.

Chatham College

AS PITTSBURGH MOVES FROM steel to software and from heavy industry to high technology, one thing remains constant: this city has always been a major educational center. Today one of its oldest and best educational institutions — Chatham College — is one of the few remaining undergraduate women's colleges in the United States.

Founded in 1869, Chatham is the oldest private educational institution in Pittsburgh. Reverend William Trimble Beatty, pastor of Shadyside Presbyterian Church, led a group of forward-thinking Pittsburghers to establish the college — then Pennsylvania Female College — to give women an education comparable to that which men received. At the new college, women would do what at that time was considered unthinkable: study challenging academic disciplines, including science.

After sitting in the basement of Chatham's library for 70 years, this original Louis Comfort Tiffany window, which was commissioned by alumnae in 1889, was restored to its original grandeur in 2000. The window, one of the oldest surviving Tiffany windows, now hangs in the Kresge Atrium of the college's science complex where it serves as a reminder of more than 130 years of women's education at Chatham.

The college's first home, overlooking Fifth Avenue in Shadyside, was an 11-acre tract at the George Berry estate, then the largest private residence in Allegheny County. Today the campus spans 32 acres surrounded by Fifth Avenue and historic Woodland Road.

Chatham was founded in 1869 to provide an education which was comparable to men, and that extended to fitness and wellness. Here, the Pennsylvania College for Women's field hockey team poses for a photo c. 1920s. Today, the college continues to promote fitness and wellness and boasts six NCAA teams, including the first women's collegiate ice hockey team in the state.

Although the college's location and mission remained constant, the name was changed in 1890 to Pennsylvania College for Women and in 1955 to Chatham College in honor of William Pitt, the first Earl of Chatham. More importantly, the curriculum was adapted through the years to reflect the changing needs of women. The arts, speech, and philosophy supplemented the initial offerings of Latin, French, German, mathematics, history, English, natural sciences, and fitness and wellness. After World War II, the college became one of the first to add a bachelor of science degree.

Today Chatham College continues to be a pioneer in women's education. Science is still a Chatham mainstay — a remarkable 25 percent of students graduate in the sciences — but the college offers its more than 1,000 students 50 programs, including undergraduate liberal arts and pre-professional majors, master's degrees, post-baccalaureate teaching certification, and other professional certificates. The college's 12-1 student-to-faculty ratio gives students the ability to learn and express their individuality in an intimate setting. Chatham also prides itself on grounding its undergraduates in a quality program of liberal arts and sciences regardless of their major, an experience capped off by the "senior tutorial" — an original research project guided one-on-one by a Chatham professor.

Since 1993 when the college first added coeducational graduate programs to its offerings, graduate education has been an important part of Chatham's mission. The college now boasts 14 master's programs — some nationally ranked by *U.S. News & World Report*. The first doctoral program was added in 2001. In 1998 Chatham College North was established in Wexford, Pennsylvania, offering undergraduate, graduate, and professional certification courses.

Chatham has long utilized its location in Pittsburgh to develop collaborations that are mutually rewarding to the college and the community. Chatham regularly partners with other Pittsburgh colleges and universities in offering special classes, seminars and lectures. For example, Chatham students can take physics and engineering courses at Carnegie Mellon University while Carnegie Mellon students can earn teacher certification at Chatham, and Chatham science students often work alongside researchers in organizations such as Magee-Women's Hospital and Bayer Corporation to gain professional research experience.

Chatham students and the Pittsburgh community also benefit from the initiatives and educational missions of the college's centers of excellence — the Rachel Carson Institute, the Pittsburgh Teachers Institute, and the Center for Women in Politics in Pennsylvania.

The Rachel Carson Institute, founded in honor of 1929 alumna and environmental activist Rachel Carson, advances environmental education and awareness. The Pittsburgh Teachers Institute, a collaboration among Chatham, Carnegie Mellon University, and the Pittsburgh Public Schools, helps classroom teachers learn new topics and further develop their curricula and teaching skills. The Center for Women in Politics in Pennsylvania is the first statewide academic center to focus specifically on women's political involvement in Pennsylvania. The center provides training and education in applied politics — a natural fit for a college whose political training and engagement of its students dates back to the early 1900s.

While Chatham's Pittsburgh connections are an integral part of its educational activity, Chatham is nevertheless a national college with international connections. *U.S. News & World Report* 2000 ranked Chatham fourth in the nation for the percentage of students who study abroad. Chatham students can travel during their sophomore year with faculty and classmates to varying destinations. Additionally, through exchange partnerships with Doshisha Women's College in Kyoto, Japan, and Seoul Women's College in Seoul, Korea, Chatham students go abroad for longer study, and international students attend Chatham.

Chatham's on-campus international initiatives are highlighted by The Global Focus Program. Since 1995 the campus has concentrated each year on one country or region of the world for study through coursework, service learning, visiting authors, scholars, experts, exhibits, and cultural events. Because all events are open to the public, the Chatham community and the broader Pittsburgh community are linked in a common area of inquiry and celebration. Leaders in the local international communities sit on the Global Focus advisory board and help plan events for each year.

A true Pittsburgh landmark, Chatham has helped pave previously unknown paths and given students from Pittsburgh and beyond the preparation they need to create their own pathways to personal and professional success.

The Chatham College campus is distinguished by historic mansions built for Pittsburgh's most prominent families. Many were donated to the college and have been converted for use as residence halls and offices. The urban campus was designated an arboretum by the American Association of Botanical Gardens and Arboreta in 1998.

Dr. Esther Barazzone, President since 1992, is an international spokeswoman for women's education and has been invited to speak in Korea, Japan and Pakistan.

Chatham College is one of only 162 colleges in the nation (and the only one in Pittsburgh) to make *U.S. News & World Report*'s list of best "National Liberal Arts Colleges." Students from across the globe come to Pittsburgh every year to attend this nationally ranked liberal arts college, one of the country's few thriving women's colleges.

La Roche College

AN INDEPENDENT, PRIVATE, CO-educational Catholic college founded in 1963 by the Sisters of Divine Providence, La Roche College has grown to become an educational institution with genuine international impact. From its scenic 80-acre campus in the North Hills of Pittsburgh, La Roche reaches out to students from the United States and other nations, offering the promise of more fruitful lives for individuals and the hope of a better world for all.

The college is named for Marie de la Roche, a French woman of noble birth who became the first superior of the Congregation of Divine Providence. From its initial role as a college for religious sisters to its current incarnation as an institution for students from around the world, La Roche offers high-quality educational opportunities that reflect its Catholic heritage and the dynamism and spirit of its founding and sponsoring congregation.

In 1965 the college admitted its first lay students and conferred degrees on its first five graduates. Two years later, the college expanded through the construction of the first college building, the John J. Wright Library.

Not long after, La Roche encountered financial difficulties. The congregation seriously considered closing the college, but such was the impact that La Roche had already made on the community, that students, state officials and community leaders urged the congregation and Sister De la Salle Mahler, the college president, to give it another chance.

The Board of Trustees responded by amending the college's charter in 1970, establishing La Roche as an independent, coeducational Catholic institution. La Roche also diversified its course offerings through its affiliation with the Art Institute of Pittsburgh, which led to new areas of study — graphic and interior design — which continue to be among the college's strongest programs.

By 1973 the revitalized college earned accreditation from the Middle States Association of Colleges and Secondary Schools, tripled its enrollment and built its first residence facility. Sister Mahler had successfully led the college through a period of uncertainty and laid the groundwork for a bright future.

A Growing, Changing Campus

The 1970s saw an enrollment boom that necessitated an ambitious building program, including the construction of two new residence halls. The college launched its first capital campaign in 1979 to finance the construction of a science building. The success of the campaign exceeded expectations and the Palumbo Science Center opened in 1980.

The college continued to grow through the 1980s with an expanded, strengthened curriculum and active building program. La Roche marked its 25th anniversary in 1987 with the dedication of the $2.5 million Zappala College Center. The Magdalen Chapel was added in 1990.

The current president, Monsignor William A. Kerr, focused his leadership throughout the 1990s on expanding the college's global reach, raising its visibility, enhancing its financial resources, and broadening its academic, cultural and athletic programs. The Kerr Fitness and Sports Center, a 1,000-seat, modern sports and fitness facility, was completed in 1993.

Athletic facilities include a baseball field, soccer field, softball field, outdoor tennis/basketball courts, aerobics room/dance studio, gymnasium, indoor track, racquetball courts and a weight room.

The Pacem in Terris Institute

With the Pacem in Terris Institute (Latin for Peace on Earth), President Kerr expanded the college's vision globally. The institute brings students from conflict, post-conflict and developing regions of the world to study at La Roche.

The program provides scholarships and assistance to international students while encouraging greater global and transcultural awareness on the part of the La Roche community. International students from 30 countries constitute 25 percent of La Roche's full-time student body. Students are chosen by their countries for their academic and personal potential and promise to return to their homelands upon completion of their studies to work for the peace and prosperity of their regions.

The institute also exposes the entire college community to unique cultures, perspectives and learning opportunities not available at colleges with less culturally diverse student populations.

The college's international impact is also reflected in its governance structures. The boards of the college and the Pacem in Terris Institute include Kim Dae-jung, president of the Republic of South Korea; Queen Rania Al-Abdullah, first lady of the Hashemite Kingdom of Jordan; and Janet Museveni, first lady of the Republic of Uganda.

Varied Curriculum and Activities

Today, La Roche College offers more than 40 undergraduate majors, 20 undergraduate minors and three graduate programs. Major areas of excellence include graphics and design, the sciences, education, nursing and the graduate program in human resources management. Nursing and health-related courses of study are augmented by affiliation agreements with hospitals and other health care institutions in the Pittsburgh area. Engineering majors can earn their degrees at La Roche through a 3/2 agreement with the University of Pittsburgh. State-of-the-art computers, labs and technology support all of these programs.

Special programs and centers at the college include the Center for International Business and Culture, the Center for the Study of Ethics, The Washington Center for Internships and Academic Seminars, the Writers' Center, the College in High School SCHOLAR Program, and the Challenge Program for Gifted Elementary School Children.

As it has grown as an educational institution, La Roche has also expanded the cultural and entertainment amenities it offers to its home community. The college's Performing Arts/Ballet Program conducts performances on campus and at area high schools. The works of student and professional artists are regularly displayed in the college's Cantellops Art Gallery. La Roche fields 12 intercollegiate athletic teams competing in Division III of the NCAA and in the Allegheny Mountain Collegiate Conference. It hosts numerous high school athletic championships and tournaments at its attractive sports facilities.

La Roche College has undergone a number of transformations throughout its history to become the vibrant institution that it is today. One thing that has remained constant throughout its history is the spirit that animates the institution. It is the same spirit that has animated the Congregation of Divine Providence since its foundation 150 years ago. It is that spirit that will lead La Roche College for many decades to come.

Penn State New Kensington

SOME YEARS AGO, THE DISTINguished president of one of the nation's oldest colleges pondered the question of how best to define his school. After a thoughtful pause, he smiled and said, "Well, what we do is make doctors and lawyers and captains of industry."

Penn State New Kensington — one of 12 regional campuses in the University's Commonwealth College system — produces some of each of those and much more. But, true to the University's long and proud traditions, the operating principle for the 72-acre campus snug in the rolling green hills 30 miles northeast of Pittsburgh focuses not on production, but rather service.

"That is our iron imperative, and what defines us best," says Dr. Carol A. Rush, campus executive officer. "We are here to serve... both our students and the people of this region."

As Pennsylvania's major land-grant university, Penn State is indeed obligated to service. Like Topsy, the university, founded in 1855, simply grew to the point that University Park (formerly "the main campus") reached its maximum capacity in the mid-20th century. That rapid growth led to the formation of Commonwealth College locations offering baccalaureate degree programs. Penn State New Kensington was one of them and in the turbulent 1960s underwent rapid development and growth.

Service, of course, usually bespeaks the need for steady growth. Penn State New Kensington is growing in any number of ways: More four-year degree programs, including the new Bachelor of Science in Business and Applied Psychology, and the Master's in Teaching and Curriculum; More students; More faculty members; More corporate partnerships to meet the needs of businesses in the region, including those with such giants as IBM, ALCOA and Oracle, all of which helped fund the school's new Information Technology Center.

Photo by Dr. John P. McNavage

The obligation to serve also has more to do than anything else in determining the school's current priorities. For example, Penn State New Kensington recently initiated new degree programs in Human Development and Family Studies and Information Sciences and Technology when research indicated a critical need in the region for well-educated workers in both fields.

Historically, Penn State and the New Kensington campus have been about responding to the Commonwealth's ever-changing social and economic needs. It is not melodramatic to say that those responses have helped shape the world... the manner in which people live, play and work.

The University touches lives in dozens of ways people never consider. Like ice cream? Penn State professors taught Ben & Jerry how to make it. Play golf? Nine of every ten courses in the country use turfgrass developed at Penn State. Need to carry an umbrella today? One of every four meteorologists in the nation is a Penn State grad.

Penn State has long been about service to its students and the community. The first African-American in space was a Penn State alum. Penn State research produced the world's first heart pacemaker and it was the first university licensed to operate a nuclear reactor. It produced the writer who wrote arguably the greatest movie ever made, *Casablanca*. Penn State even grew the first commercially successful geranium.

Indeed, the New Kensington campus owes its very existence to service. The school was founded in 1958 as the result of a study indicating a need for additional higher education in the Alle-Kiski valley.

The campus has since evolved from humble beginnings in an abandoned high school building in the industrial river valley city of New Kensington to the scenic campus on state Route 780 in Upper Burrell Township.

After classes were held in old school buildings for five years, the Aluminum Company of America (ALCOA) gave the University thirty-five acres on a heavily forested ridge four miles east of New Kensington. In September of 1966, classes convened in the Engineering Building — the first of ten university buildings — which today houses one of only three campus biomedical laboratories in the country. Two years later, the science, activities, faculty and administration, and library

Department of University Publications

needs of our growing number of non-traditional students," Dr. Rush says.

However, Penn State New Kensington also retains a number of advantages for the traditional student. More than 70 percent receive some sort of financial aid; the wooded campus is serene and quiet; and at a near all-time high of 987 students, it is still small enough to be friendly and safe. The average class size is 30 and a faculty of 41, nearly half of whom hold their doctorates, is traditionally involved with its students. The school's academic reputation is such that it draws the highest SAT scores of any of Penn State's Commonwealth College campuses. The teacher-student ratio is 23-to-1. The school's Computer Center, with a 5-to-1 ratio of students to machines, is state of the art.

"We're proud of those kinds of numbers," Dr. Rush says, "but I think the Penn State New Kensington community is most pleased with the fact that we are doing a good job for both our students and the people of this region."

buildings were completed and included additional labs and the campus art gallery.

That year, 27 additional acres were purchased from a neighboring farmer and in short order, there followed: a Health and Physical Education complex, including the PSNK Field House; a 325-seat thrust stage theatre, and a Student Learning Center. In the late 1980s, a capital campaign paved the way for a Science and Technology Center that opened in 1990 and a decade later, the Conference Center and Classroom Building was dedicated.

Students at Nittany Lion athletic contests traditionally chant, "We are Penn State." What does it mean? Well, on the New Kensington campus, that "are" has a variety of meaningful shadings.

Certainly technology would have to be considered a factor in defining the campus. Six of the 10 associate degree programs offered have to do with one form of technology or another, as do two of the five baccalaureate degree programs, IST and Electro-Mechanical Engineering Technology.

The stone lions guarding the driveway to the school are no more part of the campus than are its ten specialized laboratories and new Information Technology Center.

Still, the needs of students and the community have mandated that Penn State New Kensington develop academic virtues beyond those of a technological nature. Many students come to the campus to complete the first two years of one of the university's 160 baccalaureate degree programs and an increasing number are staying to finish baccalaureate degrees. About 90 percent live off campus; a slightly disproportionate number are non-traditional.

"One of the things we mean when we emphasize service is facilitating the academic growth and meeting the diverse

Photo by Dr. John P. McNavage

Pittsburgh Technical Institute

SINCE OPENING IN 1946, Pittsburgh Technical Institute (PTI) has made the necessary changes to stay on the razor-sharp edge of training students in fields that meet industries' needs. Sometimes growth has come student by student, sometimes by leaps and bounds, as PTI added entire programs, schools and divisions. But in five decades of change, success always has been measured by the same standards: the placement of each PTI graduate in his or her field and the performance of every PTI graduate on the job.

PTI began by offering its School of Management Engineering program in a downtown Pittsburgh hotel in the 1940s. About 20 years later, it introduced a drafting curriculum, which became its specialty. In the 1980s, PTI became the first school east of the Mississippi River to add computer-aided drafting to its curriculum. Now, the accredited, licensed post-secondary school has forged about a dozen programs to meet marketplace needs, successfully evolving from pencil-and-paper technologies to desired skills of the Digital Age, such as electronics, computer systems and Web site design. Coursework includes computer programming, electronics, graphic design, hospitality, multimedia, computer-aided drafting, computer and network systems, accounting, marketing, business, travel and tourism, and Microsoft networking.

Successful graduate employment is key to PTI's success and growth.

Under the leadership of President J.R. McCartan, faculty, students and the institution itself have focused on the growth and fields of the future. Since McCartan's arrival at PTI in 1990, the school has expanded explosively. Penn Technical Institute, a noted electronics school, joined with PTI in the 1990s, as did the Boyd School, which specializes in the travel and hospitality industries.

Internships, industry-led projects, student activities and community service projects complement the student's academic preparation.

Currently, PTI draws students from two-thirds of the counties in Pennsylvania, 14 other states and foreign countries. Its aim is to reach beyond these borders to help more students achieve their goals and to grow as the school itself has grown. Before the 1990s, PTI worked with several hundred full-time students. Within a decade, the full-time student enrollment soared to more than 2,000.

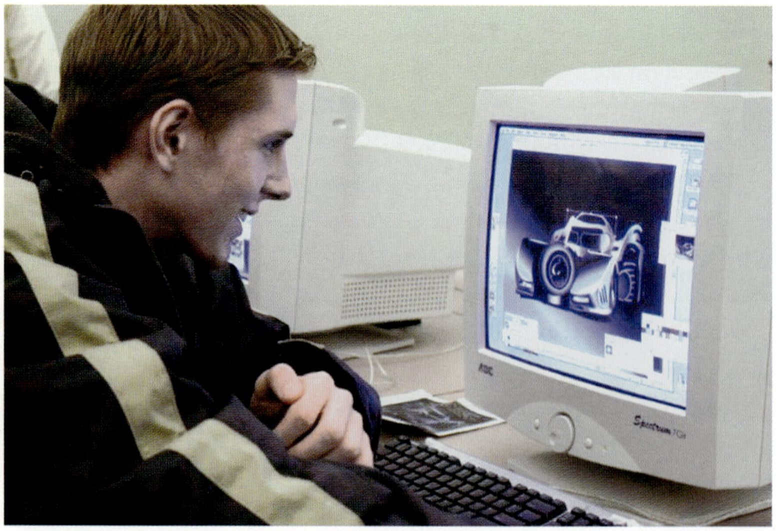

The added enrollment and programs spurred the opening of a new campus in 2000. The school continues to operate its downtown center and the new, 180-acre facility in North Fayette Township, near major highways and the Pittsburgh International Airport, has ample space for expansion. The contemporary site is equipped with more than $1.6 million in computer hardware and software, laboratories and classrooms.

Two-year degrees can be completed in morning, afternoon or evening/weekend sessions. Sessions start in July, October and January to accommodate schedules of recent high school graduates as well as those who already are in the workplace.

These changes and a multitude of others have occurred because of the school's hand-in-glove relationship with businesses needing the skills PTI students learn. The school taps working professionals to serve on advisory boards for each course of study to ensure that PTI programs keep pace with changing workplace demands.

Faculty members are required to have industry experience so they can replicate the challenges of the working world in their classrooms. Faculty members and staff maintain the school's standard of excellence with assistance from PTI's Center for Teaching and Learning, where they can update their skills in a variety of topics, from using the latest software to sharpening listening skills.

As an employee-owned institution, PTI has a staff committed to making sure the school and its students succeed. All employees, from president to student services, from house-keeping to graduate services, contribute to facilitating students' career goals by creating a learning environment that provides general and career-focused education and developing professional and life skills. Financial aid specialists assist students in applying for loans and scholarships. School-sponsored housing is available in the community and students enjoy extracurricular activities on and off campus.

As a two-year school, PTI provides the most direct route to its students' goals. Articulation agreements with four-year institutions allow PTI students to continue their education, if desired.

The required last-semester internship is far from the only bridge PTI students build with professionals in their chosen fields. In partnership with PTI, businesses bring their projects to the school for student input. These industry-led projects help businesses as well as students, who gain experience in resolving real-life situations, from developing menus for new restaurants to designing company logos or establishing Web sites.

PTI's five-year "Success Report" shows its alumni working for corporations like RPS, located just down the road from the school, for major airlines such as Northwest and US Airways, engineering firms such as Michael Baker Jr., manufacturers such as Alcoa Corp., General Nutrition Center and U.S. Steel Corp., hospitals such as UPMC, universities such as Carnegie Mellon and the University of Pittsburgh, architects such as Burt Hill Kossar Rittleman, communication firms such as Verizon and the Pittsburgh Post-Gazette, travel and hospitality firms such as Marriott, the Caribbean Information Office, even foreign embassies. Because some firms have been so pleased with the performance of PTI graduates, entire departments within certain companies are composed of PTI alumni.

Others in the business environment have recognized the school's contributions. PTI has won the Fitz Award for the Advancement of Women and consistently places among the top 100 fastest-growing western Pennsylvania companies as rated by the Pittsburgh Business Times.

After students graduate, PTI remains a touchstone. Alumni, as well as the latest class of students, are encouraged to use the school's Graduate Services Department, where more than 20 full-time staff members help to prepare students for job placement. Several staff members are specifically assigned to work with alumni seeking new employment opportunities. Alumni also can take advantage of the free brush-up courses PTI offers them. Part of the school's purpose is to continually help reposition people — and itself — as marketplaces and their needs evolve.

Students and their careers remain the focus of the school, but PTI also places importance on giving to others, whether through providing gallery space for community art shows and other functions, volunteering help to improve reading skills of local school students, or cooperating with area chambers of commerce. Through these efforts, PTI and its students establish themselves as a major support system for surrounding communities.

Community service underlines the commitment Pittsburgh Technical Institute makes to its motto: "Our greatest contribution to mankind is to be sure that every staff and faculty member cares that every student every day learns and grows and feels like a real human being."

PTI offers prospective students two Pittsburgh area locations: the North Fayette Campus, pictured left and just minutes from Pittsburgh International Airport, and the Pittsburgh Center, convienent to downtown parking and public transportation.

Slippery Rock University of Pennsylvania

FOR MORE THAN A CENTURY Slippery Rock University has fulfilled an important role in educating more than 50,000 men and women. The institution opened its doors to students on March 26, 1889, as Slippery Rock State Normal School, one of several normal schools throughout Pennsylvania that originally served as a training ground for teachers.

The university claims its name from nearby Slippery Rock Creek where, according to legend, a contingent of soldiers from Fort Pitt made a daring escape from a large party of Seneca Indians in 1779. The soldiers had intended to stop Indian raids on area settlements, but when they encountered the Senecas, the soldiers discovered they were outnumbered. Fleeing for their lives, the soldiers crossed the creek at a place where the streambed consisted of large, smooth rocks. Because of the heavy boots they wore, the soldiers crossed the creek safely. However the Senecas, who wore smooth-bottomed moccasins, slipped and fell on the rocks allowing the soldiers to escape. The Indians called the stream *Wechachochapohka*, which means "a slippery rock." The name was so colorful that it was also adopted by the surrounding village of Centreville, as the town of Slippery Rock was once known.

Slippery Rock State Normal School was founded by local residents to meet the area's educational training needs. The school's first president was James E. Morrow, the grandfather of Anne Morrow Lindbergh, wife of the famed aviator.

From Normal School to University

The Commonwealth of Pennsylvania purchased Slippery Rock State Normal School and other state normal schools in 1926 to establish a state system of teachers colleges. The Pennsylvania Department of Education assigned areas of academic focus for each of the colleges, giving Slippery Rock a concentration on health and physical education, still among the areas of expertise for which the school has established a national reputation for excellence.

For the next three decades, Slippery Rock grew as a college focused solely on teacher education. In 1960 the institution re-established itself as a liberal arts college, offering a variety of courses of study and was renamed Slippery Rock State College. The expanded curriculum sparked a period of rapid enrollment growth. From 1960 to 1970 enrollment climbed from 1,314 to 5,446.

Today Slippery Rock University of Pennsylvania is a full-fledged university, one of the 14 state-owned universities that are Pennsylvania's State System of Higher Education. "The Rock" enjoys an enrollment of 7,000 students who receive instruction from 400 faculty members (70 percent with Ph.D.s) in more than 100 undergraduate, graduate and doctoral programs.

Doctor of Physical Therapy students at Slippery Rock University learn their profession in a state-of-the-art physical therapy building opened in 2001. Slippery Rock's is the only accredited DPT program in the state.

Throughout SRU's history, enrollment growth has paralleled an active building and expansion program. One of the largest campuses in Pennsylvania, SRU is situated on 600 acres just 50 minutes north of Pittsburgh, providing students with easy access to the cultural amenities of a metropolitan city. The university's 48 buildings are located amidst woods, streams, ponds and open spaces. Recent campus additions include the Robert N. Aebersold Student Recreation Center, a garden-style apartment complex and the state-of-the-art Physical Therapy Building. Plans are underway for a new Science and

Technology Building, the new 1,500-seat Critchfield Baseball Park and restoration of Carruth-Rizza Hall.

SRU's leadership in environmental studies provides students with learning opportunities at nearby Moraine State Park, Pymatuming State Park, Jennings Environmental Education Center, McKeever Environmental Learning Center and at the Marine Science Library on Wallops Island, Virginia. The university has also established a satellite facility in Wexford, just north of Pittsburgh.

The columns of North Hall symbolize the rock solid education that has been offered at Slippery Rock University for more than 112 years.

Achieving Rock Solid Levels of Excellence

Drawing from its tradition as a teachers college with a focus on health and physical education, The Rock has built a solid reputation for excellence in related courses of study. The university offers one of the few doctoral programs in physical therapy in the world and is a leader in environmental studies. Many active coaches, athletic trainers and sports management professionals are Slippery Rock alumni.

SRU continues to build upon the excellence for which it's already known. President G. Warren Smith recently led a major reorganization of academic departments and colleges to increase visibility for nationally distinctive programs and improve coordination and enhance opportunities for interdisciplinary collaboration.

The reorganization resulted in new alignments of departments within the university's four colleges and new names for three of the colleges. The College of Business, Information and Social Sciences includes the School of Business (management and marketing, finance and economics, and accounting) and the departments of communication, computer science and information systems, government and public affairs, military science, and sociology/anthropology/social work. The College of Health, Environment and Science includes the School of Physical Therapy and the departments of allied health; exercise and rehabilitative sciences; biology; chemistry and physics; geology, geography and the environment; mathematics; nursing; parks and recreation; environmental education; and psychology. The College of Humanities, Fine and Performing Arts includes the departments of art, dance, English, history, modern languages and culture, music, philosophy and theatre. The College of Education continues the Slippery Rock tradition of giving prospective teachers a solid educational foundation.

Slippery Rock's academic programs are uniquely designed to support the university's vision statement: *Slippery Rock University will excel as a caring community of lifelong learners connecting with the world.* SRU's "World as Community" emphasis exposes students to the importance of international studies and service-learning activities.

Student and athletic life at SRU have become important facets of the community. Slippery Rock athletics are well known for excellence both locally and nationally. In fact, Rocket football scores are often announced all over the country. Athletic programs at "The Rock" include men's baseball, basketball, cross country, soccer, swimming, wrestling, football, judo, track and field, tennis, golf, water polo, and indoor track; and women's cross country, tennis, volleyball, soccer, field hockey, track and field, softball, basketball, swimming, judo, water polo, tennis, and indoor track. The College of Humanities, Fine and Performing Arts also sponsors cultural events throughout the community.

Slippery Rock University has emerged from a local teaching institution to a world-class university, achieving new levels of excellence and providing a "rock solid" educational foundation for the leaders and professionals of the future.

The national award-winning Aebersold Student Recreation Center is a focal point on the spacious 600-acre campus at The Rock.

University of Pittsburgh

ON THE FRONTIER OF THE 21ST century, the University of Pittsburgh has become one of the most highly respected institutions of higher learning in America. Founded by Hugh Henry Brackenridge, the school was chartered on February 28, 1787, as Pittsburgh Academy. More than 200 years later, the University of Pittsburgh has evolved in extraordinary ways.

Fondly known to students and alumni as "Pitt," the University is a major provider of top-quality higher education in its region, one of the nation's largest producers of pioneering research, and a leading American institution that creatively partners with the rest of the world.

The central landmark of the University of Pittsburgh campus is the 42-story Cathedral of Learning, the tallest school building in the Western Hemisphere.

Mark A. Nordenberg, the University's 17th chancellor, oversees a Pittsburgh campus of 16 undergraduate, graduate and professional schools, as well as regional campuses in Bradford, Greensburg, Johnstown and Titusville, Pennsylvania. He is the former dean of the University of Pittsburgh Law School and has been a member of the University community since 1977. "A community of intellectuals is, by definition, committed to the power of the mind and bound together by its interest in ideas. Certainly, that is one important dimension of life at Pitt," says Nordenberg. "But a university should be an institution with a heart — an institution that values nothing more than the potential that exists within its people."

Formerly a private institution, the University of Pittsburgh became state-related in 1966, establishing a relationship with the Commonwealth of Pennsylvania that has benefited both partners. Looking back over the three decades of Pitt's state-related status, Nordenberg sees an era characterized by accomplishment, growth and a steady rise in intellectual stature for the University, with far-reaching effects for the citizens of Pennsylvania.

During the past three decades, Pittsburgh has conferred nearly 200,000 degrees, more than 40 percent of them reflecting the graduate-level learning experience often essential for success in today's increasingly complex and competitive world.

In recent years, University of Pittsburgh students have achieved unusually high levels of academic attainment. For the year 2000, another student was awarded a Marshall Scholarship, and in the past 15 years, Pitt has had more Rhodes and Marshall scholars than any other college or university in Pennsylvania, public or private.

The University continues to attract the best and the brightest students. The five-year period from 1995-1999 recorded a 60 percent increase in freshman applications and superior quality:

Mark A. Nordenberg is the 17th chancellor of the University of Pittsburgh.

55 percent of the 1999 freshman class ranked in the top 20 percent of their high school class and 30 percent ranked in the top 10 percent. The combined freshman SAT score for the 1999 fall class was 26 points higher than in 1995, and 20 percent of this class was eligible for the University's prestigious Honors College. In 1999 Pitt undergraduate students were awarded four National Science Foundation Fellowships, three Goldwater Scholarships and the only Udall Scholarship in Pennsylvania.

Pitt has earned international recognition for world-class quality of programs in a diversity of disciplines such as transplantation surgery — on average one transplant is performed at the University of Pittsburgh Medical Center every 18 hours of every day — and in philosophy. The University boasts two of the top five philosophy departments in the country and the world's leading center in the philosophy of science.

Pitt has been elected to membership in the Association of American Universities, the top 60 research universities in North America. The University's recent breakthroughs in research include the development of environmentally safe "green" steel, discovery of a new planetary system within our galaxy, and the first applications of gene therapy techniques in the treatment of rheumatoid arthritis.

In 1956 at the University of Pittsburgh, Jonas Salk developed the vaccine that conquered polio. Polio had been considered the most feared disease in America.

An important dimension to the growth and development of a student is a balance between learning and co-curricula activities. The University of Pittsburgh has the proud tradition of competing in Division I sports and is a member of the Big East Conference. The Pitt Arts Program acquaints students with the fine and performing arts of the city of Pittsburgh. Cultural attractions include the symphony, opera, ballet, museums and the theater. And, for the professional sports-minded fans, the winning teams of the Steelers, Pirates and Penguins call Pittsburgh home.

Recently, Pitt's board of trustees, working closely with Chancellor Nordenberg, adopted the "University of Pittsburgh: 2000-2005" document that emphasizes the University's commitment to a continued pursuit of excellence in core academic enterprises — undergraduate education, graduate and professional education, and research. More broadly, the document asserts

The University of Pittsburgh has approximately 26,000 graduate and undergraduate students on campus in Oakland and 6,000 students at its four regional campuses.

that "by aggressively supporting the advancement of Pitt's academic mission, we will clearly and consistently demonstrate that this is one of the finest and most productive universities in the world."

Says Nordenberg, "We must become even stronger and more innovative in these challenging times — true to the work ethic of Western Pennsylvania, rich in intellectual rigor and committed in every respect to effectively preparing students for life and careers in the 21st century."

One of the largest employers in the Pittsburgh area with 9,000 employees, Pitt has a very strong institutional commitment to the people and economy of the region. Nearly 60,000 Pitt alumni live and work in Allegheny County where they earn $3.4 billion per year in salary and wages and pay millions in taxes.

In the past 15 years, the University of Pittsburgh has had more Rhodes and Marshall scholars than any other college or university in Pennsylvania, public or private.

Nordenberg affirms that "the strength of the University is directly dependent upon the strength of the region. It is also true, more than ever, that the strength of the region requires a strong University of Pittsburgh. We are a major economic force in the region. And by expanding the existing base of knowledge, we help people to lead fuller, healthier, more productive lives."

As Pitt fulfills its missions for the new century, it remains a place of enduring tradition. "Over the course of the last 213 years, this University has been the site of many high victories — individual and institutional," says Nordenberg. "But if we creatively apply our shared wisdom and have faith in our ability to successfully pursue lofty goals, I have no doubt that our greatest victories are yet to come."

Pittsburgh Theological Seminary

IN 1794 THE VISION THAT WOULD become the Pittsburgh Theological Seminary (PTS) started on the edge of the wilderness in a log cabin with six students and one teacher. The seminary flourished in this land settled by Presbyterians and evolved into a dynamic institution with farther-reaching effects through a series of mergers and acquisitions. In 1959 it grew even stronger with a consolidation of the Pittsburgh-Xenia Theological Seminary of the United Presbyterian Church of North American and the Western Theological Seminary of the Presbyterian Church in the United States of America.

Located on an estate-like campus straddling Pittsburgh's Highland Park/East Liberty neighborhoods since that merger, the seminary finds itself appropriately situated between middle-class comforts and urban challenges. The accredited seminary is a graduate institution of the Presbyterian Church (U.S.A.), with master of divinity, master of arts, master of sacred theology and doctor of ministry programs as well as joint degree programs with local universities that facilitate master's in divinity along with master's in law, social work, public health, business and sacred music. A joint doctorate degree is available in conjunction with the University of Pittsburgh.

Pittsburgh Theological Seminary, in its third century of service, works to send theologically educated Christians into the world.

About half of PTS students are Presbyterians. The ecumenically minded PTS has more than 20 denominations represented among its student body of all ages, genders, ancestry and nationalities.

Through years of serving this broad spectrum of students, the seminary has remained true to its mission of preparing men and women for pastorates, which is the cornerstone of its work. PTS remains rooted in Reformed history, faithful to Scripture and committed to Christ's Gospel. It pays serious attention to the study of Biblical languages as well as to theological, historical, ethical and practical disciplines. It provides a means for individuals to grow in skills that would allow them to continue in specific ministries through the Metro-Urban Institute; the Center for Business, Religion, and Public Life; the Spiritual Formation certificate program; and the World Mission Initiative.

A vital part of the seminary's own ministry is instructing Christian lay leaders for all phases of church outreach. PTS also encourages and supports the efforts of individuals interested in examining and strengthening their faith through its multitude of continuing education programs. Those interested in studying Biblical archaeology can do so, hands-on, at a long-running PTS dig in Jerusalem. The James L. Kelso Bible Lands Museum maintains artifacts in Pittsburgh for study by students and the public.

While seeking keys of knowledge and understanding from the past, PTS remains well-grounded in the spirituality of the present and future. Yearly, the top Presbyterian high schoolers across the country are treated to the Summer Youth Institute, which provides a taste of theological education. The seminary, which trains more than 300 pastors a year, welcomes more than 3,000 others to its campus yearly and looks to provide greater support for lay leaders, expanding into a center for religious training across the tri-state area.

At the turn of its third century, PTS finds itself poised just as it was at its humble conception more than 200 years ago: on the fringe of new frontiers.

Seton Hill College

IN 1882 THE SISTERS OF CHARITY purchased the Stokes Mansion and property in Greensburg, Pennsylvania, and renamed the home St. Mary's. The property was called Seton Hill in honor of their founder, St. Elizabeth Ann Seton. A year later the sisters established St. Joseph Academy for girls. In 1908 the first classroom building, Maura Hall, was constructed to facilitate St. Mary's School for Small Boys and academy classrooms. The academy remained in existence until 1947. In September 1914 Seton Junior College was opened. And, on June 3, 1918, Seton Hill College for women was chartered and received the distinction of being the first Catholic women's college in Pennsylvania to gain accreditation by the Middle States Association.

Situated in Greensburg, approximately 35 miles southeast of Pittsburgh, Seton Hill College is located at the summit of a winding driveway lined with sycamore trees planted by the Sisters. Amidst a rural woodland setting, 200 acres of landscaped campus are surrounded by lofty hills and lush valleys.

Traditionally a liberal arts college for women, Seton Hill College also provides program opportunities for men and had reached its highest enrollment of 1,300 students for the fall 2000 semester. A student-faculty ratio of 13-to-1 enhances the academic learning environment. For over 80 years, educators at Seton Hill College have nurtured, instructed and prepared graduates to assume professional roles in society.

Undergraduate degrees are offered in over 30 majors. The college also offers physician assistant studies, adult accelerated degrees and advanced certifications. Seven graduate programs are available: art therapy; special education; writing popular fiction; counseling psychology; elementary education; management; and technologies enhanced learning. For the 14th consecutive year, *U.S. News and World Report's* "America's Best Colleges" has ranked Seton Hill College among the top liberal arts colleges in the Northern United States.

This standing has been reinforced by the addition of two internationally recognized centers at Seton Hill College that broaden a student's global perspective. First, the National Catholic Center for Holocaust Education poses issues that stress the need for tolerance, acceptance and peace with all persons. Second, the National Educational Center for Women in Business provides information to women interested in entrepreneurial ventures and promotes networking relationships with women in the corporate arena. Regionally, these centers unite Seton Hill College and the local community in a collaborative effort to foster economic development and understanding among all people.

The legacy of Seton Hill College is evident in a heritage sustained by accountability. The success of the college's $25 million unprecedented and comprehensive capital and endowment campaign has paid for the renovation of the historic Administration Building and improvements to campus facilities, increased financial provisions for students and resulted in a substantial increase in contributions to the Annual Fund.

Seton Hill College lights the way for students to fulfill the early vision of the Sisters of Charity — to pursue academic careers in the context of moral responsibility. This is education at its finest — this is Seton Hill College.

Architect Joseph Stillburg constructed the Administration Building, the gracious centerpiece of Seton Hill's 200-acre campus, in 1889. Stillburg designed the building in Romanesque style using Pittsburgh brick and Ohio sandstone. The Administration Building is currently being renovated and restored to accommodate the college's 1,350 students, new programs and technology-enhanced learning environments.

Beautiful blue skies and students gathering on the lawn in front of Sullivan Hall confirm the approach of summer at Seton Hill College. Sullivan Hall was officially opened in 1929 and houses the college's gymnasium, swimming pool and student lounges. The hall was designed by Carlton Strong and Father Daniel Richard Sullivan in Norman Chateau style and resembles the Seton Castle in Scotland.

The Pressley Ridge Schools

PITTSBURGH IS HOME TO numerous facilities for children: museums, amusement parks and a multitude of playgrounds in nearly every neighborhood. But one of the community's more specialized children's facilities is the Pressley Ridge Schools. A leader in the treatment of troubled children, Pressley Ridge provides individualized services for children and adolescents who have been abused, neglected or diagnosed with serious mental and emotional illnesses.

The roots of Pressley Ridge were seeded in 1832 when a cholera epidemic raced through Pittsburgh, leaving children homeless and on the streets. The ladies of the local Protestant Sewing Circle quickly took action, banding together to raise funds for an "Orphan Asylum" and providing a few children with a home in a rented house. By the mid-19th century, the Protestant Home for Children was caring for several hundred children.

With the outbreak of the Civil War, a second asylum — the Home for the Friendless — was established by the congregation of the Second Presbyterian Church in a rented house on Federal Street. The home cared for more than 500 children of men killed in action and was eventually renamed Pressley House when it moved into a large building on Pressley Street in 1866. Early contributors to the Pressley House included steelmen, bankers and well-known philanthropists. One young industrialist who contributed $1000 listed himself only as "A. Carnegie."

The Protestant Home and the Home for the Friendless grew along parallel lines, operating near each other in what is now the city's north side. By the early 1950s, each saw a decrease in the number of orphans and an increase in the need for the treatment of emotionally disturbed children. In 1969 the two orphanages were merged and renamed The Pressley Ridge School.

The school soon expanded, becoming a national leader in children's mental health and social services. Today it operates in Pennsylvania, West Virginia, Ohio and Maryland and provides community and family support, therapeutic foster care, adoption services, educational services, and residential programs. It also serves children with multiple diagnoses, emotionally disturbed children who are deaf, and autistic children.

In 1991 Pressley Ridge established the Center for Research and Public Policy to evaluate the effectiveness of services and ensure ongoing program improvement. More recently, Pressley Ridge created the Pittsburgh International Children and Families Institute to develop self-sustaining programs for troubled children throughout the world.

All Pressley Ridge services are guided by the Re-Education philosophy that views treatment as teaching and requires the development of trusting relationships with caring adults. Pressley Ridge has been a pioneer in the development and dissemination of innovative treatment models such as therapeutic foster care, therapeutic wilderness camping, and wraparound services.

What started out as a refuge for orphans has evolved into a national and international leader in the treatment of troubled children. Since the 1800s, The Pressley Ridge Schools has served hundreds of thousands of children and touches the lives of more than 1,500 children and their families each day. Committed to discovering what works best, Pressley Ridge continues to create the services and therapies needed for the community's most troubled children and their families.

This mural, currently hanging in the courtyard of the school, depicts the early days of the agencies that eventually merged to form Pressley Ridge.

Carnegie Library of Pittsburgh, Pittsburgh Photographic Library

Health Care

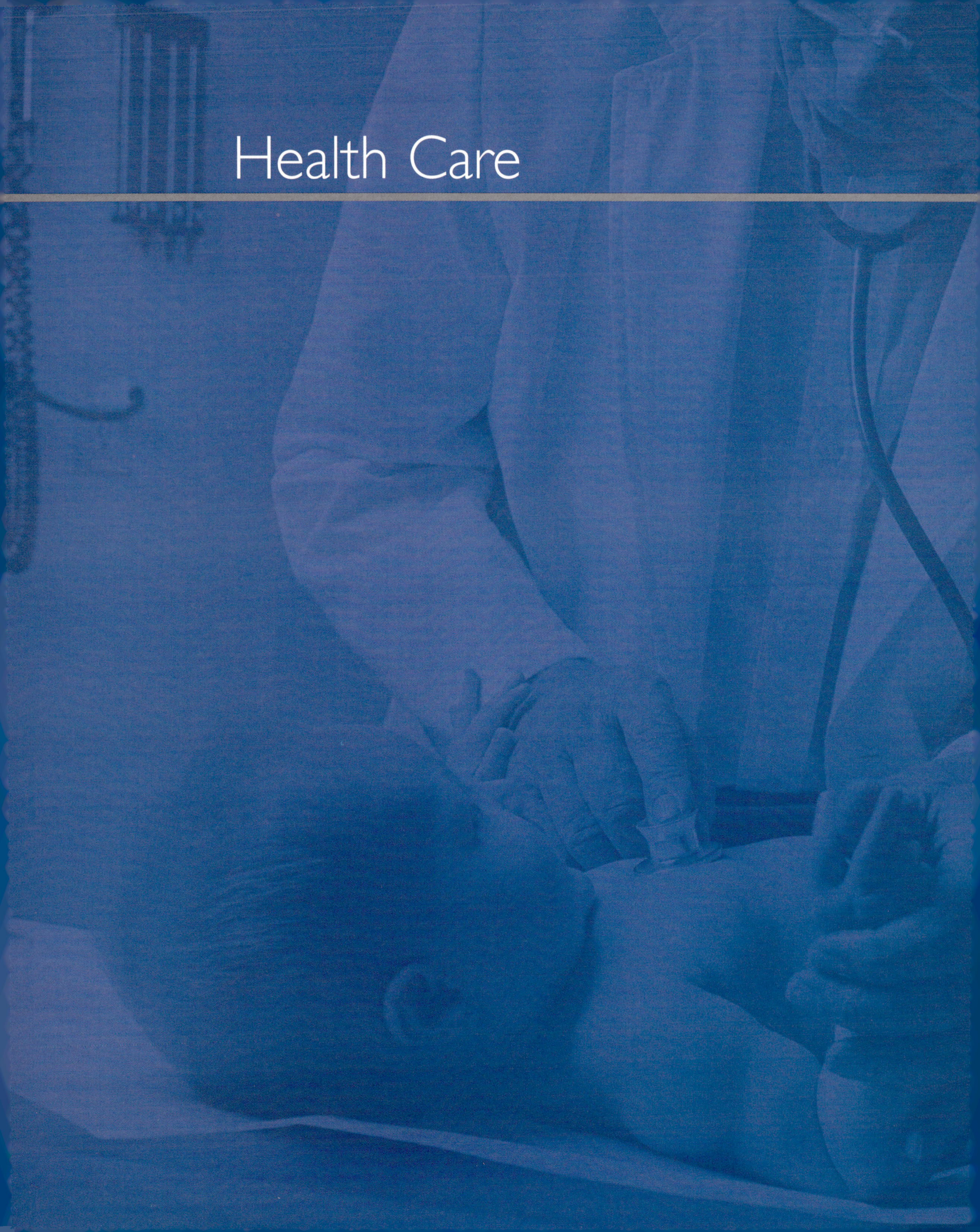

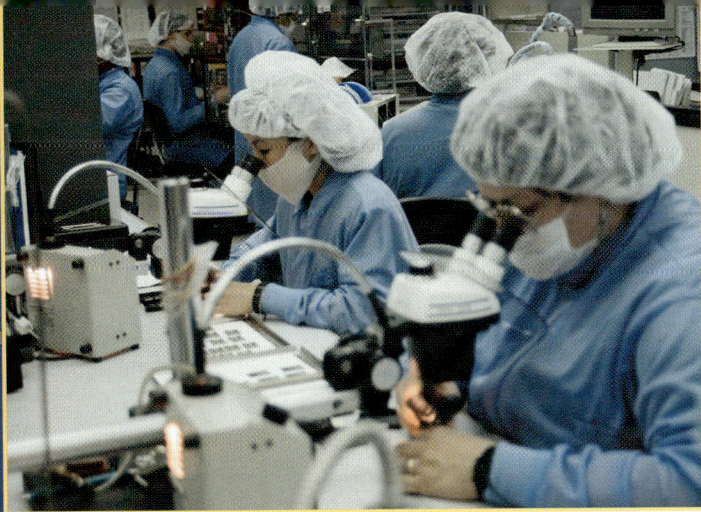

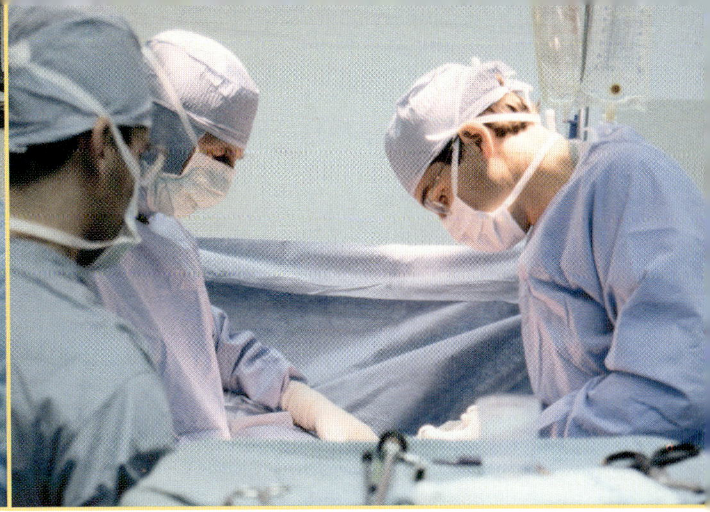

Pittsburgh's health care, insurance and pharmaceutical industries as well as its cutting-edge research facilities provide for the well-being of area residents.

Magee-Womens Hospital of UPMC Health System

MAGEE-WOMENS HOSPITAL OF UPMC Health System is one of five not-for-profit hospitals in the United States dedicated to the care of women and infants. Magee is the teaching facility for obstetrics, gynecology, gynecologic oncology and neonatology for students in the University of Pittsburgh Schools of Medicine and Nursing and for allied health professions. Magee's medical staff holds academic appointments at the University of Pittsburgh and is involved in education, research and patient care.

Magee is one of the original Centers of Excellence in Women's Health designated by the Department of Health and Human Services. Its Department of Obstetrics, Gynecology and Reproductive Sciences is among the top-funded academic departments of its kind by the National Institutes of Health for continued research and clinical trials.

Magee-Womens Hospital has grown from a health care facility focused on local women to one whose influence, reputation and knowledge are shared around the world.
John Wee

Through the Magee-Womens Health Foundation, contributions from donors who share the desire to improve the health of women and infants are managed, invested and distributed to gain the greatest benefit from contributions while ensuring that each donor's intent is honored.

Since opening in 1911, Magee has been committed to the care of women and their families. Nearly 8,000 babies are born annually at this regional referral center. The hospital's neonatal intensive care unit, the largest in Pennsylvania, treats more than 1,000 premature or critically ill newborns annually. Magee also operates nationally recognized clinical programs in breast and gynecologic cancers, genetics, infectious diseases and reproductive endocrinology.

Magee's philosophy of Womancare focuses on attributes that are unique to each woman and places her at the center of the care delivery system. The Womancare model strives to create a "hospital without walls." While the hub is Magee-Womens Hospital in Oakland, its network of comprehensive Womancare Centers offers community settings for mammography, ultrasound and other diagnostic tests and convenient physician office practices for ob/gyn and women's specialties. Womancare Centers, in partnership with UPMC Lee in Johnstown and UPMC Horizon in Hermitage, are part of Magee's regional initiatives.

Neighborhood Health Centers, located in communities that have been medically underserved, meet the primary preventive health care needs of women including many whose needs have never been adequately addressed by traditional health service models.

Through Magee Womancare International, Magee is improving health care services and conditions for women and infants around the world, offering educational programs and technical assistance in seven countries including Russia, Belarus, Ukraine, Hungary, Estonia and Jamaica.

Developments in the future of women's health are very much on the horizon. Magee is uniquely positioned to be a leader in gender-specific medicine, advancing understanding of women's health beyond reproduction. Known for its expertise in obstetrics, neonatology, gynecology, gynecologic oncology, breast care and breast cancer treatment, Magee is developing new programs in women's internal medicine and related subspecialties such as endocrinology, gastroenterology and digestive disorders, plus general, colorectal and minimally invasive surgeries, bariatrics, and continence and pelvic floor disorders.

Magee-Womens Research Institute

PAST MEDICAL RESEARCH WAS conducted primarily on the health needs of men. As attention to women's and infants' health needs increased, so did the realization that many biological processes are extremely gender specific. For this reason, the Magee-Womens Research Institute, a multidisciplinary research institute for women's and infants' research, was established in 1992. The institute emphasizes research that moves quickly from lab findings to the bedside and collaborates with more than two dozen medical colleges, health centers and health agencies in the United States and abroad. Magee-Womens Research Institute has become well recognized and respected nationally as a major force in women's and infants' health research.

Thanks to work at the Magee-Womens Research Institute, research findings rapidly move from the lab to the hospital bedside, improving the health of women around the world. *Photo by Ric Evans*

Institute members include investigators with expertise in clinical, fundamental, epidemiological and health services research. The faculty comes from the Department of Obstetrics, Gynecology and Reproductive Sciences of the University of Pittsburgh as well as other departments in the medical and nursing schools, the School of Pharmacy and the Graduate School of Public Health.

The institute conducts basic, clinical, epidemiological and behavioral research in fetal and neonatal development, pregnancy, women's cancers, family planning and sexually transmitted diseases, age-related changes in women and the advancement of women's health.

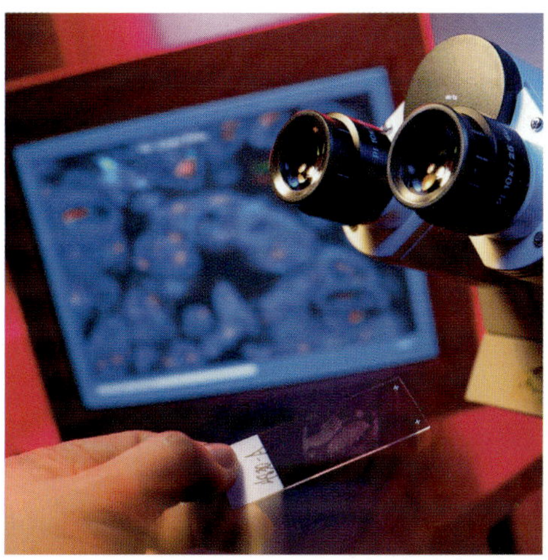

The Magee-Womens Research Institute focuses on women as scientists and patients. *Photo by Ric Evans*

Magee-Womens Hospital's large patient volume positions the institute as an ideal research center involving a broad range of women's and infants' health problems.

The Department of Obstetrics, Gynecology and Reproductive Sciences, supported by the institute, made major efforts to improve research in women's reproductive health and the training of physician-scientists. The National Institute of Child and Human Development funded the department as one of the original Women's Reproductive Health Research Career Development Programs to train the beginning scientist as a fundamental, clinical or epidemiological investigator. The institute's postdoctoral fellowship research training program for M.D. and Ph.D. scientists provides support for graduate students and proactive mentoring for young investigators. Also, the institute's summer program introduces college and high school students to women's health research, emphasizing recruitment of women and minority students into science.

Recently, the institute established the Pittsburgh Development Center to focus on human reproduction and development and the discovery of effective treatments for diseases and disabilities through the use of transgenic animal models and nonhuman primate stem cell studies. The center will collaborate with other research programs within the institute, the University of Pittsburgh, Carnegie Mellon University and the University of Pittsburgh Cancer Institute.

The institute is one of the country's largest centers for the study of sexually transmitted diseases in women, one of the few centers nationwide dedicated to family planning research, and home to the nation's largest group studying the basic biology of preeclampsia. The institute participates in several large National Institutes of Health clinical trial networks including the Maternal-Fetal Medicine Network, the Gynecologic Oncology Group, Studies of Women Across the Nation and the Incontinence Network.

The institute and hospital collaborate with RAND Corp. in the Magee-RAND Women's Health Initiative, which provides training in health services research and works with concerned organizations in Pittsburgh to assess strategies to ensure that quality health care services are available to women and their infants in southwestern Pennsylvania and nationwide.

Highmark Blue Cross Blue Shield

AS A 21ST-CENTURY INNOVATOR in health care, Highmark Blue Cross Blue Shield exceeds today's expectations by helping to ensure a healthier individual for tomorrow. More than six decades of providing quality, affordable health care coverage have built a proud tradition of achievement and success at Highmark. Steadily, the company has grown to become a premier health insurance organization serving 20 million people across the United States through its health, dental, vision and life and casualty business, as well as its Medicare Part A and Part B contracts.

Like the forging of steel, Highmark has blended responsibility, integrity and vision in the production of one of the most highly regarded consumer-oriented health care companies in the new millennium. And it all began in Pittsburgh, Pennsylvania — as a response to the health care needs of the community.

During the final years of the Great Depression, the human spirit reached its lowest point, values seemed meaningless and the will to endure was weighted by the oppression of uncertainty. In Pittsburgh this era was marked by poverty, unemployment and sickness. In December 1930 a report by Albert Kennedy on the social conditions in Pittsburgh revealed that "two-thirds of patients were unable to pay their hospital registration fee." Overcrowding coupled with financial strain forced hospitals to accept nonpaying persons in need of immediate medical attention.

Early Blue Cross and Blue Shield service representatives enrolled new members outside workplaces or public areas accessible to the community.

(Far right) Customer service representatives previously sat in a sea of desks and responded to customer inquiries on typewriters.

Accordingly, Abraham Oseroff, President of the Hospital Conference and Superintendent of Montefiore Hospital, called a meeting of the medical and hospital communities of Pittsburgh to discuss the report on health care in Allegheny County. Health care was a pivotal issue in Pittsburgh. Hospitals sought a consistent form of payment from patients, doctors depended upon reimbursement for care provided to patients, and patients desired a way to budget for medical services. The medical and hospital representatives made recommendations to the Hospital Conference for "planning, coordination and control" through a Hospital Council and a prepaid group hospitalization plan. The concept of prepayment plans was considered because it offered an alternative allowing people to meet expenses for the cost of medical services.

Planning and Development

With an unwavering belief in the premise that "ordinary working people could gain access to medical care and be able to pay for it," Oseroff and H. Lee Mason embarked on the task of developing prepaid voluntary hospitalization plans. The establishment of the Hospital Service Association of Pittsburgh began with a $20,000 loan from the Buhl Foundation.

From 1935 to 1937, Oseroff and a committee refined a group plan in Pittsburgh patterned after a New York City model. A selection of particular hospitals with complete services was offered. Proposed monthly amounts were 75 cents for an individual and $1.75 for a family, with 21 days of hospitalization.

In June 1937 the Nonprofit Hospital Act was passed. Citizens of Pennsylvania were entitled to receive hospital care at affordable charges that provided financial support to the hospitals. In order to protect Pennsylvanians from expenses incurred by commercial insurance companies, nonprofit hospital plans were initiated and known as "Blue Cross Plans." The following September, the Hospital Service Association of Pittsburgh was approved by the Pennsylvania Insurance Department. This marked the beginning of payroll deductions of premiums. On January 1, 1938, the first Blue Cross subscriber contract became effective.

By the end of the 1930s, the Pittsburgh business sector and health care were both experiencing growth, and the 100,000th subscriber was enrolled with Blue Cross. In 1939 the Pennsylvania Medical Society House of Delegates passed legislation to provide prepaid insurance to cover physician services. The Allegheny County Medical Society approved the Hospital Service Association's recommendation of $4 for "hospital care" and $2 for "medical services." This was known as Pennsylvania Blue Shield and it was a statewide organization serving the entire Commonwealth. For the first time, two coverages were available to subscribers.

Abraham Oseroff, William Robson, Cornelius Scully and Dr. William McFarland discussed the three-cents-a-day hospital plan on KQV radio.

Provisions for Workers

Social and economic change swept across America in 1941 as President Franklin D. Roosevelt began his third term. Pittsburgh prospered, and by the time the United States was engaged in World War II, the steel mills were in full operation. Subscribers increased to 500,000. The first significant contract change came in 1943. In answer to the costs of long-term hospitalization, the number of hospitalization days was lengthened from 21 to 90 at 50 percent coverage if enrolled in the program for a year or longer. Within two years subscribers had reached 1 million in number.

The year following the war brought further revisions in the plan. A nongroup enrollment with 21 days of hospitalization a year was introduced. Pittsburgh leaders reconfirmed a commitment to the community by extending insurance coverage to a greater number of persons, including those unable to afford it. Business, labor and health care providers expressed a willingness to collaborate with Blue Cross in efforts to obtain coverage for the entire community. Ten unions negotiated health plans and subscribers rose to nearly 1.2 million.

In 1947, after the Supreme Court decreed that benefit plans did come within "conditions of employment," unions were instrumental in designing benefit programs. This spirit of cooperation within the community remains a significant factor in the growth of Blue Cross and Blue Shield.

Workers and dependents receiving coverage doubled in 1950. Monthly rates were $1 for an individual and $2.75 for a family. The same year, the American Medical Association assisted in a national campaign to promote voluntary plans as the "American way."

Abraham Oseroff had nurtured the seed of affordable health care for over 25 years.

Growth and Expansion

As the torch passed to a new director, William Ford, in 1956, tremendous changes in health care were unfolding. Hospital care was the fifth-largest industry in the United States. In a decade of technological advances, subscribers asked for more services. Extended benefits and comprehensive care were a priority for nearly 2 million persons enrolled with Blue Cross.

The late 1950s introduced "experience rating" in the Master Agreement developed for the steelworkers. Rates were based on the total community, resulting in affordable charges. This was an integral element in nonprofit plans and the "community service mission" interlacing Blue Cross and Blue Shield with the health care system and society.

Before computer technology, medical claims and member information were manually filed and retrieved.

Today, Highmark Blue Cross Blue Shield Customer Service representatives receive 29,000 calls a day and respond to 7.2 million customer and provider inquiries annually. *Photo by Harry Giglio*

Increased hospital admissions stimulated innovative thinking by Blue Cross and resulted in the development of an exemplary model lowering the number of hospital stays. Known as Utilization Review, this concept was adopted 12 years later by Medicare. The Pennsylvania Economic League reviewed the accomplishments of Blue Cross in 1961. Results indicated that the contribution of Blue Cross to the people of Western Pennsylvania was "vast and remarkable." During this "Golden Age of Health Care Financing," Blue Cross responded to the requests of older adults for hospital coverage prior to the enactment of Medicare. As Medicare and Medicaid emerged, Blue Cross helped in building the framework of the "Great Society" through a Senior Citizen Agreement protecting persons 65 and older without previous coverage. For the first time, coverage to handicapped children 19 and older with parental consent was offered. In 1963 the official name became Blue Cross of Western Pennsylvania.

Early Prevention

Opportunities for unprecedented coverage proceeded in the 1970s. Searching for ways to reduce hospital stays, promote prevention and encourage early intervention through accessible primary care led to a sustaining interest in the health maintenance organization, or HMO.

Past experience led to the realization that prevention was an essential element in maintaining a healthy population. Accordingly, the HMO introduced by Blue Cross and Blue Shield highlighted early intervention to reduce the frequency of illness and hospitalization. Benefits of healthier lifestyles were reinforced with public education programs.

Response to Needs

The recession and inflation of the 1980s did not diminish the pragmatism of Blue Cross and Blue Shield. Lessons from the Depression days were not forgotten. In the 1980s, Howard W. Gindele, President of Blue Cross, stated, "Neglect of health care needs and deferral of treatment can compound the community's medical problems — and the cost of care may very well increase the longer proper care is delayed." In 1984 Blue Cross of Western Pennsylvania and Pennsylvania Blue Shield implemented a national program offering coverage to the unemployed.

Health care needs of children are of paramount concern to Blue Cross and Blue Shield. In 1985 the Caring Program provided insurance for children unable to afford coverage but ineligible for publicly funded programs. Collaboration with Blue Cross, churches and community leaders resulted in a national program of free health insurance for children.

Additional programs are: The Western Pennsylvania Caring Foundation, Inc., assisting economically disadvantaged residents of Western Pennsylvania with tax-deductible donations for health care programs; and Worksite Wellness, which implements health education in the community, schools and medical-provider settings.

The Dr. Dean Ornish Program for Reversing Heart Disease taught at Highmark's Camp HealthPLACE shows participants low-fat food selection and preparation, exercise and meditation techniques. *Photo by Harry Giglio*

Serving Customers

Leaders in the health care field, Blue Cross Blue Shield and the University of Pittsburgh Medical Center initiated the first insurance coverage of heart transplants. In 1992 Blue Cross Blue Shield Special Care was designed in Pennsylvania for low-income individuals and families. This program became a model for state and federal legislation.

In 1996 Blue Cross of Western Pennsylvania and Pennsylvania Blue Shield combined to form Highmark Inc. The company does business as Highmark Blue Cross Blue Shield in the 29 counties of Western

Pennsylvania. In the remainder of the state, it collaborates with other Blue Cross plans and operates as Pennsylvania Blue Shield.

A major health insurer in Pennsylvania and one of the largest Blue Cross Blue Shield plans in the country, Highmark Blue Cross Blue Shield provides a wide array of managed care programs, indemnity coverage for groups and individuals, and employee benefits.

Nationally, the boundaries of Highmark are extended by its subsidiary companies — including United Concordia Companies, Clarity Vision and Davis Vision, and the Highmark Life and Casualty Group — which market benefit programs for dental, vision and life and casualty coverage. Highmark also operates as a Medicare Part A fiscal intermediary and a Medicare Part B carrier.

Although the early mission of the founders of Highmark has essentially remained unchanged throughout its long history, a convergence has developed into proactive health care. The Highmark mission of today is "To help members live longer, better by ensuring access to affordable, high-quality health benefits insurance and service."

Achieving its mission is a collaborative effort with Highmark, members, physicians, and health care professionals, which assures the finest medical care available to consumers. No health insurer in the nation enlists the participation of doctors in developing medical policies and protocols more aggressively than Highmark. Some 300 practicing physicians actively consult with the company. In addition, 45 health care professionals are Highmark Corporate Members, a group of 156 company advisers from across the Commonwealth. And a total of 10 health care professionals from a variety of specialties serve on the company's board of directors.

The Highmark vision, "To be the foremost consumer-oriented health benefits insurance company in the nation," introduces members to choice, technology and education in an unprecedented forum of health insurance.

Accordingly, Highmark has employed the Internet to increase the accessibility of information and service to both customers and health providers. Members are now visiting the company Web site to take personal health assessments, change their primary care physician and download health information. Through the first Internet-based health insurance program in America, Highmark Blue Cross Blue Shield also provides members of employer groups with the ability to select health care coverage from 16 different health care plans. Health providers are using similar Internet products to submit claims, access patient eligibility for services and review benefit information.

Business operations at Highmark Blue Cross Blue Shield are streamlined by modern technology that enables nearly two-thirds of medical claims to be electronically submitted by health care providers. *Photo by Harry Giglio*

The dawn of the new millennium holds the promise of advances in medicine, healthier lifestyles and service to customers. A refined commitment of excellence of more than half a century has placed Highmark at the summit of health insurers. Through the latest strategies based on past experiences coupled with new technology, Pennsylvanians are offered innovative opportunities to receive the finest health insurance available to them. It is a tribute to the vision, principles and leadership of the founders and directors of Highmark and to the community of Pittsburgh, which has supported these efforts throughout the years.

Helping people live longer, better, Highmark Blue Cross Blue Shield sponsors community programs throughout Western Pennsylvania to improve the lives of everyone. The Young-at-Heart program helps active seniors to remain healthy. *Photo by Harry Giglio*

Children's Hospital of Pittsburgh

NOW IN ITS SECOND CENTURY OF service, Children's Hospital of Pittsburgh remains the only freestanding hospital dedicated solely to caring for infants, children and young adults in western Pennsylvania, eastern Ohio and northern West Virginia. With 235 beds and a staff of approximately 740 active physicians representing 51 pediatric specialty services and more than 2,000 referring physicians, Children's Hospital is named consistently to several respected lists of pediatric health care facilities, including ranking among the top 10 children's hospitals in *U.S. News & World Report* magazine's annual listing of Best Hospitals in America. Its staff is committed to improving the health and well-being of children through excellent patient care, groundbreaking research and outstanding pediatric medical education.

Like many great institutions, Children's Hospital of Pittsburgh began as a simple idea in the mind of a young person with foresight and generosity. In 1890, the son of a local pediatrician raised $3,000 to endow a single cot to be used exclusively for infants and children at a Pittsburgh hospital. Later that same year, Kirk LeMoyne's vision attracted enough support to open a 15-bed dedicated children's hospital in Oakland. His dream was vastly expanded in 1926 when a larger hospital was erected at the present-day site.

Over the course of the 20th century, many of the great milestones in pediatric medicine were achieved within the walls of Children's Hospital of Pittsburgh. It was here in the 1950s that Jonas Salk developed and introduced the polio vaccine. The Mr. Yuk poison prevention education campaign, credited with saving countless lives, was created at Children's in 1971. And the hospital's collaboration with the University of Pittsburgh School of Medicine and transplant pioneer Thomas Starzl, M.D., Ph.D., helped make Children's Hospital of Pittsburgh the world's largest and most advanced pediatric transplantation center. Today, more transplants are performed at Children's than at any other center in the world.

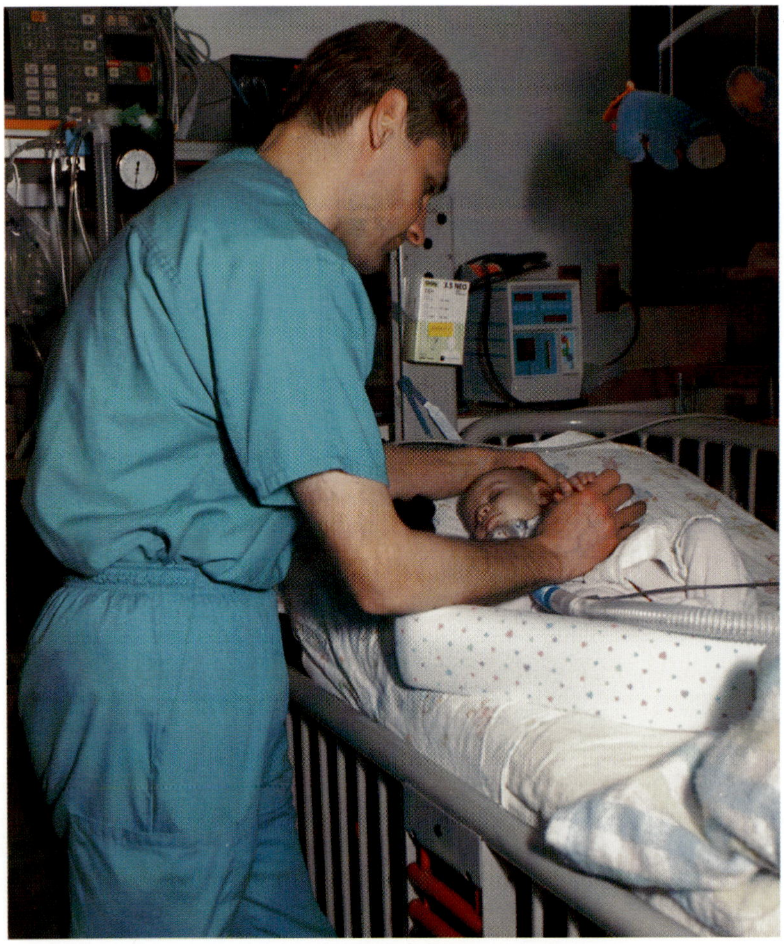

Children's Hospital of Pittsburgh has a 53-bed pediatric intensive care unit that provides care for almost 2,000 children with life-threatening illnesses and injuries each year, making it one of the busiest pediatric intensive care units in the nation.

In addition to its pioneering work in organ and tissue transplantation, the hospital is renowned for pediatric centers of excellence in areas such as cardiology, cardiothoracic surgery, critical care medicine, diabetes, hematology/oncology, molecular biology, neurosurgery, orthopaedics, otolaryngology and surgery. Children's is the only accredited Level I (highest level) Regional Pediatric Trauma Center in western Pennsylvania, treating more than 125 children daily. And its 53-bed pediatric intensive care unit has one of the highest survival rates in the country.

Children's also is one of the region's largest providers of primary care and preventive medicine for children. Through its subsidiary, Children's Community Care, the hospital offers a network of primary care pediatricians who have direct access to its dedicated pediatric specialists. The hospital offers comprehensive inpatient and outpatient services at its main campus in Oakland as well as outpatient and same-day surgical services in key regional locations north, south and east of Pittsburgh. In addition, telemedicine links Children's with outlying hospitals and provides access to the expertise of select hospital staff on a 24-hour basis.

At its heart a teaching facility, Children's Hospital of Pittsburgh offers one of the finest pediatric residency training programs in the country. It attracts physicians from around the world, many of whom go on to practice in local communities and hospitals.

Excellent patient care and medical education are enhanced by the third prong of the hospital's mission — helping children live healthier and happier lives through biomedical research. Since 1991, Children's has ranked among the top 10 U.S. children's hospitals receiving National Institutes of Health (NIH) funding for biomedical research, and annually spends $12 million on pediatric research. The state-of-the-art John G. Rangos Sr. Research Center, completed in 1990, is a model of medical and academic collaboration. The juvenile diabetes program, which was initiated more than 60 years ago, is now one of the largest in the country. Important work toward isolating a vaccine and hopefully finding a cure for juvenile diabetes takes place here every day. In addition to its juvenile diabetes and transplant research programs, Children's operates the Center for Cell Therapeutics, which is dedicated to the development of genetic approaches to improving tissue healing and regeneration. And the Otitis Media Research Center at Children's also has an international reputation as the center that has contributed the most to the current understanding of the cause and treatment of middle ear disease in infants and children.

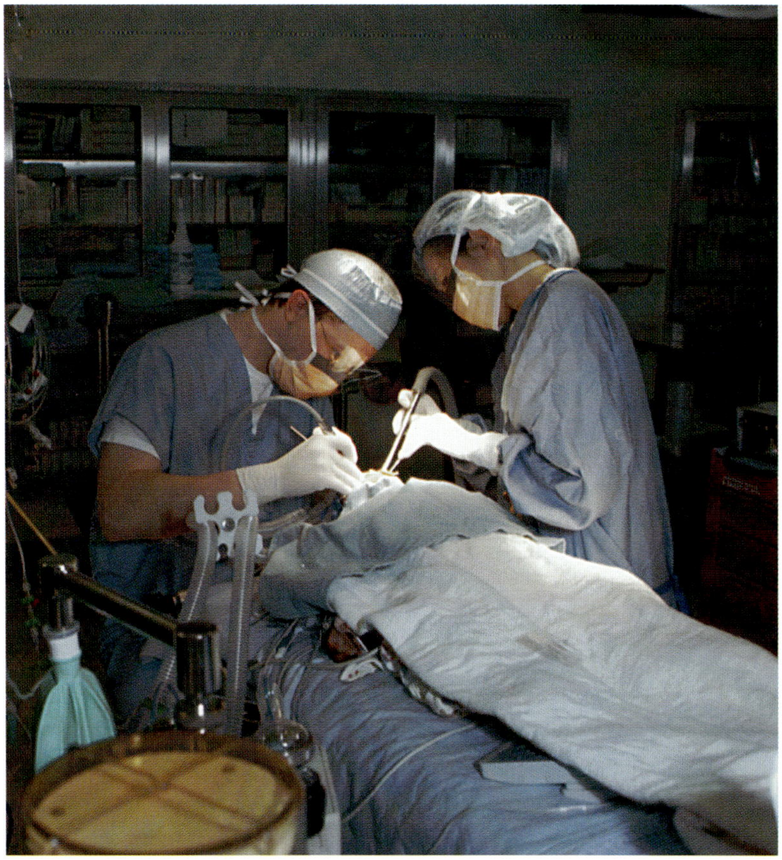

As a facility equally dedicated to patient care, teaching and research, Children's Hospital of Pittsburgh continually advances the field of pediatric medicine by developing and trialing the latest pediatric surgical techniques and procedures.

The hospital also helps children and their families through social and educational innovations. For example, Children's established the first hospital-based child abuse investigation unit. With a grant from the Robert Wood Johnson Foundation, it also established the first program to provide foster children with consistent health care. In addition, Children's offers summer camping programs that focus on children's quality of life after transplantation and while battling heart disease, sickle cell disease and childhood cancer. Its Positive Parenting classes, which offer parents practical ideas to build healthy, happy relationships with their children, have reached more than 15,000 parents in 200 community venues. In addition, Children's Web site offers a wealth of important health and safety information for parents, caregivers and children.

Children's Hospital remains committed to providing a wide array of world-class health services and will continue its policy of caring for every child regardless of the family's ability to pay for the care provided. Children's is the preferred pediatric provider for most insurers and networks and has as its goal that all children and families, regardless of insurance carrier, will have access to its pre-eminent health care services. The hospital remains firmly dedicated to providing high-quality, cost-effective pediatric health care without eliminating the essential services that make it special.

The staff at Children's Hospital of Pittsburgh know that children are not just little adults — their physical, psychological and emotional needs are very different. And nowhere else in the region will parents find such a full complement of pediatric medical professionals, including board-certified pediatric physicians, registered pediatric nurses and pediatric nurse practitioners, pediatric pharmacists and therapists, child life specialists, and even social workers and teachers. In Pittsburgh and throughout the region, the hospital's slogan has real meaning — "If you have kids, be glad you have Children's."

GlaxoSmithKline Consumer Healthcare

OVER THE PAST TWO DECADES Pittsburgh has successfully transformed itself from a smoky, Victorian industrial complex into a shimmering metropolis with an economy based on technology, research and medicine.

GlaxoSmithKline (GSK) Consumer Healthcare not only reflects Pittsburgh's rise as an international business center, but it also has been at the vanguard of its rebirth.

Tracing its roots back to the sale of Beecham's laxative pills in the late 1800s, GSK Consumer Healthcare has grown to become one of the largest manufacturers and distributors of nonprescription medications and oral products in the world. GSK Consumer Healthcare is ranked second globally in sales of both over-the-counter and oral-care products, and has a major market presence in more than 100 countries.

Like the Steelers and Pirates of the 1970s, GSK Consumer Healthcare has an all-star roster that includes such consumer favorites as Contac cold medicine, Tums antacid, Tagamet HB 200 heartburn medicine, Aquafresh toothpaste and Nicorette and NicoDerm CQ smoking cessation products.

Pittsburgh serves as corporate headquarters for GSK Consumer Healthcare Division's North American operations. It is the base from which the company serves its biggest and most important market — the United States and Canada. This market accounts for 33 percent of GSK's $5 billion in annual sales globally. GSK Consumer Healthcare operates in England, Germany, France, Italy, Spain, Japan, India, Mexico, Australia, Argentina and South America.

With its world-class airport, well-educated work force and perennial ranking as one of the best places to live in America, Pittsburgh is an ideal spot for GSK Consumer Healthcare's North American operations. In addition to its high quality of life, Pittsburgh also reflects many of the cultural values that GSK Consumer Healthcare cherishes. Like the Carnegie, Heinz and Mellon families of a century ago, GSK Consumer Healthcare employees believe in getting involved in the communities where they live, work and do business.

GSK Consumer Healthcare's civic spirit derives from its parent company, GlaxoSmithKline. Based in England, GSK is one of the world's leading research-based pharmaceutical and health care companies, with annual sales of nearly $26 billion. It is committed to improving the quality of human life by enabling people to do more, feel better and live longer.

Every second in the world, 30 people receive a GSK vaccine. Every minute, 1,100 people receive a prescription for a GSK product. And every hour, the company spends a half-million dollars on research and development.

In addition to supporting many worthwhile organizations in the Pittsburgh area, GSK collaborated with the World Health Organization in 1998 in one of the largest global disease-elimination programs ever undertaken by public health officials. GSK donated the drug Albendazole to eliminate lymphatic filariasis, one of the most disfiguring tropical diseases in the world, which has affected 120 million people in 73 countries.

The company's current roster of over-the-counter products includes a wide range of smoking cessation, respiratory tract, gastrointestinal and analgesic medicines, dermatological and hygiene products, and vitamins. One of the newest products is Abreva, an over-the-counter cold sore medication.

The path to today's GSK started with individual entrepreneurs of the 1800s, including Thomas Beecham, who developed and launched his wildly successful laxative pills in 1842; John K. Smith, who opened his first drugstore in Philadelphia, and

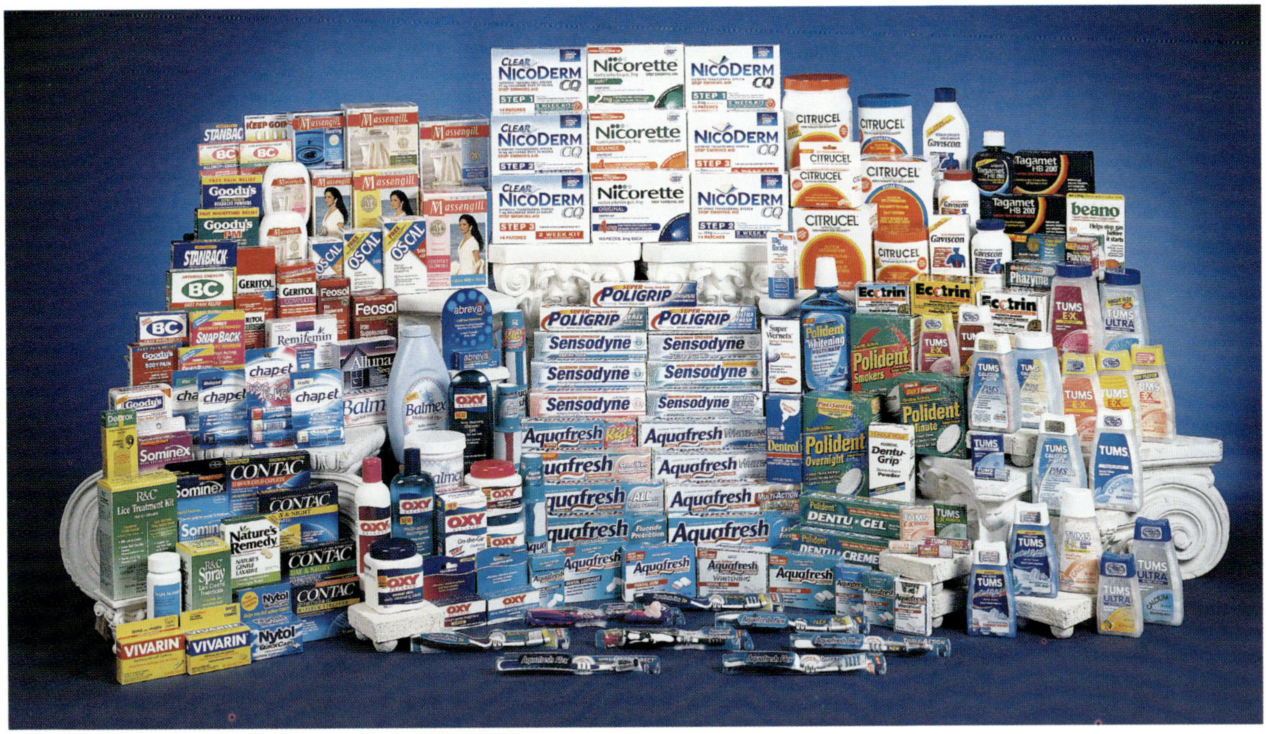

later hired Mahon Kline; Joseph Nathan, who opened a trading company in New Zealand that served as the foundation for Glaxo Laboratories; and American pharmacists Henry Wellcome and Silas Burroughs, who established the Burroughs Wellcome & Co. in London in 1880.

Their pioneering efforts laid the groundwork for growth in the companies that eventually formed today's GSK. They experienced landmark achievements in early research and development and in the discovery, manufacture, distribution and sale of pharmaceutical products, over-the-counter medicines, oral hygiene treatments and nutritional drinks. These technologically advanced products had a large impact in modifying and elevating the world's health care standards.

During the ensuing years a number of complex acquisitions and mergers occurred within each of the original organizations, greatly expanding their respective product lines and mutual positions in the marketplace. More recently, several well-known over-the-counter consumer products were added to the Beecham Group's growing product line, when in 1977 it purchased Pittsburgh-based Calgon Consumer Products Division from Merck & Co.

Maintaining Pittsburgh as its consumer health care base for North America, The Beecham Group strengthened its position in the consumer marketplace with the 1982 purchase of J.B. Williams Co., maker of Geritol multivitamins and Sominex sleep aid, and the 1986 acquisition of Norcliff Thayer Inc., maker of Tums, the calcium-based antacid, and Oxy Balance, a line of acne treatment products.

SmithKline Beecham Consumer Healthcare was created in 1989 by the merger of SmithKline Beckman, which included Contac in its product portfolio, and the Beecham Group. Following a partnership with Marion Merrill Dow in 1992, Nicorette, NicoDerm and Tagamet were added to the product line.

In December 2000 Glaxo Wellcome and SmithKline Beecham, both based in London and equally dominant players in the international pharmaceutical market, completed a merger to form GlaxoSmithKline, the Consumer Healthcare Division's new parent. The combined sales of both companies account for more than 7 percent of the world's pharmaceutical market in prescription and over-the-counter medicinal products.

With the acquisition of Block Drug Company in January 2001, makers of Sensodyne toothpaste, Poli-Grip denture adhesive and Nytol sleep aid, GSK is now the world's second-largest oral health care company and second-largest over-the-counter drug company.

The company's world-class approach to managing its business is also evident in its employees. The GlaxoSmithKline Consumer Healthcare work environment is a unique combination of innovation, energy and personal commitment.

As GSK Consumer Healthcare continues to develop new products and grow market share around the world, it will proudly proclaim Pittsburgh as the home of its North American operations.

HealthAmerica/HealthAssurance

PITTSBURGH IS A PLACE WHERE great ideas are born. It's a place of many firsts: the first Nickelodeon movies — the first licensed radio broadcast by KDKA — the first public television station, WQED — the first atomic-engine-powered submarine — and the first successful polio vaccine by Dr. Jonas Salk. So, it is not surprising that this city was also the birthplace of the first HMO in the region.

As with many firsts, the reaction to this unorthodox health plan was cautious at best. Back in 1975, the majority of Pittsburghers were unfamiliar with HMOs and were skeptical. Twenty-five years later, HealthAmerica's reputation helped to conquer the skepticism of nearly a half-million people in Pennsylvania who are now satisfied members of this health plan.

The story behind this enterprising organization that pioneered managed care in Pittsburgh a quarter-century ago and prides itself on its status as the Best Health Plan in Pennsylvania is a fascinating one.

HealthAmerica was established in 1975 as Penn Group Health Plan. However, its roots can be traced back to 1969, when a group of Pittsburgh business and labor leaders formed a nonprofit corporation — the Community Health Association of Western PA — to address the need for affordable health care benefits. Envisioning an organized system of quality health care that would be accessible and affordable, they found a working model in the health maintenance organization (HMO). HMOs place an emphasis on preventive care, based on the belief that health care services that keep people well result in lower health care costs and a healthier community. After five years of hard work and concentrated efforts, the association finally got state and federal legislation in place and formed Penn Group Health Plan.

Penn Group's first office opened in The Western Pennsylvania Hospital's Mellon Pavilion in 1975, officially launching the health plan. The first contracted hospitals were West Penn, Montefiore and other university hospitals. At the end of Penn Group's first year in business, 1,400 Pittsburghers bucked tradition and became members of the region's first HMO. The very first member to sign up was William Alberts, who was still a member at the turn of the new century in 2000.

During its first years, Penn Group fine-tuned its business practices, developing new medical and administrative strategies to improve the way medical care was provided. In 1981 Penn Group entered into a management agreement with HealthPlans Corp. based in Nashville, Tennessee, which subsequently changed its name to HealthAmerica. Penn Group Health Plan followed suit. As a result, HealthAmerica became the largest independent, investor-owned and operated HMO in the country. In 1983 membership grew to 30,000, and in 1984 HealthAmerica expanded its operations to Central Pennsylvania.

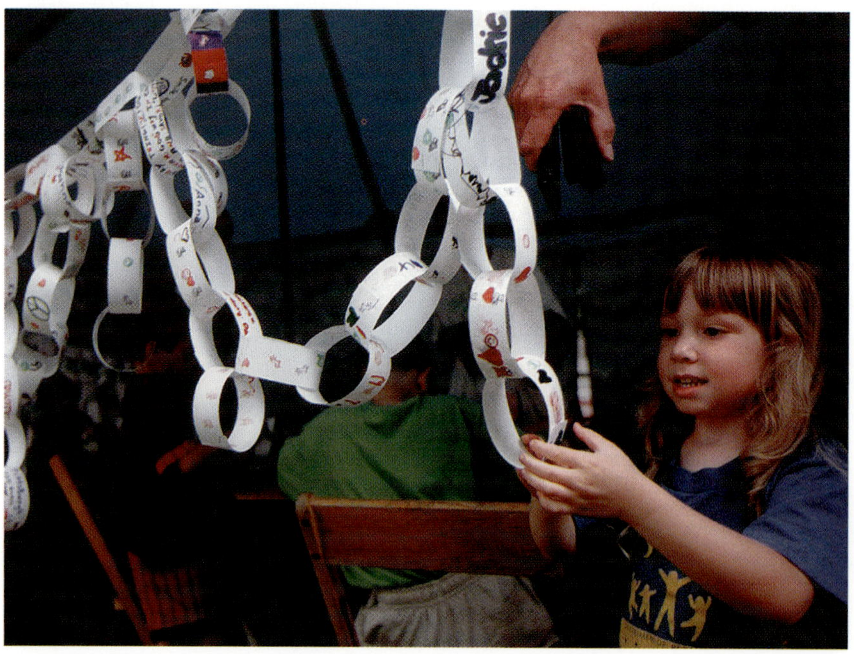

Since 1992, HealthAmerica has been a major supporter of the International Children's Festival, a dynamic annual cultural event for children. The children of Pittsburgh created and sent to the children in Kosovo refugee camps what they dubbed their "Chain of Hope," which stretched out approximately one-quarter mile in length.

Turmoil and transition characterized 1987, as Penn Group Health Plan was acquired by a nationwide chain of HMOs called Maxicare. The Pittsburgh Plan struggled to maintain its local identity despite its inflexible owner company. HealthAmerica's future brightened significantly in 1988 when Coventry Corporation, an insurance holding company, purchased the Pittsburgh and Harrisburg Plans from Maxicare and infused them with capital for ongoing operational improvements and growth.

The 90s was a dynamic decade for HealthAmerica as the organization introduced a new PPO plan: HealthAssurance. In 1993 HealthAmerica was the first area HMO to receive full accreditation from the National Committee for Quality Assurance, raising the bar for quality in managed health care among area HMOs.

In 1996 HealthAmerica became the Gold Standard for health care when *Newsweek* named HealthAmerica among the Top 10 HMOs in the Nation. That same year, HealthAmerica unveiled Advantra, a Medicare+Choice HMO that was cited for two "Best Practices in Managed Care" by Medicare. *US News & World Report* named HealthAmerica the No.1 Plan in Pennsylvania both in 1998 and 1999. *Newsweek* rated HealthAmerica the Best Health Plan in Pennsylvania as well as sixth best plan in the entire nation, best plan in the nation for child care and adolescent care and best plan in the nation for women's health. HealthAmerica received a statewide NCQA rating of 3-year "Excellent" marks. And HealthAmerica was the only health plan to rank No.1 in all nine categories for effectiveness of care in the latest *Performance Scorecard* published by the Pittsburgh Business Group on Health.

HealthAmerica's first member, William Alberts, explains his reason for staying with HealthAmerica for a quarter of a century: "When a health plan has been this good to you, you stick with it."

HealthAmerica's secret? It is as much a philosophy as it is a business. The nucleus of this eminent health care plan is its focus on people, as reflected in its mission statement:

"To be the recognized leader in providing quality, accessible and affordable health care benefits and services that maintain and improve the quality of life of all our members and the communities we serve."

Community is a key segment of HealthAmerica's business ethic. Included in its corporate creed is the organization's commitment to maintaining its role as a responsible corporate citizen in partnership with the communities it serves. HealthAmerica has partnered with a number of local organizations to implement a variety of children's programs that emphasize health, safety and preventive care. For example, the HealthAmerica Heads Up Helmet Safety Program works in conjunction with Allegheny General Hospital to promote the importance of helmets in schools and through community education. HealthAmerica received the Governor's Highway Safety Award in 2000 for the Car Seat Safety Check Program, offered in conjunction with the Pittsburgh Children's Museum.

HealthAmerica also provides financial support to many groups such as local chapters of the American Heart Association, the American Red Cross, Big Brothers Big Sisters, Juvenile Diabetes Foundation, Parent & Child Guidance Center, The Pittsburgh Children's Museum, the Early Learning Institute, YMCA, YWCA and United Way, to name a few.

As the last seconds of the 20th century ticked away, fireworks lit up the Pittsburgh skyline, the city celebrated the new millennium and HealthAmerica celebrated its 25th anniversary. Like the beautiful city of Pittsburgh, HealthAmerica also is a place of firsts: It introduced both the first HMO and the first PPO to Pittsburgh, was the first regional HMO to receive federal qualification; the first plan to enable brokers and employers to obtain premium quotes over the Internet; the first regional managed health care plan to be ranked No. 1 in the nation; and the first regional managed care program to offer discounts on complementary and alternative treatment such as chiropractic, acupuncture and herbal remedies.

Innovation, commitment and quality of life were the founding principles that guided HealthAmerica through its first quarter-century. Locally based and locally focused, HealthAmerica today is a pacesetter in the field of managed care and is poised to use its robust business ethic to promote healthy individuals in a vibrant community well into its next 25 years of growth, and beyond.

HealthAmerica/HealthAssurance employees and their families participated in a Family Fun Walk to benefit the Epilepsy foundation of western Pennsylvania. They walked in honor of a young HealthAmerica member who suffers from a seizure disorder (pictured front and center).
Photo by Dave Rentz

Jewish Healthcare Foundation of Pittsburgh

Dedicated in 1908, the first Montefiore Hospital was a converted mission in Pittsburgh's Hill District.

GROWTH OF PITTSBURGH'S JEWISH community in the 1890s and exclusion from existing services created a need for health care for this underserved population. To fill this need, community volunteer Annie Jacobs Davis met with 17 other women in 1898 to plan for a Jewish hospital in the city. Chartered two years later as the Hebrew Ladies Hospital Aid Society, the group worked with existing hospitals to improve care for Jewish patients and also brought health care into the community. They sought out the poor and the sick, rescuing victims suffering from typhoid, tuberculosis and pneumonia from cots in the cellars of the city's Hill District. Among other services, they funded the United Jewish Relief Society for treating tuberculosis, supported mental health programs and paid for a public health nurse.

Within a few years the group opened membership to men, expanded its fund raising and, in 1905, established the Montefiore Hospital Association. A year later the association paid $60,000 for a Hill District site where in 1908 it dedicated the Montefiore Hospital. Among its initiatives, the hospital opened the city's first night clinic for social diseases and made periodic health checkups possible for the underprivileged. As Pittsburgh's Jewish population continued to grow, reaching 35,000 by 1913, the volunteers planned for a larger, 196-bed hospital nearby. Opening its doors in 1929, the hospital provided facilities and staff not only to treat illness but also to conduct research, teach and lead the way in public health education and community service. In 1950 the hospital added 131 beds, a medical and surgical teaching unit, and the area's first hospital-based research laboratory.

By the end of the 1980s Montefiore Hospital faced a financial crisis as government funding contracted and many patients lacked medical insurance. To keep the institution solvent, the hospital's board agreed to transfer responsibility to the University of Pittsburgh's Medical and Health Care Division, which turned over hospital management to Presbyterian University Health Services, Inc. The agreement also led to the 1990 creation of the Jewish Healthcare Foundation of Pittsburgh (JHF), with the hospital board becoming the foundation's board. Karen Wolk Feinstein, Ph.D., was elected president.

JHF bases its programs on Jewish values and ideals as expressed through acts of social justice and charitable giving. The foundation fosters healthcare services, education and research, giving special attention to the elderly, underprivileged and underserved in both the Jewish and general populations of western Pennsylvania.

The foundation supports programs that improve the quality of health care through innovations such as the Pittsburgh Regional Healthcare Initiative; provide research, education and early detection for breast cancer, with the goal of making Pittsburgh a national center for these services; and develop initiatives that contribute to the region's emergence as an international leader in biomedical and biotechnology research. Other supported programs are designed to apply biomedical informatics, or information technology, to the healthcare industry, train healthcare professionals and prevent the spread of HIV/AIDS. JHF also supports programs to enhance the quality of life of the senior population, increase

Members of the Hebrew Ladies Aid Society, Pittsburgh's first Jewish women's volunteer association, are shown in the 1880s

public understanding of depression and support its treatment, serve the particular healthcare needs of the Jewish community in collaboration with the United Jewish Federation, and provide physical and mental health services for children.

Major accomplishments made possible with JHF support include creation of the Jewish Association on Aging, the unique Coordinated Care Network, Pittsburgh ElderHostel, the Squirrel Hill Kosher Super Pantry, Interfaith Volunteer Caregivers of Southwestern Pennsylvania and the Caregivers Training Institute to educate those serving the elderly. In women's health, in addition to its breast cancer programs, the foundation has sponsored various components of the Race for the Cure and funded community-based screening for socially transmitted diseases.

JHF is concerned with the healthcare of the entire Pittsburgh community, especially its vulnerable populations.

An exciting and far-reaching JHF innovation, the Pittsburgh Regional Healthcare Initiative (PRHI) was formed in 1997 under the leadership of President Feinstein and Paul O'Neill, chairman and chief executive officer of Alcoa, who later became U.S. Secretary of the Treasury. PRHI's goal is to establish southwestern Pennsylvania as the world model for health system performance.

PRHI's strategy calls for achieving the world's best outcomes in patient care, focusing initially on heart surgery, hip and knee replacement, cesarean sections, and treatment of depression and diabetes. By adopting quality improvement methods proven in the business world, PRHI aims to produce a healthcare system that gives patients the treatment they need when they need it, without waste or errors. The initiative empowers doctors, nurses, pharmacists and other healthcare professionals to solve problems on the spot, measure results and share what they learn.

For children at risk, JHF helped develop and establish wellness centers in more than 30 Pittsburgh-area schools. The foundation has supported the YMCA of Greater Pittsburgh's counseling program for special-needs youngsters in child-care centers. Parenting programs that JHF sponsors include Reach Out to Families — a model initiative combining home visiting, in-home physician services and community-based parent education programs — neighborhood family support centers and the Jewish special-needs care coordination project.

In support of HIV/AIDS treatment and prevention, JHF sponsors outreach and information campaigns, an adolescent resources network and other support services.

For each of its supported populations, JHF addresses nutritional needs. Toward this end, the foundation formed Food to Grow, a collaborative with corporate leaders, food-industry representatives and public officials to plan programs, educate at-risk individuals and raise funds to combat poor nutrition and hunger.

Having provided about $50 million in its first 10 years, the Jewish Healthcare Foundation plans to build on its successes and sponsor additional creative, problem-solving initiatives to benefit the entire western Pennsylvania community. This is the legacy of Annie Davis Jacobs and her friends, and of the countless professionals and volunteers who cultivated, and continue to cultivate, the seeds these women planted.

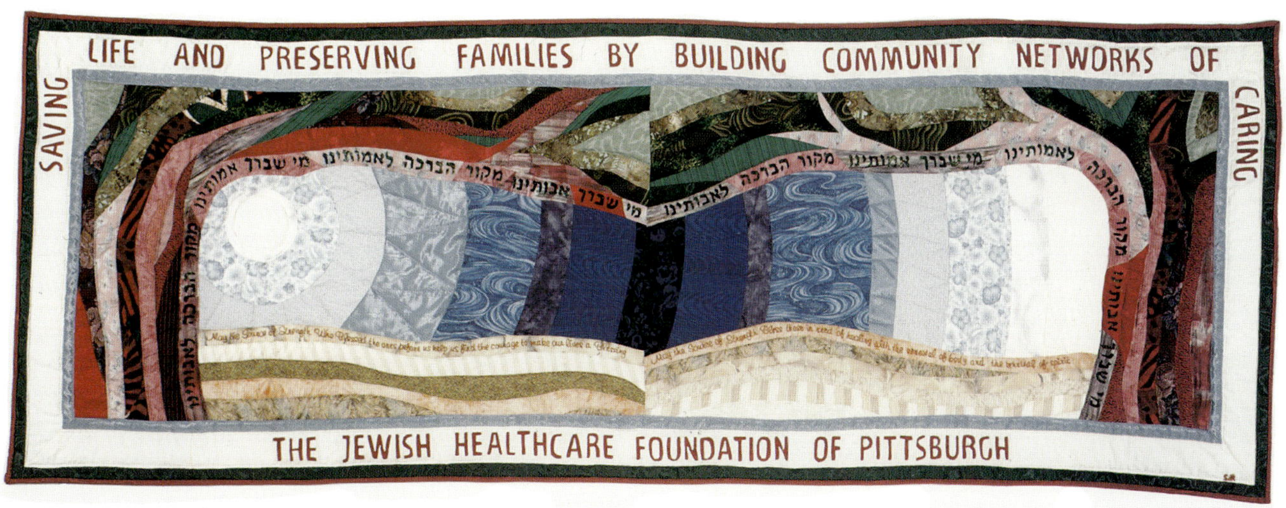

Mi Shebeirakh quilt by Louise Silk showing the Tree of Life and the Tree of Knowledge symbolizes the Jewish Healthcare Foundation's mission, which relates to life and networks.

Pittsburgh Mercy Health System

KNOWN AS "THE HEALTH CARE system closest to the heart of the city," Pittsburgh Mercy Health System has brought compassion to the defining events in Pittsburgh history. Mercy Hospital was the city's first hospital and the first Mercy Hospital in the world.

Mother Frances Warde, Mercy Hospital's founder, and six of her fellow Sisters of Mercy — a Roman Catholic order founded in Dublin to help the sick, the oppressed and the destitute — arrived in Pittsburgh in 1843 after a long, perilous journey from Ireland. This group of young, dedicated women, whose mission was to open a hospital, found themselves in a bustling industrial city that had few health care resources. These pioneering "Seven Sisters" ministered to and cared for the sick, injured and dying before opening Mercy Hospital in a portion of St. Mary's Convent on Penn Avenue on January 1, 1847. Increasing demand for their services forced the hospital to move into its own building on Stevenson Street in 1848.

Mercy established its time-honored tradition of welcoming all patients regardless of race, age, ethnicity, gender or religion, including those with no ability to pay for their health care. Doctors donated their services in rotating three-month terms, and the sisters lived in the hospital and were on duty every waking hour. Epidemics of smallpox, cholera, typhus and scarlet fever often prompted the sisters to give up their own beds to patients as well as to compromise their own health.

The Historical Heart of Pittsburgh

The development of Mercy Hospital has impacted the history of Pittsburgh and the nation in many ways. For example, the high number of battle casualties from the Civil War led to a plea from Secretary of War Edwin M. Stanton for help. In all, 27 sisters from Mercy Hospital traveled to Washington, D.C. to care for injured soldiers at the Stanton Military Hospital, where they were visited by President Abraham Lincoln.

Pittsburgh's industrial post-war boom increased demand for health care services and sparked rapid growth at Mercy Hospital, including expanded facilities, new departments, a full-time medical staff and a school of nursing. The hospital formally incorporated in 1882 and named a distinguished board of directors, which was chaired by Thomas M. Carnegie (Andrew Carnegie's younger brother). This board initiated the fund-raising activities that fueled and continued to support the hospital's growth.

When the Johnstown Flood struck in 1889, a contingent of Mercy doctors and nurses went to Johnstown to care for survivors. Three years later, the infamous Homestead Strike led to an unsuccessful assassination attempt on the life of Henry Clay Frick, who managed Andrew Carnegie's steel mills. Frick, who was cared for by a Mercy surgeon, bequeathed $1.4 million to the hospital in his will.

Throughout World War I, Mercy physicians and nurses served at U.S. Army Base Hospital No. 27, near Angers, France. When the worldwide influenza epidemic struck in 1918, the sisters were called upon to provide nursing throughout Allegheny County, not only within the walls of Mercy Hospital but also as visiting nurses within the parishes throughout the Diocese of Pittsburgh.

During the Great Depression many mills and factories in Pittsburgh closed, leaving at least one-third of the population unemployed. Mercy set up food lines at its kitchen to feed the hungry and admitted many patients who were literally starving.

Mercy physicians also had a notable presence during World War II; they again staffed Base Hospital No. 27, this time in the Pacific. One of Mercy's physicians implemented blood conservation for patient use and established the first and largest blood bank in the Pacific Theater.

Mercy entered the age of nuclear medicine in 1954 with the dedication of the Philip Murray Radiation Center, the first high-voltage radiation therapy center in Western Pennsylvania.

Changing social ideals in the 1960s and the advent of Medicare/Medicaid encouraged community-centered health care. This trend toward ambulatory care complemented the hospital's long-range plans for building and expansion. The Mercy Health Center, a medical and teaching facility, was completed in 1970, and the 13-story Mercy Tower was dedicated in 1976.

In 1983 the hospital's expanding range of services evolved to become what is known today as the Pittsburgh Mercy Health System, enabling the sisters to deliver health care directly to the outlying communities through a larger physical presence in the tri-state area. In 1998 Mercy joined Catholic Health East, one of the nation's largest not-for-profit health care systems with Catholic health facilities serving communities from Maine to Florida.

Technology, Compassion and Community

Today Mercy combines state-of-the-art technology and advanced medical care with compassion for the patient, whose dignity remains the top priority. The spirit of selfless giving and dedication embodied by the original Sisters of Mercy continues to drive the health system's commitment to service, quality and care. These principles enable Mercy to offer the full spectrum of medical and surgical services, including its renowned burn and truama treatment centers and cardiovascular services, as well as oncology, pediatrics, obstetrics/gynecology, rehabilitation, behavioral health, diabetes, neurology/neurosurgery, orthopedics and emergency care.

The health system has added new and emerging technologies, improving diagnostic and treatment capabilities, while at the same time initiating programs that focus on the whole person and that person's interactions with family and the community.

Mercy Health System continues the mission of the Sisters of Mercy through unique programs and the establishment of several community ambulatory health centers. Through a corps comprised mostly of volunteer health care professionals, Mercy's award-winning Operation Safety Net program brings health care to one of the city's most vulnerable and underserved populations — the unsheltered homeless. Volunteers make rounds of the streets five nights a week, using a medical van to provide screenings, vaccinations and primary health care services to the neediest Pittsburghers.

Mother Frances Warde, founder of Mercy Hospital

A Mercy program designed to detect domestic abuse of women entering the emergency room served as a model for statewide legislation establishing guidelines for monitoring spousal abuse. Mercy's Domestic Violence Medical Advocacy Program was recently named a Best Practice by the San Francisco-based Family Violence Prevention Fund. Phenomenal Females and Boys to Men are programs that reach out to at-risk inner city youth. The health system also sponsors the Head of the Ohio rowing regatta and the Power of the Pen, a writing forum conducted in conjunction with the Pittsburgh Public Schools and Carnegie-Mellon University. The Mercy Health System has a strong commitment to professional education and clinical research, sponsoring graduate medical residency programs and a school of nursing. Through affiliations with several colleges and universities, the health system trains additional future health care professionals.

The Sisters of Mercy came to Pittsburgh with a mission to help the needy. Today Pittsburgh Mercy Health System carries forth its mission and the vision of its founders, helping people to lead healthier lives.

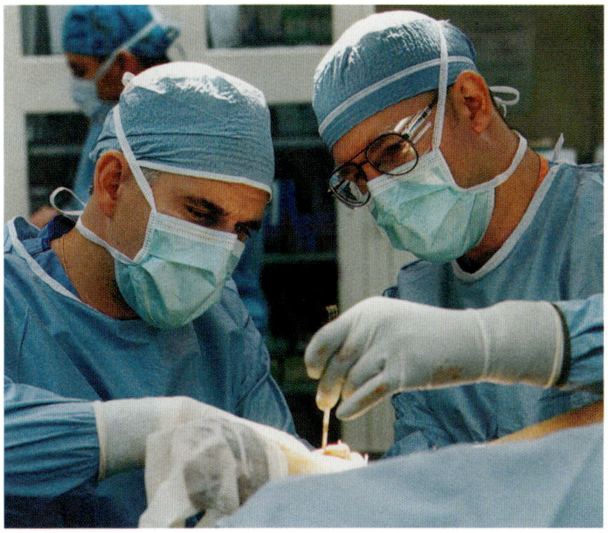

UPMC Health System

DRAWING FROM ITS RICH HISTORY of pioneering breakthroughs in the treatment of human disease and disability, UPMC Health System focuses on delivering high-quality health care throughout western Pennsylvania while conducting medical research, expanding health education and providing community support. From the eradication of polio to organ transplantation to gene therapy, the Pittsburgh region's premier health care system continues its tradition of excellence by providing health services ranging from primary health care and health-related services to comprehensive care for the most complex diseases.

UPMC Health System sets the standard for health care in the Pittsburgh region. In a recent survey by *U.S. News & World Report*, UPMC ranked among the top "Best of the Best" hospitals in the country — the only health care provider in the region ever to do so.

Affiliated with the University of Pittsburgh, UPMC Health System includes an internationally recognized academic medical center, community hospitals, regionwide outpatient treatment centers, physician practices and a range of health insurance plans. UPMC Health System is one of the largest nonprofit health care systems in the United States.

Headquartered in Pittsburgh, UPMC Health System includes 19 tertiary care, specialty and community hospitals; offers the services of more than 5,000 physicians; and provides more than 400 primary care, surgery, rehabilitation and other treatment centers. Ninety percent of the population of western Pennsylvania and eastern Ohio resides within 30 minutes of UPMC treatment, and the Health System provides treatment in urban, suburban and rural areas. But UPMC offers the region much more — the Health System's services include in-home services, retirement living options, a mail-order pharmacy and a range of innovative health insurance options.

UPMC is ranked in *U.S. News & World Report*'s honor roll of "the best of the best" hospitals in the nation. UPMC Health System is also among the top 10 recipients of National Institute for Health (NIH) research funding and sets the standard for health care and biomedical research in the region.

One of a select number of National Cancer Institute-designated comprehensive cancer centers, the University of Pittsburgh Cancer Institute is a particularly bright jewel in UPMC's crown of medical care, research and education.

Innovative Health Care Through Research

At the heart of UPMC Health System is the western Pennsylvania region's only academic medical center. Through its affiliation with the University of Pittsburgh School of Medicine and other schools of the health sciences, UPMC shares in the academic mission of the university by funding a broad range of programs in education, biomedical research, training, health promotion, diagnosis, and treatment of human disease and disability. UPMC also supports continuing education programs for more than 15,000 health care professionals each year, providing training on the most current and effective medical techniques.

UPMC Health System includes internationally renowned programs in a number of specialties such as the region's only National Cancer Institute-designated comprehensive cancer center. UPMC's Department of Psychiatry leads the nation in NIH research funding.

Pioneering research programs for organ transplantation are creating the next generation of transplantation procedures and developing artificial organs that someday may offer an alternative to donor organs.

Revolutionary UPMC programs are exploring medical applications of genetic science for the treatment of diseases as diverse as arthritis, cancer and inherited genetic diseases, as

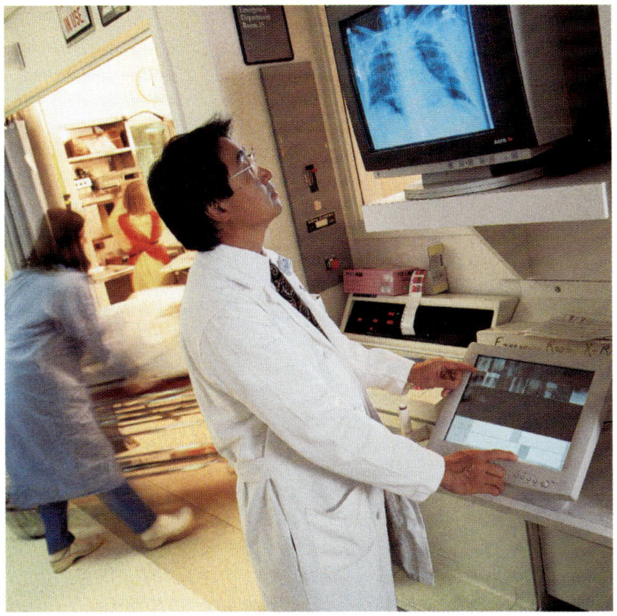

A new computer program developed at UPMC Health System gives doctors the capability to access high-quality radiographic images from personal computers located in remote sites throughout the region.

well as minimally invasive approaches to surgery. UPMC researchers are also applying technology in innovative ways, such as a computerized system that enables orthopaedic surgeons to repair injured or arthritis-inflicted joints with precision that far exceeds that of the human hand, and new brain-imaging techniques that provide researchers with a window into how the brain functions in health and disease.

UPMC Health Plan, UPMC's innovative health insurance program, was established with the belief that the people best equipped to reduce health care costs are the people who provide the care — health practitioners who closely analyze data to identify the best practices. UPMC Health Plan places coverage decisions in the hands of practicing physicians rather than insurance executives. UPMC Health Plan also allows patients to seek specialist care without referrals.

To date, UPMC Health Plan has extended medical coverage to more than 200,000 members. The plan offers insurance products for employees of small, medium and large businesses and an HMO for Medicaid recipients. It also provides coverage for Medicare recipients.

Support for the Greater Community

With more than 30,000 employees, UPMC Health System is the largest employer in western Pennsylvania. A $3.9 billion enterprise, UPMC's nonsalary spending in the region's business community amounts to nearly $750 million annually, helping to create, beyond direct employment, an additional 80,000 jobs.

As part of its commitment to the communities it serves, UPMC annually contributes uncompensated care, community services and voluntary payments valued at more than $120 million. In addition to its fundamental principles of providing affordable, accessible health care and charitable community support, UPMC Health System annually supports more than 3,000 community service initiatives to address the health and welfare of its neighbors. The Health System sponsors approximately 500 initiatives to teach consumers, patients and professionals about important health care issues through health fairs, free and low-cost lectures, and printed materials. UPMC is involved in initiatives to help prevent disease and disability, and programs that support patients and their families with counseling, support groups and subsidized services such as housing and medical prescriptions. And UPMC Health System philanthropic initiatives contribute to the success of civic, advocacy and charitable organizations through in-kind donations and leadership programs.

UPMC is using its resources to improve the community's health by designing prevention and screening programs and preserving health care services in some of the region's most disadvantaged communities. UPMC also uses its financial means to transform technological innovations into spin-off companies, bringing new products to market while helping expand employment and spur the region's economy.

Above all, UPMC remains committed to its core mission of easing human suffering, discovering new medical breakthroughs and educating tomorrow's health care professionals. This focus has enabled UPMC to achieve the many pioneering medical successes throughout its rich history and will chart the course for the region's premier health care system in the new millennium.

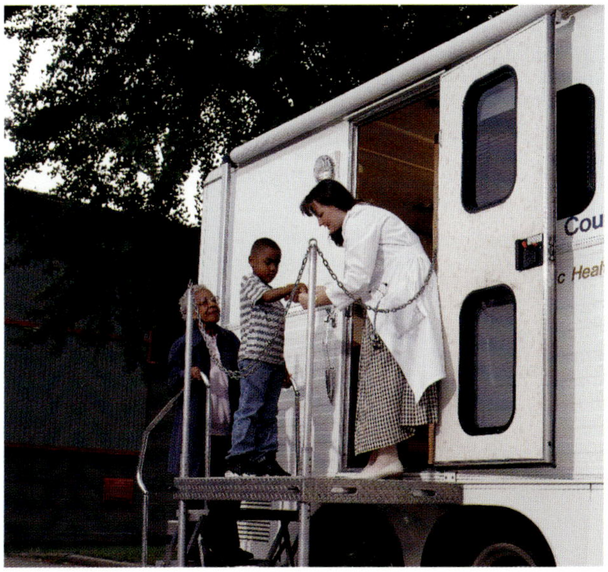

UPMC provides its services throughout western Pennsylvania's urban, suburban and rural areas, providing outpatient treatment for everything from pre-birth counseling to family-oriented community health centers to 24-hour emergency care.

St. Francis Health System

SINCE 1865, ST. FRANCIS HEALTH System has been healing the body, mind and spirit of all in need. The Heath System provides care for all from the beginning of life through senior years at its three hospitals, a skilled nursing center, and outreach locations. The flagship, St. Francis Medical Center, is licensed for 527 beds, has slightly over 2,000 employees and nearly 700 doctors on staff. It is a streamlined organization with strong values and commitment to Catholic health care and a dedicated group of core physician leaders. High-quality clinical outcomes in cardiac services as well as a traditional excellence and respect from the market in behavioral health services, St. Francis Medical Center is positioned in a geographic area appropriate for geriatric acute care. St. Francis Hospital Cranberry, the newest hospital in Pennsylvania, is located in one of the fastest-growing communities in the nation. Services on campus include a surgery center and skilled nursing facility as well as two medical office buildings. Its emergency department and laboratory and diagnostic areas command high utilization in an area that continues to promise demand.

St. Francis physicians use the most sophisticated techniques to prevent, diagnose and treat heart disease. St. Francis established The Center for Preventive Cardiology to educate people about the risk factors of heart disease and offer personal lifestyle plans to keep people's hearts in good shape. St. Francis performs more than 5,000 diagnostic heart catheterizations, stents and laser procedures annually. St. Francis introduced filmless imaging in its Cardiac Cath Laboratory to provide superior images that aid physicians in diagnosing and treating heart disease without the delay of traditional film processing. St. Francis links all facilities with 24-hour rapid access to interventional cardiologists and invasive cardiology services. Emergency air and ground transportation to cardiac labs or surgical facilities is provided in conjunction with fellowship-trained and board-certified critical care physicians. When patients need more aggressive treatment for heart disease and heart defects, board-certified cardiothoracic surgeons provide the care. St. Francis has become a leader in the surgical management of heart disease. Today, more than 800 open-heart procedures and nearly 600 non-cardiac surgical procedures are performed annually by its surgeons. Their excellence has been documented by three independent reviewers — The Pennsylvania Health Care Cost Containment Council, HealthCare Report Cards.com, and HCIA.

St. Francis Hospital Cranberry

The Institute for Psychiatric and Addiction Services at St. Francis is a world-class psychiatric and addiction center that offers a continuum of treatment, prevention, education and specialty services designed to meet individual, family and community needs in the specialties of substance abuse and mental health. Since its inception in 1880 as a nine-bed psychiatric facility, the institute has grown to a comprehensive inpatient and outpatient treatment center with 120 beds of specialized care for eating disorders, addiction, mood disorders and 24-hour-a-day emergency psychiatric services. More than 40,000 people are treated each year through more than 20 different services including mental retardation, employee assistance, mental health and addictions. It has a nationally prominent Psychiatric Residency and award-wining addiction prevention and education programs that serve as resources to the community.

Diseases of the brain, nervous system and spine can be treated at The Center for Neurosciences at St. Francis.

The Center for Physical Rehabilitation approaches treatment as a team. Physicians, therapists and rehabilitation professionals provide constant guidance — whether that means making sure a stroke patient is medically stable before entering rehabilitation, persevering with a patient who has suffered a head injury and is relearning how to walk, talk, and eat, or encouraging family members to play an active role in caring and ensuring a smooth transition when the patient returns home. Inpatient and outpatient services are provided at all locations.

Carnegie Library of Pittsburgh, Pittsburgh Photographic Library

Manufacturing & Distribution

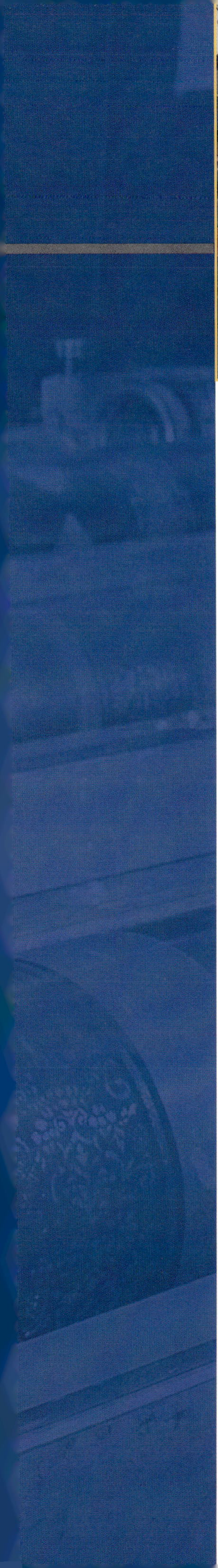

In addition to producing goods and providing services for individuals and industry, Pittsburgh manufacturing and distribution companies provide employment for area residents.

J. Allan Steel Co.

ONE STEEL BEAM, PLATE AND COIL at a time, J. Allan Steel Co. has built a reputation of meeting and surpassing customers' needs and has flourished where other steel service centers have withered.

The company started January 1, 1976, in a small office in the Frick Building as a steel brokerage firm, matching customers with the steel products they needed. Then it was a sole proprietorship, resting on the shoulders of Joe Gnazzo who had taken his first steps into the steel industry with his father, John J. Gnazzo.

Three years later the brokerage firm changed location and direction. J. Allan Steel moved into Pittsburgh's R.J. Casey Industrial Park so it could utilize 5,000 square feet of warehousing for the steel it was buying and selling. In 1983 the company rented the Power Piping Building on the North Side's Beaver Avenue and blossomed as a full-line service center for carbon steel. This happened at a time when half a dozen other steel service centers in the area were forced out of business because of the huge downturn in the industry.

Not only did J. Allan Steel survive the steel bust, it expanded to become the largest local independent service center in the Pittsburgh area. The company's growth is tied to its determination to do more for its fabricating, construction, machine and welding shop customers than any other steel service center in the area. That means J. Allan Steel will work as hard for the customer who needs a single piece of steel shipped as it does for the customer who needs an entire truckload of steel products.

This attention to customers of all sizes has paid off in solid growth for J. Allan Steel. In 1992 the company opened a division near Youngstown, in Masury, Ohio, and forged it into a prime location for stocking hot-rolled, pickled and oiled coils and strips. Located just a few miles from the Pennsylvania border near Interstate 80, the Masury division has easy access to producers and lies along the most convenient truck route between the Mid-Atlantic and Midwest.

J. Allan Steel underwent massive expansion in 1994 and relocated its main plant and warehouse to a new facility at Neville Island, about five miles from downtown Pittsburgh. The impressive Neville Island Center includes stocking and processing areas of more than 250,000 square feet and is about five times larger than its former location. The company also operates its own railroad line and barge-loading facility, which puts J. Allan Steel at the hub of highway, rail and river transportation in western Pennsylvania. The bottom line for customers is that J. Allan Steel has greater capability for meeting their delivery needs and steel specifications.

The Pittsburgh division specializes in distributing plate and flat-rolled products and

Trucks are ready to roll from any of J. Allan Steel Co.'s five strategically located service centers to customers across the East and Midwest.

keeps 26,000 tons of plate and coil inventory on hand. Computerized burning, shearing and specialized cutting capabilities offer customers options from a wide range of stock as well as individually processed sizes. Grades available include but are not limited to A-36, mild steel, HSLA, floor plate and alloy such as AR-400 and A-514. For hot-rolled, HRP&O, cold-rolled and coated coil customers, in-house slitting and leveling capabilities mean J. Allan Steel can meet virtually any width and dimensional requirements.

The Neville facility also serves as headquarters for JAS Scrap Management, which will arrange to collect, remove, transport and dispose of ferrous or nonferrous scrap from any plant or project location.

In addition to its growth in Pittsburgh in 1994, J. Allan Steel also expanded in Ohio that year. The company opened a division in Martins Ferry, across the Ohio River from Wheeling, West Virginia. Ever mindful of its proximity to steel producers and delivery systems, J. Allan Steel acquired a 40,000-square-foot facility that also has an interstate highway system and railroad at its fingertips. The heated facility specializes in slitting, with two fully operational lines.

A growing customer base in Ohio led J. Allan Steel to open a full-service center in Cleveland in 1999. Once again, the company positioned itself to provide accessible pickup or speedy delivery to better meet its customers' needs. The Cleveland location offers cut-to-size processing on structural, plate, sheet, hot-rolled and cold-rolled rounds, flats, squares, pipe and tubing.

State-of-the-art processing provides J. Allan Steel Co. with the ability to meet virtually any width or dimension requirement requested by a customer.

Specialized equipment and long-standing relationships with steel producers allow J. Allan Steel Co. to quickly deliver quality products in the quantity needed.

To better work with the mining industry, J. Allan Steel opened its Consolidated Metals Division in Cedar Bluff, Virginia, in 1997. Strategically located to serve companies in Virginia, North Carolina, Kentucky and Tennessee, the full-service center provides the same products and services that are offered at the Pittsburgh location.

With Joe Gnazzo as president and chief executive officer, J. Allan Steel remains focused on its customers, working to make their tasks easier and more profitable, and staying flexible to meet their ever-changing needs.

The reach of J. Allan Steel grows with the demand from its clients. J. Allan Steel products can be found in the Pirates Stadium on Pittsburgh's North Side, the Cleveland Browns Stadium, the Cleveland Justice Center, Millersville State University and for the renovation of the Brooklyn Bridge.

As J. Allan Steel's 255 employees celebrated the company's 25th anniversary and beyond, they remain dedicated to their vision of customers as partners. Expansion has been based on broadening the lines available to customers, adding to its customized processing capabilities and ensuring quick deliveries to clients dependent on "just in time" supplies. Because of J. Allan Steel's dedication to customer service and attention to detail, 75 percent of North America's metal producing and metalworking plants are within a 500-mile radius of a J. Allan Steel Service Center. These strategic locations allow J. Allan Steel Service Centers to remain unsurpassed in their ability to obtain, stock, process and deliver mill steel in any condition or quantity.

From its modest beginnings as a brokerage service to its growth as a steel service center titan, J. Allan Steel has not lost sight of the fact that service is half of the term "service center." J. Allan Steel remains true to its motto: "Quality service is our business."

Bacharach, Inc.

CONCERN FOR THE SAFETY OF industrial workers in the early 20th century led Herman Bacharach to found the Bacharach Industrial Instrument Company in 1909 as a provider of ventilation and gas measuring instruments for use in the mines, mills and factories of Pittsburgh.

The company — now known as Bacharach, Inc. — was the first manufacturer of gas detection instrumentation in the world and has grown to provide a complete line of instruments that detect, measure and record gas, temperature, relative humidity, air velocity, and other air quality and safety parameters. Businesses in a variety of industries around the world — heating, ventilation, air-conditioning, refrigeration, power generation, fire service, chemicals, manufacturing, etc. — use Bacharach products not only to safeguard employees but also to improve operational efficiencies and protect the environment.

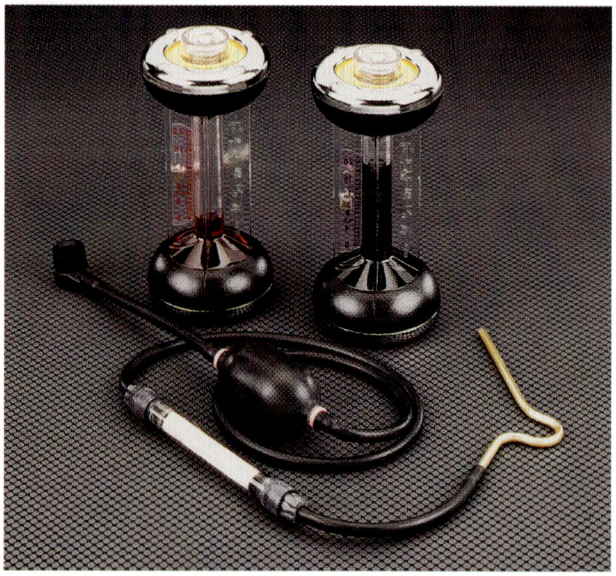

The Fyrite, a small portable gas analyzer, was the company's first heating service instrument.

Bacharach grew rapidly during its early, formative years, in conjunction with the mounting safety needs of industry, and established its first large manufacturing facility in 1915 in downtown Pittsburgh.

New Products, Markets Spark Growth

As demand for industrial instrumentation increased, Bacharach expanded into other markets with a range of new products. During the 1920s the company added manufacturing capabilities for producing temperature measuring and gas analysis instruments. Since then the company's dedication to research and development has led to important new products such as a portable combustion analyzer for determining the efficiency and safety of boilers or furnaces. When technology applicable to Bacharach business was developed elsewhere, Bacharach often acquired the developers of the desired technology to provide its customers with the most appropriate and reliable instrumentation available.

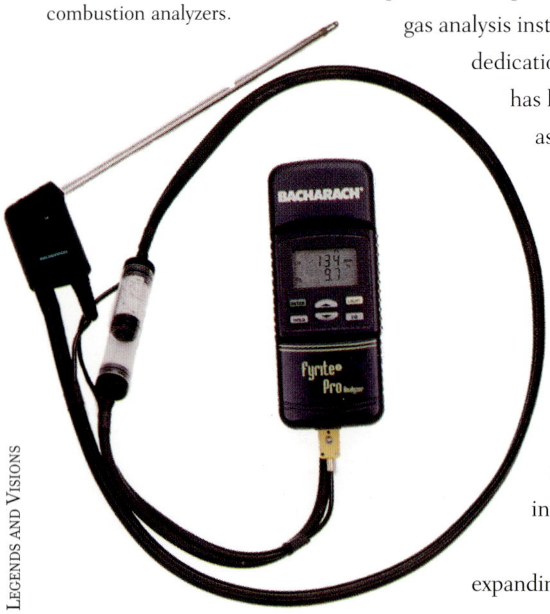

The Fyrite Pro represents the latest generation of combustion analyzers.

The commitment to a diverse, expanding product line begun by Herman Bacharach continued after his retirement in 1935. Bacharach sold his shares in the company to a progressive group of employees who introduced the first heating service instrument, a small portable gas analyzer called the "Fyrite," in 1939.

Throughout the 1940s and 1950s Bacharach established and solidified its respected diesel service instrument line, designing and building high-quality calibration equipment, testers and tools for servicing diesel engines. The U.S. Army used Bacharach calibration stands extensively during World War II. More advanced computerized calibration stands continue to be used by the armed services today.

The company acquired Johnson-Williams, a leading manufacturer of both portable and continuous monitoring systems for combustible and toxic gases, in 1965. A year later AMBAC Industries, a diversified company involved in diesel fuel systems and industrial safety, purchased Bacharach.

Continued growth precipitated the construction of a 156,000-square-foot manufacturing facility in 1968 in the Regional Industrial Development Corporation (RIDC) Industrial Park in O'Hara Township.

By the time United Technologies Automotive Group acquired Bacharach in 1978, the company's product offering had matured to support almost every area of the industrial, automotive, chemical and mining markets.

Current owner and president Paul Zito acquired the company in 1986 and has led Bacharach through its greatest period of sales increases and market expansion. Following the purchase of the complete line of Coleman analytical laboratory instruments and a high-performance liquid chromatography system from Perkin-Elmer in 1988; and GMD Incorporated, a leading producer of paper tape technology for the detection of acutely toxic gases in 1989; Zito took steps to revamp the company's distribution channel to handle the numerous new products and markets served. He established an extensive distributor network in each country where Bacharach products are sold and the Bacharach Service Centers, which provide customers with local services and support.

The ECA 450 Combustion Efficiency and Environmental Analyzer

A Commitment to Quality

The localized Bacharach Service Centers are an illustrative example of the company's commitment to providing quality products and services to its customers. The centers, which are located in five states and four countries, are designed to give customers fast, convenient access to local Bacharach operations. These facilities are staffed by full-time, factory-trained technicians, are well-stocked, and offer a full range of services including repair, maintenance, calibration, training and technical support.

In 1998 Bacharach purchased EIT, a leading producer of fixed gas detection systems, and then spun off its entire gas detection business through a joint venture with Scott Technologies, Inc., a leading provider of respiratory protection equipment and gas detection instruments for firefighting, industrial, aviation and government markets. The Scott/Bacharach venture brings together the world-class expertise of two leaders in gas detection instrumentation, providing customers with the technological benefits of the stronger, combined organization. In the Bacharach tradition, the Scott/Bacharach team of scientists is pioneering technical firsts in sensor technology and design, including catalytic bead, electro-chemical and infrared platforms. In 2000 Bacharach purchased F.T. Industries to expand its HVAC offering to include refrigerant recovery systems.

Bacharach's commitment to quality was recently validated when Bacharach received ISO 9001 quality certification from the International Standards Organization.

An Industry and Community Leader

The same concern for safety that led to the company's founding is also evident in the roles Bacharach plays in the industries it serves and the communities where it does business. The company established the Bacharach Institute of Technical Training to provide training to customers, technicians and members of the community on important safety issues such as carbon monoxide (CO) safety, combustion analysis, ventilation, combustion and venting, and building pressures diagnostics. These seminars have gained recognition as being among the best carbon monoxide and combustion testing training currently available.

Bacharach takes its industry leadership role very seriously, establishing the Carbon Monoxide Awareness Coalition and forming the National CO Advisory Council to educate people about the dangers of CO poisoning.

The company plays a similar role in the communities where it does business. Bacharach donates instrumentation and training to local utility companies and fire departments to ensure the community's instrumentation safety needs are fully met. The corporation also supports winterization grant programs for low-income families by donating the instrumentation used to identify safety problems.

Herman Bacharach was concerned about worker safety. As Bacharach, Inc. moves into a new facility in the Westmoreland County Business and Research Park in Washington Township, the company continues to develop products that not only safeguard the health of people in the community, but serve to protect industrial properties and the surrounding environment as well.

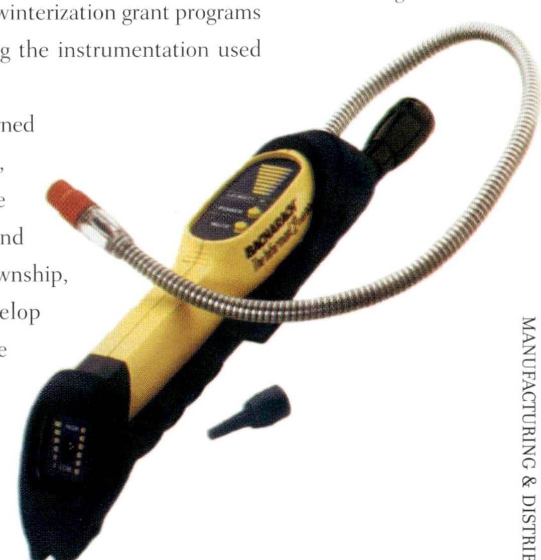

The Informant 2 Leak Detector detects refrigerant and combustible gases with a single unit.

Danieli Corporation

IN 1914 TWO BROTHERS, MARIO and Timo Danieli, founded the Angelini Steelworks in Brescia, Italy. One of the first companies to utilize electric arc furnaces for steelmaking, Danieli Corporation has achieved international prominence through innovative technological advances. Today, Danieli is headquartered in Buttrio, Italy, and is one of the three largest world suppliers of equipment to the metals industry, providing design, manufacture and installation of machinery and plants to produce aluminum, copper, brass and steel.

Through the acquisitions of United Engineering and Wean Industries in the 1990s, Danieli entered the market in the United States. During World War II United assisted the United States in the war efforts by producing artillery weapons, constructing presses for making armor plates, and manufacturing ship parts. Following the war, United employed more than 10,000 people in Pittsburgh as the "Steel City" provided a pivotal link for the supply of equipment and installation to the steel mills. With a strong sense of regional commitment and responsibility to Pittsburgh, Danieli contributes to the local economy by employing a professional work force dedicated to the highest standards in the steelmaking industry.

A Two-Stand Temper Mill built by United Engineering, which was acquired by and is now an integral part of Danieli Corporation

The Danieli United acquisition blends the expertise of United Engineering's hot and cold rolling mill technology with Danieli's meltshop and thin-medium/thin slab caster technology and outstanding performance. The production of ferrous and nonferrous hot and cold strip and plate production and downstream conditioning and finishing lines are supplied to engineering and turnkey plants by Danieli United.

Accordingly, a world leader in the design and manufacture of strip processing lines and material handling equipment, Danieli Wean has supplied over 450 plants. Specialty lines for processing stainless steel, silicon steel and nonferrous metals are also installed by Danieli Wean.

During the time steel production was flourishing in Pittsburgh, Luigi Danieli recognized the need for an international supplier of equipment for small and medium-sized steelmakers. In 1961 production increased and Danieli supplied the world's largest and fastest (400 fpm) Furnace-type Galvanizing Lines. Three years later Danieli implemented the first minimill in Germany and the first continuous casting plant in Italy.

By 1980 Danieli's corporate sales rose dramatically. Research and development projects were refined with an emphasis on cost-efficiency. The first Black Box involving the concept of continuous rolling after casting was created, and within a year, the world's largest round bloom concaster was available. By the end of the decade, Danieli controlled 80 percent of the rolling mills for long products. Danieli now has a leading role in the development of long rolling mills for commercial and specialty steels. Danieli Morgardshammer is the global supplier of rolling mills for long products. High-speed wirerod rolling, in-line heat treatment facilities for bars, wirerod and coiled rounds and high-capacity fully automatic cold finishing services complement Danieli's production of common and specialty steels and superalloys.

Technology and a series of acquisitions further strengthened Danieli's position as a major international supplier of steelmaking equipment. Companies located in Sweden,

France and the United States consolidated with Danieli in Italy and expanded product maximization. In 1991 Danieli supplied the first Turboflo™ Push Pull Pickling Line. Afterward, the first Medium Thin Slab Casters were manufactured; long products, hot strip mills and processing lines for flat products were supplied; and the world's first Liquid Pool Soft Reduction control system for bloom casters was invented. Requests for orders soared as Danieli crossed the threshold of a new frontier in steelmaking. In response to organizational growth, Danieli designated three principal factories to be located, one each in the United States, Sweden and Italy. With exportation averaging 98 percent to 78 different countries, Danieli has extended its range of supplying machines and plants for the steel and nonferrous industries around the globe.

Danieli Corporation has been located at this Cranberry Township, Pennsylvania, site since December 1999.

Recent historical milestones in the Danieli Research Center include melting processes up to 48 heats/day, rolling and in-line thermal treatment of wire rod speeds approximating 140 mps, and fume dedusting plants without emissions. Through reliable efforts of scientific testing methods and product excellence, Danieli's role in refining machinery and equipment has contributed to the overall growth of technology in the steel industry. Danieli has proven ability to supply, on a turnkey basis, complete production lines with associated services and individual machines or parts. This includes numerous and secondary cycles, which are closely interrelated. Turnkey plants designed by Danieli are given customized computer software specific to the designated industrial environment.

Modernization and expansion of existing factories are an additional dimension of service provided by the Danieli Corporation. By supporting customers in the complex details of plant operation, maintenance and training, higher productivity may be maximized. Machines are manufactured and assembled in Danieli's own workshops. Professional technicians supervise the essential steps at the main levels and carefully inspect each process. When the entire plant infrastructure is designed and supplied by Danieli, coordination is uniform, operations are streamlined and dependability is ensured. Follow-up services include personnel training, technical advice, routine maintenance, replacement parts supply and improvement proposals.

Responding to the needs of a dynamic market, Danieli plans to equip its competing manufacturing and assembly shops with the production of single components and small lots; include heat treatment and manufacture of gears; improve the utilization factor (Ku) of machines and systems; and improve machining quality. The structural steelworks production area will also be enlarged, bringing output to nearly 600 t/month. Considerable amounts of funding are annually invested in Danieli's research and development departments in order to renovate workshops, provide modern tool equipment, purchase plants for special machine use, and update the heat treatment and gear grinding shops. Danieli holds certifications in ISO 9001 and EN 729 and meets international requirements.

The mission of the Danieli Corporation is a longstanding commitment to delivering superior quality in the design and manufacture of equipment and plants to the steel industry. A proven leader in the metals industry with over 85 years of experience, Danieli skillfully combines a thorough understanding of the art of steel with scientific expertise that guarantees quality and performance. As Danieli progresses in the 21st century, future success is built upon a solid and unsurpassed reputation of manufacturing the finest steelmaking equipment in the world.

Emerald Art Glass

WITH GLASS THE POSSIBILITIES are endless — just ask Robert and Kim Zielinski. For almost 20 years they have created breathtaking and functional works of glass. In that same time span they have built a family enterprise that feels like it's been in business for generations.

Emerald Art Glass began with a Manchester apprenticeship program where Bob learned to make hand bevels — the smooth, angular edges that give glass an emerald hue. With a young family to support, Bob went to work for himself making bevels in a friend's garage. Word of mouth helped build the business until it became clear that growth would require more space.

The Zielinskis are quick to cast a wide net of gratitude for what is now Emerald Art Glass' football-field-size facility — to the friends and family who lent time and muscle; to Iron and Glass Bank, the only institution that would take a chance on them; to the landlord who trusted that the rent would eventually be paid; and to their children who ate, played and slept at the shop. But it was Bob and Kim who worked all day for customers and then most of the night on their building. They built their dream literally, by gutting and renovating the old Rexel Plumbing warehouse on Josephine Street in the South Side slopes. And they built it client by client, window by window.

Today the Emerald Art Glass showroom highlights Kim's design and Bob's engineering expertise, which combine to create their specialties — unique, custom creations in glass. Projects range from simple to spectacular in tables, mirrors, windows and door lites, glass railings, partitions and even multilayered ceilings and free-standing art glass pieces. Emerald provides many specialty edge works to the glass along with etched, v-grooved and beveled designs in glass and mirror. Kim helps homeowners, architects and designers with new concepts in glass for homes and businesses, whether new construction or renovations. Emerald's specialty is total, unique custom creations to fit customers' needs and tastes.

In the production area, Bob and his staff turn ideas into reality. His equipment ranges from the most primitive hand bevelers to high-tech, state-of-the-art machinery, giving him the widest range of ability to cut and fabricate to his customers' specifications. No matter how large or small the job, he applies the same level of dedication and perfectionism. He and Kim built the business on word of mouth and dedication to quality, and they rely on the same for the majority of their business today.

To the Zielinskis, success isn't measured in sales volume or even in the critical praise they receive from designers and customers. Their business has been a labor of love. It is an integral part of their marriage, a legacy for their children and an outlet for their creativity from the first bevel to the most elaborate, custom window that will be cherished in someone's home tomorrow.

H.J. Heinz Company

WHEN MOST OF THE WORLD THINKS of ketchup, the first name that comes to mind is Heinz. This is grand testimony to a combination of the product's superior taste and flavor, effective and innovative brand advertising and marketing, consistent availability and outstanding quality — as well as firm confirmation of founder Henry John Heinz's original maxim: "To do a common thing uncommonly well brings success."

Company founder Henry J. Heinz

The H.J. Heinz Company has been practicing this principle from its early beginnings in the small town of Sharpsburg, Pennsylvania — producing quality food products with unparalleled, universal consumer acceptance. What began in 1869 as a very small neighborhood business, operated by a young entrepreneur selling a home-grown product from his family's garden, has developed and evolved into today's successful global enterprise marketing No. 1 and No. 2 brands in more than 50 countries with approximately 46,900 employees, and manufacturing and distribution facilities in over 200 major market locations worldwide.

Today, the sun never sets on the business of the H.J. Heinz Company. At any given point in time, somewhere in the world someone is producing, selling, buying or consuming one or more of the company's processed food products. In support of its seven core product categories of ketchup, condiments and sauces; pet food; tuna; infant foods; frozen foods; soups, beans and pasta meals; and organic/nutritional foods, the company has continued its strategy of international growth by acquiring key businesses throughout the world.

Heinz North American and frozen food complex on Pittsburgh's North Side

Recognized as a pioneer in the food processing industry, over the years the H.J. Heinz Company has influenced and led subtle shifts in the eating habits of a great many consumers both domestically and internationally. Earning the public's trust was and remains the dedicated goal of the company. Once convinced of the purity, taste and quality of these brand-name reciped convenience foods, consumers came to appreciate, in large numbers, the products produced by the H.J. Heinz Company. Henry J. Heinz proudly displayed his first product, horseradish, in clear, transparent glass bottles so as not to deceive the purchaser, departing from the unscrupulous manufacturing practice of adding fillers to the product and concealing the product from view in green glass jars. In later years, this ardent dedication to quality was also instrumental in the passage of the Pure Food and Drug Act of 1906.

As Heinz markets have expanded from local to national to global in scope, and from one product to thousands — made famous in large part through the turn-of-the-century "57 Varieties" slogan — quality and product purity have been the driving force of the company's outstanding success. Upon the death of founder Henry J. Heinz in 1919, Howard Heinz, the son of Henry J., assumed the leadership role in the company as well as his father's unfaltering commitment to product quality. Through Howard, an unprecedented regime of scientific product processing, research and quality control methods and procedures was instituted. Although the company struggled through the Great Depression, it was during this era of Howard's presidency that baby foods and ready-to-serve soups were added to the company's product line.

It was not until after World War II that Henry J. Heinz II, who became president in 1941, presided over the company's transition from a family-run operation to that of a professionally managed company. Under his leadership, the H.J. Heinz Company went public and finally began its globalization policy, launching post-war operations in Holland, Japan, Italy and Venezuela. This policy of growth through expansion and acquisition continued to flourish for the next 20 years, during

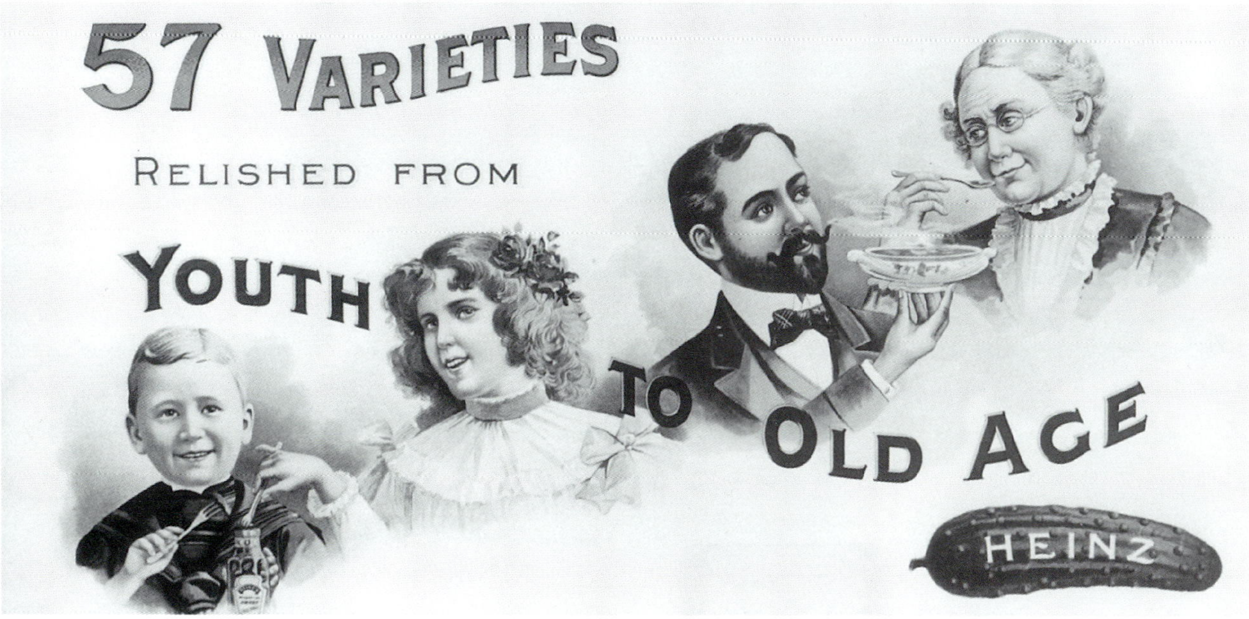

An early "57 Varieties" ad, c. 1896

which time the company acquired additional operations in Italy, Portugal, Mexico and the United States.

In 1965, R. Burt Gookin, an accountant and company manager, was named president and chief executive officer, becoming the first non-Heinz family member to hold this office. Under Gookin's expert management, the pace of acquisitions and growth quickened, and by 1972, Heinz had achieved the $1 billion mark in sales. He introduced advanced financial and management practices, restructured the company under an international management team and hired young Anthony J.F. O'Reilly to serve in the newly created post of senior vice president for North America and the Pacific. Architect of the modern Heinz era, Gookin presided over two key domestic acquisitions, StarKist and Ore-Ida. Under the direction of Dr. O'Reilly, the company acquired Weight Watchers International in 1978 and expanded operations to Spain, Portugal, New Zealand, South Korea, China, India, Egypt and Zimbabwe.

In 1998 William R. Johnson became president and chief executive officer of the H.J. Heinz Company. He continued the company's international growth strategy by developing joint ventures in Indonesia and the Philippines and by strategic acquisitions to significantly expand Heinz's European frozen foods business. Johnson also launched Heinz's organic/nutritional foods category, turning the company into the fastest-growing segment in the food industry. In 1999, Pittsburgh gained even greater prominence at Heinz with the relocation of headquarters for Ore-Ida Foods and Weight Watchers Gourmet Food Company from Boise, Idaho, to the city's North Side as a newly combined Heinz Frozen Food Company. The following year, Heinz moved its StarKist and Heinz Pet Products affiliates to Pittsburgh from the Cincinnati area, forming a unified Heinz North America.

The modern H.J. Heinz Company stands poised for breakthrough advances and accelerated global growth under the direction of a new generation of leadership in key markets around the world. When Henry J. Heinz first envisioned the opportunity to provide a superior-quality food product, perhaps little did he realize the enormous impact his small company would eventually have on the world marketplace. The H.J. Heinz Company that exists today is, unquestionably, one of the most respected marketers of quality food brands in the world — a testament to both the genius of its founder and premier Pittsburgh native, Henry John Heinz, and the enduring dedication and skill of generations of Heinz employees around the world.

Heinz today: a world of leading brands

Matthews International Corporation

FROM DISTINCTIVE BRONZE memorials to its role in the development of UPC bar code symbol technology, Pittsburgh-based Matthews International Corporation has arguably gained top ranking as the premier leader of manufactured items that identify people, places, products and events. It also enjoys the distinction of being Pittsburgh's oldest continuously operating company.

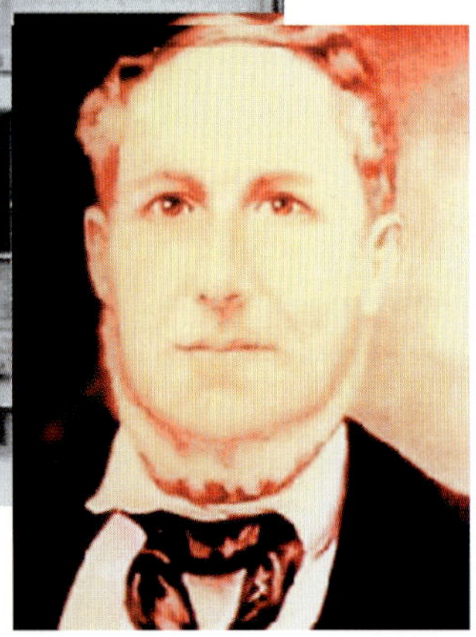

John Dixon Matthews, founder of Matthews International Corporation

Although the company makes its headquarters on Pittsburgh's north shore, its presence is seen in grocery stores where UPC codes are scanned, on the crest for the Sultan of Brunei's 747 hangar — even at the summit of Pikes Peak where a bronze plaque includes the words to "America the Beautiful." That's a long way up for a company whose founder came to Pittsburgh bearing steel stamps, stencils, branding irons and a big dream.

The creation of a Matthews bronze memorial combines an age-old casting process with the latest technology.

John Dixon Matthews, a native of Sheffield, England and a skilled engraver, immigrated to America and eventually opened a small shop in Pittsburgh in 1850. He focused on becoming the foremost provider of superior quality identification products and services. Production at the shop created materials for personalization, including military stamping dies, branding irons, ornate engravings and stamps for wooden crates.

The business flourished through the late 1800s and by the turn of the century in 1902, Matthews went from a partnership to a corporation.

Throughout the 1920s Matthews continued to grow, receiving accolades along the way for its high-quality identification capabilities. Out of that growth emerged three separate operating units: the Bronze Division, the Graphics Imaging Group, and the Marking Products Division.

Since casting the first flush bronze memorial in 1927, the Bronze Division has become the world's leading manufacturer and marketer of cast bronze memorials and architectural plaques. Every memorial and architectural order is custom-made. Some of the most notable include: the cast bronze inductee plaques for the National Baseball Hall of Fame; the 100-foot by 30-foot doors for the Saudi Arabia Monetary Authority; the plaques for the 1984 Summer Olympics in Los Angeles as well as the 17-foot-high bronze sculpture that has been credited with sheltering many people from the bomb explosion in Olympic Park during the 1996 Summer Olympics in Atlanta; and bronze memorials for celebrities such as Lucille Ball, Red Skelton and Elvis Presley.

The Graphics Imaging Group continues to be a leader in pre-press services used by consumer product companies and manufacturers of corrugated and flexible packaging to create packaging graphics designed to improve sales and recognition of their clients' products. Products and services have been expanded to offer creative design, digital scans, color separations, and color retouching. The Group also has a global reach through facilities located both in North America and Europe that are connected via high-speed internet lines. This enables simultaneous marketing of a client's corporate image and products through a variety of capabilities and controls. With worldwide accessibility and distribution, the Graphics Imaging Group bills itself as a full-service supplier to clients that include Anheuser Busch and Proctor & Gamble.

The Marking Products Division's employees manufacture an array of equipment for industrial marking in the packaging, automotive, rubber, building products, metals, plastics and glass industries. Companies worldwide count on Matthews to mark their products for identification, traceability, compliance and operational purposes. The Marking Products Division has even made use of covert marking with invisible inks to combat counterfeiting. It has counted among its equipment the simple steel stamps John Matthews used in 1850 as well as environmentally friendly inks and fully-automated ink-jet and laser printing systems.

In 1994 Matthews became a public company, and in April 2000 it celebrated its 150th anniversary with an exhibit at the Senator John Heinz Pittsburgh Regional History Center. The display completely filled the History Center's Third Floor Gallery and garnered a profile in the Pittsburgh Post-Gazette. And, for the first time, the National Baseball Hall of Fame allowed the plaque commemorating hometown Pittsburgh Pirates great Roberto Clemente to be displayed outside its Cooperstown, New York site.

Today, the company employs more than 2,300 people in 26 manufacturing and marketing facilities in seven countries on three continents. Even as Matthews International continues to grow, it considers its employees its most important asset. Many long-time Matthews employees state that the company was founded on its commitment to both its customers and its own employees. For example, in the early 1900s, James H. Matthews, the youngest son of the company's founder, introduced health insurance and a profit distribution program. And in a company newsletter from July 1942, employees were recognized for events such as engagements and births to the sons of employees who served aboard the U.S.S. Bunker Hill. One piece of advice casually mentions, "If you have any teeth that need pulling, see Bill Evans, the expert tooth yanker from Memorial Bronze."

Local officials have long recognized Matthews' influence on Pittsburgh, its success as a company and its employment of Pittsburghers. Mayor Tom Murphy declared June 25, 2000 "Matthews International Corporation Day," and Allegheny County followed with "Matthews International Week" for the week of July 9, 2000.

With an eye toward growth and acquisitions and continued innovation in the identification industry, Matthews International celebrates more than 150 years of literally making its mark on the world.

(Left)
Matthews International Corporation makes its headquarters on Pittsburgh's revitalized north shore.

Matthews designs, manufactures, and markets custom-made products used to identify people, places, and events. The company's products and operations are comprised of three business segments: Bronze, Graphics Imaging, and Marking Products.

Pitt Ohio Express

IN THE HISTORY OF TRANSPORTING goods by ground carrier, much more has changed than just the mode of conveyance. Today's operations of Pitt Ohio Express, a leader in regional LTL (less-than-truckload) transportation, are a long haul from the original business, Hammel's Express, that Charles Hammel Sr. and his wife, Marie, established in 1919. In that early industrial era, the business was a horse-and-buggy operation that made a 20-mile trek from Pittsburgh north to Aliquippa, Pennsylvania, supplying provisions to the J&L Steel Company store.

Hammel's Express remained a small local carrier until Charles Jr. took the reins after World War II. The company expanded to become a leading carrier in the Pittsburgh region and as it prospered, Charles Jr. broadened his territory. In the 1960s it expanded to serve a 25-air-mile radius in western Pennsylvania.

In the 1970s, as local warehouses were closing, Charles Jr. foresaw that the future lay in interstate hauling. Seizing an opportunity in 1979, he bought a dormant Interstate Commerce Commission certificate, which enabled him to conduct state-to-state business. This certificate led to his founding of Pitt Ohio Express, which he then turned over to his sons, Charles "Chuck" Hammel III, president; Robert, executive vice president; and Kenneth, who retired in 1996.

Today the privately held Pitt Ohio Express is Pittsburgh's largest trucking company and employs more than 2,000 drivers, terminal workers and support staff. The company directs a fleet of nearly 1,000 trucks from its modern headquarters building in the city's Strip District. Pitt Ohio serves all of the Mid-Atlantic states and parts of the Midwest and South.

Just as his father had done earlier, Charles III and other Pitt Ohio executives spotted an industry trend — just in-time (JIT) deliveries — that changed the way the company did business. Customers were shifting to a production and sales operation that relied heavily on JIT delivery of goods to save money previously tied up in inventory.

In JIT delivery, retail stores notify manufacturers when they sell a product and it is replaced almost immediately. Pitt Ohio picks up the product from the manufacturer and delivers it to the retail store the next day, eliminating the need for stores to have a huge warehouse space to keep inventory in stock. Pitt Ohio delivers more than 97 percent of its freight overnight.

Familiar sights throughout the Pittsburgh region are the big rigs of Pitt Ohio Express, the city's largest trucking company.

To make overnight delivery possible, the company operates 18 terminals in Pennsylvania, Maryland, West Virginia, New Jersey, Ohio and Virginia. Through selective partnerships, Pitt Ohio also can receive and carry shipments from other parts of the country. The strategic locations of its terminals and its partnerships give Pitt Ohio a strong competitive edge, as does the reliability of its drivers. All of the company's drivers are selected for their entrepreneurial spirit and dedication to excellence.

President Hammel and Pitt Ohio continue to be innovators in the transportation industry by staying in the forefront of information technology. The rapid development of electronic commerce with the Internet has caused information to be the key element to customer satisfaction. The company is leading the way in this arena with development of proprietary computer software to track its shipments. The Pitt Ohio Imaging System (POIS) electronically scans freight bills and delivery receipts at terminals, which eliminates time-consuming paperwork. Computer systems then transfer the electronic images to a central office for processing and order tracking.

Still active in his own trucking firm, Charles Hammel Jr. (right) founded Pitt Ohio Express, which is run by sons Robert (left) and Charles III.

Safety is a top priority at Pitt Ohio Express, and the company is leading the way in transportation safety studies. For example, Pitt Ohio volunteers its resources to support the Drowsy Driver program of Carnegie Mellon University's Robotics Institute. This advanced research project developed a device that measures a driver's blinking rate and sounds an alarm when the rate indicates drowsiness.

The company and its employees have received accolades for their safety, performance and innovation. Among the most important is the coveted American Trucking Association President's Trophy for an outstanding safety record. Pitt Ohio is the only carrier to have won this prestigious award twice in less than five years. In addition, it is the only company named by General Electric Company as Carrier of the Year three years in a row. It has also received Carrier of the Year honors from other major companies.

Pitt Ohio is heavily involved with many civic and charitable organizations. President Hammel serves on the boards of the Boy Scouts, Greater Pittsburgh Community Foodbank and the Lawrenceville Development Corporation, which supports a neighborhood near the company's headquarters. Pitt Ohio and its employees donate their time to many annual projects, such as the MS 150 Bike-A-Thon, for which drivers volunteer to haul 1,000 bicycles from Erie, Pennsylvania, back to Pittsburgh. In addition, Pitt Ohio sponsors the Pittsburgh Penguins cystic fibrosis fund-raising dinner. It also transports all the goods collected in the Pittsburgh area for the Scouting for Food campaign and delivers Christmas trees for a fund drive for the Little Sisters of the Poor in Charleston, West Virginia.

A strong work ethic is an important family value that the Hammels pass on to every generation. In their early teens, the three sons of Charles Jr. broke into the family business by working on Saturdays and during summer vacations. Learning the trucking industry from the bottom to the top, the brothers started out by washing trucks, fixing turn signals, and loading and unloading freight. Charles III and Robert have passed this tradition along to their own children.

In their role as the company's leading executives, the Hammel brothers devote a portion of their time to studying transportation trends, with the aim of continuing to lead industry change. They believe the future belongs to lean regional companies that are swift in adapting to such developments. As a result, Pitt Ohio Express is basing its future not only on modern equipment but also on computer technology.

A prime example of Pitt Ohio's innovation to meet rapidly changing needs is its recently formed logistics operation, which lays the groundwork for its evolution as an information clearinghouse. The aim is to allow customers to monitor every shipment in its point-to-point journey. A vital part of the future of Pitt Ohio Express, this "see-all" computer-based information system will track shipments by every mode of transportation in every corner of the world.

Koppers Industries, Inc.

CARBON PITCH, RAILROAD TIES, furnace coke and creosote are top commodities at Koppers Industries. But respect and loyalty are the reason employees and customers stay. Of 475 Pittsburgh employees, many have worked for Koppers their entire career, and employees own almost 40 percent of the company.

In the early 1900s beehive ovens supplied a majority of the coke necessary for steel production. Unfortunately, the coke was poor quality and lacked uniformity, causing blast-furnace inefficiencies. In addition beehive ovens burned off valuable chemicals. Enter U.S. Steel and Heinrich Koppers, a German engineer who invented a chemical recovery coke oven in 1906 that improved on wasteful American beehives.

Koppers ovens were efficient machines that produced higher quantities of better quality coke. Coke uniformity was achieved, as was the recovery of coal gases, tar and chemicals. U.S. Steel brought Heinrich Koppers to America and contracted with him to build a 280-oven coke plant in Joliet, Illinois. A few years later, Koppers moved his operation to Chicago and incorporated under the name H. Koppers Company.

This tough, astute entrepreneur had a flair for taking risks and helping his associates, particularly his young apprentices when they showed talent and ability. After World War I, Andrew Mellon caught wind of a genuine business investment from colleagues — Heinrich Koppers was looking to sell controlling interest in his company. Mellon's group bought the H. Koppers Company in 1914 and moved the headquarters to Pittsburgh by 1915. At that time, the company's 15,000 stock shares were valued at $1.5 million.

Headquartered in the 35-story, National Historic Landmark Koppers building since 1929, some businesses of the old Koppers Company changed hands in 1988 in a leveraged buyout, resulting in the current global company, Koppers Industries, Inc.

Koppers Industries produces carbon compounds and treated wood products, like railroad ties, for use in a variety of markets including the railroad, aluminum, chemical, utility and steel industries. Now a worldwide player, Koppers Industries still believes in its employees and maintains close relationships with several large customers, including CSX and ALCOA. Research is underway to create specialty carbon pitch products for multiple uses, from batteries to car brakes.

Employing over 2,100 people worldwide with operations in the United States, Europe and Australasia, Koppers Industries has grown steadily, mostly through acquisitions. Improving customer satisfaction with better products and productivity means that every company Koppers buys will improve. With the 2000 acquisition of Tarconord A/S, now known as Koppers Europe, and a joint venture in China, Koppers Industries sees its place in the global marketplace continuing to expand over the next several decades while keeping its headquarters in Pittsburgh.

Providing high quality carbon materials and chemicals efficiently for a low cost is what brought Koppers Industries to life in the early 20th century. Satisfied customers, hard work and employee dedication are the reasons the company will continue to thrive into the 21st century.

L.B. Foster Company

LEE B. FOSTER WAS JUST 20 YEARS old when he started the company that bears his name. Financed in 1902 with a $2,500 loan from Foster's father, which was repaid within six months, L.B. Foster Company grew over the next century to become a national leader in the manufacture, fabrication and distribution of surface transportation infrastructure products.

Foster founded the company to fulfill a transportation need he first observed while growing up around his father's oil business in Titusville, Pennsylvania. Many inquiries came to his father's company from mines, logging camps and quarries regarding the relaying of rails. Because no truck transportation existed at that time, rail spurs, both temporary and permanent, represented the only means for transporting heavy materials. New rail was cost prohibitive, so Foster initiated the practice of selling "used" rail — taken from abandoned and replaced railroads and urban transportation systems — to meet this transportation need.

What set L.B. Foster Company apart in those early years and contributed greatly to the firm's success was the Foster Guarantee: "If the material is not up to the standard represented, ship it back and we will pay the freight both ways." This dedication to customer satisfaction is a core company value, and the Foster Guarantee is still in force today.

Lee's success attracted the notice of his three brothers, Reuben, Sydney and Byron, who all joined the company upon completion of their education. The four brothers worked well together (Lee changed his sole proprietorship into a four-way partnership) and expanded the company into new markets and regions, opening offices in New York City in 1922 and Chicago in 1926.

The company, which became publicly traded in 1981 (NASDAQ: FSTR), continues to supply products for rail markets, offering a full line of new and used rail, trackwork, and accessories to railroads, mines and industry. Today, the company's core business shares focus with products used in the construction of transportation infrastructure, including pilings, bridge decking, expansion joints, overhead sign structures, mechanically stabilized earth wall systems, precast concrete modules and pipe-related products.

Lee B. Foster II, the founder's grandson, became president and chief executive officer of the company in 1990, providing a vital link between the company's past and present as he expands the firm's core competency and develops niche markets.

In 1999 the firm acquired CTX Inc., a leading manufacturer of engineered concrete products for the railroad and transit industries. The acquisition better positions L.B. Foster Company to serve rail and transit customers with a mix of products and services, delivering comprehensive project capabilities on even the largest projects.

The company's products have been used in many well-known national projects, such as the rail used to serve the Port of Los Angeles and materials used in the Brooklyn Bridge rehabilitation. Locally, L.B. Foster products were used on the Smithfield Street Bridge and Hot Metal Street Bridge rehabilitation projects.

As Pittsburgh and America have grown, L.B. Foster Company has provided the products necessary to help build the infrastructure of a city and a nation.

LTV Copperweld

LTV COPPERWELD IS THE LARGEST North American manufacturer of superior-quality steel and stainless tubing products, steel pipe and conduit, and a world-leading producer of bimetallic wire and strip products. It is a unit of The LTV Corporation, a manufacturing company with interests in steel production, metal fabrication and advanced steel technologies. Formed in 1999, LTV Copperweld is the result of a myriad of acquisitions, facility expansions and finally, the merger of three premier pipe and tubing manufacturers — Copperweld Corporation, Welded Tube Company of America and LTV Tubular Products Company. The new LTV Copperweld employs 3,600 and has 22 manufacturing facilities strategically located in prime market and distribution areas throughout the United States and Canada.

(Far right) A lab technician at LTV Copperweld's Elizabethtown plant checks the weld from a cross-section of LaserTube[tm] stainless steel tubing.

LTV Copperweld is the largest producer of high-quality steel tube and pipe in North America, and the world's leading manufacturer of bimetallic wire products.

Copperweld Corporation was formed in 1915 in Rankin, Pennsylvania, and manufactured a line of copper clad steel wire and strand products. Originally called the Copper Clad Steel Company, it was renamed in 1924 to promote its patented molten weld process of bonding copper to steel. Copperweld entered the mechanical steel tubing business in 1952 when it acquired the Ohio Seamless Tubing Company. It acquired Chicago's Regal Tube Company in 1972 to further extend its product offerings with structural tubing. In 1975 IMETAL, a French firm, acquired a major interest in Copperweld. During the same year, an advanced bimetallic wire production facility was opened in Fayetteville, Tennessee. Several expansions occurred over the next several years, enlarging the scope of the company's basic market position. In 1993 it expanded its interest in the welded mechanical tubing business by acquiring Miami Industries Division of Armco, Inc., and in 1995 acquired Metallon Engineered Materials Corporation, a producer of bimetallic products. Finally, in 1997 Copperweld purchased two major manufacturers of steel tubing in Canada, Sonco Steel Tube and Standard Tube Canada, and New York-based Tube and Steel Company of America.

The Welded Tube Company of America was formed in 1946 in Philadelphia, Pennsylvania. Originally it manufactured steel tubing for hammock frames and car jack parts. Two additional plants were acquired during the 1950s because of a growing market demand for increased structural steel tubing applications. A new manufacturing facility was constructed in Chicago during the 1970s and is one of few operations in existence capable of producing tubing in up to 16-inch square sizes.

LTV Tubular Products Company was a pioneer in welded specialty tubing with production beginning nearly 80 years ago, and quickly developed into a leading manufacturer of structural and mechanical tubing and steel conduit and pipe. Products produced at LTV Tubular Products Company complemented those of Copperweld and Welded Tube, providing an opportunity to span virtually the entire range of steel tubing and pipe products.

The formation of LTV Copperweld offers outstanding benefits and opportunities to its valued customers, employees and communities in which it serves. The company is committed and dedicated to providing leading-edge product and facility technology in an atmosphere of total environmental compliance and safe working conditions. LTV Copperweld will confidently face the future with assurance that it will perform according to the highest standards of corporate responsibility.

Marshall Elevator Company

A FRONTIER LAND CONFRONTED

John Marshall in 1818 when he immigrated to Pittsburgh from Avon-on-Trent, England, seeking better opportunities for his family and his business. That year, just two years after the city was incorporated, Marshall set up a blacksmith shop and foundry not far from where Fort Pitt stood at the Point.

His three sons — John, Michael and Joseph — took over the business in 1845 and built a larger factory up the road. In 1875, as the region continued to grow steadily and new buildings rose constantly, the brothers entered the fledgling business of making elevators. Hoisted by hand or water- or steam-powered systems, the small lifts were vital for multistory factories and office buildings, mainly to haul freight and equipment. The advent of electricity brought elevators that could go higher, move faster and carry larger loads of people and freight. There is no doubt that electric-powered elevators raised the face of America.

In 1902 the business was incorporated as Marshall Elevator Company and moved to its present location on Pittsburgh's South Side. It turned another page some decades later with the invention of the automobile grease rack. In 1942 President Ralph Marshall formed an association with Dover Elevator Company, a successor to Rotary Lift Company, the rack's inventor. The partnership led to production of passenger elevators powered by hydraulic lifts, which proved to be much less costly than cable systems when used in small buildings. To this day, Marshall is a franchised distributor of hydraulic lifts.

Now in its third century of operation, Marshall Elevator Company remains a family-run business. Under the leadership of Robert S. Jamison Jr., a son-in-law who is president and chief executive officer, the company sells freight and passenger elevators, escalators, stage lifts, dumbwaiters and wheelchair lifts for installations throughout western Pennsylvania. The lifts are essential for factories, hospitals, schools, office buildings, towers and homes, as well as landmarks like the Pittsburgh Steelers' new football stadium.

A subsidiary, Marshall Electronics Division, makes electronic control and communication equipment for automated warehouse vehicles, cranes and similar machinery around the world.

Contributing to his community, Jamison serves on the board of Family Guidance, Inc., and several business and religious organizations. He also supports civic groups that are working to rejuvenate the South Side, a lively neighborhood that mixes residences, retail shops and light industry.

As the company builds on its amazing longevity, its 100 employees take pride not only in their historic contributions to western Pennsylvania, but also in farther-afield jobs such as the company's man lift that carried workers up the outside of the St. Louis Arch during its construction in the early 1960s. Among its other contributions, the company designs and produces a unique elevator for tall transmission towers.

Jamison plans for future growth by attending to the historic pattern set by John Marshall and his successors. This family blueprint calls for the company to develop the right products for selected market niches, constantly improve every aspect of the business and, above all, provide solid leadership in an indispensable industry.

Carrying construction workers to and from their job during construction of the famed St. Louis Arch in the early 1960s was an external lift built and installed by Marshall Elevator Company.

Fans at the Pittsburgh Steelers' new football stadium, shown during construction, will be whisked from level to level on Marshall Elevator's escalators and elevators.

MetPlas Incorporated

RUSSELL FINSNESS, FOUNDER and President of MetPlas Incorporated, developed ideas on how to grow and evolve a fabrication business while working as the general manager of an Oakmont plastics fabrication company. He realized that making his ideas come to life, however, required measures of freedom and flexibility he could never attain working for someone else.

In 1981, working with three partners and 10,000 square feet of leased industrial space in Glenshaw, Finsness founded MetPlas. Like most new ventures, the early years were a time of struggle. Through the hard work, dedication and commitment of the work force combined with his vision and hands-on management style, Finsness grew a successful company.

MetPlas began operations as a plastics fabricator but quickly took on metals fabrication as well. Finsness says metal came naturally because the same equipment is used to fashion both metal and plastic components.

The company soon outgrew its Glenshaw facility. In 1988 the company broke ground on a new, 24,000-square-foot building on four-and-one-half acres, becoming the first facility in the Highlands Industrial Park in Natrona Heights, which is located northeast of Pittsburgh. Business growth led to the construction of an additional 11,000-square-foot facility in 1999.

Finsness bought out his partners' interests and continued evaluating and implementing new technologies. Using robotics, business automation and computer-driven CNC machining technologies, MetPlas has consistently improved its cycle time in machining plastic and metal components under contract and has established a reputation for the highest quality products and on-time delivery. MetPlas customers have recognized the company's superior performance through numerous "valued supplier" awards and increased business volume. During the 1998-2000 timeframe, MetPlas sales revenues increased 67 percent, further proof of the confidence regional OEMs have in MetPlas.

MetPlas is committed to supporting its employees and the community through its involvement in many area initiatives. The company sponsors a local sprint-car racing team whose members include MetPlas employees: driver Scott Preister, his father and his father-in-law. Employees and their families cheer on the team at the annual Race Night at nearby Lernerville Speedway. MetPlas also supports the Northern Area Multi-Service Center of Allegheny County, contributing to the center's Community Assistance Program and Restore Food Pantry, which provide services and food to more than 100 families each month. The company is a member of the Allegheny Valley Chamber of Commerce, and Finsness is on the board of the Southwestern Pennsylvania Industrial Resource Center.

Finsness founded MetPlas on the belief that a plastics fabricator could do more. The company has grown to become a leading contract machine shop through his commitment and dedication to his company, his employees and the Southwestern Pennsylvania area.

TRACO

THE STATUE OF LIBERTY HAS BEEN shining more brightly over New York Harbor ever since its salt-encrusted crown was fitted with new bronze windows in 1986. Their maker was TRACO, a global manufacturer living up to its motto: "The windows and doors that greet the world."

Using the exacting methods of the original French craftsmen, TRACO artisans handcrafted the 25 polished bronze replacement windows in the Statue of Liberty's crown.

During Lady Liberty's refurbishing, TRACO developed and produced 25 miniature handcrafted windows made with safety glass. The polished bronze windows shine like jewels in the statue's crown.

The statue's restoration was among the company's many achievements since 1943, when Mae and E.R. Randall founded the firm as Three Rivers Aluminum Company. Evolving with postwar Pittsburgh — from a commodities maker of affordable building products to a high-tech producer — today's TRACO manufactures high-performing, energy-efficient windows, doors, skylights, folding glass walls, solariums and sunrooms for the commercial and industrial markets. Based in suburban Cranberry Township, Pennsylvania, the company operates seven manufacturing facilities around the world, with offices and distribution centers across the United States. In 1999 TRACO became a global manufacturer when it established a joint venture in Wuhan, China, to produce aluminum and vinyl windows for Pacific Rim nations.

Making exciting things happen remains the foremost goal of the company's 1,700 team members, according to the founders' son, Robert Randall, TRACO's president and chief executive officer. On into this new century, the company's commitment is to develop innovative products for buildings. Its major markets comprise education and health care facilities, multifamily residences, offices, hotels and motels, and renovation projects, including historic landmarks.

For new or replacement window applications, TRACO's team of professionals develops and produces unique customized designs. The company's capabilities include glass tempering, anodizing, paint finishing, aluminum extruding and glass insulating.

Developing innovative products to confront extremely challenging environmental or building conditions is another specialty of the technical team. The TRACO operation in Miami, for example, develops and manufactures unique "hurricane" products designed to meet the toughest weather challenges. The impact-resistant windows and doors are built to withstand hurricane-force wind loads up to 200 mph.

TRACO team members recognize that rising operating costs are of extreme concern to the owners and operators of office structures, apartment buildings and condominium complexes. The company's team works with architects to develop efficient windows that cut energy costs that usually pay for themselves over the life of a building.

Health care providers and owners of educational buildings — from grade schools through universities — also look to TRACO's team to meet their specific needs. Team members incorporate cost-reducing features in their custom products as well as aesthetic properties that improve the quality of life for people using the facilities. Such products include laminated glass and other special glazing to enhance sound control as well as make buildings safer and more secure.

With the Statue of Liberty and the Empire State Building as just two of the stars in its firmament, TRACO aims to carry on the proud traditions of its founders — especially their dedication to quality and innovation in technology.

At its Cranberry Township, Pennsylvania, headquarters and other facilities worldwide, TRACO's 1,700 team members contribute to production, sale and distribution of high-performance, energy-efficient windows and doors.

Mine Safety Appliances Company

THEIR EXPERIENCES AS engineers with the U.S. Bureau of Mines, including a 1911 mine explosion in Colorado, during which they could "hear the screaming of children and the desolation of wives and mothers," prompted John T. Ryan and George H. Deike to found Mine Safety Appliances Company (MSA) in 1914. MSA's founders had witnessed the human destruction in the mines and noticed the lack of quality safety equipment for protecting workers. They resolved to start a company with the mission of producing equipment and instruments that enabled every man and woman to work in a safe, healthy environment.

MSA's safety expertise leverages advanced technology. Firefighters use MSA's Thermal Imaging Camera (TIC) to see through dense smoke and locate victims and fellow firefighters.

The two founders discovered a kindred spirit in America's greatest inventor, Thomas Edison. The association with Edison produced MSA's first product: the Edison Electric Safety Cap Lamp, which the federal government approved in 1915 as a replacement for the dangerous flame lamps that miners had worn previously.

While MSA's initial focus centered on products for the mining industry, World War I began MSA's long association with the American armed services. From the primitive breathing equipment used by those digging under the trenches to the sophisticated respirators used during The Persian Gulf War, MSA has safeguarded U.S. service men and women. Today MSA is the leading supplier of respiratory protection for defense preparedness for those defending our homeland against terrorists and the consequences of their actions.

Since its formative years, MSA has grown to become the leading manufacturer of safety products and instrumentation in the world. John T. Ryan Jr. directed MSA's expansion into new markets and around the globe. Products used to protect miners and soldiers were redesigned for other purposes and new products were developed to meet emerging safety needs. Today MSA products are used in more than 120 countries to meet safety needs in the firefighting, industrial manufacturing, chemical, steel, construction, hazardous materials, offshore refining, power plants, utility, shipbuilding, agricultural and paper industries. MSA manufactures and distributes safety products and equipment in concert with its 29 international affiliates.

Under the leadership of John T. Ryan III, chief executive officer for more than a decade, MSA has adapted to a changing world where traditional heavy industries are significantly less of a factor in the global economy. The fire service has become clearly the company's largest customer area and instrumentation to protect against toxic and combustible gases is of increasing importance. MSA has expanded into the consumer marketplace, under the MSA Safety Works brand, and into new technologies, such as Thermal Imaging Cameras to enable people and fire sources to be seen through dense smoke. MSA's key product areas are respiratory protection equipment, instrumentation, personal protective products (including eye, ear, face, head and fall protection equipment) and specialty chemicals.

A publicly held company traded on the American Stock Exchange, MSA sales total more than $500 million annually. The company employs more than 4,000 people worldwide.

MSA's concern for people extends beyond work environments to communities throughout North America through the efforts of the MSA Charitable Foundation, which has contributed millions of dollars to health, welfare and cultural organizations for more than half a century.

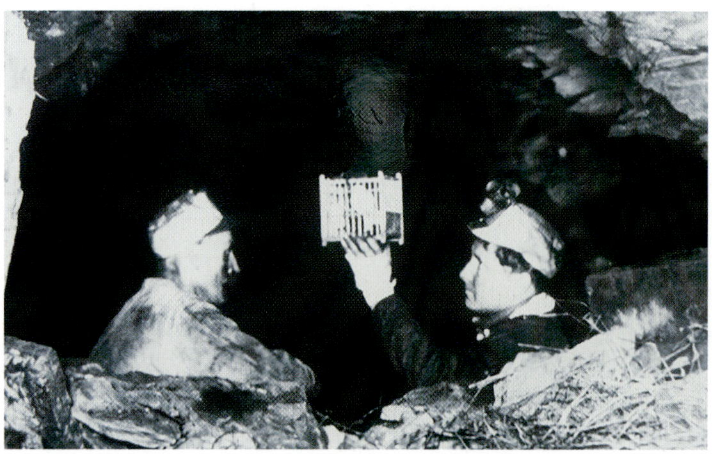

At the scene of a mine explosion in 1911, John T. Ryan Sr. holds a caged canary to detect carbon monoxide. Experiences like this led Ryan to found MSA with George H. Deike in 1914.

Pittsburgh History & Landmarks Foundation

Marketplace

Pittsburgh's world-class retail establishments and service industries offer an impressive variety of choices for residents and visitors.

American Eagle Outfitters

AMERICAN EAGLE OUTFITTERS (AE), a Pittsburgh retailer, started in 1977. The original store carried national brands that had a rugged, outdoorsy inspiration. Jerry Silverman, who started the company, had seen other chains developing that were devoted to camping and outdoor goods and decided to try implementing the concept using resources from another chain he operated, Silverman's. The original American Eagle Outfitters and Silverman's were both headquartered in the same Marshall Township building that is home to American Eagle Outfitters today. The first AE store was opened on October 22, 1977, in Twelve Oaks Mall in Novi, Michigan; this store still ranks in sales in the top 15 percent of the company's stores.

AE and Silverman's operated uneventfully during the 1980s, until Merry Go Round bought all 120 Silverman's stores in 1989. The Silverman's stores were doing poorly, so Jerry Silverman sold the stores to concentrate on the success of AE. At this time, Jerry Silverman and the Schottenstein family were 50/50 partners in AE. In March 1991 the Schottenstein family, led by Jerome Schottenstein, took control of all assets and liabilities of American Eagle Outfitters. Under the strong direction of Jerome Schottenstein, the company began operating more profitably with a longer-range vision for the future.

In 1995 the Schottenstein family, now led by Jay Schottenstein, took American Eagle Outfitters public (NASDAQ: AEOS). The brand strategy continued to develop and the company set up a design center in New York City. The company became a leading lifestyle retailer for men and women between the ages of 16 and 34, with women's merchandise making up 60 percent of the line. American Eagle designs, markets and sells its own brand of relaxed, clean and versatile clothing, providing high-quality merchandise at affordable prices. AE's lifestyle collection offers casual basics like cargoes complemented by fashion looks in stretch, denim and other modern fabrications. In the last four years, American Eagle Outfitters has expanded its operation to 556 stores in 47 states. By year end 2000, sales were estimated to exceed $1 billion.

Along the way, American Eagle Outfitters has celebrated several major milestones. The AE Clear Card was launched in 1996 as a way to build the brand through a private-label credit card. In 1997 the company finished the initial rollout of its AE University Training system, a user-friendly program with an introductory video that uses a self-paced learning approach for employees. AE also launched its Web site in 1997, which has grown to become its own division, AE Direct. In April 1998 AE

The new store design launched in 1999 is constructed of natural elements like wood, wrought iron and river stone and has a relaxed, inviting feeling like an old beach house or cabin.

aggressively launched e-commerce on its site, which now receives approximately 29 million hits, 8.3 million page views and 450,000 unique user sessions each month. Circulation of the company's catalog, the AE Magazine, has grown to a distribution of over 6 million per year.

In 1998 AE also changed its state of incorporation from Ohio to Delaware; on April 7, 1999, AE completed a reorganization plan to implement a holding company structure.

In September 2000 AE introduced personal care products, including the unisex fragrance Alive. In January 2000 AE acquired importing operations from Schottenstein Stores Corporation and integrated SSC importing expertise into its own supply chain process.

American Eagle Outfitters is still looking ahead and planning future growth. Leaders in the area of marketing at American Eagle Outfitters acknowledge that they must evolve and react quickly to the ever changing retail environment. AE's marketing campaign has grown steadily in the past few years to include both print and electronic media. The company's long-term goals include continuing its rapid growth by expanding the Internet business and opening new stores throughout the United States and Canada. AE executives hope stores already open will continue to increase their sales figures each year. AE's growth strategy also includes the possibility of developing through acquisitions. In October of 2000, AE purchased two specialty retail operations in Canada. Headquartered in Toronto is the 117-store chain Thrifty/Bluenotes selling casual apparel to the teen through 20s customer. The other business was converted to AE-Canada with 47 stores opening in 2001. The company has already invested in expanding its distribution and headquarters facility to achieve its goal of improving efficiency in replenishment and processing new orders. A related goal involves increasing the capacity of the Warrendale distribution facility to serve 700 stores.

In the near future, American Eagle Outfitters will break ground on a state-of-the-art, 42,000-square-foot distribution facility in Kansas. When this second facility is fully operational, the company will be able to supply about 1,400 stores. This development is a powerful sign of the confidence AE executives have in the brand's future. Additionally, the company plans to spend approximately $9 million to install new hardware and software systems for its stores, corporate office and existing distribution facility.

White Christmas — On him: cotton expedition sweater in butternut over cotton rugby in burgundy and paired with cotton standard issue khaki pant in cavalry; on her: wool snowflake hoodie in polar paired with heavy-duty cotton denim mechanic jean

Head in the clouds — On him: nylon freestyle snowboarder jacket with microfleece lining in orange soda, paired with nylon avalanche pant in blue moon/stone

Hardy & Hayes

THE TURN-OF-THE-CENTURY horse-drawn carriages that stopped at the Hardy family's jewelry establishment in Pittsburgh's Golden Triangle transported some of the city's leading citizens. Founded in 1887 by President J. Alex Hardy, with Harry B. Hayes as vice president, Hardy & Hayes served steel barons, coal producers, glassmakers, bankers, lawyers, politicians and others who were to carve their names in the city's history. Then, as now, Hardy & Hayes basked in its reputation as the sole purveyor of many world-class names in jewelry between western Pennsylvania and Philadelphia, New York and Washington.

Hardy & Hayes adopted the griffin — said in mythology to possess hoards of fabulous treasure — as its logo representing its high standards of craftsmanship in fine gifts. During their more than 50 years of running the store, Hardy family members built up that treasure by traveling throughout the United States and Europe to add fine names to their roster of top makers of jewelry, watches, crystal, leather goods and other giftware.

In 1950 the Hardys sold the business to the Morrow family, who operated the store for three decades. After having been overseen by family owners for more than 80 years, the business experienced several ownership changes in the 1980s, including sale to a British corporation. In late 1989 local family ownership returned when the Betres family purchased the firm.

Since then, Mark Betres has served as president of Hardy & Hayes. He is assisted by Rhonda McGuire, vice president, and a staff of seven, most of whom have worked in the jewelry industry for 20 years or more. Betres and McGuire both learned the retail trade by managing card stores. The jewelry store's parent firm, the Betres Group, also operates card shops, restaurants and other area businesses.

Among the challenges Betres faced in restoring the firm to its former luster were a weak area economy and a decline in recognition of the Hardy & Hayes name. He concentrated on restoring customer awareness as well as expanding the lines of high-end merchandise. The firm's brand name exclusives now include Patek Philippe watches, Buccellati handmade jewelry and silver, Van Cleef & Arpels jewelry and watches, Tous Spanish jewelry and leather, Cartier watches, Bulgari Italian jewelry and watches, John Hardy silver, Cathy Waterman exclusive jewelry, William Yeoward English crystal, Cede and Wellendorff German jewelry, Fabergé jewelry, Hoya Japanese crystal and Paul Morelli jewelry.

To preserve their prestige and assure personal service, most of these world-quality brands shy away from Internet sales, thereby strengthening Hardy & Hayes' role as the sole vendor in the Pittsburgh area for virtually all of its product lines. In light of the exclusive names it carries, Hardy & Hayes' competition comes primarily from other fine jewelry firms across the nation and in the Caribbean islands and Europe.

Now restored to its former reputation, the firm operates an elegant headquarters shop in Pittsburgh's One Oxford Centre, where it relocated in 1986. The spacious, 1,600-square-foot store is enclosed in glass walls that sparkle

Located in downtown Pittsburgh's prestigious One Oxford Centre, Hardy & Hayes has provided fine jewelry to the city's carriage trade since 1887.

Sparkling display cases in the Hardy & Hayes headquarters shop set off exclusive jewelry, timepieces, silver, leather and other giftware from world-class specialists.

like a jewelry case. In 1997 Joe Hardy, a descendent of the original owners, asked Betres to open a satellite store in the newly constructed Chateau LaFayette at his famed Nemacolin Woodlands resort and spa. Located 65 miles southeast of Pittsburgh in the Laurel Highlands of western Pennsylvania, the resort has hosted U.S. presidents and numerous other prominent figures. Set near a giant crystal chandelier in the chateau's shopping complex, the store's front features elegant wood panels framing spacious display windows.

As it has been since Hardy & Hayes' founding, Pittsburgh remains a big jewelry town. Although the firm still caters to the carriage trade, its modern mix of clientele includes not only industrialists, lawyers and bankers but also — reflecting the changing economic base of the Pittsburgh region — electronic-commerce moguls, medical researchers and practitioners, developers and entrepreneurs. With success coming earlier to some, younger people also make up a larger portion of the jeweler's customers.

For clients visiting the city for a short time, Hardy & Hayes offers timely service in providing the right item or producing custom-designed jewelry. Numbered in this group are the many film stars and directors who are making movies in the region. Film producers are attracted to Pittsburgh's hills, valleys, rivers and colorful neighborhoods, which not only offer a scenic backdrop but also serve as look-alikes for many other locations throughout the country. Along with movie folk, sheiks and other luminaries drawn to the city's pioneering medical facilities patronize the store during their short stays.

When the store's clientele request a custom design, as they often do, Hardy & Hayes draws on its own jewelry craftsmen, who hand-pick the stones and fashion the jewelry to the customer's requirements or design. For bigger pieces, the firm maintains working relationships with New York craftsmen.

The Betres family is active in community affairs, and a family member serves on the board of the Pittsburgh chapter of the Leukemia & Lymphoma Society. For this organization, Hardy & Hayes donated jewelry and held many events, with proceeds going to the society. The firm also has donated jewelry to the Shadyside Academy as well as other nonprofit groups and events.

To maintain Hardy & Hayes' reputation in its third century of operation, Betres continually seeks out new lines from world-class names specializing in exclusive jewelry and giftware. He intends, as well, to preserve the tradition of excellence established by the earlier family owners who built their business on personal service and superb-quality merchandise to satisfy the ever-changing members of western Pennsylvania's carriage trade.

Pittsburgh Brewing Co.

WITH EACH BEER IT MAKES, Pittsburgh Brewing Co. serves its customers a sip of history that stretches back more than 140 years.

The brewery, perched between the industrial bustle of the city's Strip District and the collegiate and medical world of Oakland, is the second-oldest in the country.

Pittsburgh Brewing Co. grew up with the city, flourishing before the Civil War, surviving Prohibition, renewing itself in Pittsburgh's Renaissance and retooling into the Digital Age. For more than 140 continuous years, generations of workers have been processing a product that has become synonymous with the city itself.

Pittsburgh Brewing Co.'s roots reach back to 1818 and Wainwright beer, but because the brand was discontinued, its official history does not begin until nearly 50 years later. In 1855 Edward Frauenheim and another German immigrant, Leopold Vilsack, discussed a brewery partnership. Six years later, they had completed a namesake brewery in the city's Lawrenceville section. Their surnames still can be seen, carved into the stone at the original red-brick brewery at Liberty Avenue and 34th Street, along with the company motto: "Integrity — Quality — Tradition."

As the rest of the city grew up around the iron and steel mills that would make Pittsburgh famous, the owners decided to capitalize on Pittsburgh's boomtown vitality and rename their growing concern the Iron City Brewing Co. By the end of the 1890s, every neighborhood in the city held at least one brewery of its own; more than 200 beer makers sent their sweet, grainy smells into the city's air.

In 1899 Iron City and 20 other breweries merged to form Pittsburgh Brewing. The merger turned Pittsburgh Brewing into a powerhouse, the biggest brewery in the state and the third-largest in the country. As horse-drawn beer trucks rolled out the barrels, the company added one of its many firsts to its history: Pittsburgh Brewing became the first beer maker to ship its product. Its beer went into the city of Allegheny, now part of Pittsburgh's North Side, as well as to the far reaches of Birmingham, on the 'Burgh's South Side.

From the heyday of industrial Pittsburgh to the Roaring Twenties, beer flowed from the plant into Pittsburgh's many neighborhoods. Prohibition turned off the tap, but the company managed to stay in business by producing ice, ice cream, soda and near beer. When Prohibition was repealed in the 1930s, Pittsburgh Brewing was well-poised to again start delivering the products that had built its reputation.

At the 1958 World's Fair in Brussels, Pittsburgh Brewing brought home the medal that proclaimed it "The World's Premium" lager. The tradition of excellence continued through the city's Renaissance. Pittsburgh Brewing and its signature Iron City beer had long been associated with Pittsburgh sports teams. When the Pirates and Steelers became world champions in the 1960s and 1970s, so did Pittsburgh Brewing.

With a tradition stretching more than 140 years, Pittsburgh Brewing Co. and its signature Iron City products are synonymous with the city itself.

Golden milestones are strung through the brewery's history like nuggets in a miner's pan. Pittsburgh Brewing was the first in the business to produce snap-top cans in the 1960s. It was the first industrywide to imprint its cans with scenery and the likenesses of professional athletes. It was the first beer maker to offer its customers the convenience of resealable, twist-off bottles. It was the first to package draft beer in cans.

In 1978 the brewery broke new ground. Pittsburgh Brewing marketed the first-ever lower-calorie beer with the same alcohol content of its regular product. This dazzling little number with one-third fewer calories wore the simple, recognizable name of IC Light. It infused Pittsburgh Brewing with new business at a time when liability laws were creating a downturn in the marketplace. In the process, it happened to revolutionize the beer-making industry.

These adaptations are merely extensions of how Pittsburgh Brewing honors its past while stepping into the future. For instance, the Ober Brau Haus, once a stable for those wagon-pulling delivery horses, has been renovated into a modern meeting room with an expansive bar and big-screen TV, yet keeps its turn-of-the-century charm. This is the home for the company store, which feeds the public demand for sports gear and clothing bearing the vintage Iron City logo, and produces specialized gift baskets of Pittsburgh Brewing products that can be sent around the globe.

This building seems to belong to the community as much as to the company. Nonprofit organizations meet here for free. The rental fee received from others is donated to various local charities.

Joseph R. Piccirilli is Pittsburgh-proud of the brewery that he is leading into a new millennium.

These are just some of the ways Joseph R. Piccirilli, vice chairman of the company since 1995, has found to give back to the loyal Pittsburghers who form the backbone of Pittsburgh Brewing's market and those dedicated to making its products.

Many of these second- and third-generation workers have shared photos and memorabilia showing how their family history is entwined with the company's past. The Ober Brau Haus holds cases of collectibles, such as Iron City songbooks, Pittsburgh Brewing commemorative plates, special-issue cans, even a scaled-down replica of a beer wagon, all items given by affiliates or saved by the company. Elsewhere, the company vault protects its 19th-century ledger and the flowery calligraphy that tells of the company's earliest days.

Records and recipes now are all computerized. Kegs are made of metal instead of wood. Automation moves 1,200 cans through production lines each minute. In the 1990s, Pittsburgh Brewing continued to win awards and recognition from the brewing industry for its products. Its in-house marketing department can lay claim to awards as well, beating out Madison Avenue for the top honor in the Beverage Packaging Global Design Awards.

Iron City beer is being served in cities' sports stadiums built in areas where the horse-drawn beer delivery wagons once trekked for their out-of-town deliveries. Now, out-of-town deliveries include shipments to China, Cambodia, Korea and Australia, even though Pittsburgh Brewing is considered a regional brewery. The brewery started by two German immigrants more than 140 years ago remains among the 10 largest in the country.

Pittsburgh Brewing's latest introduction to the local market, Augustiner, caters to the trend toward darker beer with a lighter taste.

As tastes change, the industry evolves and globalization spreads, Pittsburgh Brewing remains true to the motto engraved into its walls nearly a century and a half ago: "Integrity — Quality — Tradition."

Westin William Penn Hotel

IN THE TRADITION OF WILLIAM Penn, founder of the colony of Pennsylvania, a hotel bearing his name remains steadfast in the history of Pittsburgh. The inscription on the ancestral crest of William Penn, "As long as I hold the helm," characterizes the integrity of the Westin William Penn Hotel. Tracing a lineage to March 9, 1916, the Westin William Penn Hotel is reminiscent of 18th-century classical grandeur. Renowned architects Janssen and Abbott designed the last building venture of Henry Clay Frick, Pittsburgh industrialist, for $6 million. Constructed in the shape of the letter "E," the 20-story hotel was described in the April 1916 edition of *The National Architect* magazine as being "ahead of the times." It was considered the finest hotel between New York and Chicago. Since the day it was built, the Westin William Penn Hotel has been in the vanguard of architectural style, modern amenities and international acclaim.

The renowned Westin William Penn Hotel, built by Henry Clay Frick, is the ultimate setting for Pittsburgh's most prestigious social events.

The exterior of the building is designed in Renaissance Revival architecture, and the first three stories feature white Indiana limestone on a granite base. Ornate arches in terra cotta frame the lower windows. Fifteen stories of red brick with terra-cotta decoration provide a layered contrast. The uppermost stories consist of red brick with window ornamentation that mirrors the first level. A parapet, cornice and frieze provide finishing touches to the hotel.

At the hotel entrance, the Palm Court Lobby is cloaked in Italian Renaissance architecture emanating a fine European heritage. Romanesque arches and walnut pillars dominate the 25-foot-high room that melds with a ceiling modeled after the Chateau de Fontainebleau. Inlaid with 65 coffers, the ceiling is embossed with shields and rosettes monogrammed with "WP." Throughout the lobby, polished Westfield Green Marble accents the floors, wainscoting and the lower walls. High tea is served in the afternoon in a lobby that has welcomed guests from Theodore Roosevelt to the Rolling Stones. A traditional social venue, the lobby atmosphere often resonates with sounds of tinkling glassware, engaging conversations and an affluent mix of high society. The Palm Court Lobby affords an elegant setting for prominent Pittsburghers to gather and socialize.

An indoor parterre leads to the Terrace Room, which is the main dining room. Vaulted arches in Edwardian style reveal a rich patina of walnut paneling beneath an intricately detailed plaster ceiling. Pittsburgh's early years as a trading post are vividly portrayed in a panoramic mural of George Washington being welcomed to Fort Pitt. A dynamic center of activity for business transactions, the dining room daily pulsates with informal meetings, discussions and deals. Well-known personalities, corporate leaders and power brokers are some of the recurrent patrons.

The Palm Court Lobby welcomes guests to an impressive atmosphere of understated elegance.

Special occasions are enhanced with Renaissance-style reliefs decorating the upper walls replacing scenes of a harvest and a mythical centaur on Beaux-Arts murals entitled "The Seasons." The menu once featured Egyptian quail, Biscuit Glace Demidoff and Turkish coffee.

In earlier days, guests passed through hallways of lavish muraled wallpaper leading to their rooms. Daily rates ranged from $2.50 for a single room to $4-6. Reproductions in mahogany, walnut and white enamel from the period designs of Louis XVI and the Adam Brothers decorated 900 guest rooms. Furniture, draperies, glassware, silverware, carpeting and ceilings were imprinted with the crest of William Penn. Guest floors operated independently and were equipped with offices, pantries and linen rooms. First-time guest amenities were ventilation, iced drinking water, electricity, clocks, telephones and private baths. In the 1900s, these innovations were considered technological advancements in hostelry.

Clearly an urban village, a print shop, bakery, barbershop, manicure parlor, drug store and billiards room were located in the hotel. Quarters for staff and a "Bachelor's" floor with a sitting room and library were available. And in the 20s, KDKA and WCAE radio stations were broadcast there.

On the 17th floor, the palatial Grand Ballroom glitters with hand-cut antique Baccarat crystal chandeliers pinned to plaster medallions that sparkle amidst the backdrop of red velvet draperies, gilt-filigreed design balconies and Renaissance-style reliefs. An impressive guest list always complements the eloquence and grace of this resplendent ballroom that accommodates 1,200 persons.

When flappers danced, Art Deco was arty and speakeasies were noisy, Joseph Urban, an Austrian who was both an architect and Art Deco artist, designed the Urban Room. Previously, he had designed the Ziegfield Theatre in New York, sets for the Ziegfield Follies and the Metropolitan Opera. A historic landmark located within a historic landmark, the Urban Room reflects the roar of the 1920s. Bright colors and geometric design detail the "Tree of Life" ceiling mural with female Ziegfield musicians painted in lasting fame. Black Carrara glass walls complement hand-painted panels and black velvet draperies. The Urban Room, with its Art Deco motif, is the only room that remains of three Moderne rooms created by Joseph Urban in the late 1920s.

A view from the gilt-filigreed balcony of the magnificent Grand Ballroom

When prohibition ended in 1933, guests were "In the Mood" for the sounds of Big Band music at the Chatterbox Supper Club. Another design of Joseph Urban, the former club is now the location of the William Penn Ballroom in the lower lobby.

The Urban Room epitomizes the characteristic design of the Art Deco period of the 1920s.

Adaptability defines the Westin William Penn Hotel. Change is a part of growth, and the hotel has undergone several renovations in its long history. The most recent was a $20 million refurbishment of sleeping rooms and meeting space that was completed in 1999.

The leading hotel in Pittsburgh, the Westin William Penn Hotel maintains the spotlight for hosting weddings, corporate events, socialite gatherings and charity fund-raisers. It is said, "If it happens in Pittsburgh, it happens at the Westin William Penn Hotel."

A landmark in Pittsburgh, the Westin William Penn Hotel has outlasted its contemporaries while experiencing a flourishing renaissance of its own. In the midst of a bustling American city with an exciting past, the hotel is a respite of Old World charm, sophisticated elegance and generous ambiance defining hospitality well into a new century.

Café Allegro and Club Café

SINCE CAFÉ ALLEGRO FIRST FIRED up its grills in 1986, it has become a Pittsburgh legend. Located in the city's South Side, a unique mix of trendy and funky shops in a working-class neighborhood, this go-to place has a vibrant spirit in keeping with its name.

Owner Antoinette Cardamone greets visitors with a toss of her trademark headful of curly locks. She seats her livelier guests in the bar-dining room. There a window-wall looks outside to the people parade on the sidewalk. Across the room, the wide-open kitchen window frames a performance of Chef de Cuisine Gloria Fortunato and her crew.

Those seated on the half-dozen stools at the bar choose from a solid wine list offering many vintages by the glass. Across from the bar, couples sit at banquettes, but when a large group arrives, tables are pushed together party-style. Decorated with Picasso prints and ringed with festive mini blue lights, the room is one happening place.

The bright blue awnings of Café Allegro carry its Riviera theme out to the street.

Club Café's sleek, sophisticated look reflects its sophisticated musical ambience.

In the quieter, nonsmoking dining room, both regulars and out-of-towners sit at cozy tables where mushroom garlic cheese pate and warm, homemade rustic breads are immediately served while diners peruse the menu.

Café Allegro's menu, the creation of Executive Chef Joe Nolan, is billed as Riviera style, offering in-season foods with a coastal French-Italian accent served in the European manner. Favorite dishes include the Swiss Chard Casserole, exquisitely seasoned with tomatoes, wine and fennel and topped with toasted cheese and bread crumbs, and the Riviera Antipasto Platter, offering marinated mussels, caponata, roasted herb goat cheese and smoked trout.

Diners complete a delightful meal with a selection from one of many tempting desserts including chocolate chocolate, a rich concoction whose name speaks for itself, and cherry sorbet, savory sorbet served in a wine glass, drizzled with raspberry sauce and topped with fresh berries.

While Café Allegro sates the appetite, its sister spot located just across the street, Club Café, offers Pittsburgh residents the best in musical entertainment, booking musicians and bands ranging from Dixieland to reggae to classic rock 'n' roll. And added to these South Side jewels is the new Allegro Hearth Bakery in Squirrel Hill, which bakes creative breads in more than 30 varieties.

For those who can't decide where to linger — at scrumptious Café Allegro for dinner or at Club Café for grooving — the answer may be both.

Emphatics

AMONG PITTSBURGH'S MANY well-kept secrets is Emphatics, a collection of fashions that is not only unparalleled in Pittsburgh but, which rivals the most sophisticated fashion retailers in the world.

Until they walk through the doors, passers-by might assume that Emphatics is an intriguing boutique — something different, exclusive and chic. But only the lucky few realize that right here in Pittsburgh dwells a true style-maker and fashion-influencer. The clothing artfully displayed at Emphatics is selected by owners James and Karin Legato from ready-to-wear collections directly off the Paris runways. It is for the woman who seeks striking looks and definitive fashion statements — who is not afraid to stand out.

The Legato's are among the few retailers who can truly say their clientele are among the best-dressed in any city. The collections of Azzedine Alaia, Jean Paul Gaultier, John Galliano, Stella McCartney, Nicholas Ghesquiere, Thierry Mugler and Issey Miyake are regularly featured at Emphatics — and nowhere else in Pittsburgh or the region. The ability to merchandise these European couture collections is only possible through close personal relationships with the design houses, not to mention a great deal of time spent in Paris and New York researching and selecting garments that will please the women back home.

James Legato has known these women all his life. As the son of a hair stylist and later a stylist and salon-owner himself, he built a career around giving women the looks they want. His sense of style was self-taught and is constantly honed.

After opening a salon with his brother Anthony in the Jenkin's Arcade in 1963, James began to notice that his taste and style pushed the envelope toward the avante-garde and the risky. By 1969 he realized that his creativity could be best expressed through women's fashion, and the brothers opened a boutique, also in the Jenkin's Arcade.

In 1983 the Legato's unveiled their vision of a "Theater of Fashion" at their current location in Oxford Centre. To its owners, the uncommon design of Emphatics' retail space is essential for the illumination and appreciation of modern high fashion. Through shape, light, color and texture, clients are literally placed on center stage at Emphatics. The far right side of the store is dominated by an actual stage of marble and enhanced by a remote control console that operates an intricate lighting system. Throughout the rest of the store, customers can glide among garments that signal fashion's latest mood on Italian marble floors under a 15-foot domed and vaulted ceiling.

Cultivated over 30 years and now serving the sophisticated tastes of two generations of clientele, James and Karin Legato's Emphatics continues to bring the true creators of fashion to Pittsburgh. Their products are works of art, interpreted into body coverings and then turned loose on a city whose sense of style is just beginning to blossom.

James and Karen Legato bring modern fashion direct from the runways of Paris to their boutique in the heart of downtown Pittsburgh.

Emphatics' "Theater of Fashion" is a truly unique retail experience for the discerning Pittsburgh shopper.

Forest City Enterprises

FOREST CITY ENTERPRISES FIRST began landscaping urban communities in 1921. Back then it provided lumber to homeowners for garage construction. Today that simple venture has evolved into a $4 billion real estate development and management enterprise — one of the largest in the country — with developments in 40 states.

Shown is a rendering of Bessemer Court Plaza and the entrance to the River Landing at Station Square, a classic boardwalk area that will be the site of summer carnivals, games, live entertainment, fireworks displays and a breathtaking view of downtown.

From the beginning Forest City has focused on revitalizing cities. Concerned with more than just property, it works hard to ensure its developments will be community assets, generating growth and improving the quality of life. As Pittsburgh enters its third renaissance, Forest City is keeping the momentum going with three exciting projects.

Concurrent with the city's Convention Center expansion, Forest City is expanding the Liberty Center/Westin Hotel, an office, retail and hotel complex developed by Forest City in the early 1980s. The $100 million expansion includes 500 more hotel rooms and an integration of the light rail system, both of which are key to the city's efforts to increase its convention business.

The Mall at Robinson is a $35 million project that enhances and diversifies Greater Pittsburgh's retail district. Located less than 10 miles west of downtown in Robinson Township, the two-level enclosed mall is 1.2 million square feet of premier shopping.

Forest City's most distinctive project is the revitalization of Station Square. Working with a public/private partnership with the city, it helped to develop a Master Plan that will integrate and build upon the relationship of the North Shore, South Shore and Golden Triangle that already exists at the confluence of Pittsburgh's three rivers. The plan is to interconnect business, living, culture, history, entertainment and shopping areas to create "The Platinum Triangle," a network of amenities that will make Pittsburgh stand out as a business, cultural and tourist destination.

On the south shore of the triangle is Station Square, 52 acres of narrow land on the Monongahela River. With spectacular views, a Sheraton Hotel, popular dining, shopping, and entertainment venues, it is Pittsburgh's number one tourist destination. Forest City first began purchasing the site in 1994 and by 1997 had full ownership. Planning activities for the revitalization began in 1998.

Started in 2000, the redevelopment of Station Square includes Bessemer Court, a riverfront restaurant, plaza and festival area that serves as the centerpiece attraction; an expansion of the Sheraton Hotel; a cover over the outdoor amphitheater; new amenities for the Freight House Shops and an outdoor deck for the East Warehouse, along with other improvements.

New to Station Square is the Scenic Trail and River Landing, public amenities that combine to provide vital connections to the river, the trail network and other tourist destinations. Included is a 1.2 mile trail lined with historical artifacts, an Artifacts Park, stair towers and elevators for the Duquesne and Monongahela Inclines, and a Monongahela Incline bridge. Centered in front of Bessemer Court is the River Landing boardwalk and public boat docks. This combination of new development and public amenities is the strength of this unique mixed-use project.

These three projects are only the beginning of the partnership between Forest City and the city of Pittsburgh. The company looks forward to continuing its commitment to Pittsburgh's renaissance and supporting the redevelopment of cities around the country.

Gateway Clipper Fleet

FOR THE FIRST HALF OF THE 20th century, Pittsburgh's three rivers were not pretty sights. The city's steel industry, which played a pivotal role in the development of the United States, also played a role in polluting the Allegheny, Monongahela and Ohio rivers. The once beautiful rivers had become filthy, and something had to be done to restore the three rivers to their natural beauty.

During the 1950s, civic attention was focused on the city's polluted rivers. In 1955, when John E. Connelly was appointed treasurer of the Allegheny County Sanitary Authority (ALCOSAN), the rivers found a champion. ALCOSAN's purpose was to cleanse the polluted rivers and make them an attractive part of Pittsburgh, and Connelly saw the three rivers as the lifeblood of the city.

A man of vision, Connelly recognized the need for an excursion boat to show off the revitalization of the city and its rivers. Enlisting the aid of his nephew, Capt. Jack Goessling, Connelly began the search for a boat on which passengers could sail and enjoy the city's rivers. Connelly accompanied Capt. Jack to Erie, Pennsylvania, where Connelly bought the *Bridget Ann*. On May 17, 1958, with Capt. Jack Goessling at the helm, the redesigned fishing boat was christened the *Gateway Clipper* and made its first excursion on Pittsburgh's rivers from the Monongahela Wharf.

Since that maiden voyage, the Gateway Clipper Fleet has become a major Pittsburgh attraction and one of America's most successful riverboat companies, greatly contributing to the atmosphere of a dynamic city. Carrying more than 800,000 passengers each year, the fleet continues to grow and maintain an interest in the health and vitality of Pittsburgh's rivers.

The original *Gateway Clipper*

The fleet moved its docking location from the Monongahela Wharf, on the city side of the Monongahela River, to its present location adjacent to Station Square in 1982. The company has grown from a single boat to a full-fledged fleet of six riverboats: the 1,000-passenger *Majestic*, the 600-passenger *Gateway Party Liner*, the 400-passenger *River Belle*, the 400-passenger *Keystone Belle*, the 400-passenger *Liberty Belle*, and the 150-passenger *Good Ship Lollipop*.

Today, the Gateway Clipper Fleet, under the helm of Terry Wirginis, Connelly's grandson, has continued to offer just about every kind of cruise imaginable: from Sightseeing and Dinner Dance Cruises to Nationality, Family Fun, Sunday Brunch and Private Charter Cruises. The fleet navigates the three rivers from Pittsburgh to Kittanning, McKeesport, and Wheeling, West Virginia, and provides shuttle services to and from Pirates and Steelers games on the North Shore of the Allegheny River. The fleet also sponsors special events, such as the USS Nightmare haunted boat during the Halloween season, and supports local community initiatives, such as Sharing & Caring, Inc., which serves local hospitalized veterans; the Girl Scouts of America; and Project Bundle-Up, which provides winter clothing for disadvantaged children.

As interest in Pittsburgh's revitalized rivers grows, the Gateway Clipper Fleet continues to fulfill Connelly's vision, offering unique views and entertainment opportunities while floating on Pittsburgh's beautiful three rivers.

The flagship of the fleet, the 1,000-passenger *Majestic*

Hilton Pittsburgh

THE HILTON PITTSBURGH STAKES its claim to a fistful of firsts. Within the Hilton family, it is recognized as the first Hilton to be conceived and designed by Conrad Hilton, founder of the hotel chain. In the early 1950s the company had been expanding through both mergers and acquisitions. Then in 1956 Hilton bought the Statler Hotel Co., which was planning to build a hotel near Point State Park in Pittsburgh's booming downtown. Conrad Hilton proceeded with these plans and was involved with the design and construction for this hotel from the ground level up.

The building was the first structure designed and constructed of anodized aluminum by fellow Pittsburgh giant Alcoa. The hotel's reputation spread when Alcoa and the Hilton featured the Pittsburgh hotel's innovative architecture in a national advertising campaign.

When the Hilton Pittsburgh opened its doors in December 1959, it was touted as the largest hotel between Chicago and New York City. It boasted 815 rooms and the biggest ballroom east of the Mississippi.

The sun takes a shine to the Hilton Pittsburgh, the golden building in the city's glorious skyline.

On opening night, the hotel served a memorable prime rib dinner — from a prize steer that had been seen grazing at Point State Park for the two weeks prior to the gala event. The opening of the new Hilton was a Hollywood affair, drawing luminaries such as Liz Taylor and Joe DiMaggio and an accompanying entourage of onlookers and press.

When the hotel opened, Al Zugger was general manager. For a hotel that considers itself a family, it is fitting that 40 years later Al's grandson Tim Zugger is resident manager. Conrad Wangeman currently serves as Hilton Pittsburgh's general manager.

THE HILTON'S STRIKING FAÇADE REFLECTS THE LATE AFTERNOON SUN AND OFFERS GUESTS AN UNFORGETTABLE VIEW.

The Pittsburgh hotel today retains its original grace. The ballroom still bears the traffic of dancing feet and remains the biggest dance floor in the region. The hotel's four food and beverage outlets boast fresh and exciting menus, serving breakfast, lunch and dinner. The concierge and 713 rooms cater mainly to business travelers, though weekend guests are likely to frequent the area's festivals and attractions.

Now, as in the early days of the Hilton, its most prized asset is location. The gold-tinged building can be spotted easily from vantage points around the city amid the gray and glass giants of Pittsburgh's Golden Triangle, home to many Fortune 500 corporations. The Hilton's striking façade reflects the late afternoon sun and offers guests an unforgettable view. The hotel faces Point State Park, a sprawling grassy space where the Ohio River begins. That puts the Hilton a long ball and a river away from Three Rivers Stadium, PNC Park and the Carnegie Science Center. Point State Park houses a frontier museum and also hosts many of the city's celebrations, placing the Three Rivers Arts Festival, Fourth of July festivities and the Three Rivers Regatta virtually in the Hilton's front yard.

No other spot in the city can compare with the Hilton's. It has one eye on corporate headquarters in parklike Gateway Center and the other on the panoramic view of rivers that made Pittsburgh famous.

Pittsburgh City Bed & Breakfast Association

THREE OUTSTANDING BED AND breakfast inns comprise the Pittsburgh City Bed & Breakfast Association: Morning Glory Inn on Sarah Street on the South Side, Victoria House Bed & Breakfast on Western Avenue on the North Side and The Appletree Inn on South Negley Avenue, in Shadyside. They are the elegant, shining jewels of Pittsburgh's stylish, historical past. Representing the essence of warm, relaxing hospitality, each offers a different experience to the traveler. Old-world charm, exceptional accommodations and impeccable personal service combine to make any traveler feel welcome in these inviting surroundings.

In 1995, shortly after purchasing the building that would become the Morning Glory Inn, Nancy and Dave Eshelman perceived the need for an organization to market the concept of the bed and breakfast as an alternative accommodation, especially for the business traveler. Owners of the other city bed and breakfasts were receptive to the idea and the Pittsburgh City Bed & Breakfast Association was formed. The concept has proven successful for each of the association's members, due in large part to the noncompetitive referral system established among the operations. Collectively, association members have attracted visitors from all over the world to their bed and breakfast locations as the result of unified marketing efforts directed toward Pittsburgh's business establishments.

The Pittsburgh City Bed & Breakfast Association is unique in what its members offer to the visitor and business traveler. The innkeepers' sincere interest in meeting the individual needs of their guests transforms the brick and mortar of the bed and breakfast into a "home away from home." Each captures the heart and personality of the neighborhood in which it is located, providing guests with the unusual opportunity of bearing witness to the luxurious lifestyle of an often opulent, descriptive past. Members of the association quietly and effectively serve as unofficial ambassadors to the city of Pittsburgh and its various cultural activities and community events, as well as its other historically interesting neighborhoods.

> The innkeepers' sincere interest in meeting the individual needs of their guests transforms the brick and mortar of the bed and breakfast into a "home away from home."

Astute members of Pittsburgh's business community have recognized the merits of utilizing this bed and breakfast atmosphere in selling new employee recruits on the benefits of working and living in the Pittsburgh area. Keeping business organizations continuously informed of the activities and special events that occur within the city's neighborhood communities is an integral part of the Pittsburgh City Bed & Breakfast Association's success. The weekday breakfast atmosphere has become an invaluable networking workshop for the business traveler and allows the innkeepers to accomplish what they do best — interact with their guests in planning and providing an eventful, memorable and enjoyable visit to Pittsburgh.

The innkeepers pride themselves on providing guests with the amenities travelers need: private baths, private telephone lines, voice mail, computer ports, Internet access, fax services, cable television, video cassette players and more. The inns also provide a unique, intimate atmosphere for business meetings, catered executive luncheons, cocktail parties, private receptions as well as wedding and anniversary parties. The innkeepers are experienced and knowledgeable in the planning and preparation of these types of events.

Holiday Inn Pittsburgh Airport

SINCE OPENING IN 1973 THE Holiday Inn Pittsburgh Airport has been a mainstay for travelers and a gathering place for the local community. It sits mere minutes from the airport and only 17 minutes from downtown Pittsburgh. That much hasn't changed.

What has changed is the look of the place, a unique look that has captured the very essence of Pittsburgh and altered forever the experiences guests can expect.

One step into the lobby is a transforming moment for guests and a hint of treasures to come. Pittsburgh has brought many "firsts" to the world and the Holiday Inn Pittsburgh Airport, a leading corporate citizen for two decades, celebrates these achievements through its "themed experience" concept.

Behind the registration desk, a grand mural depicts the city's connection to the first railroad air brakes and nuclear submarines. When guests enter their rooms, radios are tuned to KDKA to remind them they're in the hometown of the first commercial radio broadcast. Instead of finding mints on their pillows, guests enjoy a local confection called the Clark Bar, another Pittsburgh invention.

The celebration of the city continues in the dining room where a mural depicts the city's bridges. The Ferris Ballroom — named after the Ferris Wheel's inventor, Pittsburgh's own George Ferris — is illuminated by translucent skylights and crested by blue-coated girders that mimic the sky.

Meyer Jabara Hotels, which owns and operates the 11-story, 255-room full-service hotel along with 22 others in the U.S., is a company with a culture that believes in the value its associates (employees) bring to the business; redesigning the hotel was no different. Not only did associates discover many Pittsburgh firsts — from Bingo to Big Macs — but each is eager to talk to guests about them.

Clearly, the hotel's theme — "In a City of Firsts, You're Our First Priority" — comes shining through, offering guests a distinctive experience they will remember for a lifetime.

Matching the hotel's $6 million investment in 2001 is emphasis on creating that memorable experience through memorable service. Each guest room is equipped with high-speed Internet access. The Concierge Level features executive workstations with computer, scanner, color printer, fax and other upscale amenities.

Given all this, it's no surprise that in 2001, Meyer Jabara Hotels was ranked in the "Top 10" among Pennsylvania's Top 100 Best Places to Work, the only hotel company to achieve this recognition. The company attributes its success to the dedication of its associates and its culture — the "MJ Way" — which motivates and empowers associates to adopt an "I'd be happy to help" attitude. Meyer Jabara "storybooks" are filled with anecdotes of associates going above and beyond to create memorable guest experiences.

In a company that strives for legendary service, Meyer Jabara understands that a great employee experience translates to a great guest experience. That management philosophy has brought Meyer Jabara considerable success in the competitive hotel industry.

The personality of a city and its people linger in a traveler's memory long after a visit. The Holiday Inn Pittsburgh Airport, with its focus on hometown pride, outstanding service and a distinctive themed experience, invites guests to return again and again.

Poli

JOINING THE IMMIGRANT WAVES of the early 1900s, 14-year-old Joseph Poli left his family farm in Lucca, Italy, in 1911, bound for Pittsburgh. He sought a better life and money to send home. Living with an uncle, Joseph sold fruit and roasted chestnuts in Pittsburgh's Strip District. In 1921, having worked hard and saved the $600 construction cost, he built a luncheonette in Squirrel Hill to serve workers laying streetcar tracks to Kennywood Park.

Married four years later, he and wife Mary worked continually to expand their business and in 1930 they converted their luncheonette into a dinner restaurant. Over time, inspired by his love of fishing during family trips to Eastern shores, Joseph brought the flavors of the seacoast back to Pittsburgh.

Fresh from college in 1950, son Larry devoted himself to burnishing the Poli restaurant image and expanding the business. He added a second dining room in 1953 and created an elegant atmosphere, transforming sawdust floors into wall-to-wall carpeting and paper napkins and table coverings to cloth. Drawing on their travels, Larry and his wife, Dolores, introduced many new dishes, which they adapted to their customers' tastes. By the 1960s he had established Poli not only as a purveyor of fine Northern Italian cuisine but also as the city's premier seafood restaurant. In 1976 Larry again renovated the restaurant and built a state-of-the-art kitchen and banquet facility.

Third-generation members have carried on the tradition. Joseph Poli II entered the business in 1974 and served as maitre d' and bar manager until 2000. Following graduation from the Culinary Institute of America in 1981, Larry Poli Jr. also joined the staff and worked with his father, who passed away in 1992. Subsequently, Larry ran the business with mother Dolores, who served as president, banquet administrator and afternoon hostess until her death in 2001. He now has sole responsibility, overseeing a staff of 55 who serve an average of 3,000 guests weekly.

Appealing to passersby, the restaurant's renowned brass lobster door handles open to an interior adorned with fine cherry woodwork throughout, as well as spectacular silk sails draped from the ceilings. In two side dining rooms, hand-painted Italian seascapes complete the elegant environment.

Rated best seafood restaurant by *Pittsburgh Magazine*'s readers for 18 years, Poli also has earned that tribute from numerous other publications. Maintaining his forebears' tradition, Larry Jr. and Chef David Conley travel broadly to stay abreast of cuisine trends from the East and West coasts.

A board member of the Pittsburgh chapter, Leukemia & Lymphoma Society, Larry has chaired a golf tournament for nine years, raising $100,000 for research. Among his other volunteer work is a Community Food Bank fund-raiser in which restaurants serve their signature dishes. In 1995 Larry received the Squirrel Hill Urban Coalition Community Renewal Award for his dedicated service. Professionally, he founded and is an advisory board member of the Pittsburgh chapter, Young Entrepreneurs' Organization. Larry also has volunteered for many years as a member of the board of directors of the Western Chapter of the Pennsylvania Restaurant Association.

For the future, Larry intends to continue to enhance the restaurant's famed high-quality cuisine, which he blends with value orientation, hospitable service and a refined, relaxing atmosphere.

Founder Joseph Poli converted his Squirrel Hill luncheonette into a dinner restaurant in 1930.

Renaissance Pittsburgh Hotel

IN CITIES ACROSS THE NATION, debate rages over progress versus preservation. Pittsburgh is no exception. Although technology and the new sports stadiums along the north shore have become a large part of Pittsburgh's revitalization, preserving the city's rich architectural and cultural history is just as vital. The March 2001 opening of the 300-room Renaissance Pittsburgh Hotel in the landmark Fulton Building offers that sought-after balance of old and new.

The Renaissance Pittsburgh Hotel, located in the city's Cultural District on the corner of Sixth Street and Ft. Duquesne Boulevard

The Fulton Building was one of five buildings commissioned by notable Pittsburgher Henry Phipps, partner of industrialist Andrew Carnegie. Built in 1906, the building was a home for office and retail space. Today it remains a fixture of the unique Pittsburgh landscape at the corner of Sixth Street and Ft. Duquesne Boulevard.

The redevelopment of the building by Denver-based Sage Hospitality Resources, LLC brings to life the splendor envisioned by original architect Grosvenor Atterbury.

Built of granite, brick and copper, the building has original Renaissance Revival detail, including mythical winged dragons flanking the marquee. Inside, rich marble, mosaic tile, glass and cast-iron elements reflect the painstaking care that has been taken to preserve detail and authenticity.

When restoration began in 2000, far more than old office supplies were discovered. The secrets left behind in the building revealed a past rich in history. Workers were surprised to discover that the huge glass dome in the rotunda had been covered with a heavy rubber shield during World War II so that light from the lobby would not attract air attacks. The shield remained in place until its removal during the restoration. Also cleared away were 300 pounds of coal dust from the dome — a relic of Pittsburgh's days as an industrial leader.

Transformation of the building into an upscale hotel was an extraordinary undertaking. The copper on the building was cleaned with 40,000 pounds of baking soda. The building required the largest copper restoration project on the East Coast since the Statue of Liberty, made with 100 tons of copper, was refurbished in 1986. The building's granite exterior hails from the same quarry in Connecticut that supplied stone for the base of the Statue of Liberty. Uncovered on the floor at the base of the grand staircase was an original Fulton Building medallion that is now displayed inside the entrance. Three marble "F" logos were designed to match. They sit above the hotel elevators.

The hotel's unique U-shaped design allows many guests to enjoy views of the Allegheny River as it flows to its estuary at The Point. A seven-story lightwell offers breathtaking views from almost every room.

The Renaissance Pittsburgh Hotel marries history with modernity. It offers all the amenities expected of an upscale hotel without sacrificing any of the building's 20th-century grandeur. It is an impressive coupling of history and progress, and an integral part of a city rich in tradition.

Renaissance Hotels have a strong global presence, with more than 40 properties in the United States and 55 properties throughout Europe, the Middle East and Asia.

Zambelli Fireworks Internationale

ZAMBELLI FIREWORKS Internationale works to make other people happy, in a big way. The fireworks manufacturing company has moved into its second century of putting together displays that illuminate special occasions: Fourth of July, the new millennium, presidential inaugurations, papal visits, Super Bowls, The Kentucky Derby, troop parades, world fairs and corporate events.

In 1893 Antonio Zambelli brought his artistry from Italy to New Castle, the nation's Fireworks Capital, establishing one of the country's oldest and largest fireworks companies. George Zambelli Sr., one of Antonio's seven children, started rolling firecracker tubes at age 7 and setting off displays at 16. After receiving his college degree in accounting, George returned to the company and, in 1957, took over. With his drive and his dreams, he has created the most well known name brand of fireworks in the world, earning Zambellis the nickname of the "First Family of Fireworks."

Zambelli Fireworks Internationale, one of the country's oldest and largest fireworks manufacturers, lights the skyline of Pittsburgh.

The Zambelli family tradition carries on with all five of George and wife, Connie's, children involved in the business. The corporation has grown to include a southern office in Boca Raton, Florida, and a western office in Shafter, California. The Zambelli Internationale marketing area has expanded into Europe, Central and South America as well as North America, but Zambelli Fireworks Internationale maintains its U.S. corporate headquarters in New Castle, about 60 miles north of Pittsburgh.

At Zambelli Fireworks Internationale, work is done the old-fashioned way with experienced pyrotechnicians making shells by hand, one at a time, at a remote 360-acre site. With the layering involved, each shell takes about three weeks to carefully wrap. Some of the shells still are hand-fired by pyrotechnicians; others explode electronically at carefully timed intervals, often choreographed to music. The company was the first in the business to use the blazing emblems of corporate logos at promotional shows and since has added laser light shows to its repertoire. Both Pittsburgh and Zambelli earned a notation in the Guinness Book of World Records for fireworks being launched from the highest altitude, the U.S. Steel Building.

Fireworks have gained popularity over the years, but the Fourth of July remains the biggest boom in the business. Every year Zambelli, his family and staff produce more than 1,800 firework shows across the country for the nation's birthday, launching more than a million shells for this holiday alone.

Marking the millennium made Zambelli Fireworks Internationale explode with excitement at more than 400 shows including New York City, Boston, Baltimore, Cleveland, Miami, Houston, California, Ecuador, Belize City and St. Croix. The company's Pittsburgh show was the biggest in the world.

George Zambelli's personal favorite remains a display at the Statue of Liberty Anniversary Celebration on July 4, 1986, when the company set off about 26,400 shells in New York City's harbor, lighting the entire Manhattan skyline.

The quest to make others happy has brought George Zambelli a Congressional citation for excellence. The quest to make memories for others, celebration after spectacular celebration, is what keeps Zambelli Fireworks Internationale sparkling.

Family and fireworks are central to Zambelli Fireworks Internationale, which has produced outdoor fireworks displays, indoor pyrotechnics and special stage effects around the world. Family members are, from left, standing, Dr. George R. Zambelli Jr., Connie Zambelli, George R. Zambelli Sr., Danabeth Zambelli; sitting, Marcy Zambelli and Dr. DonnaLou Zambelli; kneeling, Annlyn Zambelli and Michael Richards.

Networks

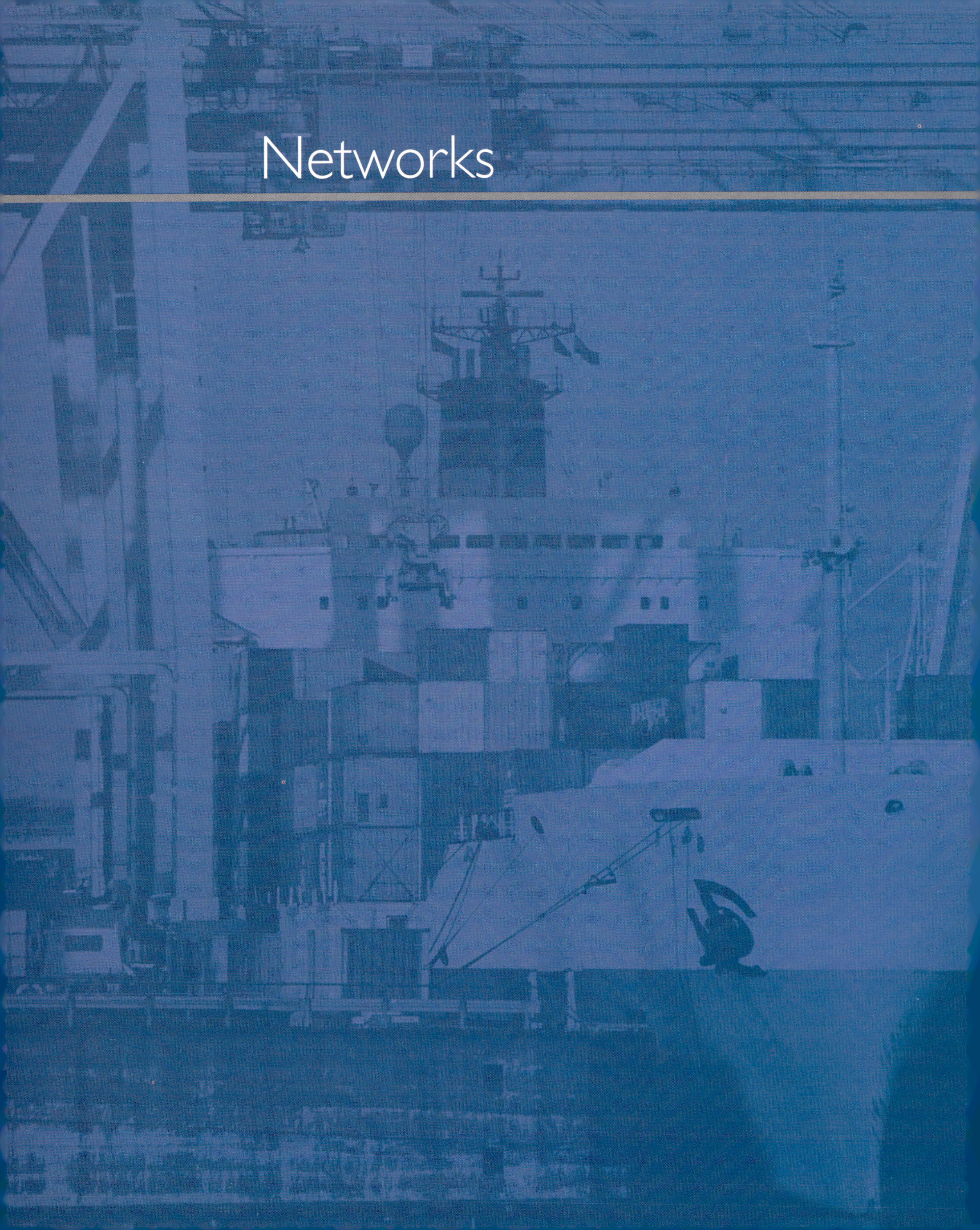

Pittsburgh media, telecommunications, transportation and energy companies keep information, people and power circulating throughout the region.

Columbia Gas of Pennsylvania

ONE OF THE OLDEST NATURAL gas utilities in America, Columbia Gas of Pennsylvania, Inc. traces its origins to the founding of Manufacturers Natural Gas Company in 1885. Throughout its more than 100-year history, the company has contributed greatly to the development of the Pittsburgh region. Through mergers and acquisitions Columbia Gas has emerged as one of the largest natural gas utilities in the state and has maintained its commitment to provide innovative energy solutions and high levels of customer service.

The first of many mergers occurred in 1903 when Manufacturers Light & Heat Company — the company was renamed to reflect its main business of lighting Pittsburgh's cobblestone streets and heating the city's homes — merged with six other natural gas companies. Soon afterward, gas lighting began to disappear due to the advent of more affordable electric lighting, prompting the company to concentrate on serving the heating and gas-powered appliance markets.

In 1915, 13 affiliated yet independently run companies serving Pennsylvania, eastern Ohio and the northern panhandle of West Virginia merged into Manufacturers Light & Heat. The expanded company fueled the tri-state area's booming steel, pottery and porcelain industries.

Ohio Fuel Corporation acquired Manufacturers Light & Heat in 1924. Two years later, the holdings of Ohio Fuel Corporation and Columbia Gas & Electric Corporation were consolidated to form Columbia Gas & Electric Corporation. By 1930, Manufacturers had grown to comprise 25 separate companies.

The company's commitment to technology and customer service resulted in many industry firsts. For example, in 1937 Manufacturers became the first utility to store an oversupply of summer gas underground to meet higher winter demand. The first underground gas storage facility, which was located at Cross Creek in Washington County, ensured reliable, affordable gas service when customers needed it most.

A third major merger occurred in 1944, when Manufacturers Light & Heat combined with Manufacturers Gas Company, Pennsylvania Fuel Supply Company and Greensboro Gas Company. The new company extended direct service to Warren and other towns in north-central Pennsylvania. In 1948 Manufacturers acquired the assets of Gettysburg Gas Corporation. Three years later, the company purchased the Pennsylvania and West Virginia properties of The Natural Gas Company of West Virginia.

By 1962 a new company, Columbia Gas of Pennsylvania, assumed responsibility for Manufacturers Light & Heat distribution operations throughout Pennsylvania. Columbia acquired York County Gas Company in 1969, further extending the company's service area throughout the state.

In 2000 Columbia Gas of Pennsylvania became part of NiSource, Inc., as a result of a $6 billion merger. NiSource, Inc., is a holding company with headquarters in Merrillville, Indiana, whose operating companies engage in all phases of the natural gas business from exploration and production to transmission, storage and distribution, as well as electric generation, transmission and distribution. With more than 10,000 employees, NiSource businesses provide energy to 3.6 million customers located in the high-growth energy corridor from the Gulf of Mexico to the Midwest to New England.

Delivering the Future

Through the years, Columbia Gas has delivered value to its customers. With operations that span 27 Pennsylvania counties and as a subsidiary of the third-largest natural gas distribution company in the country, Columbia Gas of Pennsylvania is poised to meet the demands of an ever-changing marketplace.

Columbia Gas offered Pennsylvania's first natural gas choice pilot program and continues to find ways to better serve its customers. Columbia advises its residential customers on how best to equip their homes and stretch their energy dollars and offers businesses a wealth of efficient energy options. The company works with state and city officials and chambers of commerce to attract economic development.

The company also delivers the future by keeping the past alive. For decades, the Eternal Light Peace Memorial, a gas-fueled, flaming monument, burned brightly at Gettysburg National Battlefield — a symbol of hope that the carnage that had occurred there would never happen again. The energy crisis of the 1970s and a moratorium on natural gas use for anything other than necessities extinguished the flame in 1973.

Columbia management believed this symbol of hope was too important to die, so the company relighted and rededicated the monument in 1988 during the 125th anniversary of the Battle of Gettysburg. The flame has shone brightly ever since, and Columbia is committed to donating the gas to keep this beacon for peace burning for years to come.

A Leader in Labor-Management Cooperation

Columbia not only has fueled the industrial growth of Pittsburgh but also has set new standards for labor-management cooperation in an area with a turbulent labor past. The company initiated an interest-based bargaining process during negotiations with the United Steelworkers of America in 1998. Unlike traditional bargaining, which focuses on taking and defending positions, Columbia's approach emphasizes reconciliation of interests through techniques that promote open communication.

Columbia and USWA Local 7139-03 used the process to implement a safety program that improved workplace safety practices and increased employee safety awareness. The efforts of the company and its union were recognized in 1999 with the Governor's Award for Labor-Management Cooperation, which recognizes companies and unions that promote economic success through partnering.

Reaching Out to the Community

Columbia Gas of Pennsylvania has led the way in giving back to the communities it serves through numerous outreach and cultural enhancement programs. The company's WarmChoice program, which is designed to weatherize the homes of low-income customers, was one of the first of its kind in the country. Additional customer outreach programs assist the disadvantaged and the elderly with energy costs and repairs.

FrontRow! is a unique, cooperative venture with the region's six leading performing arts organizations — Pittsburgh Ballet Theatre, Pittsburgh Civic Light Opera, Pittsburgh Dance Council, Pittsburgh Opera, Pittsburgh Public Theater and Pittsburgh Symphony Orchestra. Funded with a Columbia grant, the program brings the performing arts closer to the community through special student-oriented offerings at area schools.

In addition to contributing to local United Way campaigns, the Western Pennsylvania Conservancy and regional performing arts organizations, Columbia partnered with the City of Pittsburgh and the Urban Redevelopment Authority on the South Side Works Project, a reclamation of the old J&L Steel site, by donating the installation of gas lines to serve the development.

Despite the number of mergers throughout its history, Columbia Gas of Pennsylvania has continued its leadership role in providing safe, reliable gas service to its nearly 400,000 customers. The company has succeeded since the birth of the utility industry by remaining focused on customer service, by leveraging technology and through its commitment to the communities it serves.

Dominion

DOMINION'S ROOTS IN WESTERN Pennsylvania run long and deep. It has been serving customers in the Pittsburgh area for more than 100 years. Dominion's local ties go back even further — to George Washington, who played a prominent role in the founding of both Pittsburgh and Dominion.

Business magnates John D. Rockefeller and Frank Jay Gould built up parts of what is now Dominion. Company predecessors operated canal barges and streetcars. Others were at the center of legendary natural gas field wars, industry innovations and landmark court cases.

Today's Dominion is the result of the merger in January 2000 of Pittsburgh-based Consolidated Natural Gas Company (CNG) with Dominion Resources, Inc., of Richmond, Va. The merged entity is the largest energy producer in the Northeast, and it delivers natural gas and electricity to nearly four million homes and businesses. While the corporate headquarters are in Richmond, Pittsburgh remains a business center for Dominion's energy distribution and marketing businesses, as well as a hub for its new telecommunications operations.

Dominion is involved in a wide array of community service, charitable giving and employee volunteer programs, including sponsorship of the Western Pennsylvania Conservancy's "Gateway Gardens" program.

Fueling Pittsburgh's Industrial Boom

Joseph Newton Pew, a real estate trader from Mercer, Pa., and Edward O. Emerson, a Titusville, Pa., banker, founded The Peoples Natural Gas Company — now known as Dominion Peoples — in Pittsburgh in 1885. They came to Pittsburgh because of the significant natural gas finds around Murrysville, in Westmoreland County. The Murrysville discovery drew a rough-and-tumble crowd. A dispute over ownership of one nearby gusher resulted in a riot in which one man was killed. Along with being prodigious, the wells were long-lived. Peoples Natural Gas Well No. 1 was drilled in 1886 and continues to produce today.

At about the same time, a subsidiary of Rockefeller's Standard Oil Company discovered large quantities of natural gas in West Virginia. The resourceful Rockefeller built pipelines to bring the gas to the booming industrial centers of Pittsburgh, Akron and Cleveland. Emerson and Pew sold Peoples Natural Gas to Standard shortly thereafter.

As the 1900s unfolded, increased government oversight of business figured prominently in the company's history. The Sherman Antitrust Act of 1911 forced the breakup of Rockefellers' Standard Oil empire. Standard Oil of New Jersey became the holding company for Peoples Natural Gas and several other natural gas affiliates. Pressed by another federal law and a U.S. Supreme Court decision, Standard was forced in 1943 to spin off its natural gas pipeline and distribution businesses into the new, independent Consolidated Natural Gas Company.

Father of a Country and a Company

The Virginia leg of today's Dominion began as a transportation company. While still serving as the nation's first president, Washington joined James Madison and others to start the Upper Appomattox Company in 1795. The company was created to promote navigation on the Appomattox River. It entered the electricity business in the 1880s by taking over hydroelectric plants. Gould bought a successor company, adding it to a string of electric streetcar lines and electric and gas utilities. New York engineering firm Stone & Webster acquired what was then called Virginia Railway and Power Company (VR&P) in 1925. VR&P later became Virginia Electric and Power Company (VEPCO). The same federal law that brought about the birth of CNG caused VEPCO to become an independent company.

Through the last half of the Twentieth Century, CNG and VEPCO grew and prospered. CNG became one of the first natural gas companies to venture offshore and drill in the Gulf of Mexico. VEPCO put its first nuclear power unit into service in the 1970s. VEPCO later renamed itself Virginia Power and was put under the umbrella of a holding company, Dominion Resources.

Dominion Tower, located in the heart of Pittsburgh's Cultural District, serves as Dominion's headquarters in western Pennsylvania.

A Fully Integrated Energy Company

The merger of CNG and Dominion Resources under the Dominion name created the nation's largest fully integrated energy company. It has annual revenues of more than $10 billion and the ability to produce more than 3 trillion British Thermal Units (BTUs) of energy per day. The company has a power generation portfolio of more than 22,000 megawatts, which is expected to grow to more than 29,000 megawatts by 2006. Dominion also is one of the largest independent oil and natural gas exploration and production companies in North America, with 4.6 trillion cubic feet equivalent of natural gas reserves.

The company has 7,600 miles of natural gas pipeline and operates the nation's largest underground natural gas storage system, with more than 950 billion cubic feet of storage capacity. Dominion also owns a managing equity interest in Dominion Fiber Ventures LLC, owner of Dominion Telecom. Dominion Telecom plans to expand its fiber-optic network from its current 35,000 fiber miles to more than 800,000 miles.

Dominion's strategy is to focus on the northeast quadrant of the United States, which accounts for 40 percent of the nation's energy consumption. By being involved in the energy business from wellhead to burner tip and from power station to light switch, Dominion has an unparalleled set of options every day.

Serving the Community

Dominion is more than a leading energy provider. The company is committed to improving the lives of people in the communities it serves through an array of community service, charitable giving and employee volunteer programs. For example, most of Dominion's 16,000 employees are eligible to take a day off with pay each year to participate in charitable work of their choice.

In addition, hundreds of company employees take part annually in "Dominion Volunteers: Putting Our Energy to Work for the Environment" projects. Dominion is a regular participant in the Habitat for Humanity program, helping to build new homes for families in need. It has organized many community service projects as part of the United Way's annual "Day of Caring." The Dominion Foundation provides financial support to numerous worthy causes. And, as part of its environmental stewardship, Dominion manages its pipeline rights of way to help restore Pennsylvania's elk herds.

The CNG-Dominion merger was more than the combination of two historic companies. It marked a continuation of a longstanding commitment to serve the people of western Pennsylvania as an energy provider, community contributor and trusted neighbor.

The Peoples Natural Gas Flynn No. 2 well in Ligonier, Pa., was the world's deepest natural gas well — 7,765 feet — when it was drilled in 1922.

Hoechstetter

AS A SHY HIGH SCHOOL STUDENT in the 1960s, Harvey Hoechstetter was enthralled with the power of the press. While his classmates were working to buy a car, Hoechstetter traded the used car he had bought with odd-job earnings for a printing press. He installed his press in the family's row house in Squirrel Hill and began his career by printing flyers and circulars for local businesses. Upon earning his degree in printing management from Carnegie Mellon University in 1963, he opened his first print shop above a movie theater in Squirrel Hill. As his business grew, Hoechstetter moved his presses to a larger site in Pittsburgh's East Liberty in 1970 and to its present location in Point Breeze in the early 80s.

Among its many innovations, the Hoechstetter Printing Company installed the region's first phototypesetting equipment in the early 70s. The move allowed the firm to carve a niche printing college journals and periodicals because the technology was faster and cheaper than the previous Linotype machines that clanked out hot metal type. As other printers acquired phototypesetting, Hoechstetter moved into another niche market: art prints. The company's staff developed processes that used permanent ink pigments and acid-free papers to produce high-quality reproductions, and the firm turned out limited-edition prints for artists and publishers throughout the United States.

In the early 80s Hoechstetter entered another precision market, that of printing wildlife stamps. To ensure success in this business, the company developed a printing operation that allowed for perfect registration of multiple small images in a variety of colors. Later, Harvey Hoechstetter developed and printed Strictly Pittsburgh, a move-around-the-city board game, which he also marketed to various other cities under their names.

To fund additional modernization and expansion, Harvey Hoechstetter sold the business in 1988 to Graphic Industries of Atlanta. He remained president until his retirement in 1990 when Stephanie Firtko succeeded him. Among contributions to the printing industry in which he takes the most pride are bringing more women into a previously male-dominated trade, hiring promising individuals who had little or no technical or work experience, and seeing his protégés thrive and advance to leadership posts.

Since 1999 the Hoechstetter Printing Company has operated as an independent subsidiary of Wallace Computer Services. Its current leadership team consists of Jake Zoller, president; Tom Phillips, vice president of operations; Carrie Zdobinski, vice president of administration, and Jim Ford, vice president of manufacturing.

With about 245 employees at its headquarters plant, today's Hoechstetter has built upon its expertise in niche markets to become the preeminent general commercial printer in the Pittsburgh region. From this base, the company serves the entire northeastern United States and also handles national printing jobs. Customers range from small organizations to major companies, and printing runs vary from a few hundred business cards to millions of product brochures. For USAirways, the company makes runs of 15 million for pocket-folded ticket holders.

Founder Harvey Hoechstetter, left center, shakes hands with Mayor Richard Caliguiri in the new plant opened in 1986 in Pittsburgh's Point Breeze section.

Remaining in the forefront of technology to benefit its customers, the company maintains all-electronic prepress systems, which it updates continually. The prepress operations convert a customer's artwork on electronic disks into printing plates for the presses. Included among the firm's varied presses are seven and eight-color sheet-fed presses, with ultraviolet drying capability, and a six-color continuous-paper or web press. In-line finishing operations allow for remoistenable or permanent gluing, page folding, pocket folding and trimming. Other capabilities include die cutting, foil imprinting and embossing as well as complete bindery operations. Its unique specialty capabilities have allowed Hoechstetter to attract business from other geographical regions. They also helped the firm boost its sales by more than 200 percent in six years — from $11 million in 1995 to $35 million in 2001.

Several jobs completed in 2001 demonstrate the range and scale of the company's printing capabilities. On a Wednesday afternoon, Hoechstetter's sales representative in Cincinnati called with an order for 10 million promotional postcards to be mailed to a retail firm's potential customers by the following Monday morning. Working around the clock, the printing plant's staff located a paper supplier who could deliver three truckloads by Thursday evening. That night, the staff arranged for Internet transmittal of the electronic disk containing the type and graphics from a Baltimore printer, which had abandoned the project, and sent a proof copy by overnight express to the customer. The job went on press Friday morning and the first completed postcards were delivered to a mailing house on the West Coast on Saturday afternoon. The next delivery was to the Midwest on Sunday morning, and the final truckload traveled to an East Coast mailing house on Sunday evening.

Still running daily is the 1960s Heidelberg press behind Hoechstetter's leadership team: from left, Jake Zoller, Tom Phillips, Carrie Zdobinski and Jim Ford.

Another order in 2001 called for rapid printing, binding and delivery of 200,000 company annual reports. Hoechstetter and a sister plant in Boston printed the job on web presses, then the reports were bound at the Pittsburgh plant and shipped to the customer in Akron, Ohio — all in three days.

Throughout its history, Hoechstetter has been active in civic affairs in the Pittsburgh community. Among its newest endeavors, the company sponsored its first annual competition for visual artists in 2001. Works of the seven winners were showcased in a printed portfolio and a limited-edition book entitled *Impressions: Three Rivers, Four Seasons.* Other community activities include the annual March of Dimes Walk America, with more than 100 employees participating and company trucks delivering water. Hoechstetter is also a corporate benefactor of the Carnegie Museums of Pittsburgh.

Looking ahead, Zoller plans to emphasize a closer relationship through partnering with customers in the local market and to continue installing new presses and other advanced-technology equipment. He also intends to build on Harvey Hoechstetter's legacy of expanding into promising new markets that demand high-quality printing as well as giving job opportunities to those dedicated individuals who share the founder's love of printing.

A colorful PT Cruiser transports Hoechstetter's customers to and from its plant.

Port Authority of Allegheny County

A LOCAL FOLK SONG, "YOU CAN'T Get There from Here," pokes fun at the hapless traveler trying to negotiate Pittsburgh's hills and valleys, strange bends and sharp curves, bridges, tunnels, snowstorms and potholes. If only someone had given him a Port Authority route map highlighting bus, light rail, incline and mini-bus service connecting virtually all points in Allegheny County.

Although it serves the 22nd-largest metropolitan area, Port Authority is the 12th-largest transit system in the United States. Over half of downtown commuters use it. So do more than half of downtown shoppers. And everyone benefits from reduced traffic and parking congestion and improved air quality.

Early public transportation in Pittsburgh

Mini-bus service introduced to Monroeville in June 1998

The urban industrial community of Pittsburgh has always relied heavily on mass transit for its economic well being. From 1900 to mid-century the Pittsburgh Railways Company was the primary provider of trolley service. At its peak in 1918, 99 routes and 606 miles of track carried 600,000 passengers daily.

After World War II, the urban population of Pittsburgh began its migration to the suburbs. By the mid-1950s some 37 independent bus companies served the city and its outlying communities. Although they fulfilled the basic transportation need, few of these often family-owned lines could afford to adequately maintain or update their vehicles.

This increasingly untenable situation prompted government and civic groups to call for public ownership of a unified, countywide transit system. In 1956 an Act of the Pennsylvania General Assembly created the Port Authority to develop port facilities to serve Pittsburgh, and in 1959 that Act was amended, empowering the organization to acquire privately owned transit facilities and operate them as a public system. By August of 1964 the planning and acquisition phases were complete. For the first time in history, a unified fare and transfer system became effective throughout Allegheny County.

Traditional transit ridership changed and shifted during the 1960s and 70s and Port Authority kept up through strategic expansion. In 1977 Port Authority completed the South Busway, which bypassed Liberty Tunnel congestion. Work on the Martin Luther King, Jr. East Busway was about to begin and would eventually reduce the trip between Wilkinsburg and downtown from 45 minutes to a mere 15. But obsolescence was fast approaching the popular South Hills trolleys while suburban communities voiced their demand for system expansion from all directions.

In 1980 Port Authority broke ground on a new light-rail system that would incorporate Pittsburgh's first subway. The impetus for a downtown subway system dates back to 1902 and was revived in 1926 and again in 1932. But each time the plan was abandoned for lack of consensus. This time, enthusiastic support from Pittsburgh corporations, which were busy building no less than five major office towers downtown, ensured that the "T" was welcomed as a major component of the city's latest renaissance. Twenty years later, another building boom is following the same trend with Mellon's new operations center on top of the Steel Plaza station and PNC's new operations center at what will be Port Authority's newest T station at First Avenue.

In 1989 service and ridership to the northern suburbs was significantly improved by the HOV lanes of the North Hills Expressway (I-279). In 1996 mini-buses were first used to serve the important airport corridor and have proven to be so popular and cost-effective that they have been expanded to other areas of Allegheny County and now make up one out of every 10 vehicles operating at peak hours. The West Busway and Wabash HOV facility will continue the western leg of Port Authority's expanding service to all points on the compass.

A Port Authority light rail vehicle

Port Authority focuses not only on where but also on whom it will serve. Since 1979 the Port Authority-sponsored ACCESS program has been a model paratransit service for senior citizens and persons with disabilities, and wheel-chair accessibility on its regular routes increases each year. Unique contractual relationships with the University of Pittsburgh and Carnegie Mellon University provide unlimited access to Port Authority services for all students and staff. This opens the entire county to the university population and generates a whole new generation of transit riders. And for tourists and pleasure seekers, the North Shore Project will tie the light-rail system with the new ballparks, the expanded Convention Center and the Cultural District.

Port Authority has become much more than a transit system. It is a billion-dollar construction company with significant impact on the economic development of the community. It is an economic partner with the likes of the Convention and Visitors Bureau, the Airport Corridor Transportation Association and the Heinz Endowments. It employs 3,000 employees, including operators, maintenance workers, transit police, communications specialists and administrators. And it is on a path to become the premier public transit system in the country — the articulated vision of Port Authority Chief Executive Officer Paul Skoutelas.

A low-floor bus introduced into Port Authority's fleet in 1999

"Certainly this is an ultimate vision and goal," says Skoutelas, who took the helm in 1997. "But even when we get there, we will still look for ways to improve our services. We will always need to make choices about where to employ our resources and how to best serve our customers."

Providing an exciting glimpse into the future of mass transit in Allegheny County is the Regional Transit Vision Plan, a joint effort led by Port Authority and the Southwestern Pennsylvania Commission in partnership with Heinz Endowments. This study will look closely at the emerging needs of all stakeholders in public transportation and create a blueprint for the future. It will involve a great deal of public participation and a strong focus on the changing economic base of the community as well as emerging technology.

"There is a feeling that the new service and technology-based economy will create a better, stronger Pittsburgh," says Paul Skoutelas. "What we do and how we do it has to keep pace with the new economy and the new rider."

Port Authority has been a presence in and a partner with the community since 1956. It has helped the people of Allegheny County get through the mountains and over the rivers; to the office, to the factory, to Kaufmann's and to Heinz Hall; from class at the university to the movies on McKnight Road; and from north to south, east to west and everywhere in between.

Port of Pittsburgh Commission

BEFORE PITTSBURGH WAS A CITY, it was a port. Indians settled along the riverbanks because canoes afforded easy transportation and trade. The British fought the French for control of the Ohio knowing that it opened the gateway to the continent's inland wealth and a future empire.

When Lewis and Clark began their canoe exploration of the western rivers nearly 200 years ago, a person could walk across the Ohio at only a foot and a half of natural depth. Early commerce was restricted to a rush of flatboat barges during the dangerous spring rise in the river. The U.S. Army Corps of Engineers built locks and dams, some of which are now 100 years old, and gave the region safe navigable pools, reliable sources of drinking water, river recreation and industrial transportation infrastructure. With this, Pittsburgh entered into the Industrial Revolution.

The Port of Pittsburgh stretches along 200 miles of waterways in western Pennsylvania and has access to more than 10,000 miles of markets along the inland waterway system.

Early river transportation gave birth to boat building, metal making and glass making industries. Later, steel magnates would know that the abundance of raw, natural materials moving on liquid highways would make Pittsburgh the center of industry that it became. Today, chemical, plastic, pharmaceutical and power generation industries bring raw materials to Pittsburgh, the "Point of Arrival and the Port of Manufacture." Nearly one in six in southwestern Pennsylvanians owes his or her livelihood to an industry dependent upon these advantages of waterway transportation. The Monongahela, Allegheny and Ohio Rivers are the reasons that Pittsburgh exists and that it emerged as an industrial powerhouse.

In 1994 the Commonwealth of Pennsylvania created the Port of Pittsburgh Commission for the 10-county district of Allegheny, Armstrong, Beaver, Butler, Clarion, Lawrence, Greene, Fayette, Washington and Westmoreland to promote the commercial use and development of the inland waterway and intermodal transportation systems and to integrate these systems into the economic, environmental, recreational and intermodal future of southwestern Pennsylvania. In the first six years of the Commission's existence, traffic increased by 20 percent.

Pittsburgh is one of the busiest inland waterway ports in the world, leading to 10,000 miles of inland markets. It is the 11th-largest port of any kind in the nation. The Port of Pittsburgh moves more than 50 million tons of cargo each year. This cargo brings nearly $14 billion worth of business to the area and generates another $6 billion in indirect business.

Waterway transportation remains the most economical and environmentally friendly form of surface transportation. A single barge moves the same capacity of cargo as 58 trucks or 15 rail cars. It uses about one-tenth the amount of fuel as trucks.

Water quality is returning to the rivers, just as new demands are being placed on the system. As residents beautify, develop and take greater recreational advantage of the cleaner rivers, shippers explore new markets of moving passengers and higher value goods on the river system.

Although the rivers remain a limited resource, their safe use continues to provide multiple benefits. As the rivers once again change the region, the Port of Pittsburgh Commission will help define the characteristics of that change.

Pittsburgh History & Landmarks Foundation

Professional Services

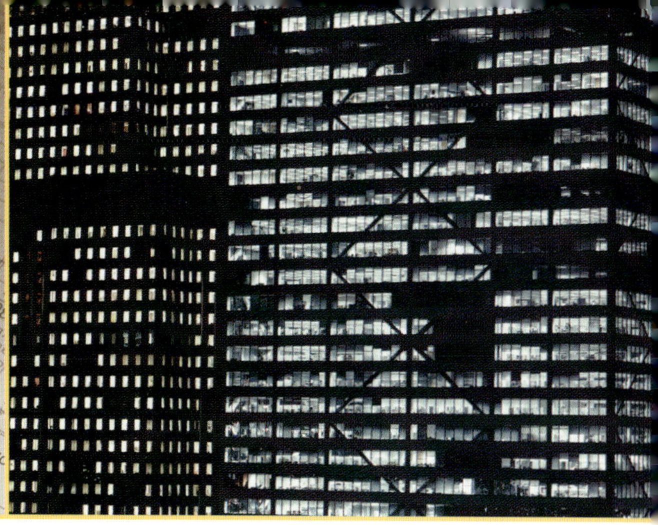

A variety of professionals provide essential services to the Pittsburgh area.

CelliFlynnBrennan Architects and Planners

OVER THE PAST 50 YEARS, CelliFlynnBrennan Architects and Planners has built an international reputation for design excellence, outstanding quality and exceptional client service as one of the region's pre-eminent architectural, planning and construction management consulting firms.

Founded as Celli-Flynn Architects (CFA) in McKeesport, Pennsylvania, in 1950 by two brothers, Mario Celli, FAIA, and Raymond Celli, AIA, along with William V. Flynn, AIA (all graduates of the Carnegie Institute of Technology), the firm has grown by attracting and retaining top-notch associates who come together as a tightly integrated team to provide superior architectural design and intelligent project management services.

Entrance court to the Paterno Library at Penn State

In 1957 Mario Celli introduced his son, Thomas, to the firm and its professional values. After earning an architectural degree from Cornell University in 1967, Thomas C. Celli, AIA, joined the firm as a design architect. Since 1985, CFA and Thomas Celli have been synonymous. He became president of the company that year, a position he still holds, and received the coveted Arthur Ross Award from Classical America for the completion of the East Wing of the Pennsylvania State Capitol. In 1999 William P. Brennan, AIA, joined the firm, precipitating the name change to CelliFlynnBrennan.

Unlike other professional services firms, whose principals serve primarily as salespeople and managers, the principals at CelliFlynnBrennan have always taken an active role in architectural work. Since the beginning, the firm has stressed a commitment to personalized service from its principals. That basic value has enabled the company to win repeat business, attract new clients and work on many highly visible projects.

An Industrial Beginning

CFA began as a leading national architectural expert in the design and construction of paper mills. During its early days, the firm designed and managed the construction of paper mills in Wisconsin, Tennessee, New Hampshire, Arkansas, Georgia and Florida. CFA also consulted on specific aspects of design with representatives of the Japanese paper industry.

The company has designed and managed the construction of building projects in 17 states, and the firm's expertise has been carried to Brazil, Argentina and Italy through the international efforts of Mario Celli, who represented the United States on the Educational Buildings Commission of the International Union of Architects, and through lectures given by Thomas Celli at various conferences, including those sponsored by UNESCO and ABCEM (the Brazilian Iron and Steel Institute), among others.

East Wing addition to the Pennsylvania State Capitol

Schools and Churches

Even though industrial work helped to establish and sustain CFA, the firm earned its reputation for architectural excellence on the design and construction of educational and religious facilities and the restoration of area churches. Today, educational and transportation projects, college and university facilities, and corporate offices and hotels make up the firm's workload in six states.

The firm's first educational project was the Jefferson Morgan High School in Greene County, followed by many high schools and elementary schools, including South Park, McKeesport, Highlands, Elizabeth-Forward, Norwin, Slippery Rock and Belle Vernon. CFA also managed the major renovations and additions to Taylor-Allderdice High School, a prominent institution in the Pittsburgh City Schools, and five high schools for the Diocese of Pittsburgh.

The company's parochial work led to major renovations of historic churches throughout the Pittsburgh region, including Blessed Sacrament Cathedral in Greensburg; St. Joseph's Cathedral in Wheeling, West Virginia; First Westminster Presbyterian Church in Steubenville, Ohio; and the preservation of the Bellefield Presbyterian Church in Pittsburgh, which won many international awards for historic preservation.

Numerous college and university projects — including the restoration of Seton Hill College's Administration Building, which was originally built in 1888; the restoration of Westminster College's Thompson Clark Hall, which was originally built in 1893; the design of the new Student Center at Robert Morris College; the design of new science buildings at Susquehanna University, Carlow College and University of Charleston; and the development of a Master Plan for Allegheny College — have enhanced the reputation and geographic reach of CelliFlynnBrennan.

Other state and regional projects include the East Wing of the Pennsylvania Capitol in Harrisburg, the Hillman Library and Posvar Hall at the University of Pittsburgh, the National Flag Foundation's headquarters, the Boy Scouts of America's Heritage Reservation in Fayette County, and the Paterno Library at Pennsylvania State University. The ranking of the Duquesne Club as the finest private club in America was partially due to the firm's successful design of the club's Health and Fitness Center.

CelliFlynnBrennan's list of successful projects has resulted in numerous national, state and regional awards for architectural design and historic restoration.

Design Expertise Amidst Change

The firm has changed much since the days of its founders. Offices were relocated from McKeesport to downtown Pittsburgh. Thomas Celli assumed the reins of the firm from his father, Mario, and still leads the corporation. More recently, William Brennan, AIA, with extensive credentials in historic preservation, commercial design and project management, joined the firm as a principal.

Interior restoration of the Bellefield Presbyterian Church

Nowhere is change more evident at CelliFlynnBrennan than in the deployment of technology in the design of buildings and the management of construction. Long gone are the drafting tables and pencil sharpeners of the past, replaced by a state-of-the-art computer-aided-design (CAD) system and Web-based project management applications. The firm was the first in the Pittsburgh region to design on a computer, leveraging technology as part of its commitment to client service.

The face of Pittsburgh has changed dramatically since the days of smokestacks and heavy industry. CelliFlynnBrennan has changed with it. Even though the faces and tools have changed at CelliFlynnBrennan, the firm's commitment to doing quality work with high ethical standards, integrity, and personalized service from the principals remains the same for each and every client.

Science and Technology Center at Carlow College

Aon Consulting Inc.

THE GAELIC WORD "AON," MEANING "unity" and "oneness," is especially fitting for Aon Consulting Inc.'s Pittsburgh operation because the company helps others unify their business and human resource strategies. Aon Consulting has assembled a group of innovative professionals from around the globe to offer area employers a broader, more strategic approach to resource management consulting services.

Aon Consulting, a division of Aon Corporation, one of the world's leading insurance services organizations with nearly $7.1 billion in revenue generated through more than 550 offices worldwide, absorbed the human resources, employee benefits and risk management expertise of two of the region's top consulting firms (Godwins, Booke and Dickenson; and Alexander and Alexander Insurance Services), which Aon acquired in the mid-1990s. Aon Consulting has three distinct consulting groups: employee benefits, compensation and management consulting. Through the greater Aon Corporation, the consulting company can also offer all of the products and services provided by the parent corporation, including brokerage services, specialized insurance coverages, risk management solutions, insurance underwriting, and comprehensive extended warranty and consumer service programs. This interdependency, better known as "One Aon," offers customers broad, efficient access to capital, human resources and risk management solutions so they can focus on driving their businesses forward.

The Aon executive team specializes in linking people strategies with business strategies. Pictured are: (front row, left to right) Candice Mill, Carole Lyon-Orr, (back row, left to right) Michael Garofalo, Darryl Blecher, Michael Higgins, Christopher Young, Pete Hess and Joseph Balash.

The "One Aon" philosophy is an important part of the corporation's culture, one in which fairness, integrity, client advocacy, teamwork and an entrepreneurial spirit combine to provide unsurpassed levels of service and groundbreaking business solutions.

Aon Consulting specializes in linking human resource strategies with business initiatives to achieve improved performance. Whether a company needs to fashion employee compensation packages to attract or retain employees who are in demand or contain its own rising benefits costs, Aon helps clients to develop and implement appropriate employee benefits strategies.

Aon Consulting leverages the latest technology, including Internet/Intranet applications, to help clients more efficiently and cost-effectively communicate employee information — total compensation statements, benefits statements, executive statements, early retirement programs and stock option information, to name just a few. Aon can even help customers manage their human resource data.

In addition to its three consulting groups, the company offers a wide range of services, including organizational analysis; job design and competency modeling; recruitment and selection; compensation and reward systems benefits design and management; and training and development programs. Aon's integrated consulting approach ensures that clients are effectively attracting, retaining and utilizing their people resources. Aon Consulting applies an objective, global perspective that provides customized solutions and consistent administration.

Every year Aon Consulting sponsors "United States @ Work™: The Work Force Commitment Index," a national study on employee and organizational commitment. The study explores trends affecting work force commitment and offers solutions, such as behavioral indicators of a committed work force and the steps an organization can take to help improve work force commitment. By understanding the forces impacting employee loyalty, Aon helps customers to link their people strategies with their business strategies.

With Aon Consulting, a company that celebrates and upholds the meaning of its name, customers unite with an expert in all facets of resource management so they can concentrate on what they do best: running their businesses.

Burt Hill Kosar Rittelmann Associates

WHEN PITTSBURGH THRIVED amidst a swirl of steel and smoke, Burt Hill Kosar Rittelmann Associates was there. As the city has evolved through three Renaissances to embrace the New Economy of the Digital Age, Burt Hill has continued to stand as western Pennsylvania's leading architecture and engineering firm, leaving its indelible mark on the built environment.

Embodying WHYY's new vision of itself as a visible, accessible and cutting-edge operation, this new public broadcasting facility showcases advanced digital technology and presents a very transparent and interactive face on Philadelphia's Independence Mall.

The first challenge for G. Edwin Howard, when he began his architectural practice in 1936, took him to the Oval Office of the White House, which he restored for the architect of the Capitol. Howard's practice in Butler welcomed Ralph Burt and Alva Hill in 1952, just as the baby boom was ushering in a school building boom. The firm responded and staked a claim in the K-12 market, which it continues to service today. Over the years, the practice has broadened, propelling Burt Hill into diverse market sectors, from public schools to higher education, commercial to residential, hospitality to health care, and historic renovations to advanced laboratories and other technologically intensive environments. These new challenges have led Burt Hill from its Butler headquarters to growing offices in Pittsburgh, Philadelphia, Boston and Washington, D.C., with projects as far away as Moscow and the United Arab Emirates. Yet despite its geographic expansion, Burt Hill has remained firmly rooted in western Pennsylvania, where it employs over 230 of its 320 employees.

Burt Hill's commitment to leading-edge design and delivery systems drives both its internal management and its project delivery. By integrating a full range of services in-house, from research and engineering to interior design and landscape architecture, the firm is able to bring the best thinking of each discipline to devise the most innovative solution for each situation. Burt Hill has pioneered use of the Internet for design, delivery, and ongoing facilities management and remains a Beta site for new technologies and software, folding its technological savvy into the marketplace. Likewise, Burt Hill has led the pack in the development and application of "green" or sustainable design principles aimed at creating healthy buildings and promoting environmental responsibility.

Technological leadership and innovation is reflected in a number of prominent projects that carry the Burt Hill stamp. The firm's award-winning design for WHYY, the new public broadcast facility in Philadelphia, incorporates the latest in digital editing and broadcast technology in a building designed to encourage public participation in the broadcasting process. By revolutionizing work spaces and ultimately impacting how business is conducted, Burt Hill has helped clients such as law firm Buchanan Ingersoll and accountants Deloitte & Touche improve their productivity and bottom lines. Burt Hill engineering innovation has been applied to Pittsburgh's David E. Lawrence Convention Center, making the building "green" by maximizing daylight and incorporating gray water recycling to cool the building from the rooftop down.

Today the firm enters its fourth generation of leadership and continues to rely on its original principles of client service while trailblazing innovation into the millennium and beyond.

As one of six new buildings in a 1.38 million-square-foot technology park designed by Burt Hill, 200 Minuteman Place in Andover, Massachusetts, provides an inspiring workplace setting for advanced-technology tenants.

Civil & Environmental Consultants, Inc.

CEC provided permitting services for inland dam construction for the Braddock Lock and Dam rehabilitation.

CIVIL & ENVIRONMENTAL CONSULTANTS, INC. (CEC) is a professional engineering and environmental science consulting firm headquartered in Pittsburgh, Pennsylvania. Established in 1989 by James M. Roberts, Ph.D., P.E.; James P. Nairn, P.G., L.R.S.; Kenneth R. Miller, P.E.; and Gregory P. Quatchak, P.E., CEC has rapidly expanded into a successful management-owned corporation. Initially one office with six employees, CEC now has a national presence with over 225 employees and seven offices located throughout the Eastern, Southern and Midwestern regions of the United States.

Principal level involvement is the CEC hallmark that guides its tradition of uncompromising standards and business excellence. For three consecutive years, *The Pittsburgh Business Times* selected CEC for the "Pittsburgh 100" list of fastest-growing companies. In addition, a survey by the *Central Penn Business Journal* ranked CEC in the top four "Best Places to Work in Pennsylvania" for medium-sized firms.

CEC serves a broad client base. Manufacturers, metals producers, electric and natural gas utilities, waste management firms, and the mining industry represent key market sectors. CEC is also known as a respected adviser to many clients within the legal community. Developers, architects and engineers are also provided with comprehensive engineering services.

Ecological restoration of slag slopes for future expansion of Frick Park, part of the Brownfield Development at Nine Mile Run

To date, more than 8,000 projects have been successfully completed by experienced CEC specialists in the civil and environmental disciplines. Trails and greenway development, comprehensive site development, including landscape architecture and planning, surveying, geotechnical engineering, municipal engineering, jurisdictional wetlands, investigative engineering, water resources, and municipal solid waste design projects demonstrate the company's versatility as a civil engineering firm.

A unique focal point within CEC is its highly successful environmental practice. Projects such as subsurface investigations, site assessments, site remediation, regulatory compliance audits, hazardous waste management, permitting, risk assessments, and brownfield development are typical of CEC's extensive environmental management capabilities. CEC also offers a full range of services in the life sciences, including turnkey wetland services, fishery surveys, benthic macroinvertebrate surveys, watershed assessment studies, ecological risk assessments, wildlife surveys, habitat evaluations, and threatened and endangered species studies.

Projects are carefully reviewed, analyzed and monitored by project managers from the initial phase to completion. Cost-effectiveness is a prime consideration in the overall approach and is always coupled with design and implementation components in the planning stages.

Prominent local projects are the Prime Outlets at Grove City, Pennsylvania, and the Pittsburgh Technical Center and South Side Developments (former LTV Pittsburgh Works). CEC has received repeated recognition for outstanding projects including two Brownfield Awards for environmental cleanup and restoration of former industrial properties. A regional project of significance was providing fast track and innovative engineering solutions to restore the Rumpke Sanitary Landfill near Cincinnati, Ohio, after a catastrophic landslide.

Named as one of the top 500 design firms and one of the top 200 environmental firms by *Engineering News-Record*, CEC views a strong client focus and ethical business practices to be essential for the integrity and growth of the organization. CEC is dedicated to providing quality professional engineering, environmental science, life science, and design-build services to its clients. A proven commitment to excellence and client satisfaction inspires the growth of CEC.

HMS Hallmark

IN 1968 HALLMARK ADVERTISING was founded on the strength of just two accounts: Dad's Pet Foods and The Hoover Company (vacuum cleaners). Much has changed over the ensuing 32 years, yet those two accounts have remained and have grown with the agency. This three-decade relationship is rather unusual in the advertising world of today, but it is a testament to the importance of insightful strategic thinking, quality work and commitment.

Throughout its history, Hallmark Advertising has acquired or merged with several advertising agencies. Each acquisition and merger has added a complementary body of experience and clients. Today, the original retail and sales promotion agency known as Hallmark Advertising has grown to become HMS Hallmark, a multiregional, full-service agency with more than $215 million in annual billings.

Headquartered in Pittsburgh, Pennsylvania, HMS Hallmark has offices in Columbus, Ohio; Orlando, Florida; and Tampa, Florida. HMS Hallmark provides brand planning/management, advertising, public relations, direct marketing, Web site design and event marketing to more than 40 clients, including Adelphia Communications, Allegheny Energy Systems, Anthem Blue Cross and Blue Shield, Dad's Pet Foods, GTE Communications, Huntingdon Bank, Kings Family Restaurants, Roomful Express, Southern Brick Institute, Supervalue (Shop 'n Save and Foodland stores), The Hoover Company and Universal Studios - Orlando.

The work created by HMS Hallmark is driven by one overriding objective: to build strong personal relationships between its clients' brands and consumers by changing beliefs and behaviors in order to produce measurable results for its clients. This objective has fostered the development of three of HMS Hallmark's proprietary marketing concepts: Brand DNA, The Unbundling of America℠ and H/T Bridge Marketing℠.

Over the years, the marketing pendulum has often swung from promotional selling to branding and then back to promotional selling. But in today's highly competitive marketplace, HMS Hallmark believes that there must be an intrinsic link between branding and promotional selling, and this belief was the genesis of the H/T Bridge Marketing concept.

Supporting the Pittsburgh community has also been important to the agency. When the nationally respected Pittsburgh Aviary faced a funding problem in the late 1980s, the agency donated creative services to help privatize the institution as a National Aviary. The effort succeeded, and HMS Hallmark continues to promote the facility. In addition, agency employees take part in the community's annual "Christmas in April" program of refurbishing the homes of elderly people.

The advertising industry will continue to change. For this reason, HMS Hallmark is committed to developing strategic paradigms that will continue to produce results for its clients in the marketplace as well as exploring acquisition opportunities that will expand its areas of expertise. But, in the midst of all the changes that will sweep the advertising industry, one constant remains for HMS Hallmark: the belief that strategic planning is at the core of every great creative concept. One could say that this belief is the hallmark of HMS Hallmark.

CEO Bill Binstock with new products and packaging from Hallmark Advertising's original and still growing accounts: Dad's Pet Foods and The Hoover Company

Kvaerner

KVAERNER'S TIES TO SOUTHWESTERN Pennsylvania and the city of Pittsburgh are extensive and reflect a network of strategic company acquisitions and business transactions spanning more than 100 years. This relationship began shortly before the turn of the century when in 1890 Andrew Carnegie's Carnegie, Phipps and Company, Limited signed a contract with Davy Brothers, Limited to design and furnish a forging press for its growing metals producing operation. Davy Brothers was headquartered in Sheffield, England, and specialized in equipment supply and engineering services for foundries, mills and railroads. This business connection was the beginning of a long-term association in servicing the region's burgeoning steel industry.

Kvaerner's E&C Division is located in Pittsburgh's Strip District.
Photo by Tom Barr

Following the successful completion of its initial order in the United States, and recognizing a significant business opportunity, Davy began to orchestrate an aggressive acquisition program. By purchasing several engineering and construction firms in the Pittsburgh area, Davy established itself as a major contributor to the growth and development of the region as a major producer of steel. Davy acquired the A.G. McKee Corporation in 1978, the Swindell Furnace Group in 1981, Dravo Engineers and Constructors in 1988 and finally Comstock Engineering in 1990, solidifying the company's role as a major source of engineering, design and construction services in the global marketplace.

Galvanizing line at U.S. Steel Fairless Works, Fairless, Pennsylvania
Photo by Tom Barr

In 1991 Davy was acquired by Trafalgar House, a United Kingdom-based international group of companies with interests in engineering and construction. In 1996 Trafalgar House was acquired by Kvaerner ASA headquartered in London, England, forming one of the world's largest and strongest engineering and construction companies with significantly expanded operations and capabilities worldwide.

Kvaerner's E&C Division specializes in providing process technology, engineering, design, project management, construction and commissioning services for the iron, steel, non-ferrous and precious metals, pharmaceutical, oil and gas, chemical, power generation, nuclear, minerals, mining and transportation industries. Worldwide, it employs more than 9,000 experienced personnel who work in over 30 key markets. Recent projects span the globe in more than 20 countries and include engineering, construction and management of a copper smelter in Peru; pelletizing plants in India, Mexico and Brazil; a blast furnace reline in Canada; and a greenfield steel plant and five soda ash projects in the United States. The Pittsburgh office of Kvaerner, serving the iron, steel, process and energy industries, is an integral part of the E&C Division.

Kvaerner has made a long-term commitment to the city of Pittsburgh and its employees with the creation of a state-of-the-art office facility located in the city's Strip District. The newly refurbished office complex includes an open central atrium, modular furniture systems and electronically linked workstations, and reflects management's progressive approach to an open exchange of information within its operation.

Kvaerner's E&C Division, recently formed through the amalgamation of the Process and Metals Divisions of Kvaerner ASA, possesses the strength, ability and imagination to provide cutting-edge technology in serving its customers worldwide. With the support of the extensive resources of its parent firm, Kvaerner can look forward to a successful future as a global force in the highly competitive field of engineering, design and construction.

L.D. Astorino Companies

ADMITTING THE BRILLIANT ITALIAN sky through its windows, the Chapel of the Holy Spirit in Vatican City "brings in God's light and mystery." The chapel's designer and architect, L.D. Astorino Companies (LDA), has expanded its international presence through such projects, but it still remains true to its Pittsburgh roots.

Founded in 1972 by Pittsburgh native Louis D. Astorino, a fellow of the American Institute of Architects (FAIA), LDA now employs more than 200 people at its city headquarters and branches in State College and Greensburg, Pennsylvania. Its professional staff works in architecture and interior design, environmental consulting and engineering.

LDA contains a deep family structure. Founder Astorino is chairman and chief executive officer while brother Dennis, AIA, is chief operating officer and heads the architectural division. Other staffers include mother Anne, who works in accounting, daughter Christine Astorino Del Sole, a landscape architect, and son Louis, a civil engineer.

With works across the United States and in other countries, the firm's staff ensures that all projects accomplish the LDA philosophy: "To capture a building's essence, to create visionary yet pragmatic solutions that meet deeply felt needs."

Another guiding principle is to create distinctive and appropriate architecture — buildings that are well suited to their site. A prime example is PNC Financial Services Group's vari-storied operations center in Pittsburgh's Firstside district, a rich and complex urban setting. The architects ensured that the glass-banded structure fits its historic site like a hand in a glove. Engineers on the LDA team worked with the architects to make the structure environmentally friendly, energy efficient and cost-effective to operate.

Bathed in bright sunlight, the Chapel of the Holy Spirit in Vatican City was designed by LDA architects to create an environment of holiness, serenity and contemplation.

For its Pittsburgh home, LDA restored a warehouse and adjoining buildings into unique "signature" offices that provide adequate work space for the firm's growing staff.

The LDA approach also extends to restoration projects, as exemplified by the company's Firstside headquarters complex. The structures epitomize the firm's aim of not only preserving buildings' historic value but also extending their useful life. The challenge was to restore a rundown 19th-century warehouse and two adjoining buildings while creating adequate work space to meet LDA's growing needs. To capture the spectacular view of sunlight reflecting off the nearby Monongahela River, the architects faced the warehouse building with a bay window façade and added a terrace and rooftop garden. The new headquarters displays the attributes that LDA's staff brings to all projects. Its design is original, enduring, creative, functional and cost-efficient.

As it continues to grow, LDA plans to emphasize sports, hospital and education facilities. Its project roster includes such prominent sports facilities as PNC Park, the Pittsburgh Pirates' new old-time ballpark; McKechnie Field, the Pirates' spring-training home; and Space Coast Stadium, the Florida Marlins' training facility. One shining example of LDA's work in the medical field is a transplant hospital in Palermo, Italy, affiliated with the world-renowned University of Pittsburgh Medical Center, a leader in organ transplants.

In addition to the contributions his business has made in the development and restoration of Pittsburgh, Louis Astorino expresses his commitment to the area through his devotion to community affairs, and he encourages his staff to become involved as well. And while LDA plans to expand its work geographically, the firm remains dedicated to transforming the face of Pittsburgh and surroundings, a region Astorino regards as brimming with strength and vitality.

Parsons Brinckerhoff

ONE OF THE WORLD'S FOREMOST engineering firms, Parsons Brinckerhoff (PB), provides a multi-dimensional array of complex services in a highly technical marketplace. From developing a network of bridges connecting interstate highways, to tunneling roads deep into the earth's crust, to designing tracks for a bolting rapid transit system, PB is a proven leader in infrastructure design, construction and implementation. With over 116 years of experience in world-class projects, PB has devised transportation systems on nearly every continent.

Stage I Light Rail Transit designed by PBGH — light rail vehicles cross the Panhandle Bridge.

PB has provided Continuous Airport Master Planning for Pittsburgh International Airport.

Founded and headquartered in 1885 in New York City by William Barclay Parsons, chief engineer of the RT (IRT) New York City subway in the early 1900s, the company established the world's first standard for underground rail construction.

National projects include the Pittsburgh Light Rail Transit System (LRT) in Pennsylvania, Oahu's H-3 highway in Hawaii, and San Francisco's BART (Bay Area Rapid Transit) rail and bus system in California. Internationally, PB's work includes the Greater Cairo Metro in Egypt, the West Coast Main Line of the British rail system in England, and the Taipai Rapid Transit System (TRT) in Taiwan.

PB's experience in both steel and concrete bridge design and rehabilitation includes segmental, cable-stayed, truss, suspension, arch, movable and floating, and multilevel and urban interchanges. Noteworthy projects include the Newport Suspension Bridge in Rhode Island, the Charles River Crossing in Boston and construction management for the Sunshine Skyway Bridge in Tampa.

In Pittsburgh, Pennsylvania, PB primarily directs its engineering expertise to the redevelopment of the city. Projects in "The City of Bridges" have involved the design of the Rankin Bridge, 62nd Street Bridge and the Fleming Park Bridge. PB was one of the original designers of the Pennsylvania Turnpike System and conducted the financial analysis for the commonwealth.

Highway design places PB in the forefront of transportation systems connecting roads in the 21st century. Highway services are addressed with regards to construction, reconstruction and restoration, toll facilities, complex interchanges and vehicular tunnels. Location planning responds to the community, environment and safety issues.

Among the prestigious awards PB has received are the First Place, Gold Award for Water Resources from the Consulting Engineering Council of West Virginia; Project of the Year for the Monongahela Connecting Railroad Bridge from the ASCE, Pittsburgh Section and the ABCD Outstanding Rehabilitated Bridge of the Year Award; and recently attained finalist status for the PennDOT PQI Awards for the Kennerdell Bridge over the Allegheny River.

From planning to completion, projects conform to architectural, structural, civil, building, mechanical, electrical, and environmental engineering requirements. PB's Operations and Maintenance consulting programs improve the operations of existing facilities, target maintenance and repair, and instruct staff in techniques and operations. Additionally, Fleet Maintenance Consultants, a division of PB which has designed more maintenance facilities than any other firm in the United States, contributes support to the operations and maintenance sector. Business interaction is enhanced through PB's new e-Business solution Project Solve, facilitating intercommunication of customized project solutions.

Employing a professional support staff of 9,000 people with 250 offices on six continents, PB is an engineering leader in the global sphere of transportation and infrastructure. Rated one of the leading transportation-engineering firms in the world by *Engineering News-Record*, PB is a model of vision and expertise in design, operation and implementation of infrastructure projects. The award-winning efforts of PB provide progressive solutions to contemporary transportation planning.

Tucker Arensberg, P.C.

WHEN PARTNERS THOMAS Patterson, Ross Sterrett and Mark Acheson founded their new law firm in 1900 and set up shop in downtown Pittsburgh's Frick Building, they counted among their fellow tenants legendary businessman Henry Clay Frick himself. While Frick already was an established presence in Pittsburgh, the fledgling practice was not. That soon would change. The law firm dedicated itself to building a practice based on client service and community involvement, a combination that proved to be very successful.

In 1902, Patterson, then president of the Allegheny County Bar Association, helped organize the predecessor to the University of Pittsburgh Law School. By the time Harvard Law School graduate Charles F.C. Arensberg joined the firm in 1911, its client roster included the Pennsylvania Railroad and First National Bank predecessor to PNC Financial Services Group. The practice continued to grow.

Though the 1930s marked an economic downturn for Pittsburgh and the nation, the firm — then Patterson, Crawford, Arensberg & Dunn — enjoyed new milestones. The firm welcomed its future partner and firm namesake Richard B. Tucker Jr. to the practice. Shortly thereafter, Ella Graubart became the firm's first female attorney. She later won a hard-fought case for the dependents of 38 workers who died in a tank explosion in the late 1940s.

Community involvement was one of the driving principles of the firm, and working for civil liberties became a particular passion for Arensberg. In 1942, under his tenure as president of the Allegheny County Bar Association, African-American lawyers became eligible to join the association for the first time. And during the era of McCarthyism in the 1950s, Arensberg formed a panel that protected civil liberties lawyers from explosive McCarthyist charges.

Throughout the second half of the 20th century, the firm's client list continued to grow and included Peoples-Pittsburgh Trust Company, The Bell Telephone Company of Pennsylvania, Erie Railroad, United Engineering Company, Coca-Cola Company, the University of Pittsburgh and Lawyers Title Insurance Company. It was also during this time that the practice forged family with business. Richard Tucker became a partner in 1955 and his son, Richard Tucker III, joined the practice in 1976. Charlie Arensberg, who joined the firm in 1938, continued his father's passion for carrying out the fight for social justice. In 1964 he traveled to Jackson, Mississippi where he spent several weeks living with and defending African-American activists. He later published an account of his time in the south in the *Pittsburgh Legal Journal*.

One PPG Place in downtown Pittsburgh, where the law firm of Tucker Arensberg, P.C. makes its headquarters

In the early 1980s the growth of Tucker Arensberg, P.C. led to the opening of branch offices in the Pittsburgh suburb of Moon Township and in Harrisburg, the state's capital.

Today the firm has 70 attorneys and 22 paralegals. Staying mid-sized and independent has permitted the firm to offer clients the highest levels of professional service, while maintaining the efficiencies that have been an important part of the firm's success over the past 100 years. The firm is organized into four primary practice groups — banking and finance, litigation, business and estates, and administrative law and government relations. Within these areas, the firm has developed specialized areas such as real estate, labor and employment, technology, municipal law and health care.

Economic, technological and legal changes dictate the future of law. The law firm of Tucker Arensberg adapts to these changes and has made the latest technology an integral part of its practice. However, the law firm continues to focus on the principles on which it was founded over one hundred years ago: client satisfaction, efficiency, practical and effective legal and business solutions and community involvement. It's a tradition of service to the region's business community that will lay the groundwork for another successful one hundred years.

Quality of Life

Religious, cultural, entertainment and service organizations contribute to the quality of life enjoyed by Pittsburgh residents and visitors.

Carnegie Museums of Pittsburgh

A TRUE RENAISSANCE MAN, STEEL industrialist Andrew Carnegie loved being a member of the Egypt Exploration Society, which sponsored many archaeological digs under the desert sands. While traveling to Egypt with his wife, Louise, in the mid-1890s, he sent back to Pittsburgh a mummy and decorative coffin, which became the first exhibits for his new museum. Shortly after, he had a 3,800-year-old Egyptian boat excavated and shipped back.

Carnegie Museum of Natural History is world-renowned for its collection of dinosaur fossils and publicly displayed dinosaur skeletons.

From this modest beginning and Carnegie's broad vision evolved four unique museums, each making a distinctive contribution to science and the arts. Ranked second only to the Smithsonian Institution for their diversity and public outreach, the quartet of Pittsburgh institutions consists of Carnegie Museum of Natural History, Carnegie Museum of Art, The Andy Warhol Museum and Carnegie Science Center. The museums primarily serve Allegheny, Westmoreland, Butler and Washington counties, although the yearly 1.6 million people they serve also include travelers from around the world. Besides an endowment and fund raising, more than 28,000 members and donors support the museums and their staff of 1,200.

Remaining faithful to Carnegie's philosophy of helping those who seek self-education, Carnegie Museums serve a diversity of people in community settings. Each year the institutions enroll nearly 90,000 people in formal on-site education programs, and their outreach programs involve more than 400,000 others. The museums also provide special programs and free admissions for underserved community members, other free or reduced-rate programs for economically disadvantaged audiences, special programs for at-risk youth and seniors, and scholarship programs.

Adopted in 2000, Carnegie Museums' vision statement describes strengthening relationships with its many audiences as the overarching goal: "With uncompromising quality, Carnegie Museums of Pittsburgh will set the national standard among museums for integration into the communities it serves, for our mutual advancement."

Carnegie Museum of Natural History

Opened in 1895 in Pittsburgh's Oakland district, Carnegie Museum of Natural History continued to broaden its Egyptology collection well into the 20th century and also branched into paleontology with staff digs that made important finds in Utah, Montana and Wyoming. Today the museum owns one of the world's largest dinosaur and mammal fossil collections, including more recent finds from the Canadian Arctic and China. Delighting youngsters and adults alike, the exhibits include 13 complete dinosaur skeletons and numerous other fossils, as well as interactive technology and video displays explaining the fossilization process that produced the dinosaur collection.

The museum's curators conduct internationally acclaimed research and stage exhibits and programs from long-established departments devoted to anthropology, insects, minerals, mammals, mollusks, birds and geology. In all, the museum displays more than 16,000 objects, and another 10,000 items make up the museum's educational loan collection, which is used by schools throughout the region. They represent a tiny fraction of the more than 22 million objects the staff has scientifically catalogued for research.

Carnegie Museum of Art

Opened at the same time as the Museum of Natural History was the adjoining Carnegie Museum of Art, which Andrew Carnegie planned as a gallery for contemporary artists — the "old masters of tomorrow." The first two paintings he acquired were Winslow Homer's *The Wreck* and Whistler's *Arrangement in Black: Portrait of Pablo de Sarasate*.

Contributing to the founder's vision of promoting the future of art is the triennial *Carnegie International*, which, from its origin in 1896, has grown to become the most important exhibition in the United States for new artwork from around the globe. Matching the *International* in mass appeal is an exciting 21st century innovation: "blockbuster" exhibitions that bring together hundreds of objects and artworks to explore a topic in its many facets. In the winter 2000-2001 season, *Aluminum by Design* highlighted the role of aluminum in contemporary architecture and the design of such diverse objects as jewelry, sculpture, chairs, dresses, automotive, train and aircraft components, and coffee pots and other ordinary household items.

Carnegie Museum of Art is the Pittsburgh region's pre-eminent center for contemporary visual arts.

The Andy Warhol Museum is the largest single-artist museum in the country, with seven floors that house more than 1,500 drawings, 400 photos and 77 sculptures.

In spring-summer 2001, the museum and Amsterdam's Van Gogh Museum mounted the joint exhibition *Light! The Industrial Age 1750-1900*. The display mingled more than 300 works of art, science and technology, demonstrating how light changed the artist's studio, the inventor's laboratory, city streets and the home. It mixed paintings by Van Gogh, Monet, Toulouse-Lautrec and other masters portraying naturally lit scenes at different hours with such diverse objects as a Tiffany lamp, a lighthouse magnifying lens and early cameras.

Carnegie Science Center

Along the Ohio River on Pittsburgh's North Shore stands Carnegie Science Center, which has expanded continually since its founding in 1991. The center's attractions include more than 250 hands-on exhibits, an interactive planetarium, an OMNIMAX® theater and a World War II submarine, the *USS Requin*.

Visitors to Carnegie Science Center interact with hundreds of hands-on exhibits and have access to the four-story Rangos Omnimax Theater, Buhl Planetarium, a real submarine and three live demonstration theaters.

Among the center's major displays are the SciQuest exhibits, which help explain waves, the physics of flight and the forces of nature. Exploration Station displays digital drums, a laser harp, a chick hatchery and a "build-a-critter." Opened in 2001, *UPMC SportsWorks* focuses on the science of sports illustrating balance, centers of mass and gravity, and other natural laws. Visitors can enjoy a climbing wall, golf and basketball, and virtual and mechanical simulators offer them the thrills of bobsledding, hang gliding, snowboarding, skiing and auto racing. A planned expansion could more than double the size of Carnegie Science Center.

The Andy Warhol Museum

A few miles away on the North Shore, The Andy Warhol Museum honors one of Pittsburgh's most prominent sons, born Andrew Warhola in 1928 not far from the site. Attracting thousands of visitors from around the world each year, the seven-level museum houses more than 1,500 drawings and 400 photos by the artist, as well as 77 of his sculptures. Its artwork and broad variety of personal material make the museum a major resource for the study of Pop Art and contemporary culture, as does a daily screening program of movies and videos by Warhol, who died in 1987.

With a mission to be "more than a museum" and "ever changing," The Warhol augments its art collection with a rich blend of performing arts and community events. Among these, the museum hosts Friday evening happy hours — Good Fridays — that combine avant-garde performing art with the visual art of Andy Warhol and other artists. The Andy Warhol Museum also has created successful traveling exhibitions of Warhol art, which since 1996 have been viewed by more than three million people worldwide.

Greater Pittsburgh Literacy Council

TODAY THERE IS MUCH DISCUSSION in economic development circles about the need for a skilled workforce in Pittsburgh. One organization that has made a major contribution to workforce development is the Greater Pittsburgh Literacy Council. Its adult education programs provide a wide range of training to thousands of Pittsburghers every year. The Council has been named as an exemplary program by regional and national organizations and it has grown rapidly to meet a heavy demand for its services.

The joy of reading stories in English is a family affair for Lucija Marina, a refugee from Bosnia, and her two sons. Greater Pittsburgh Literacy Council is teaching English language skills to many immigrants and refugees from foreign countries. These classes enable the immigrants to become productive citizens of the United States.

It all began in 1965 with Mary Yardumian. The Florida woman heard an inspiring speech about adult literacy given by author and educator Frank Laubach and she began teaching entry-level workers to read. After moving to Pittsburgh in 1971, Mary looked for opportunities to continue her pioneering work. She quickly became a consultant and trainer, setting up programs around the region. Out of her Mt. Lebanon home, Mary single-handedly activated the adult literacy movement in Western Pennsylvania.

By the early 1980s demand had far exceeded the resources of Mary's fledgling organization. With help from a long-range planning committee and an inaugural board of directors, the Greater Pittsburgh Literacy Council (GPLC) was incorporated, establishing an office and hiring staff members. Today GPLC employs 35 full-time staff and annually serves over 2,500 adults in 14 neighborhood-based programs around the region. Its services include basic skills as well as GED preparation, English as a Second Language, job preparation, on-site literacy training for employees of local companies, computer literacy and computer assisted instruction, family literacy programs and training for the staff and volunteers of other literacy programs.

Executive Director Donald G. Block notes that people voluntarily and eagerly seek GPLC's services. They want to get their GED or diploma, to better support their family, to help their kids with schoolwork, to advance in the job they have or get a better job. Some simply want to get a driver's license or fill out a job application. Others want personal growth and a chance to get ahead.

Almost half of GPLC's clients are enrolled in the English as a Second Language program, reflecting the growing need for this type of instruction in Pittsburgh's communities. Professional instructors and volunteers are trained in English as a Second Language methods. They help immigrants and refugees with conversational language practice as well as the day-to-day issues of living in a new culture. This in turn helps clients find jobs and support their families.

Created in 1995, GPLC's Families for Learning program is designed to blend adult literacy and early childhood education while helping to develop parenting skills and fostering the concept that parents are a child's first teachers. Participants work five days a week with professional educators who incorporate job preparation, technology and problem-solving into the curriculum.

Research strongly supports the family literacy model. It shows that the best predictor of a child's school performance is the educational attainment of the mother. "The demonstrated intergenerational patterns of illiteracy can be broken by intervening for families and giving them tools and skills to achieve real success in school, at work and in life," adds Donald Block. "Some have learned a whole new way of parenting at the same time."

Incorporated into all of GPLC's programs is access to its two Computer Learning Centers in downtown Pittsburgh.

Created to be accessible, responsive and to serve adult learners at all skill levels, the centers offer instruction and test-taking in reading, math, history, science and other academic and life-skills topics as well as training in computer literacy, the Internet and a wide variety of software titles. Mastery of these skills is a great asset when clients go out to seek jobs. It also helps parents relate to their computer-savvy children.

A staff member of Greater Pittsburgh Literacy Council shares the joy of learning with an adult learner in one of the council's computer centers. The Literacy Council is a leader in teaching job-related skills and computer literacy to adults and families.

The work of the GPLC has an impact on workforce development and a very real connection with the region's economy. It moves people off of public assistance, helps them find jobs, trains them in technical skills and builds a quality workforce that will attract and retain business and industry for the region. GPLC's Workplace Skills Development Program provides custom educational programs to employers in the service, manufacturing and high-tech sectors. By helping employees gain higher-level comprehension, problem-solving, analytical reasoning, communication and interpersonal skills, the program helps the employer increase productivity, improve morale and reduce turnover.

Although GPLC has 600 trained volunteers, it relies on its professional staff and a myriad of community partnerships to stay constantly in tune with the growing, changing needs of clients and the community. For example, the health care industry is becoming acutely aware of how patients with low literacy utilize health care systems. Unable to understand doctors' instructions or read complicated directions on medication, these patients use the emergency room to manage their health care. GPLC is participating in research to study the connection between health and literacy, and it plans to develop programs to address it.

The Greater Pittsburgh Literacy Council and its students have received state and national recognition for their work. GPLC was the first program in the nation to win accreditation by Laubach Literacy Action and was a nominee for the U.S. Department of Education's Adult Education award. It was selected by the federal government to direct and coordinate the Literacy AmeriCorps-Pittsburgh project, one of four in the nation, which places volunteers with literacy programs throughout the area. In addition to providing training and consulting services to 35 adult education programs in a seven-county area, GPLC provides assistance to programs throughout the country on adult literacy issues.

Those involved with GPLC believe that everyone has the right to participate fully and productively in today's society and to reach his or her potential. As it has grown from a group of committed volunteers to a comprehensive professional team, the Greater Pittsburgh Literacy Council has expanded the scope of its services to serve adults, families, employers and the region at large.

Frank Davitian, a recent immigrant from Bulgaria, is studying English with the Greater Pittsburgh Literacy Council. He is able to function in his job as an electronics engineer thanks to the language instruction he is receiving. The Literacy Council helps thousands of adults to contribute to the local economy through the adult education that it provides.
Photo courtesy of Pittsburgh Post-Gazette

Phipps Conservatory and Botanical Gardens

JUST DOWN THE STREET AND OVER the bridge from Andrew Carnegie's library, in Mary Schenley's park, lies another sparkling jewel left behind by industrial barons and wealthy landowners of turn-of-the-century Pittsburgh. Henry Phipps' conservatory endures as a celebration of the tranquil and inspiring beauty of plants and flowers.

In 1891 Henry Phipps, who made his fortune in steel and real estate, petitioned Pittsburgh Mayor H.I. Gourley for permission to erect a conservatory in Schenley Park. With unanimous approval of the Select and Common Councils of the city of Pittsburgh, Phipps began the $100,000 project by employing Lord and Burnham of Irvington-on-Hudson, New York, to design and construct Phipps Conservatory.

The full-blooming Aquatic Gardens reach their peak in the summertime, when visitors seek out the relaxing beauty of its serene pools of flowering water lilies. *Photo by Craig Thompson*

Visitors admire the East Room as it changes from season to season. Here it transformed into an azalea dreamland, complete with a moongate and a stream. *Photo by Craig Thompson*

Described as a Victorian crystal palace, the nine original glasshouses were completed in 1893. Phipps' creation was the largest conservatory in the United States at the time. Its entrance was of Amherst sandstone in the Richardsonian Romanesque style. The glasshouses, including the Palm House — the largest of the original nine houses — featured glass ogee, fleur-de-lis and exterior ornamental metal work. Filled with tropical plants acquired when the 1893 Columbian Exposition in Chicago closed, the conservatory was home to the largest and most extravagant botanical collection of the time.

Henry Phipps emphasized that his conservatory be "a source of instruction as well as pleasure to the people." To ensure that all could enjoy it, he mandated that it stay open seven days a week to accommodate the working people of Pittsburgh. In 1901, at the request of local high school botany teachers, Phipps added Phipps Hall of Botany to provide laboratory space for instruction.

In 1902 the new Cacti House, now the Desert Room, gave many their first glimpse of the flora of the American Southwest. Over the years the popular orchid room grew in stature through several notable bequests of rare plants. These additions helped the conservatory maintain its position on the forefront of botanical facilities in the United States.

From its earliest days and continuing today, fans eagerly anticipate the conservatory's annual flower shows. They were started by the first conservatory manager, John Wynn Jones, who caused a stir in 1893 with his exotic plant collections. In 1934 Adolphe "Doc" DeWerth and his assistant and successor, Frank Curto, became the conservatory's horticulturists. Their combined talents along with those of landscape architect Ralph Griswold developed the elaborate themes that today define the annual flower shows. The first Christmas Flower Show was held in 1938.

Beginning in 1935 the Pittsburgh Park and Playground Society, later the Pittsburgh Horticultural Society, raised money for the upkeep and improvement of the conservatory. Their first and only project was to install lighting so that the conservatory might remain open in the evening.

When Frank Curto became chief horticulturist in 1946 it marked the beginning of a period of creative growth and high attendance that would last until his retirement in 1970. During Curto's tenure, the conservatory was a gathering place for the people of Pittsburgh and quite literally a breath of fresh air in the "Smoky City."

Many philanthropic-minded people have made a valiant effort to maintain the conservatory's glory through the years. The conservatory was placed on the National Register of Historic Places in 1976 and underwent a major facelift in 1978. But during the 1970s and 80s, it became difficult for staff and supporters to keep up with growing signs of decay. A group of volunteers called Phipps Friends took over the task of preserving the facility's grandeur during the 1980s, and their efforts resulted in the privatization of Phipps Conservatory in 1993.

This was an invigorating change for the conservatory, now a nonprofit corporation with a 100-year lease from the city of Pittsburgh. Immediately, the board and first executive director, Richard V. Piacentini began work on capital improvements and staff development. The horticultural staff started the process of organizing the collection's accession records. Between 1993 and 1999, the conservatory's annual attendance increased from 110,000 to 185,000 and expanded its name to better reflect what the future holds, Phipps Conservatory and Botanical Gardens

Phipps Conservatory and Botanical Gardens espouses a four-pronged mission including display, education, research and conservation. In addition to three major flower shows in the spring, fall and winter, the conservatory has permanent displays in the glasshouses, a garden railroad and butterfly exhibit during the summer months, the outdoor perennial garden, Japanese Courtyard Garden, Discovery Garden and Aquatic Gardens.

Between flower shows, the conservatory presents exciting interpretive exhibits in the Serpentine Room. With titles like "Urban Home Gardening" and "Orchid Fever," they give visitors practical plant and gardening tips to use at home. The conservatory keeps a full calendar of workshops for young and old, lectures on plant life and conservation, and even musical programs and plant sales. It has also become a favorite wedding and party venue.

Phipps Conservatory and Botanical Gardens continues its important work as a living laboratory. Future partnerships with hospitals and universities will allow the conservatory to conduct botanical research on medicinal plants, and currently a biodiversity project called "The Frozen Garden" is helping to preserve plants native to Western Pennsylvania.

A Victorian crystal palace in the heart of Pittsburgh's Schenley Park — Phipps Conservatory and Botanical Gardens. *Photo by Craig Thompson*

Old picture postcards vaunted one of Pittsburgh's crowned jewels — the front entrance and original Palm Court structure of Phipps Conservatory and Botanical Gardens.

Since 1998 the organization has been working on a master plan for expansion, and in July 2000 it launched Campaign 2000, a $35 million capital campaign. To better serve its visitors, the conservatory ultimately will expand its facilities to include a Welcome Center, enlarged gift shop, cafe, rental facilities and new display and classroom areas. Interactive educational programs will enhance the conservatory's eye-opening experiences. And all of these improvements will increase revenue and attendance for Phipps Conservatory and Botanical Gardens, assuring its prosperous future.

"In my lifetime, Phipps Conservatory and Botanical Gardens has boldly capitalized on all the space it has. The vision of Campaign 2000 is not only to maintain the historic integrity of my great-uncle's splendid building, but also to provide more beauty, space and knowledge for our visitors," says Henry Phipps Hoffstot, one of the honorary chairs of Campaign 2000. While it is true that each day brings a new bloom, a new visitor and a new accomplishment to Henry Phipps' conservatory, the future holds the potential to bring Phipps Conservatory and Botanical Gardens into full flower.

The annual Spring Flower Show delights thousands of visitors and Kneeling Venus welcomes each and every one.

The Pittsburgh Foundation

THE PITTSBURGH FOUNDATION has a direct and long-term connection to Pittsburgh and Western Pennsylvania in its philosophy of philanthropic grant-giving. The concept of endowment-giving was originally developed by Andrew Carnegie in Pittsburgh during the early stages of the 20th century. It was modernized by Ames Coney, head of the Mellon Bank Trust Department, some 40 years later when in 1945 he introduced the concept of the community foundation movement to Pittsburgh bankers and lawyers, and encouraged H.J. Heinz II, Leon Falk and principals of the Buhl Foundation to provide administrative funds totaling $60,000 for the creation of The Pittsburgh Foundation.

More than half a century later, The Pittsburgh Foundation is alive and thriving in serving Pittsburgh and Western Pennsylvania communities as a resource for helping individuals, families, organizations and corporations realize the dream of creating a philanthropic, charitable legacy to benefit those in need. As receiver, manager and giver of these benevolent funds, The Pittsburgh Foundation, by providing expert leadership, has helped financial and legal advisers, donors, investment managers and grantees participate in making the Pittsburgh region a more livable community for all of its residents.

After 55 years of successful growth and with endowment assets of over $500 million, The Pittsburgh Foundation is the 11th-largest community foundation of more than 600 similar foundations located throughout the United States. Classified as a community foundation by the federal government, its donors benefit from considerable tax savings while their fund continues to grow and function in perpetuity as a source of generosity for each of the needy recipients. In 2000, through the generosity of its donors, The Pittsburgh Foundation provided over $20.3 million in grants that met the needs of individuals, families, children and elderly by supporting the arts, culture, humanities, health care and educational institutions as well as community and environmental development. This was the largest amount distributed in the history of The Pittsburgh Foundation.

The various funds established at The Pittsburgh Foundation are primarily endowment funds tailored to the particular donor's

The Pittsburgh Foundation and Union Trust Company organization meeting on January 30, 1945, included (left to right): William B. McFall, Edmund C. Stone, Leon Falk, Jr., Clarence Stanley, Arthur E. Braun, James C. Rea and H.J. Heinz II.

wishes. Each year, a portion of income earned by the funds (approximately 5 percent of the previous three years' average) is spent on grants to nonprofit organizations. The balance is returned to principal, allowing remaining funds to grow and meet evolving needs of the Pittsburgh community for generations to come.

The Pittsburgh Foundation is staffed by experienced, knowledgeable personnel concerning the various charitable organizations that seek to improve the Pittsburgh region, including highly skilled professionals in the areas of finance and administration, development and donor services, and grant-making. While The Pittsburgh Foundation has the option of making grants throughout the country, its primary focus is the Pittsburgh region. As a community foundation, The Pittsburgh Foundation is not subject to excise taxes or other restrictions imposed upon private foundations. Thus, a greater percentage of charitable assets are available for distribution to those in need within the community.

For maximum return, foundation gifts are managed by several financial fund managers and closely supervised by The Pittsburgh Foundation's financial personnel to insure that prudent investment strategies are maintained for long-term growth of endowment fund principal. This efficient management style insures a consistent level of annual grants to charity.

Funds established at The Pittsburgh Foundation usually fall into one of seven categories: (1) Unrestricted Funds offer the broadest option for charitable giving. These funds constitute the core of The Pittsburgh Foundation's ability to meet the community's needs during the present as well as emerging needs in future years. (2) Field of Interest Funds provide grants within the overall direction of the donor's wishes. This type of fund allows donors to support a broad area of concerns. (3) Donor Advised Funds enable the donor to make specific suggestions about where grants should be directed. (4) Designated Funds allow the donor to determine eligible organization(s) to receive annual charitable grants as long the organization(s) are tax-exempt. (5) Scholarship Funds enable students to pursue their academic goals. (6) Organization Endowment Funds hold assets for a named charitable organization and provide income to that entity. In the event the original purpose of a fund becomes obsolete, the board of directors of The Pittsburgh Foundation redirects the assets of the fund to the most closely related use.

Although The Pittsburgh Foundation functions as an independent, charitable grant-making organization, several Pittsburgh-headquartered philanthropies have found it advantageous to affiliate with The Pittsburgh Foundation and support its overall objectives. The William J. Copeland Fund (formerly the Forbes Fund) was created in 1982 as a supporting organization to provide grants to nonprofit human service groups experiencing crises or facing urgent needs. Another supporting organization, The Pittsburgh Partnership for Neighborhood Development, was incorporated in 1988 as an intermediary that pools funds and makes investments addressing poverty and disinvestment in Pittsburgh's distressed communities. Funds are raised from foundations, banks and corporations to support this initiative. The Cahouet Charitable Trust was created in 1996 as a supporting organization to benefit the donor's intent and to perform the functions of and carry out the purposes of The Pittsburgh Foundation. For tax purposes and avoidance of costly administrative and reporting requirements, private foundations often find it more cost-effective to transfer part or all of their assets to The Pittsburgh Foundation.

(Left to right) Alfred W. Wishart, Jr., president of The Pittsburgh Foundation, James S. Broadhurst, current board chairman, and William J. Copeland, past board chairman, present James C. Roddey with the 1998 Isabel P. Kennedy Award for volunteer service.

In 1999 financial fund managers experienced an impressive double-digit return on investments with endowment assets showing an increase of approximately 15 percent, and a five-year return of over 18 percent, with the number of funds totaling almost 700. President and Chief Executive Officer Alfred W. Wishart, Jr. states that as a dynamic, vibrant organization, The Pittsburgh Foundation's long-term objective is to double its grant-making capability from the current level of $20 million to $40 million within the next decade. Aware that the Pittsburgh and Western Pennsylvania region is rich in resources, generosity, spirit and compassion, and possesses an enviable history of public/private partnering, The Pittsburgh Foundation looks forward to serving the future needs of deserving communities and its citizens by providing comfort and financial aid through its support of worthy, vital causes.

Pittsburgh History & Landmarks Foundation

SAVING THE BEST OF OUR PAST; giving new life to old buildings; strengthening historic neighborhoods by engaging people in the process of renewal — long-term policies such as these have made the Pittsburgh History & Landmarks Foundation (Landmarks) "one of the most innovative and accomplished local preservation organizations in the United States," according to Richard Moe, president of the National Trust for Historic Preservation.

Landmarks' offices and reference library are located on the fourth floor of The Landmarks Building at Station Square, just across the Smithfield Street Bridge from downtown Pittsburgh. *Photo by Jim Judkis*

Landmarks was founded in 1964, at a time when vast amounts of public money were spent to replace some of Pittsburgh's most historic neighborhoods and commercial areas with characterless architecture, parking lots and roadways. After more than three decades of work in Allegheny County, the grassroots, nonprofit historic preservation organization has shown that architectural landmarks and historic neighborhoods are community assets and that historic preservation can be a catalyst for urban renewal.

Landmarks is known across the nation for its pioneering work in restoring inner-city neighborhoods without dislocating the residents. In 1966 Landmarks established the Revolving Fund for Preservation with a $100,000 grant from the Sarah Scaife Foundation. Monies from the fund were used primarily on the North Side and South Side of Pittsburgh to purchase and renovate historic inner-city properties. These properties were then rented or sold to low- and moderate-income families. Landmarks' Revolving Fund has grown into a major funding source, providing loans to over 30 Pittsburgh neighborhood organizations and technical assistance to preservation groups throughout the United States.

Landmarks was the first historic preservation group in the nation to undertake a countywide survey of architectural landmarks. Co-founders Arthur P. Ziegler, Jr. and James D. Van Trump began that survey in 1965. As a result of a second, more comprehensive survey completed by Landmarks' staff in 1984, more than 6,000 architecturally and historically significant sites in Allegheny County have been documented. Close to 400 of those sites are distinguished by one of Landmarks' "Historic Landmark" plaques. Landmarks also has surveyed steel industry sites, African-American historic sites, and historic parks and gardens, and has prepared thematic National Register nominations on Pittsburgh public schools and bridges.

The data and research collected during these surveys has provided much original material for major books and brochures. Current titles from Landmarks include *Pittsburgh's Landmark Architecture: The Historic Buildings of Pittsburgh and Allegheny County* (1997) and *Pittsburgh's Bridges: Architecture and Engineering* (1999), both by Walter C. Kidney.

PHLF News, a quarterly membership newsletter, includes feature articles on current preservation issues and major programs.

The 1300 block of Liverpool Street in Manchester, slated for demolition in the 1960s, was saved through the efforts of Landmarks, the Manchester Citizens Corporation and neighborhood residents. *Pittsburgh History & Landmarks Foundation*

"Woodville," the Neville House of c. 1785, is owned by and is a museum of the Pittsburgh History & Landmarks Foundation. *Photo by William Rydberg, Photon*

Over the years, the trustees, staff and members of Landmarks and neighborhood organizations have successfully campaigned to save the North Side Post Office (now The Pittsburgh Children's Museum), the Union Station rotunda in downtown Pittsburgh, the Neill Log House in Schenley Park, the Burtner House in Harrison Township, the Rachel Carson Homestead in Springdale, and the Neville House in Collier Township, among many other places. Thanks to year-end contributions from its members in recent years, Landmarks has awarded grants to more than 60 historic religious properties in Allegheny County for bricks-and-mortar projects.

As a result of Landmarks' leadership and assistance, numerous local preservation and civic groups have been organized to manage the day-to-day business of caring for historic neighborhoods. These include the Manchester Citizens Corporation, the South Side Local Development Company, and the Pittsburgh Community Reinvestment Group (PCRG), among others. The PCRG now includes more than 30 neighborhood groups that work with every major financial institution in Pittsburgh; these banks have committed some $2.4 billion dollars to inner-city neighborhoods in compliance with federal regulations.

Station Square gave Landmarks the opportunity to put its urban planning principles into practice. Aided by an initial generous gift from the Allegheny Foundation in 1976, Landmarks adapted five historic Pittsburgh & Lake Erie Railroad buildings for new uses and added a hotel, a dock for the Gateway Clipper fleet, and parking areas. Now shops, offices, restaurants and entertainment complexes anchor the historic riverfront site on the south shore of the Monongahela, opposite the Golden Triangle. Station Square is one of Pittsburgh's premiere attractions. It reflects a $100 million investment from all sources, with the lowest public cost and highest taxpayer return of any major renewal project in the Pittsburgh region since the 1950s. The sale of Station Square in 1994 created an endowment to help support Landmarks' ongoing restoration efforts and educational programs.

Each year the staff and docents of Landmarks introduce more than 10,000 people — teachers, students, adults and visitors — to the architectural heritage of the Pittsburgh region and to the value of historic preservation. Through student/teacher workshops, tours, exhibits and a variety of educational programs, Landmarks encourages people to notice and appreciate the historic buildings, parks, public spaces, bridges, streets, etc. that make up the city and its neighborhoods and compose the special character of the Pittsburgh region. By exploring and discovering something about local history and architecture, people are more likely to preserve old buildings and thoughtfully consider the impact of new building proposals.

Through its work, Landmarks is improving the quality of life for Pittsburghers and attracting visitors to the region. Today, homes in neighborhoods such as Manchester, stores on main streets such as East Carson, and the historic buildings housing shops and restaurants at Station Square survive and flourish and attract people by their architectural uniqueness, human scale and urban character, thanks in large part to the work and determination of Landmarks.

Touring the Mexican War Streets on Pittsburgh's North Side *Pittsburgh History & Landmarks Foundation*

Pittsburgh Presbytery

KNOWN AS THE PRESBYTERIAN Valley, the Pittsburgh area has for many generations been a home of Presbyterianism in the United States. With over 160 Presbyterian churches in Allegheny County alone, Presbyterianism is the largest protestant denomination in Western Pennsylvania. Missionary zeal built the Presbyterian heritage and continues to thrive today in Pittsburgh Presbytery. Christ's admonition to spread the gospel inspires the churches of Pittsburgh Presbytery to reach out in evangelism and service to the people of Pittsburgh's numerous communities.

The vitality of Pittsburgh Presbytery is found in its congregations, which are called to reach people for Jesus Christ through providing vibrant worship experiences and participating actively in mission. A renewed commitment to support congregations is the vision of Pittsburgh Presbytery. Congregations are reaching their communities for Jesus Christ through programs such as the Youth Outreach Street Workers at Grace Memorial Presbyterian Church in the Hill District.

Fun in the clay pits at Crestfield Camp and Conference Center

Heritage United Presbyterian Church mission trip to El Papilla, Mexico
Photo by Dick Thomson

A foundational principle of the presbytery is, "Our God is a missionary God; we are a missionary people." Presbytery's mission is:

To serve congregations so they are healthy and vital as evidenced by their

- success in bringing others to Christ
- vibrant worship and
- active participation in the mission of Christ's church.

Currently the presbytery supports 43 local mission agencies, which provide food, clothing, shelter, counseling and support. It operates the Crestfield Camp and Conference Center where numerous children, youth and adults have personal experiences of faith each year. The presbytery reaches out in global mission through its Malawi Partnership.

Western Pennsylvania has a rich history of Presbyterianism. Beginning with the Reformation movement spreading from Holland to Scotland and Ireland, the early Presbyterian church flourished in the 17th century under the influence of the Calvin and Knox theologies. From settlements in Northern Ireland, thousands of Scots-Irish Presbyterians immigrated to the English colonies in the New World.

John McMillan, known as the Father of Presbyterianism in Western Pennsylvania, was a direct descendant of these early Presbyterians. As a newly ordained minister in 1774, McMillan's first mission was to evangelize a pioneering community located in Southwestern Pennsylvania. He ventured forth with a profound zeal for imparting the gospel in the rural wilderness. Fellow Presbyterian leaders assisted and followed the call of evangelism and education on the emerging frontier. By 1790, McMillan had organized four Presbyterian churches for the settlers.

While laying the foundation of the church, the newly formed presbytery directed its attention to education for the pioneers west of the Allegheny Mountains and throughout the upper Ohio valley. With a firm belief that education is necessary in a democracy, coupled with a concern for the spiritual formation of children, the Presbyterian General Assembly implemented a policy to establish parochial schools in all congregations. Bible and catechism instruction was included in the daily school curriculum at the primary, secondary and college levels. A structure of academies, the first educational institutions west of the Allegheny Mountains, was created.

Many of the historic Presbyterian seminaries, academies and colleges remain in existence today. Reverend Dr. William H. McGuffey, well-known educator and author of the *Eclectic Readers*, was a graduate of the Greersburg Academy. Some of the log cabin schools founded by Presbyterians are known today as: Allegheny College, Chatham College, Davis and Elkins College, Grove City College, University of Pittsburgh, Washington-Jefferson College, Pittsburgh Theological Seminary and The College of Wooster.

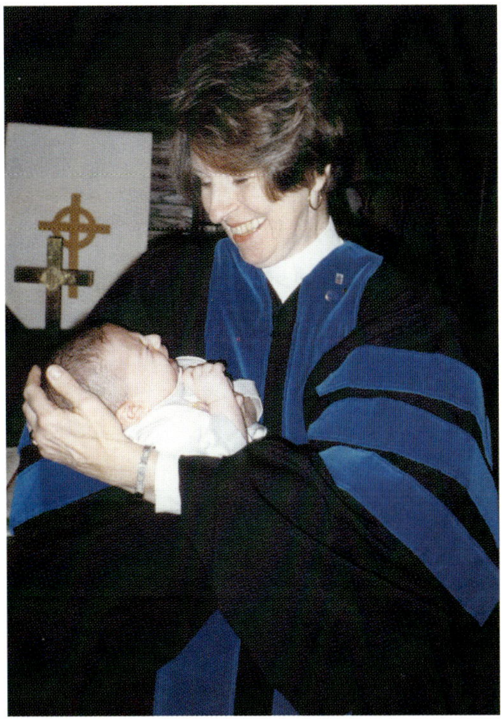

Infant baptism at The Presbyterian Church of Mt. Washington

As Presbyterian educational efforts progressed in the 19th century, the Ohio Presbytery and the Presbytery of Pittsburgh united to become Pittsburgh Presbytery. During this time, several of Pittsburgh's famous Presbyterian industrialists, including Mellon, Negley and Carnegie, engaged renowned architects and designers to build lasting "cathedrals" for worship, Christian education and mission. The monumental East Liberty Presbyterian Church, known as the Cathedral of Hope, maintains an active congregation today.

The characteristic Presbyterian service to others has always driven ministry to the poor, the sick and the aged in society. At the turn of the last century, the establishment of the Presbyterian Missionary Training School, Presbyterian Hospital, Presbyterian School of Nursing, and the Presbyterian Home for the Aged helped to improve health and living conditions in Pittsburgh.

Furthermore, the unwavering Presbyterian commitment to mission outreach sought to dispel racial injustice. When the United Presbyterian Church of North America formed in 1858, it was with a declaration of opposition to slavery. This historic denominational union took place in the city of Pittsburgh. In 1870 Grace Memorial Presbyterian Church became the first African-American Presbyterian congregation founded in Allegheny County. Inner-city mission efforts in African-American congregations promoted social justice and cultivated the work of former civil rights leaders Maida Springer, Rev. Dr. James Robinson and Rev. Dr. Leroy Patrick, who voiced the anguished cry of African-Americans. Today, long-range mission initiatives of Pittsburgh Presbytery include plans for congregational development in predominantly African-American communities. Seminary scholarships are offered to African-American students preparing to become Presbyterian pastors.

Pittsburgh's role as a center of Presbyterianism again became clear when the city hosted another historic reunion in 1958, this time between the United Presbyterian Church of North America and the Presbyterian Church in the U.S.A. to become the United Presbyterian Church in the U.S.A.

In many aspects, there are similarities between the colonial Presbyterians and contemporary Presbyterians. The same God who impassioned John McMillan and the early Presbyterian leaders to minister to the settlers still speaks in the communities of Pittsburgh. God's words continue to call Presbyterians to missionary opportunities for sharing Christ's love within Allegheny County and throughout the world. The response of Pittsburgh Presbytery is to lead congregations to establish Christ's mission, provide educational opportunities for all ages, and embrace the disenfranchised in society. Through this calling, Presbyterians obey Christ's command to "make disciples of all nations." Through the fervor of new pastors and vital congregations, the flame of evangelism is passed to future generations. Under the guidance of the Holy Spirit, the same missionary spirit of the early Presbyterian leaders thrives in Pittsburgh Presbytery today.

New believer in Christ at Mulberry Community Church

United Jewish Federation of Greater Pittsburgh

FROM HISTORIC SYNAGOGUES TO its sprawling Jewish Community Center, the Squirrel Hill section of Pittsburgh is arguably the physical epicenter of the city's Jewish community. It is a community driven by a tapestry of programs, fund-raising and outreach efforts. It is a community whose philanthropy travels beyond Squirrel Hill into surrounding counties and countries. It is a community whose continued vitality is the mission of the United Jewish Federation of Greater Pittsburgh (UJF).

For over 90 years UJF has been central to the Jewish community's planning and fund-raising efforts, working to touch the lives of Jews in the Pittsburgh community, in Israel and beyond. In the spirit of *tikkun olam* (the healing and repair of the world), UJF has placed its emphasis on families, community and Jewish heritage by working with local agencies and a committed core of volunteers to identify and address Jewish needs in areas such as health, education and social welfare.

The roots of this expansive organization were formed in the early 20th century in social agencies that continually grew with and adapted to the changing climate of Pittsburgh's Jewish community. In 1912 community leaders first created the Federation of Jewish Philanthropies (FJP), an agency that eventually merged five family welfare programs into today's Jewish Family & Children's Service. Two years later, FJP helped create a community foundation — now known as the United Jewish Federation Foundation — to secure bequests, endowments, and trusts. By 1932 the Great Depression caused increased fund-raising and service demands and led FJP to join the Community Chest, the precursor organization to the United Way.

UJF beneficiary agencies provide a variety of services to Pittsburgh's senior adults, including enrichment programs and assisted living facilities.

When the fires of Nazism began to burn in the late 1930s, the United Jewish Fund was created. It raised funds and distributed them to aid and rescue European Jewish refugees from the ravages of the Holocaust. The fund continued to help Holocaust survivors even after World War II, most notably in 1948 when the fund provided support to meet the human needs associated with establishing the state of Israel. In 1955 FJP and the United Jewish Fund merged into what is now the United Jewish Federation.

In the following decades, Pittsburgh's Jewish community grew. To meet demand UJF stepped up its fund-raising efforts. Its Annual Community Campaign raised millions of dollars for social, health and educational causes locally and in 60 countries worldwide, and it continues to do so today.

While UJF's programs touch the lives of people around the world, its local efforts are especially strong. UJF has responded to community needs with the creation of a variety of agencies. The Career Development Center of Jewish Family & Children's Service helped those left unemployed by the virtual demise of the steel industry and continues to provide career assistance today. The Jewish Association on Aging provides the continuum of care required by Pittsburgh's growing aging population. And Jewish Residential Services assists families who have members with special needs.

Other local programs continue to flourish under UJF's auspices. From support for formal Jewish education including congregational and day schools to informal efforts such as camps, youth groups and Israel trips, UJF works to fund and organize high-quality Jewish learning experiences. Some of the most important lessons learned from history are preserved at the UJF-established Holocaust Center, Western Pennsylvania's only educational resource center on the Holocaust.

Other efforts to build the community were born out of the Renaissance Campaign. Launched in the mid-1990s, the capital campaign touched nearly every major agency in the community by raising more than $50 million for infrastructure improvements, including creating new facilities and revitalizing aging ones.

UJF's efforts extend far beyond local borders. In times of war and peace, UJF has responded to Israeli needs and forged a special bond with its people. Two decades ago, innovative programs enabled Pittsburgh Jews to join a nationwide effort to make an impact on the development of disadvantaged communities in Israel. Those efforts have been extended today with the Partnership 2000 program, which nurtures personal and professional relationships between North American Jews and the people of Israel in a new and thriving way. The program fosters the exchange of knowledge, ideas and experiences through work with teachers, summer camp counselors and business professionals and is helping to build people-to-people and economic connections in Israel with the city of Karmiel and the surrounding Misgav region.

For the past 50 years UJF has provided financial and human resources to meet overseas Jewish needs beyond Israel as well. In 1990 UJF launched Exodus: the Campaign to Rescue and Resettle Soviet Jews. More than $14.5 million was raised locally to rescue Jews from the former Soviet Union. Several thousand Soviet immigrants have since been brought to freedom in Pittsburgh. This was part of a wave of tens of thousands that resettled nation-wide and one million in Israel. Additionally, the UJF has suppported the resettlement of 90,000 Ethoiopians to Israel. And a special connection was formed between members of Pittsburgh's community and those in the country of Moldova in the former Soviet Union (FSU) where efforts have helped to rekindle Jewish communities through a variety of collaborative programs.

Elsewhere in the FSU, other UJF-supported programs have helped those who live in vulnerable communities by opening up opportunities for Jewish learning and expression. Programs receiving UJF support range from kindergartens and Hillels for young adults to Hesed Centers that provide food, health services and programming for the elderly to training for Jewish communal professionals.

Today, UJF continues to enhance the growth and vitality of Pittsburgh's growing Jewish community. UJF helped fund a new Jewish Community Center in Pittsburgh's southern suburbs and also helped create a new facility for Hillel Jewish University Center, located between Carnegie Mellon University and the University of Pittsburgh campuses. And the Shalom Pittsburgh project was developed to attract young Jewish adults to make their home in Pittsburgh. More recently, a 2001 community study was commissioned to help shape the direction of Pittsburgh's Jewish population.

As a unifying force in the Jewish community, the UJF has been effective at quickly mobilizing the Jewish community in response to crisis situations. In the twelve days after the Sept. 11, 2001 terrorist attacks in New York, Pensylvania and Washington D.C., the UJF organized a community reponse by working with law enforcement agencies to coordinate security measures for community facilities. The UJF also provided venues for the community to gather for prayer and support. This included a gathering attended by more than 5,000 people, to express abhorrence of terrorism, as well as their support for the victims of terrorism and their families.

From developing financial resources to meeting the social needs of the community, the United Jewish Federation of Greater Pittsburgh continues to build on its nearly century-old vision of sustaining, educating and enriching the lives of Jews in Pittsburgh, Israel and worldwide. With more than 70 agencies and programs locally, nationally and overseas receiving its support, UJF of Greater Pittsburgh is not just keeping its finger on the pulse of the Jewish community — it's helping to keep that beat steady and strong.

Educational programs, Jewish summer camps, and trips to Israel are just a few of the many programs UJF sponsors to help strengthen Jewish identity.

For over 90 years, UJF has built a legacy of service to the Jewish community. Shown here are some of the Jewish immigrants who helped build Pittsburgh, c. 1921.

Manchester Bidwell Corporation

WHILE GROWING UP IN THE 1960s, William E. Strickland Jr., like many inner-city teen-agers, needed a mentor. The person he found — a high school ceramics teacher, Frank Ross — transformed Strickland's life. He ignited in Strickland a passion for the arts and encouraged him to apply to the University of Pittsburgh. While a student there in 1968, Strickland founded the Manchester Craftsmen's Guild (MCG), a center to motivate at-risk youth through the arts, in a basement on Pittsburgh's North Side.

Employing the arts as a motivator for lifetime learning, Manchester Craftsmen's Guild trains young people in ceramics, photography, computer imaging and drawing.

Today, MCG is one of several subsidiaries that Strickland oversees as president and chief executive officer of the nonprofit Manchester Bidwell Corporation. MCG is a world-class multi-disciplinary arts and learning organization that includes the enterprise units MCG Jazz, MCG Youth Development and MCG Denali. MCG Jazz is a premier site for live jazz recording, and its concert program features the masters of jazz. The program has included performances by Dizzy Gillespie, Nancy Wilson, Joe Williams, Herbie Hancock, Billy Taylor and the Count Basie Orchestra, to name a few. In 1997 and 1999, MCG Jazz received two Grammy nominations and one Grammy Award. MCG Youth Development is dedicated to educating and inspiring urban youth through the arts on their road to becoming productive citizens. Approximately 80 percent of MCG's students matriculate to college. The MCG Denali initiative is a national enterprise that equips and educates leaders to achieve their entrepreneurial potential in the social, nonprofit sector.

Guided and inspired by its president and chief executive officer, William E. Strickland Jr., Manchester Bidwell Corporation is a leader in art and vocational education for young people and adults in southwestern Pennsylvania.

In 1972 Strickland was asked to take over the Bidwell Training Center, an accredited post-secondary institution that offers short-term accelerated programs geared to equipping students with the necessary skills for employment in today's ever-changing marketplace. Bidwell students enjoy increased employment opportunities in the high-tech, medical, culinary and scientific fields. The institution's majors include business travel counselor, chemical laboratory technician, culinary arts, information sciences, medical claims processor, medical coder/abstractor, medical secretary, medical transcriptionist, pharmacy technician and plastics processing technician. The Bidwell Training Center operates on the belief that education offered in an intelligent, planned and financially sound way will bear results for the students and the community as a whole. The facility, along with a deeply committed corporate board, will continue to offer to southwestern Pennsylvania the high standard of professional training demanded by its students and the area's economy.

During the last 30 years, Manchester Craftsmen's Guild and Bidwell Training Center have been the leaders in the fields of art and vocational education for inner-city youth and adults. For everyone served by Manchester Bidwell's varied programs, Strickland is an inspiring role model. Among his many honors are a MacArthur Foundation Genius Award for leadership and ingenuity in the arts. In 1998 Strickland received the prestigious Kilby Foundation Award and the White House "Coming Up Taller" Award. In 1999 he was presented with the Commonwealth of Pennsylvania Arts Leadership and Service Award. Strickland sits on the board of the Institute for Social Enterprise of the Harvard Business School and is a trustee of the University of Pittsburgh.

Manchester Bidwell Corporation's William Strickland, who began at a potter's wheel, is now molding the lives of thousands and shaping a future for entire communities.

The Pittsburgh Children's Museum

THE PITTSBURGH CHILDREN'S Museum is a unique facility on Pittsburgh's historic North Side where children can explore their creativity, curiosity and joy through hands-on exhibits, fascinating collections, live performances and art activities.

The Children's Museum was founded in 1983 by the Junior League of Pittsburgh, Inc. to serve children with their families and community groups in Western Pennsylvania. Originally located on one floor of the historic landmark Old Post Office Building, the museum expanded into the entire building in the late 1980s to better accommodate its permanent and temporary exhibits. In 1998 the Children's Museum underwent a major renovation to provide improved exhibits, services and spaces where children can create, play and learn.

The museum's hands-on exhibits are geared to a wide age range and different learning styles, and focus on gross motor development, language arts skills, health education, self-esteem and personal responsibility. Children are welcomed by the museum's signature piece, The Kids' Climber, a two-story climbing sculpture which invites children to climb towards the sky, then slide back down to earth. They can devise and launch their own flying machines, explore health and anatomy with the museum's mascot Stuffee™, board a real school bus to learn safety rules on Safety Street, and take a ride in a human-powered elevator.

The Children's Museum's collection of artifacts features the work of three prominent Pittsburghers — Fred Rogers, Andy Warhol and Margo Lovelace — as well as original puppets from Jim Henson. *Mister Rogers' Neighborhood: A Hands-On Exhibit* opened in 1998. This successful exhibit later became the first major traveling exhibit designed and built by the Children's Museum.

Children can apply their creativity in new and varied ways through puppet activities, interactive performances and art classes in silk-screening, sculpting, weaving, photography and painting in the multimedia studio. The Children's Museum's Outreach Program brings its resources into the community by offering more than 50 different learning activities to schools, libraries and community festivals.

On the first floor of The Pittsburgh Children's Museum, the Rotunda area features The Kids Climber (right), and two flying machines (left). *Photograph by Roy Engelbrecht*

The Pittsburgh Children's Museum is currently involved in a $25 million capital campaign for an expansion project linking its current 100-year-old home with the adjacent Buhl Planetarium. The world-class facility will incorporate an expanded Children's Museum, an outdoor Children's Park and the Pittsburgh Children's Center, a space for other children's organizations to offer services, hold activities and share resources. The expanded museum's exhibits will follow the philosophy of "Play with Real Stuff." Settings include the Kitchen, Studio, Garage/Workshop, Attic, Theater, Backyard, Nursery, Office and the permanent installation of Mister Rogers' Neighborhood. This project strives to revitalize the museum's North Side neighborhood while creating a new town square for children and families.

The Pittsburgh Children's Museum is housed in the Old Post Office, built in 1894 on Pittsburgh's North Side. *Photograph by Roy Engelbrecht*

With its many activities and exhibits that inspire children to better understand themselves, each other and the world around them, The Pittsburgh Children's Museum serves as a vital resource for the region. As its vision for the future takes shape, the museum will offer children and families a one-of-a-kind experience to play, explore new ideas and subjects, and create important memories for many generations.

The Pittsburgh Cultural Trust

THE PITTSBURGH CULTURAL TRUST is a legacy of Pittsburgh civic leader H.J. "Jack" Heinz II, who envisioned the development of a restoration project in the renowned Cultural District in the city of Pittsburgh.

In 1967, while searching for a new location for the Pittsburgh Symphony, the Howard Heinz Endowment purchased the deteriorating Loew's Penn Theater for renovation. Reopened as Heinz Hall for the Performing Arts in 1971, the elegant performing arts center was situated in the midst of a declining business section. In response, Jack Heinz collaborated with the Allegheny Conference on Community Development, and the formation of a cultural district was planned for downtown Pittsburgh.

The Agnes R. Katz Plaza in the heart of the Cultural District was commissioned by The Cultural Trust and designed by Louise Bourgeois, artist; Michael Graves, architect; and Daniel Kiley, landscape architect. *Photo by Clyde Hare*

To implement these plans, The Pittsburgh Cultural Trust was founded in 1984 and later named Carol R. Brown as president. Emerging as a visible meld of the arts and the public/private sector, this liaison provided the foundation for subsequent successful revitalization projects in the Cultural District. Preservation of the historical integrity of the district, located in a 14-square-block area bounded by Liberty Avenue, the Allegheny River and 10th and Stanwix streets, resulted in 51 buildings being designated a National Historic District.

The first project of The Pittsburgh Cultural Trust was the restoration in 1987 of the 1928 Stanley Theater, which became the Benedum Center for the Performing Arts through a lead gift from the Benedum Foundation. Resident companies include Pittsburgh Ballet Theatre, Civic Light Opera, Pittsburgh Dance Council, and Pittsburgh Opera.

Recent Cultural Trust projects include the Fulton Theater, originally a vaudeville house, reopened in 1991 and renamed the Byham Theater in 1995 through a gift from the Byham family of Pittsburgh. A mural by artist Richard Haas is painted on the north facade of the theater. Wood Street Galleries became downtown's first visual art galleries. The Art Cinema became Harris Theater, home of Pittsburgh Filmmakers. The O'Reilly Theater is the residence of Pittsburgh Public Theater with Michael Graves as the architect.

The Agnes R. Katz Plaza displays a 25-foot fountain and eyeball-shaped benches by Louise Bourgeois. Daniel Urban Kiley, landscape architect, created the landscape design in the model of a formal European park with Michael Graves as the consulting architect. A sculpture by Alexandr Brodsky is temporarily exhibited in an adjacent sculpture park.

An overall theme for the Cultural District was commissioned to Robert Wilson, artist-designer, and Richard Gluckman, architect, who plan to integrate natural and artificial light for animation. And in 1998, Ann Hamilton, artist, and Michael Van Valkenburgh, landscape architect, created an ecological pathway above the river's edge in the two-tier Allegheny Riverfront Park.

The Pittsburgh Cultural Trust has received international recognition and design awards for developing a master plan that interweaves the performing and visual arts with the business community. Through cultural venues, The Cultural Trust nourishes the arts, enriches the urban environment and cultivates appreciation for performing and visual arts.

Today, approximately 1.2 million visitors attend over 1,200 performances held in the district annually. Internationally recognized architects, artists, designers and performers portray a colorful texture on the canvas of Pittsburgh. The Cultural District, with the guidance of The Pittsburgh Cultural Trust, is becoming a work of art inspired by the brushstrokes of Jack Heinz.

The Benedum Center for the Performing Arts, the flagship project of The Cultural Trust, is a faithful historic restoration from the flashing-lights marquee in the front to the proscenium stage. *Photo by Dennis Marsico*

Pittsburgh Symphony Orchestra

ON FEBRUARY 27, 1896, A CROSS section of the people of Pittsburgh was united in celebration. The occasion was the Pittsburgh Orchestra's inaugural concert at Carnegie Music Hall. Thus was born one of the city's most important cultural landmarks, long recognized as being as much a part of what makes Pittsburgh great as its majestic rivers, ethnic neighborhoods, prospering industries or champion sports teams.

In its first 14 years, under the direction of Victor Herbert and later Emil Paur, the orchestra was the subject of high praise from many fronts including composer and guest conductor Richard Strauss, who commented, "The one mistake I made of this, my first American tour, is that I did not engage the unapproachable Pittsburgh Orchestra for every one of the concerts I was engaged to conduct."

Financial adversity and World War I placed the orchestra on extended hiatus from 1910 until 1926, when the Pittsburgh Symphony Society was established. This auspicious moment marked the convening of a group of individuals, privately held businesses, corporations and foundations whose untiring support have fostered decades of success for the Pittsburgh Symphony Orchestra (PSO).

After Braddock native Antonio Modarelli's popular success as music director, the orchestra board decided it was time to take a step toward world-renown. They hired the first of many conductors of international reputation — Otto Klemperer — in 1937. He and his successors each added another component to the orchestra's prestige.

During the Fritz Reiner years the orchestra built an extensive portfolio of important recordings and world tours. The William

Victor Herbert took the Pittsburgh Symphony Orchestra through its first turn of the century as music director from 1898 to 1904. The Irish-born cellist, composer and conductor was known for his energy, flamboyance and musicality.

Steinberg years expanded the orchestra's repertoire back to the early 17th century and brought the sound of modern music to the ears of loyal patrons. André Previn brought a less traditional but no less brilliant baton to the podium from 1976 to 1984. And from 1989 to 1996 Lorin Maazel, who had once conducted the Pittsburgh orchestra at age 12, continued to refine its international reputation. All continued to record and tour with the orchestra, to commission and premiere new works, and to please audiences with well-loved traditional offerings.

In 1971 the orchestra moved from its Oakland home at the Syria Mosque to the heart of the city. Once a vaudeville theater and movie house, the Loew's Penn Theater was transformed into Heinz Hall for the Performing Arts, a concert hall both aesthetically and acoustically superior and home to the Pittsburgh Symphony Orchestra.

In 1996 the PSO entered its second century with the announcement that Mariss Jansons would become music director. Under his leadership, the orchestra has maintained its rich traditions while courting a new generation of music lovers through unprecedented educational and outreach efforts. As the PSO's first principal pops conductor, Marvin Hamlisch has helped to cultivate new audiences through his own great charisma and showmanship.

The PSO looks to a future filled with challenges and opportunities. The challenges will be to foster new audiences willing to explore the depths of classical music. The opportunities, supported by an ever-growing endowment fund, lie in the Pittsburgh Symphony Orchestra's vital role in Pittsburgh's latest renaissance.

Mariss Jansons, whose musical style has been described as "intense and abandoned," took the artistic helm of the PSO in 1997 and has captured the hearts of listeners at home and abroad.

Technology

Diverse businesses have gathered to make Pittsburgh one of the country's leading centers of technology innovation, development, manufacturing and employment.

Penn Telecom

WHEN FRANK REESE, FORMER president of North Pittsburgh Systems, Inc., came up with the idea for an independent subsidiary to serve the expanding business, network and specialty telecommunications needs of communities north of Pittsburgh, he continued the commitment to Pittsburgh that had been made by the founding fathers of the North Pittsburgh Telephone Company in 1906.

Headquartered in Cranberry, Penn Telecom began operations in 1979 as a provider of business telecommunications systems and supplies. The success of that business spawned the establishment of a related finance division that helped customers fund the purchase of business telecommunications systems.

Reese envisioned that Penn Telecom would grow and prosper under the deregulated telecommunications environment of the 1980s by offering innovative products and services that complemented the parent telecommunications carrier's core business. In many ways, Penn Telecom's growth has paralleled the explosive boom in economic development that has characterized Pittsburgh's northern communities over the past 20 years.

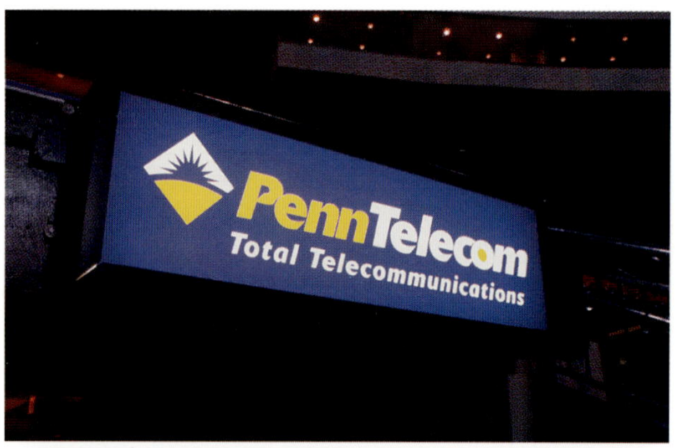

Penn Telecom is the official telecommunications provider of the Pittsburgh Penguins Hockey Club, sponsoring the Penn Telecom Lounge East and the Penn Telecom Lounge West at the Mellon Arena.

When the Pittsburgh Pirates moved into a new home at PNC Park, the team looked to Penn Telecom to meet its local and long-distance service needs.

As deregulation of the telecommunications industry continued throughout the 1980s, Penn Telecom took steps to extend its business offerings and modernize its network infrastructure to meet the expanding telecommunications needs of the metropolitan Pittsburgh area.

Long-Distance and Local Service

In 1982, when deregulation opened the door to competition among long-distance carriers, Penn Telecom entered the market by reselling long-distance services that were purchased at a volume rate from major carriers to local business and residential customers. This facet of the business has continued to grow and includes additional products and services, such as calling cards, toll-free 800-number service and operator services.

As a Competitive Local Exchange Carrier (CLEC), Penn Telecom offers competitively priced local telephone service throughout the metropolitan Pittsburgh area irrespective of past regulated boundaries. By adding long-distance and local telephone service to its offering, Penn Telecom provides solutions to all business telecommunications needs, from phone equipment and data services to telephone services.

Laying a Fiber Foundation

Penn Telecom has embraced technology as a key driver in the growth of its network infrastructure and business offering, partnering with other technology providers to upgrade telecommunications links in the metro Pittsburgh area. In the early 1980s, Penn Telecom partnered with Qwest Microwave to establish the first microwave radio link between Gibsonia and downtown Pittsburgh.

However, the emergence of fiber-optic technology in the early 1990s proved to be an important milestone in the evolution and growth of the company. Penn Telecom management made a strategic decision to invest heavily in fiber-optic technology, envisioning future telecommunications needs for greater bandwidth. Partnering with the communications arm of a local energy provider that was building five major fiber-optic rings around Pittsburgh, Penn Telecom expanded its fiber-optic network that was in place from Pittsburgh to Butler.

This fiber-optic network proved to be a critical element in the growth of Penn Telecom's business. Initially, the company sold access to the network to end users at competitive rates while completing fiber connections to important Pittsburgh buildings, such as Oliver Plaza and The Pittsburgh Information and Technology Center. Penn Telecom management leveraged revenue from this arrangement to complete a ring of fiber around downtown Pittsburgh. As a facility-based provider with its own fiber backbone, Penn Telecom not only doubled its footprint capacity but also laid the foundation for offering a robust range of services in the Internet Age.

Penn Telecom is committed to providing excellent service to customers throughout the Pittsburgh metropolitan area.

Broadband for the Internet Age

The advent of the Internet proved propitious for Penn Telecom and its investment in a fiber-optic infrastructure because the bandwidth provided by the network prepared the company to compete immediately in the growing data telecommunications services market. Today, Penn Telecom offers a full line of network and broadband data services.

Penn Telecom was one of the first telecommunications providers in the Pittsburgh area to offer digital subscriber line (DSL) technology for fast, reliable access to the Internet. DSL permits data access speeds as high as 768 kbps over an existing telephone line without disrupting voice communications. In other words, customers can surf the Web at a rate nearly 14 times faster than they could with a 56 kbps modem, while simultaneously carrying on a telephone conversation.

In addition to DSL service, Penn Telecom offers the full range of high-speed data access technologies to meet the needs of businesses of varying size. These technologies include DS1, DS3, OC-3c, PRI, Frame Relay and transparent local area network (LAN) connections. Penn Telecom also offers LAN and wide-area network (WAN) engineering services to assist customers in setting up their computer networks.

A Continuing Commitment to Pittsburgh

Throughout its history, Penn Telecom's approach to business has stressed a commitment to Pittsburgh and the city's business community. By working through interrelated arrangements with its sister companies — the North Pittsburgh Telephone Company, a local exchange carrier; and Nauticom, an Internet service provider (ISP) — Penn Telecom provides unique value to the Pittsburgh market by offering alternative, affordable, cost-effective solutions to its customers.

Penn Telecom is the official telecommunications provider of the Pittsburgh Penguins Hockey Club, sponsoring the Penn Telecom Lounge East and the Penn Telecom Lounge West at the Mellon Arena, where the Penguins play their home games, and also has been selected as the Pittsburgh Pirates' choice for local and long-distance service. The company is an active member in the Pittsburgh High Technology Council, the Pittsburgh Chamber of Commerce, the Cranberry Township Chamber of Commerce, the Butler Chamber of Commerce and the Monroeville Chamber of Commerce.

Since its beginning as an idea in Frank Reese's mind, Penn Telecom has continued the North Pittsburgh Systems tradition of focusing on the needs of and opportunities in Pittsburgh as it charts its course in the exciting telecommunications industry of the new millenium.

Penn Telecom's Cranberry headquarters

ALCOSAN

THE TRANSFORMATION OF Pittsburgh's rivers and streams from open sewers devoid of aquatic life to waterways safe for recreation and thriving habitats is testament to the success of the Allegheny County Sanitary Authority.

Incorporated in March 1946 under the Pennsylvania Municipal Authorities Act, the sanitary authority known as ALCOSAN was created to protect public health through environmentally sound wastewater collection and treatment. The impetus of ALCOSAN's formation was an order by the Pennsylvania State Sanitary Board to 102 municipalities and 90 industries to quit discharging untreated sewage into waterways. By 1947 the equivalent of 4 million bathtubs full of sewage was discharged daily into Allegheny County rivers and streams. Diseases and conditions caused by the ever-present water-borne bacteria included typhoid fever, dysentery and infectious hepatitis.

In 1958 a 30-inch pipe encased in concrete is lowered into the Allegheny River near 16th Street in Sharpsburg.

The first executive director, chief engineer and chairman of the board, the late Col. John F. Laboon, P.E., began planning for the construction with years of engineering, laboratory and financial studies. In 1947, ALCOSAN's in-house lab was selected as one of the six outstanding sewage research labs in America.

The creation of ALCOSAN had to overcome numerous obstacles. Rural municipalities rejected a comprehensive report recommending a countywide sewage plan. Some communities wanted to join the service area while others didn't. And political infighting continued over responsibility for collection systems. Laboon didn't give up and, with the assistance of the city of Pittsburgh, a final project was adopted in August 1948 which included the city and 67 surrounding communities.

A 1957 Plymouth Belvedere sits inside a 10-foot-diameter pipe which carries wastewater directly into the ALCOSAN treatment plant.

ALCOSAN was presented with a sales agreement for a site for the treatment plant from the city of Pittsburgh for 16.85 acres plus 20 building lots for $250,000. The site represented one of the lowest points in the county, allowing the majority of the wastewater to flow by gravity. The site formerly housed factories and a little village of rowhouses called Verner Town. By 1956, 23 area banks combined forces to create a loan totaling over $100 million for ALCOSAN to construct the treatment plant, intercepting sewers and related systems.

Former Pennsylvania Gov. George M. Leader said of ALCOSAN at the April 1956 groundbreaking ceremony, "It holds the promise of things to come — improved sources of water supply, more abundant fish and aquatic life, and the development of new recreational areas. I am confident that under the Authority's direction, the completed project will prove to be the outstanding engineering achievement we expect it to be." The efforts to design and construct the plant received notoriety in 1960 when the American Society of Civil Engineers awarded ALCOSAN an honorable mention as the second-best outstanding civil engineering project of the year.

After three years, 11 strikes and two fatalities, the primary treatment facility minus the 200-foot smokestack was completed at a cost of $16 million. The primary (mechanical) treatment process began operating January 1959, however, the official dedication wasn't held until October 1, 1959. Customers were charged 30 cents per 1,000 gallons of water used.

Expansion of the system continued when in 1966 a billing department was added. The Pennsylvania Sanitary Water Board then ordered ALCOSAN to begin providing an increased level of treatment, not because of its operations, which were commended, but due to the nationwide trend toward higher water-quality standards. In response, construction began in 1970 on $45 million in additions to provide sludge processing and secondary (biological) treatment. The sludge dewatering building was completed in 1972 and secondary treatment began the following year.

ALCOSAN CONTINUES TO RECEIVE ENVIRONMENTAL AWARDS AND ACCOLADES FOR ITS SYSTEM DESIGN AND OPERATIONS. THE STAFF, COMPRISED OF A WIDE VARIETY OF PROFESSIONALS, PROVIDES EXPERTISE THROUGHOUT THE COUNTRY ON WASTEWATER AND TECHNICAL ISSUES.

Although ALCOSAN was originally designed to prevent water pollution, its environmental scope grew to include both land and air. An experimental land application was launched in 1980 to test liquid sludge as fertilizer for sod production. Results were positive, demonstrating that the time to produce mature sod was cut in half using sludge over commercial fertilizers. That summer, ALCOSAN created an experimental garden of vegetables and 10,000 flowers to evaluate the sludge as a general crop fertilizer. Again, the results were positive, prompting ALCOSAN in 1991 to begin beneficially reusing the sludge as a soil amendment to abandoned strip mines and agricultural sites. As of 2000, the product, known as ALCOSOIL, has shown positive growth on 15,000 acres in Western Pennsylvania and Eastern Ohio.

An October 2000 aerial view of the ALCOSAN treatment plant along the Ohio River

In 1996 a $400 million, 10-year program began to upgrade the treatment process and interceptor system. The projects include odor control, treatment capacity and planning for control of wet-weather flows. Treatment tanks were retrofitted or added to increase daily treatment capacity from 200 million gallons to 275 million gallons, primary process tanks were covered, systems were increased or added, and state-of-the-art control systems were installed. Renovations over the years have expanded the treatment facility to 56 acres, with ALCOSAN providing wastewater treatment service to 320,000 customers in 83 communities.

ALCOSAN's legacy of cleaning up area rivers and streams through sound wastewater treatment will continue to be strengthened in the future as the organization undertakes arguably the most important project of its history. Planning for the control of wet-weather flows, which can overwhelm the sewer pipes and treatment plant, allowing the discharge of untreated diluted sewage into area waterways, has been under way since 1992. It is estimated that it will cost the region $3 billion to meet environmental regulations to address wet-weather issues.

ALCOSAN continues to receive environmental awards and accolades for its system design and operations. The staff, comprised of a wide variety of professionals, provides expertise throughout the country on wastewater and technical issues. At $2.23 per 1,000 gallons of water used, customers still receive excellent service at one of the lowest rates in the country. Development has substantially increased since the Authority's inception due to the availability of sewage service. Today ALCOSAN continues its success with the premise on which it was founded — to provide environmentally sound wastewater collection and treatment.

Compunetics/Compunetix

INNOVATION HAS BEEN THE career hallmark of Giorgio Coraluppi ever since he earned his doctorate in electrical engineering in 1958. A respected research scientist in his native Italy, he immigrated to Pittsburgh in 1964 to join the Space Defense Division of the American Optical Company. While there, he served as senior project engineer for a special-purpose digital computer to control the NASA Lewis Flight Simulator. He also was designer and project engineer for a satellite attitude simulator now installed at NASA's Ames Research Center. In 1967 Coraluppi joined Carnegie Mellon University.

In 1968 Coraluppi established a small operation for hardware engineering and manufacturing in a shopping center in suburban Penn Hills. A year later, he moved the growing business to a larger facility in Monroeville Industrial Park, about 15 miles east of Pittsburgh. One of the company's early developments was a system of cameras connected to computers to measure hot steel slabs in preparation for cutting. The system's accuracy reduced waste and improved operating flexibility in the steel industry.

Today Compunetics produces state-of-the-art circuit boards for commercial and military markets. Its sister company, Compunetix, activated in the early 1990s, designs, manufactures, installs, and supports teleconferencing systems for commercial, industrial, civilian government, and military applications. Compunetics has a staff of 95 and Compunetix employs about 265 people. The bulk of the two firms' work force consists of software and hardware design engineers along with technical and quality control personnel.

With continued growth, Compunetix moved its headquarters in 1996 to its present facility occupying a modern, six-story building in Monroeville. Besides its U.S. operations, the company has sales offices in Australia, United Kingdom, and Hong Kong. The two firms' research and development teams work directly with customers' engineers to design and develop new products.

In support of the next generation of technical professionals, Compunetics and Compunetix sponsor internships and co-op programs for students of the University of Pittsburgh, Penn State University and Carnegie Mellon University. They also provide funding for WDUQ, Pittsburgh's outlet for National Public Radio.

As a long time supporter of local organizations, Compunetics was one of the founding members of the Pittsburgh Technology Council. Today Compunetix not only continues as an active member of the Pittsburgh Technology Council but is also a voting member of the Pittsburgh Digital Greenhouse.

This modern, six-story building in Monroeville, Pennsylvania, houses headquarters and other facilities of Compunetix.

COMPUNETICS

Compunetics provides custom-engineered circuit boards for such major corporations as Westinghouse and IBM. Among its vital products, the company has designed and manufactured circuit boards to control the emergency shutdown rods in commercial nuclear power plants.

The Printed Circuit Boards division of Compunetics, which is located in Monroeville Industrial Park, designs and manufactures high-tech circuit boards. It is one of the few operations in the United States that can produce highly compacted circuitry.

The Advanced Interconnect Products division serves the emerging market of fine-pitch interconnects between circuit board components. The operation produces high-density, high-speed interconnect products, including flexible circuits, multichip modules and multilayer printed circuit boards.

COMPUNETIX

Among its many honors, Compunetix received the Boeing and NASA 1999 Exceptional Company Performance Award for the high quality of its product and technical support. In addition, the World Trade Council named Compunetix Exporter of the Year in 2000, and the Pittsburgh Technology Council designated the firm as one of the 50 fastest-growing technical companies in the region.

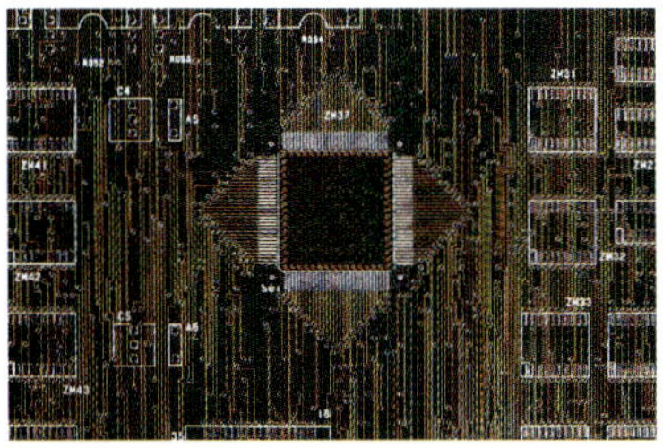

The Communications Systems Division designs and manufactures CONTEX audio teleconferencing systems for telephone companies, government agencies, corporations and distance learning centers. Its teleconferencing products range from small, 24 port systems to large central office systems. The newest CONTEX product will provide up to 10,000 ports in a single system. The Communications Systems Division also produces a web-controlled interface for its teleconferencing systems as well as an integrated reservation, scheduling, and billing system. Among its major clients are WorldCom, Sprint, Verizon and telephone companies in Great Britain, Japan, the Netherlands, New Zealand, Norway, South Africa, Germany, Hong Kong, Australia and Mexico. For three years in a row Compunetix has been named market leader for audio conferencing equipment.

The Federal Systems Division designs and manufactures audio teleconferencing equipment for the military and civilian government agencies for mission-critical applications. Its customers include the U.S. Navy, the National Oceanographic and Atmospheric Administration, the Federal Aviation Administration, INTELSAT and NASA. At the Goddard Space Flight Center, Compunetix systems play a vital role in coordinating space launches, allowing all authorized personnel at various locations to pick up a phone line and be connected immediately with the teleconferencing network. In addition, the Federal Systems Division provides equipment for the Boeing control center at Huntington Beach, California, which monitors space shuttle launches and the International Space Station.

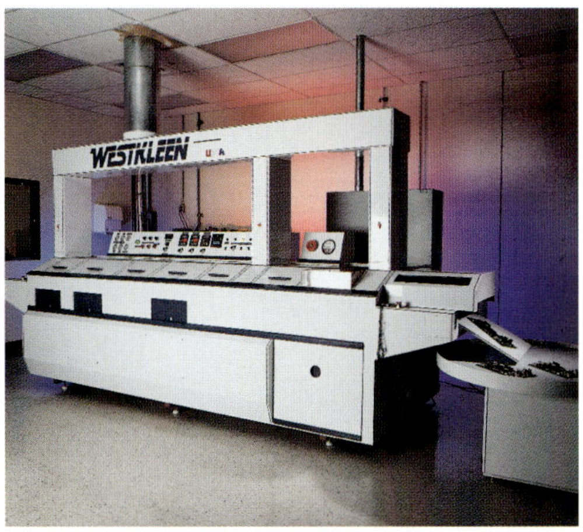

The Video Systems Division designs and manufactures Compunetix's video conferencing systems, which are used by teleconferencing service providers as well as distance education, telemedicine, government, and corporate communications clients. Its videoconferencing products range from the VIRTUOSO, a small 8 port enterprise system, to the large central office system called the ORCHESTRATOR that scales up to 160 ports. The newly released hybrid videoconferencing products provide fully integrated audio, video, and data conferencing capabilities. Major customers include the United States Department of Justice, Novell, Tele Danmark Communications, and Telecom Italia.

The Instrumentation Systems Division assembles circuit boards including components of Compunetix's teleconferencing systems. Among its notable products, the Instrumentation Systems Division manufactured components of the IBM Big Blue chess-playing computer that defeated world chess champion Gary Kasparov. Compunetix also designed these cards, which interconnect Big Blue's microprocessors.

Another groundbreaking enterprise in which Compunetix played a vital role is the "virtual reality cave" constructed at Brown University in a cooperative project with IBM. The cave consists of a room with four large video screens for walls. Each video screen is connected to four computers. Each computer transmits one layer of video graphics to a screen and compositor cards designed and manufactured by Compunetix combine the layers to produce multidimensional visual effects.

Planning for the future, Coraluppi is gearing up for major growth in several new markets, including air traffic control, emergency response, date conferencing, and other collaborative technologies.

High-tech printed circuit boards are designed and manufactured by a Compunetics unit for company products as well as outside customers.

The Virtuoso videoconferencing control system can connect up to eight parties at separate locations.

Advanced equipment operated by Compunetix' Instrumentation Systems Division removes solder and flux from printed circuit boards following assembly.

Seagate Technology

THE WORLD TODAY RUNS ON information. Every time people surf the Internet, hit "send," trade a stock online, watch the latest Hollywood blockbuster movie or use an ATM, they create, access and share tremendous amounts of digital information. And for over 20 years, Seagate Technology has been developing the technology and manufacturing the products that help make it all happen.

With the recent addition of its Pittsburgh-based research arm – Seagate Research – the company is poised to further its success. That's no small feat considering this industry leader was formed just 20 years ago on an educated gamble, a slender $20,000 initial investment and a very aggressive plan.

Seagate is the world's largest manufacturer of disc drives, magnetic discs and read-write heads and a leader in Storage Area Network (SAN) solutions and server appliances. Seagate storage products are where the Internet lives, and the growth of the Web has led to worldwide demand for storage doubling every nine months. When Seagate was founded it helped create the PC revolution. Now it is positioned to capitalize on the growth of the Internet.

With the recent addition of its Pittsburgh-based research arm — Seagate Research — the company is poised to further its success. That's no small feat considering this industry leader was formed just 20 years ago on an educated gamble, a slender $20,000 initial investment and a very aggressive plan.

In the late 1970s, Seagate founders Al Shugart and Finis Conner recognized the emergence of personal computing and the resulting imminent need for data storage. So they set out to build the world's first 5 1/4-inch rigid disc drive. It would offer 15 times the capacity of a floppy disc at only three times the cost.

Seagate burst out of the starting gate with new drives for a new concept called the PC, and the company hasn't looked back since.

Throughout its history, Seagate has relied on a strategy of vertical integration: designing, developing and producing the key enabling technologies that go into its storage products, rather than relying on outside suppliers. This isn't easy because building disc drives is widely recognized as the "extreme sport" of the technology industry. It requires expertise in physics, tribology, aerodynamics, fluid mechanics, information theory, magnetics, process technology and numerous other disciplines. And in recent years the increasing pace of technology has led Seagate to amend its thinking.

Seagate Research occupies 190,000 square feet in a new, state-of-the-art, research facility on the Allegheny River near Pittsburgh's Strip District.

Recognizing the increasingly strategic role storage was playing in the networked world, new company CEO Steve Luczo took the reins and guided Seagate onto a new path, while still maintaining a commitment to vertical integration. However, instead of using the old business model of building the lowest-cost drives without leading-edge technology, the company shifted its focus to quality, technology and time-to-market leadership.

This new focus has significantly increased the company's commitment to research and development in order to strengthen its lead in technology and get more advanced products to market faster than the competition. By owning and developing the core technologies that make data storage possible, Seagate can do it better and faster, in addition to doing it at less cost.

Cheetah X15 is the world's first drive to operate at 15,000 revolutions per minute (RPM) and deliver 3.9 msec average seek times — the fastest in the world. The Cheetah X15's performance is equivalent to a person reading the entire works of Shakespeare in less than .15 seconds.

Now research and development is the foundation of Seagate's business, and the company has some of the brightest minds in the technology industry working to ensure that it stays on the leading edge. Seagate's technology advantage has enabled the company to consistently set and then shatter world records with the highest-performing disc drives in the industry. And it also provides the highest capacity disc drive in the world, a 3.5-inch drive capable of storing information equivalent to a stack of typed pages three times the height of the Empire State Building.

Looking beyond these accomplishments, Seagate Research has its sights four to 10 years into the future, exploring what kinds of technology it will take to put the world's information at people's fingertips. From hand-held computers and Web phones, to intelligent storage that knows what information people want and when they want it, to home networks that deliver entertainment, education and services on demand — Seagate has the know-how and the resources to develop the technologies required for tomorrow.

The Pittsburgh site of Seagate Research is committed to finding new solutions and new technologies in data storage technology, pushing it further than anyone could have imagined when the company had its humble beginnings 20 years ago. With a bold mission and a clear vision, Seagate Research, along with the center's director, Dr. Mark Kryder, is dedicated to advancing future information storage technologies.

Seagate believes that the growing demand forecast for storage can be addressed by only a handful of companies, and owning the technology to enable future generation storage devices is critical. In both the enterprise and consumer markets, Seagate is the leader. With a focus on innovation, time-to-market, ownership of enabling technologies and a proven strategy of

WITH A FOCUS ON INNOVATION, TIME-TO-MARKET, OWNERSHIP OF ENABLING TECHNOLOGIES AND A PROVEN STRATEGY OF VERTICAL INTEGRATION AS WELL AS RESEARCH AND DEVELOPMENT, SEAGATE IS THE DOMINANT PLAYER IN THE MARKET TODAY AND BEST POSITIONED FOR THE FUTURE.

vertical integration as well as research and development, Seagate is the dominant player in the market today and best positioned for the future. With the race on to discover newer, faster ways to store, access and manage information, look for Seagate Technology to continue to surge to the front of the pack.

ServiceWare Technologies, Inc.

LONG DOMINATED BY COAL, STEEL, glass and aluminum, Pittsburgh-area river towns are now welcoming new neighbors from the world of high-tech commerce. At the forefront of the region's evolution is ServiceWare Technologies, a leader and innovator in Internet-based customer service solutions for the competitive arena of electronic business. Founded in 1991, ServiceWare stemmed from ideas conceived by two computer scientists at the Carnegie Group, a spinoff from research and development efforts at Pittsburgh's Carnegie Mellon University. While at the Carnegie Group, ServiceWare founders Jeff Pepper and Rajiv Enand had developed software systems to manage corporate knowledge — every piece of information a company acquires about its customers, products, partners, markets, employees and other important facets of doing business. They also explored how to increase the value of that knowledge and re-use it productively.

Founded and based in Oakmont, Pennsylvania, ServiceWare is a leading provider of electronic-service knowledge management solutions for the service and support industry.

Pepper and Enand believed that software systems for knowledge management could have a powerful impact on a company's profitability if the systems could be used to improve service to customers, thereby increasing their satisfaction and loyalty. In a flash of insight, they foresaw the impact the Internet would have on business and that Internet-based customer service solutions could provide a tremendous competitive edge to companies engaged in commerce on the World Wide Web.

The founding partners launched ServiceWare as an knowledge management consulting firm in the Allegheny River town of Oakmont, Pennsylvania, a few miles northeast of Pittsburgh. In the ensuing years, the company has evolved into a world-class provider of innovative software and content solutions that allow organizations to give customers fast and accurate answers to their inquiries, whether by Internet, e-mail, phone, fax or in person. In the short time since its founding, ServiceWare has expanded its operations to locations throughout the US and into Europe. Major US offices include include Parsippany, NJ, and Redwood Shores, California. The company also operates in Europe through its subsidiary, ServiceWare International, based in Reading, England.

Since September 2001, ServiceWare has been led by President and Chief Executive Officer Kent Heyman, who has established the company's mission: to deliver knowledge-based software that defines excellence in the electronic commerce industry. Heyman is building on a rich history. In 1993 ServiceWare pioneered the industry's first technical-support knowledge base to provide answers to commonly asked questions about the use of personal computers. Since then, the company has expanded this software — the Knowledge-Pak product family — to include desktop applications and hardware, network operating systems and enterprise applications. Shortly after the product's launch, *Call Center Magazine* named the Knowledge-Pak family its Product of the Year. Knowledge-Pak Architect, an administrative tool, was added in 1997.

In 1999 ServiceWare broadened its product spectrum when it acquired the Molloy Group. The addition of the Molloy-developed MindSync technology set ServiceWare apart from its competition as the only provider of automated service

IN A FLASH OF INSIGHT, THEY FORESAW THE IMPACT THE INTERNET WOULD HAVE ON BUSINESS AND THAT INTERNET- BASED CUSTOMER SERVICE SOLUTIONS COULD PROVIDE A TREMENDOUS COMPETITIVE EDGE TO COMPANIES ENGAGED IN COMMERCE ON THE WORLD WIDE WEB.

With the MindSync laying the groundwork, ServiceWare achieved another industry first in 2000 with the introduction of the eService Suite product set, which integrated the company's leading-edge knowledge management software and its Web-based tools.

solutions backed by artificial intelligence. A patented, sophisticated neural network, the MindSync mimics human thinking and learns from experience every time it is used.

Also in 1999, ServiceWare introduced RightAnswers.com, a Web-based technical support portal believed to be the most comprehensive such system in the world. The system allows users from organizations of any size to gain access to a continuously updated database that presents hundreds of thousands of electronic problems and corresponding solutions. In late 2000 the company expanded this system by adding 10 new software titles. Shortly after, in early 2001, the firm Control-F1 made RightAnswers.com available to its customers worldwide as part of its electronic-support product suite. In July 2001 ServiceWare divested the RightAnswers.com division of the business.

With the Cognitive Processor laying the groundwork, ServiceWare achieved another industry first in 2000 with the introduction of the eService Suite product set, which integrated the company's leading-edge knowledge management software and its Web-based tools. The product met the market's demand for a system that was easy to use and to administer. By means of the MindSync, the eService Suite allows each new user to benefit from the experience of everyone who has used the system previously. As an example, the 50th person to ask a question gains the benefit of the answers given to the first 49 people who asked the same question. In short, the system gets smarter with use.

Among the many honors ServiceWare has received for its pioneering developments, Technology Marketing Corporation presented the company with its 2000 CRM Excellence Award for its innovative products and leadership in customer relationship management (CRM). The award also honored ServiceWare for demonstrating the highest standards and continually striving to revolutionize customer service by means of its interactive products. In early 2001, in conjunction with the Software Support Professional Association's annual program, supportgate.com presented ServiceWare with a WebStar Service Award for superior service to its online customers.

Perhaps best illustrating ServiceWare's success is its customer base, which represents a cross section of industry leaders in the financial services, technology, manufacturing, health care, entertainment, education and government sectors. More organizations have implemented ServiceWare solutions, including H&R Block, Amgen, Northeast Utilities, Respironics, Marconi, Qualcomm and Stream International.

Well into the current century, ServiceWare plans to continue investing in research and development to keep its products and services on the cutting edge in the fast-growing electronic-service market.

Perhaps best illustrating ServiceWare's success is its customer base, which represents a cross section of industry leaders in the financial services, technology, manufacturing, health care, entertainment, education and government sectors.

Sony Technology Center

ON APRIL 18, 1990 NEWSPAPER headlines shouted the good news — "Sony Says Yes," blared the *Pittsburgh Tribune Review,* while the *Post Gazette* hailed "Sony To Hire Up To 1,000."

With the entire eastern half of the United States vying for the prize, Sony had selected Mount Pleasant, Pennsylvania, as the site of its newest domestic assembly plant for large-screen televisions. Just 30 miles east of Pittsburgh, the new Sony Technology Center-Pittsburgh (STC-P) would be conveniently located near two major interstate highways and within a two-day drive of over 60 percent of Sony's North American markets. The industrial site — a former auto assembly plant — was highly conducive to Sony's operational and technical needs, and the region offered relatively low utility costs and taxes. Perhaps the most important factor in Sony's decision, however, was the region's experienced, motivated and loyal work force whose long industrial history and strong work ethic makes it one of the region's greatest assets.

Sony's newest models, the 40-inch FD Trinitron® Wega television set and the 57-inch wide-screen projection set.

By the Center's 10th anniversary, the original 1,000 employees had grown to 3,300. At peak seasons for worldwide television set purchases — around Christmas, the Super Bowl, the Olympics and World Cup Soccer — thousands more temporary workers are hired to help Sony meet demand. STC-P is truly a regional employer, drawing its highly skilled work force from Westmoreland, Fayette and Allegheny counties and seven other counties in Pennsylvania.

Sony's impact on the local economy extends beyond its positive effect on employment figures. The facility contracts for parts, materials, services and equipment with more than 1,500 local suppliers and vendors within a 100-mile radius. One hundred percent of the mechanical parts used for projection televisions are purchased within 300 miles of the facility. And in its first 11 years alone, Sony invested nearly $700 million in STC-P. In 1991 *Executive Report Magazine* named Sony Electronics as the first recipient of its "Best Deal Award" for having made a significant corporate impact on the Pittsburgh region.

STC-P is the world's first vertically integrated television production plant. It is the only facility in the U.S. capable of completing the entire television manufacturing process in one place. Directly across the street from the television production area, American Video Glass Company, a joint venture of Sony Electronics Inc. and Corning Asahi Video Products, produces high-quality television glass from sand and other raw materials. Cathode Ray Tubes (CRTs). Aperture Grilles, a key componant of Trinitron televisions and other components are manufactured and assembled at STC-P, and the facility's logistics center sends its products to markets and consumers around the world.

Television products produced at STC-P include the large-screen, rear-projection Videoscope® and High-Scan® televisions in 43-inch, 48-inch, 53-inch and 61-inch models. In 1998 the

An STC-P employee guides a finished 36-inch FD Trinitron Wega off the production line.

(Far right) A Company Member scans a bar code of a finished television in STC-P's warehouse. The bar code was made at Sony Chemicals Corporation of America — global headquarters for Sony Chemicals Corporations thermal transfer ribbon business.

facility began producing the newest generation of CRTs for the 32-inch and 36-inch FD Trinitron® as well as the 36-inch FD Trinitron® Wega sets. They were the first of their kind to be manufactured outside of Japan; their distinctive flat screens provide a truly distortion-free picture. In 1999 the facility began to produce Sony's first High Definition projection television, a state-of-the-art, 65-inch set that was designed and built at STC-P. In 2001 STC-P began producing the world's largest direct view television, the 40-inch FD Trinitron® Wega.

STC-P is the world's first vertically integrated television manufacturing facility. The site is capable of going from sand to glass to television picture tube to finished television set — all in one location. Sony Electronics Inc. and Sony Chemicals Corporation of America comprise approximately 2.8 million square feet of space on STC-P's 650 acres. American Video Glass contributes 750,000 square feet.

Sony brings to Pittsburgh an innovative management style and a generous spirit of corporate citizenship. For its smaller-volume orders, crew cells build a television set from start to finish. This approach necessitates a high degree of flexibility in the manufacturing process. Ongoing employee education is another important element of the life of this facility. An in-house training department offers courses from basic computer skills, writing and presentation course to hightly technical training.

A Company Member completes the final inspection of the picture quality of a big screen projection television using one of STC-P's most valued assets — the human eye.

Sony believes that cooperation and teamwork extend beyond the workplace. It is a meaningful participant in the surrounding communities, adopting local schools, taking part in Adopt-a-Highway programs through Penn DOT, and encouraging employees to participate in volunteer experiences like America's Promise.

American Video Glass manufactures television panels and funnels from sand from central Pennsylvania. Funnels and panels are shipped either to other Sony facilities in North America or are brought across the street where they are made into a CRT and then a finished television set.

Sony and STC-P are leaders in developing environmentally friendly manufacturing methods. When Aperture Grille production began at the plant in 1995, Sony environmental experts found a beneficial use for iron chloride waste that resulted from the manufacturing process. The iron chloride generated at STC-P is safely managed and sold to a local treatment plant which uses it to control pollutants in waste water by removing harmful sediments before the water is returned to local streams and rivers. STC-P has also eliminated lead from the front panel of all picture tube glass.

Sony Technology Center-Pittsburgh has become the North American engineering center for large-screen, rear-projection television sets and continues to expand its electronics capabilities and products. But with 2.8 million square feet of industrial space, Sony has also located the North American headquarters and a manufacturing facility for Sony Chemicals Corporation of America at STC-P. The facility produces coated thermal transfer ribbon, used for bar coding applications in manufacturing, inventory control, logistics and distribution, and is Sony's world headquarters for this product. It also produces a variety of industrial adhesive products.

As a result of Sony's many innovative solutions, Arthur D. Little, Inc. recognized STC-P as one of America's top 20 companies in its 1995 "Best of the Best" program in manufacturing management. Both Sony Chemicals and Sony Electronics have earned ISO 9001 and 14001 certification as a result of their environmental efforts.

Sony also maintains a factory outlet in Grove City, Pennsylvania.

Allegheny Technologies

FROM KITCHEN SINKS TO JET engines to heart stents, Allegheny Technologies plays a pioneering role in developing and supplying stainless steel and high-technology superalloys designed to meet the demands of vital industries around the world.

The company traces its roots to 1901, when a small group of steelmakers established the Allegheny Steel Company to operate a plant along the Allegheny River in Brackenridge, Pennsylvania. In the 1920s the firm became the first U.S. maker of stainless steel, a versatile metal that had been developed several years earlier in Sheffield, England.

Among early uses of the company's stainless steel in architecture were the dome and trim of the Chrysler Building and the trim of the Empire State Building. In 1929 the rust-resistant metal was specified for all bright parts of Model A Fords.

In 1938 Allegheny Steel merged with Ludlum Steel, then one of the world's leading producers of high-quality alloy steel, to form Allegheny Ludlum Steel Corporation.

Several major transformations in the 1990s elevated the company's standing as a global leader in specialty materials. In 1996, under the leadership of Richard P. Simmons, Allegheny Ludlum's board chairman, the company combined with Teledyne, which expanded its specialty materials capabilities and added other businesses, including aviation, electronics, and industrial and consumer products. Since 1996 the company, now known as Allegheny Technologies, has acquired additional specialty materials companies and divested operations not related to specialty materials.

Ranking today among the world's largest and most diversified specialty materials producers, Allegheny Technologies plans continued growth through global expansion and initiatives in electronic commerce. Among its products, the company makes metal alloys that are vital to aerospace, transportation, energy production, medicine and the processing industries, including food, dairy, pulp and paper, chemical and pharmaceutical.

For the aerospace industry, Allegheny Technologies produces nickel-based and titanium alloys for the most demanding applications. Among them are jet engines, airframes and landing gear. For transportation, the company supplies stainless steel for such critical uses as catalytic converters and multilayered head gaskets.

One of the world's most productive stainless steel rolling mills, the 60-inch-wide unit at Allegheny Technologies' Vandergrift, Pennsylvania, plant is equipped with advanced-technology process and shape controls.

This electron-beam melting furnace produces titanium ingots and slabs for high-performance metal components at the Richland, Washington, facility of Allegheny Technologies.

A broad product spectrum for the energy industry includes high-performance alloys for offshore drilling platforms, fusion reactors and gas turbines. Important applications of Allegheny Technologies materials also are found in medicine, including hip implants and magnetic resonance imaging (MRI) equipment.

Tied to western Pennsylvania throughout its history, Allegheny Technologies operates three plants in Washington, Pennsylvania, and plants in Brackenridge, Latrobe, Leechburg and Vandergrift. Additional operations are located throughout the United States and at 17 locations overseas, including major facilities in Sheffield, England; Shanghai, China; and throughout Europe.

Historically, the company has been deeply involved in supporting community organizations in the Pittsburgh region, including the Pittsburgh Symphony and public television, and in other locations that are home to its 11,500 employees. Adding to its corporate sponsorships is a matching gifts program, which encourages individual employee involvement in the community.

From its early work with stainless steel in the 20th century, Allegheny Technologies now also produces sophisticated superalloys and other exotic materials for ever-changing and expanding applications of the 21st century.

CoManage Corp.

DAVE NELSEN AND ANDY FRALEY, former executives at FORE Systems, a leading telecommunications equipment provider now known as Marconi Communications, were making their last run during a ski trip in Jackson Hole, Wyoming, in early 1998 when the idea for CoManage Corp. was born.

The pair, who had spent the early parts of their careers in California, realized telecommunications service providers needed a software system to manage the plethora of computer networking equipment that is used to run telecommunications and data networks. At the time, a heterogeneous network management system that could manage different types of equipment from many manufacturers did not exist. Nelsen and Fraley understood the need for network management solutions as a result of their work at FORE Systems.

(Left to right) Dave Nelsen and Andy Fraley, founders of CoManage Corp.

The two entrepreneurs could have started their new company anywhere but chose to settle in Pittsburgh because of the area's positive business climate, world-class cultural amenities and software talent pool.

Beginning with \$4.2 million in financing from local venture capitalists, CoManage opened its doors for business on July 4, 1998, in Wexford, which is located just north of Pittsburgh. Since then, the company has successfully completed two additional rounds of financing — raising \$12.6 million and \$39 million — and launched its flagship product, Integrated Service Manager (ISM), in May 2000. Just one month later, ISM won the Best New Telecom Management Software Award at SuperComm, the largest telecommunications trade show in the country. ISM supports the corporation's mission to deliver software solutions that help service providers increase their managed service revenues and improve their customers' service experience while reducing costs.

Today, the privately held company, one of five startups founded by former FORE Systems employees, has grown its work force from two founders to more than 150 employees, and secured major telecommunications customers such as AT&T Canada and AT&T Broadband Network Solutions.

Like most technology startups, CoManage has embraced a progressive corporate culture, which encourages a dynamic work-hard, play-hard environment, to attract and retain the best software talent available. The company's kitchens and recreational areas, where bread is baked fresh daily, feature video, pinball and foosball games. The company hosts a movie night every two weeks for employees and their families, and sponsors weekend outings such as mountain biking, white-water rafting and paintball trips.

CoManage is active in Pittsburgh's high-technology community as a charter member of a newly formed technology club in Pittsburgh, where venture capitalists, business leaders and students can network the ideas that continue to grow Pittsburgh's technology sector. CoManage professionals participate as judges in the city's annual Enterprise Business Plan Competition, where local students and entrepreneurs prepare business plans for the technology startups of the future.

The company also encourages community involvement. CoManage employees support the Light of Life Mission, a nondenominational ministry, by donating money and merchandise for single mothers and disadvantaged children.

As a leader in the network management systems market, CoManage Corp. continues to support the dreams and aspirations of Pittsburgh's entrepreneurs, two of whom believed in an idea formulated on a ski slope and then realized one of Pittsburgh's growing technology companies.

MetalSite Inc.

"WHY CAN'T I SELL STEEL THE WAY Saber and Apollo sell airline tickets?" was the question that launched a revolution in the metals industry, sparked by MetalSite, the first and premier independent Internet site for steel and other metals. The rhetorical question was posed in autumn of 1995 by former Weirton Steel Corporation President and CEO Richard Riederer to his then-CIO Patrick Stewart as the two were discussing strategies to take costs out of the metals supply chain.

After two years of research and testing, MetalSite opened its doors for business in August of 1998 as an independent e-marketplace where all suppliers and buyers of metal goods could securely and confidentially conduct business anytime of the day or night, from any location in the world, through the power and speed of the Internet. By December of that year, MetalSite made history as the first independent Web marketplace to facilitate the sale of metal goods online. Today, MetalSite conducts thousands of transactions each month and posts millions of tons of metal each year for buyers and sellers around the world. MetalSite's Web portal also offers daily news and metals-related information from world news leader Reuters and other sources to help customers make better-informed business decisions.

Patrick B. Stewart is president and CEO of MetalSite Inc., the world's first and leading independent Internet marketplace for the $900 billion global metals industry.

MetalSite is led by Patrick Stewart, who has served as company president and CEO since it was founded. Richard Riederer, who retired from Weirton Steel in 2000, is MetalSite's chairman of the board. The company is perfectly suited for the Pittsburgh region, blending the area's rich history in the steel and metals business with its growth in the fields of high technology and e-commerce. MetalSite is headquartered in Robinson Township, minutes from Pittsburgh International Airport and downtown Pittsburgh. It employs a staff of 90 professionals, including one of the region's most talented teams of software engineers and Web developers who internally develop and implement all MetalSite e-commerce technology.

MetalSite is privately held and receives funding, expertise and product commitments from several top U.S. metals companies, including Bethlehem Steel Corporation, LTV Steel Corporation, Steel Dynamics, Weirton Steel and North America's largest service center, Ryerson Tull, Inc. In 1999, Internet Capital Group, Inc., a leading business-to-business e-commerce company, became a major MetalSite investor.

In 2000 the company was set on a path of explosive growth, adding two subsidiaries to its fold. By May, MetalSite launched a new Web site, ScrapSite, to facilitate the buying and selling of ferrous and nonferrous scrap metal and scrap substitutes on a global scale. In August, MetalSite joined forces with Japan's leading trading houses, Itochu, Marubeni and Sumitomo, to form the MetalSite Japan Corporation to support business-to-business e-commerce for Japan's metals marketplace.

Also in 2000, MetalSite formed a partnership with a technology leader to deliver supply chain solutions for its customers. Along with partner i2 Technologies, MetalSite is working to deliver collaborative planning and advanced order status solutions.

By focusing on the customer and driving business efficiencies, MetalSite has become the leading force in metals e-commerce with the most active metals community, the largest product inventory and the most online transactions. MetalSite's vision is to continue to bring greater efficiencies to the entire metals supply chain by reducing costs and connecting supply chain partners faster and smarter.

Spinnaker Networks

LIKE THE TRIANGULAR SAILS used on racing yachts from which the company takes its name, Spinnaker Networks whips along a powerful, downwind run as it charts its course through the burgeoning network storage server market.

Founded in 1999 by six entrepreneurs with links to Carnegie Mellon University (CMU) and several successful Pittsburgh technology companies, including FORE Systems (now Marconi Communications), Transarc Corp. (now IBM Transarc Labs) and Scalable Networks (acquired by FORE in 1996), Spinnaker Networks is committed to the development of storage-server-specific technologies for accelerating the performance and reducing the cost of network storage.

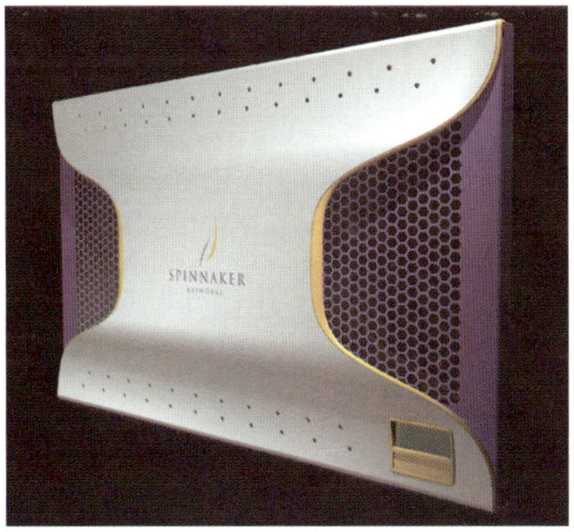

Spinnaker's first industry-leading network storage server

Operating with $20.4 million in financing from two leading West Coast venture capital funds — Norwest Venture Partners and Menlo Ventures — Spinnaker Networks develops hardware and software for accelerating the delivery of data, voice and video over computer networks and the Internet at its headquarters in the Regional Industrial Development Corporation (RIDC) Park in O'Hara Township.

In addition to a common passion for sailing, the six founders of Spinnaker Networks share backgrounds in both networking and storage technologies. Those experiences helped to crystallize their vision for a storage-server-specific computing platform, according to Spinnaker Networks President and CEO Ronald P. Bianchini, Jr.

Bianchini, a former CMU professor who continues as an adjunct professor in the electrical and computer engineering department at CMU, says he passed up a promotion at his previous company to found Spinnaker Networks. With his co-founders, Bianchini saw the opportunity to enter the network storage server market, which is projected to become a multibillion-dollar market, at the outset.

Network storage servers, which enable corporations and organizations to store and safeguard data that is generated in multiple distributed locations at a centralized location, are for the most part general-purpose PCs. Spinnaker Networks aims to pull network storage servers out of a general-purpose computing platform, as the founders did with routers, and develop a new computing platform for network storage only. Through a combination of hardware and software, the company offers network storage solutions with industry-leading performance at breakthrough prices.

Bianchini says the founders decided to establish the company in Pittsburgh because of the region's growing technology community, large talent pool and national prominence in data storage. The National Science Foundation has designated Pittsburgh and CMU as a Center of Excellence for Data Storage.

The Spinnaker team is committed to the development of storage-server-specific technologies for accelerating the performance and reducing the cost of network storage.

Spinnaker Networks is a member of the Pittsburgh High Technology Council and Pittsburgh Digital Greenhouse, a state-sponsored effort to develop system-mounted chip technology. The company gives back to the community through sponsorships of the Habitat for Humanity Marathon, Pedal Pittsburgh (a community development organization) and National Public Radio on WDUQ-FM.

A spinnaker on a racing yacht indicates speed and power, and also serves as a symbol of the company's drive for the same in network storage server computing.

Bibliography

Adams, Mrs. Marcellin C. "Pittsburgh's Great Fire of 1845." *Western Pennsylvania Historical Magazine*, March-June 1941.

Alberts, Robert C. *Pitt: The Story of the University of Pittsburgh, 1787-1987.* Pittsburgh, 1986.

Allegheny Centennial Committee. *Story of Old Allegheny City.* Pittsburgh, 1941.

Arensberg, Charles F. C. "The Pittsburgh Fire of April 10, 1845," *Western Pennsylvania Historical Magazine*, March-June 1945.

Ashe, Thomas. *Travels in America.* London, 1808.

Baldwin, Leland D. *Pittsburgh: The Story of a City 1750-1865.* Pittsburgh, 1981 (Reprint).

Blythe, Mrs. Ellen H. Two letters written to her brother John C. Green, July 22, 1834, and June 9, 1835. In Carnegie Library of Pittsburgh.

Bolden, Frank E., with Laurence A. Glasco and Eliza Smith Brown. *A Legacy in Bricks and Mortar: African-American Landmarks in Allegheny County.* Pittsburgh, 1995.

Brown, Eliza Smith, Project Director. *African American Historic Sites Survey of Allegheny County.* Harrisburg, 1994.

Brown, Eliza Smith. *The African-American Legacy in Allegheny County: A Timeline of Key Events.* Pittsburgh, 1997.

Brown, Eliza Smith. "In Search of a Breathing Place: A History of the Allegheny Commons." Unpublished manuscript for the Garden Club of Allegheny County, 1996.

Brown, Mark, with Lu Donnelly and David G. Wilkins. *The History of the Duquesne Club.* Pittsburgh, 1989.

Carlisle, Ronald C. *The Story of "Woodville:" The History, Architecture, and Archaeology of a Western Pennsylvania Farm.* Pittsburgh, 1998.

Church, Samuel Harden. *A Short History of Pittsburgh: 1758-1908.* New York, 1908.

Cohen, Harold W. "Plays at Fort Pitt Were Forerunners of Pittsburgh Theater." *Pittsburgh Post Gazette,* September 26, 1936.

Collins, F. S. *Stringtown on the Pike (The Story of East Liberty).* Ann Arbor, 1966.

Collot, Victor. *A Journey In North America.* Originally printed in Paris in 1826. In Reprints of Rare Americana, No. 4. Firenze, 1924.

Craig, Neville B. *The History of Pittsburgh.* Pittsburgh, 1851.

Crevecoeur, J. Hector St. John. *Letters from an American Frontier.* 1782.

Demareest, David Jr., Ed. *The River Ran Red: Homestead 1892.* Pittsburgh, 1976.

Dickens, Charles. *American Notes.* 1842.

Edmunds, Arthur J. *Daybreakers: The Story of the Urban League of Pittsburgh.* Pittsburgh, 1983.

Elder, Margaret. "Pittsburgh Industries that Used to Be." *Western Pennsylvania Historical Magazine,* October 1929.

Elkus, Leonore R., Ed. *Famous Men and Women of Pittsburgh.* Pittsburgh, 1981.

Evans, Henry Oliver. "Life in Pittsburgh in 1845." *Western Pennsylvania Historical Magazine*, March-June 1945.

Fahnestock's Pittsburgh Directory, 1850.

Fox, Arthur B. "The Ups and Downs of Pittsburgh's Inclines." *Pennsylvania*, July/August 1999.

Galvin, Martin. "French Travelers in the Ohio Valley, 1788-1792" *Western Pennsylvania Historical Magazine*, Vol. 59.

Gangewere, Robert J. *The Bridges of Pittsburgh and Allegheny County.* Pittsburgh, 2001.

Glazier, Willard. *Peculiarities of American Cities.* Philadelphia, 1883.

"The Great Flood." *Pittsburgh Press*, April 18, 1936.

Harper, Frank C. *Pittsburgh: Forge of the Universe.* New York, 1957.

Harris, Helen L. *Trinity & Pittsburgh: The History of Trinity Cathedral.* Pittsburgh, 1999.

Harper, Frank C. *Pittsburgh of Today: Its Resources and People.* New York, 1931.

Hays, Samuel P. Ed. *City at the Point: Essays on Social History of Pittsburgh*. Pittsburgh, 1989.

Hoerr, John P. *And the Wolf Finally Came: The Decline of the American Steel Industry*. Pittsburgh, 1988.

Iacone, Audrey Abbott. "Early Printing in Pittsburgh, 1786-1856." *Western Pennsylvania Historical Magazine*, Vol. 73.

Jones, Samuel. *Pittsburgh in the Year 1826*. Pittsburgh, 1826.

Kellogg, Paul Underwood. *Civic Frontage: Pittsburgh Survey*. 2 vols, New York, 1914.

Kelly, George E. Ed. *Allegheny County: A Sesqui-Centennial Review, 1788-1938*. Pittsburgh, 1938.

Kidney, Walter C. & Ziegler, Arthur P. *Allegheny*. Pittsburgh, 1975.

Kidney, Walter C. *Landmark Architecture: Pittsburgh and Allegheny County*. Pittsburgh, 1985.

Kidney, Walter C. *Pittsburgh's Landmark Architecture: The Historic Buildings of Pittsburgh and Allegheny County*. Pittsburgh, 1997.

Killikelly, Sarah H. *The History of Pittsburgh, Its Rise and Progress*. Pittsburgh, 1906.

Kinard, Agnes Dodds. *Celebrating the First 100 Years of the Carnegie in Pittsburgh*. Pittsburgh, 1995.

Kuncio, Gerald M. "Golden Age in the City of Bridges." *Western Pennsylvania History*, Summer 1999.

Lorant, Stefan. *Pittsburgh: The Story of an American City*. Garden City, NY, 1980 (Third Edition).

"Losses of the Fire of 1845." *Western Pennsylvania Historical Magazine*, September-December 1943.

Lubove, Roy. *Twentieth Century Pittsburgh*. Pittsburgh, 1969.

"Mr. Mellon's Patch." *Time Magazine*, October 3, 1949.

Olmsted, Frederick Law, Jr. *Pittsburgh: Main Thoroughfares and the Down Town District*. Pittsburgh, 1911.

"Our Flood in Pictures." *Pittsburgh Sun-Telegraph*, April 3, 1936.

Palmer, Robert M. *Pictorial Pittsburgh and Prominent Pittsburghers Past and Present*. Pittsburgh, 1905.

Pittsburgh Quarterly Trade Circular. Pittsburgh, 1857.

Rishel, Joseph F. *Founding Families of Pittsburgh: The Evolution of a Regional Elite 1760-1910*. Pittsburgh, 1990.

"Rivers Drop: Crest 46 Feet, Thousands Awaiting Relief." *Pittsburgh Post-Gazette*, March 18, 1936.

Roberts, Paul, Ed. *Points in Time: Building a Life in Western Pennsylvania*. Pittsburgh, 1996.

Royall, Mrs. Anne. *Mrs. Royall's Pennsylvania, or Travels Continued in the U.S.* Washington, 1829.

Stryker, Roy with Mel Seidenberg. *A Pittsburgh Album 1758-1958: Two Hundred Years of Memories in Pictures and Text*. Pittsburgh, 1959.

Swetnam, George. "There Was a Tavern." Pittsburgh Press, May 9, 1958.

Thomas, David. *Travels Through the Western Country in the Summer of 1816*. Auburn, NY, 1819.

Thurston, George H. *Pittsburgh & Allegheny in the Centennial Year*. Pittsburgh, 1876.

Toker, Franklin. Pittsburgh: *An Urban Portrait*. University Park, PA, 1986.

Trice, Harley Niles, "Wall to Wall to Wall," exhibition catalog, 1998.

Trimble, William F. "From Sail to Steam: Shipbuilding in the Pittsburgh Era, 1790-1865." *Western Pennsylvania Historical Magazine*, April 1975.

Uptown: Greater Pittsburgh's Classic Section; East End: The World's Most Beautiful Suburb. Pittsburgh, 1907.

Van Trump, James D. "And Always the Play: Historic Theaters of Pittsburgh." *Carnegie Magazine*, 1967.

Van Trump, James D. "Henry Phipps and the Phipps Conservatory." *Carnegie Magazine*, January 1976.

Van Trump, James D. *Life and Architecture in Pittsburgh*. Pittsburgh, 1983.

Vexler, Robert I. *Pittsburgh: A Chronological and Documentary History, 1682-1976*. Dobbs Ferry, NY, 1977.

Weisberg, Gabriel P., DeCourcy E. McIntosh, Alison McQueen. *Collecting in the Gilded Age: Art Patronage in Pittsburgh, 1890-1910*. Pittsburgh, 1997.

Ziegler, Arthur P. *Birmingham: Pittsburgh's South Side*. Pittsburgh, 1968.

Index

Index of Partners & Web Sites